INTRODUCTION

SEE MORE AT: WWW.THEGAMEOFTRUTH.COM

1/3/16
LUNGS SEARING...
HUF HUF HUF HUF HUF
SNOT OOZING OUT OF NOSE....
BUT I HAD FUN.
2ND!
RAD!
1/4/16
SO MUCH TO DO, CAN I REMEMBER IT ALL? NO.
I FORGOT.
I MAKE LISTS, BUT I THINK IT'S GOOD NOT TO SOMETIMES.
LET'S SEE... WHAT WAS IT?
LIKE ONES BODY, MEMORY RESPONDS WITH STRENGTH TO A GOOD JOG.
OH YEAH! NOW I REMEMBER!
1/5/16
MAN, IT'S STUCK.
LET ME SEE... NO PROBLEM!
KEEP IN MIND I DO THIS EVERY DAY.
YOU'RE WEAK SON!
I KNOW.

1/6/16
OH YEAH, I FOUND THIS JACKET IN THE STREET!
RAD!
EVERYTHING I GOT ON IS A FREEBIE OR A DISCARD!
WHEN ARE PEOPLE GOING TO GET IT THAT IT JUST DOESN'T MATTER.
1/7/16
ARE YOU DOING YOUR WRITINGS?
NOT NOW. NO. I HAVE THEM IN MY HEAD.
YOU'RE A GOOD WRITER, A NATURAL.
NO I'M NOT A NATURAL. I HAD TO WORK AT IT A LONG TIME.
I KNOW PEOPLE THAT CAN DO EVERYTHING I CAN DO, BUT BETTER THE DIFFERENCE IS I KEEP TRYING.
1/8/16
AS YOU GET OLDER YOU JUST KNOW.
OH..WHYS THAT SORE?
WHEN YOU HAVE AN INJURY. YOU SELDOM KNOW THE REASON.
WHEN DID I HURT THAT?
BUT YOU KNOW IT WILL BE A WHILE BEFORE IT STOPS HURTING.
FEELS LIKE 6 MONTHS ON THAT ONE.

1/9/16
CAN WE BORROW YOU FOR A MINUTE?
OK?
WOULD YOU LET MY DAUGHTER TAKE HER PICTURE WITH YOU? WE HAD SUCH A GOOD EXPERIENCE WE WANT TO GET A PHOTO.
I GUESS. I'M JUST DOING MY JOB.
1/10/16
2ND!
LATER.. 1ST SHOW.
PAY ATTENTION!
AND SO ENDS A TOTALLY RAD DAY!
NOTHING IN LIFE IS A GIVEN EXCEPT YOU WILL DIE.
SNIFF.
WHAT YOU GET OUT OF IT IS UP TO YOU. THERE ARE NO EASY ANSWERS, JUST ENDLESS QUESTIONS.
AM I HAPPY?
IS IT WORTH IT? THAT IS ONE THAT CAN BE EASILY ANSWERED...
YES!

1/13/16
HOW'S IT GOING P.J.?
NO GOOD. I GOT FOOD POISONING!
YOU'RE AT WORK? GO HOME!
I'VE... NEVER... ...MISSED... A... DAY..
OH. WELL I UNDERSTAND THAT FOR SURE.
WHAT IS TRUTH? IT IS A LIE - A SNAPSHOT THAT FOR A MOMENT IS TRUE.
RING!
TRUTH IS A GREAT WAVE OR A LEAP INTO THE AIR. A MOMENT YOU TRY TO HANG ONTO.
BUT CAN'T.
STILL DRAWING YOUR COMICS?
YEAH.
I THINK THEY'RE GOOD FOR YOU.
WELL AT LEAST MY DRAWINGS HAVE IMPROVED.
I GET ONE ACT OF POIGNIANCY FOR EVERY 100 OR SO DRAWN.

1/15/16
I DID SO LITTLE AFTER WORK TODAY., JUST RE-WIRED MY TRUCK STERO. I FELT SO LAZY.
GO DO SOMETHING..
I HATE MYSELF FOR BEING LIKE THAT. THERE IS SO MUCH I NEED TO DO.
WHERE TO BEGIN.
WELL PERHAPS DOING NOTHING IS SOMETHING TO DO.
HO HUM.
OK - IT'S 29 BUCKS.
29... WILL YOU TAKE 24?
NO.
DON'T YOU WANT THE BUSINESS?
SURE...
BUT AT SOME POINT IT'S JUST NOT WORTH SELLING. SEE YA.
DICK.
1/17/16
DINGO'S CLOSING IN. HE GETS ME EVERYTIME!
DON'T STOP! FASTER!
!
SNOT.
MAN, YOU BEAT ME!
YEAH, ONLY TOOK 8 YEARS!

1 | 18/16
I THINK LOVE TERRIFIES PEOPLE. IT OVERWHELMS THEM IN IT'S POWER, EXPOSES ALL FRAILITY, ALL WEAKNESS. SO PEOPLE OFTEN RUN FROM IT.
I LOVE YOU.
LOVE CAN BE A FORCE OF DISTRUCTION - IT CAN RUIN YOU. THIS I KNOW. SO PEOPLE HIDE FROM IT, RUN FROM IT, AVOID IT BY GUARDING THIER HEART. THE FEAR LOVES POWER.
KLANG!
A FEW ARE NOT AFRAID, THEY KNOW ONLY THE TRULY BRAVE RUSH IN KNOWING THE POWER OF LOVE IS GREATER THAN THE FEAR OF IT. ONLY FOR THE STRONG.
AIM FOR THE HEART!
OH COME ON! YOU KNOW YOU WANT IT!
IT'S JUST NOT BEEN GOOD LATLEY.
AM I BECOMING A COFFEE SNOB? I HOPE NOT. YOU'VE BEEN GOOD TO ME... TRUE.
BUT I'M FEELING SMOTHERED.
1 20/16
YOU REMEMBER MY BIG GRAY POODLE?
THE POODLE LADY
NO
DO YOU REMEMBER ALL THE BIKES I HAVE?
OK THEN.

1/21/16
WHAT ARE YOU DOING? COME PLAY WITH US!
A RAD LADY WOULD BE... RAD.
DAH!
IT'S TRUE. COFFEE & BICYCLE ARE MY BEST FRIENDS... MOST LIKELY ALWAYS WILL BE.
BUT THERE'S MORE THAN ONE KIND OF LOVE. I CAN'T LOVE YOU THE SAME WAY.
YES YOU CAN!
NO. GROSS.
1/22/16
JUST WORK HARDER.
YOU CAN, OR YOU SHOULD WORK HARD AND YOU MAY HAVE A CHANCE...
OR DON'T AND THEN YOU WON'T.
TOO LATE.
1/23/16
I LOVE CHECKLISTS.
WITH A CHECKLIST, YOU DON'T FORGET A THING...
OH YEAH. PUMP.
AND AS YOU CHECK THINGS OFF YOU GET A SMALL TOKEN OF JOY AND A SENSE OF ACCOMPLISHMENT.

1/24/16
OH TODAY I HAD SO MUCH FUN FINISHING AN EVENT. I GOT THE GIGGLES SO GOOD.
HE HE HE HE HE HE
I REMEMBER A TIME WHEN I COULDN'T LAUGH AT ANYTHING
HANGING ON TO SADNESS IS SUCH A JIP. YOU RIP OFF YOUR OWN LIFE.
HE HE HE HE HE HE
1/25/16
LET ME CHECK OUT YOUR SKETCH BOOK.
SURE.
OH YEAH MAN...
YOU'RE BAT-SHIT CRAZY!
1/26/15
COOL!
LOOKS GOOD, HOWS IT RIDE?
OH WELL SEE!

1/27/16
HEY YOU LOOK FRESH! THAT SHIRT...
I DO?
OH WELL IT'S NEW SO ME LOOKING CLEAN IS A FLOOK.
GIVE IT TIME.
1/28/16
YOU CAN TAKE MELETONEN FOR SLEEP...
NO WAY.
BUT IT'S NATURAL.
STILL, YOU'RE CHANGING WHO YOU ARE.
IT'S NATURAL FOR ME TO ROLL AROUND ALL NIGHT. WHAT DO I LOSE IF I TAKE SOMETHING TO SLEEP?
1/29/16
I CALL IT PERMAGREASE.
YOU CAN SCRUB ALL DAY BUT AFTER A WHILE THE GREASE ON YOUR HANDS IS IN YOUR HANDS.
SINCE GETTING IT OFF MEANS REMOVING YOUR SKIN, AND IT WILL JUST BE BACK THE NEXT DAY IT'S BETTER NOT TO WORRY ABOUT IT.

1/30/16

KEEP THINGS MOVING AND THE MOTION WILL MAKE THE JUGGLING ACT ALL THE EAISER.

DO THINGS OR YOU SUFFER THE FATE OF ALL THINGS THAT DO NOT MOVE: RUIN.

BE THE AGENT OF ACTION, NOT THE REACTION.
NA-NA-NA NA NA!

1/31/16

LOOKING AT THE WORLD IS A BUMMER. I GET SAD.
THAT BLOWS.

SOMETIMES YOU WANT TO DO SOMETHING TO HELP SO BAD, BUT WHAT? WHERE? THERE'S SO MUCH THAT IS WRONG WHERE DO YOU START. IT'S OVERWHELMING...

CAT VIDEOS DO ON THE OTHER HAND CAUSE YOU TO LAUGH AND FORGET. IS IT WRONG TO SQUANDER A NIGHT ON SUCH TRASH? OR IS IT OK TO TAKE A MOMENT TO LAUGH BECAUSE YOU CAN?
HA NA HE HE
HA HE

2/1/16

I SHOULD BE SO HAPPY RIGHT NOW BUT - NO? WHY?
MEH.

I'VE HAD THE CITY ON MY ASS FOR MONTHS, IT'S BEEN A HUGE BALL OF STRESS.

NOW IT'S OVER, I CAN BREATHE EASY AND YET I WORRY...
STOP IT.
WUMP!

2/2/16
DEEP INSIDE ONE'S MIND IS A SWITCH.
MOST PEOPLE LOOK AND LOOK BUT NEVER FIND THE SWITCH IT IS SO YOU CAN TURN OFF AN IDEA OR FEELING.
- CLICK! -
THOSE THAT HAVE FOUND THIS SWITCH CAN MOVE FORWARD WITH GRACE. MOST OF US CANNOT.
MAKE IT STOP!
2/3/16
BELIEVE IN SOMETHING. HAVE FIRE. HAVE CONVICTIONS. BE REAL.
GO TO MOVIES...
NO.
BE AMBIVELMENT, TAKE THE EASY ROAD. INDULGE. BE SELFISH.
CRACK?
SURE.
YOU CAN ASK YOURSELF WHAT DO YOU BELIEVE IN? COULD YOU?
2/4/16
WELL I COULD SEE WHAT WAS GOING ON...
THAT'S COOL TELL ME MORE...
OK.
IT SEEMED LIKE THIS GIRL WAS TAKING A LIKING TO ME. THE WAY SHE LEANED IN ON THE COUNTER SO CLOSE. BUT NO.
OH MY...
I FELT MY HEART QUICKEN BUT AS A RULE, NO FUNNY BUSINESS AT WORK.
OH WELL.

2/5/16
TWO SLEEPLESS NIGHTS IN A ROW AND I'M WHOOPED.
I'VE BEEN A TERRIBLE SLEEPER AS LONG AS I REMEMBER, IT IS PART OF WHO I AM AT THIS DOING GOOD OR BAD.
WIDE AWAKE AGAIN.
WHILE I STRIVE TO CHANGE THINGS ABOUT ME I DON'T LIKE. SOME THINGS EVEN IF NOT GOOD SHOULD BE LEFT ALONE AS THEY MAKE UP PART OF WHO YOU ARE.
HO HUM.
2/6/11
LET'S DO THIS.
SPEAKER BOX MADE FROM DRAWER
AFTER MUCH WIRING...
OK.
YES, A CASSETTE PLAYER.
THEY CALL ME A WORKING MAN!
2/7/11
NO. WE GO UP THAT.
PARKING LOT
MAN, THAT WAS SO HARD! BUT ON A SINGLE SPEED—WHY?
TO SEE IF I COULD!

2/8/16
HEY! NEW BIKE!
YEAH.
THE ROAD
GOING UP THE CAB?
LATER.
HEY! YOU OK?
OH YEAH UM...
PICTURE TIME.
OH. ALRIGHT THEN.
2/9/16
DO YOU HAVE PLANS FOR WHEN YOU DIE?
DEATH SALESMAN
REALLY? WHAT?
YEAH I GOT IT COVERED.
FILL MY HOUSE FULL OF WHITE FLUFFY CATS SO WHEN I DIE THEY EAT ME AND BECOME PINK FLUFFY CATS!
YOU ROCK!
2/10/16
I DON'T WANT TO HEAR ANYONES OPINIONS ON WHAT I SHOULD DO, I DON'T NEED THAT CRAP.
KEEP YOUR IDEAS TO YOURSELF, I DON'T NEED YOUR BULLSHIT.
HUMANITY REALLY NEEDS TO FUCK OFF AND FOCUS UPON THEMSELVES. PEOPLE CAN DO WHAT THEY WANT.
YOU SHOULD..
NO.
AS LONG AS IT DOES NOT INVOLVE GIVE ME ADVICE.
LIVE YOUR OWN LIFE MAN - NOT MINE.

2/11/16
THE IDEA. IT POSESSES ME.
MOUNTIAN BIKE WITH DROP BARS...
ANOTHER NIGHT NOT SLEEPING
UNLIKE MOST, I MAKE MY IDEAS REALITY.
COOL.
SOMETIMES, THEY DON'T MESH TOO WELL.
SCARY!
2/12/16
OH, THESE PEOPLE ARE DOOMED.
THERE'S SO MUCH MAGIC IN THE WORLD. SO MUCH AROUND YOUR LOCAL IS WORTH LOOKING INTO. BUT NO.
PEOPLE WOULD RATHER JUST IGNORE THE WORLD AROUND THEM FOR LITTLE BOXES OF LIGHT.
2/13/16
DON'T YOU THINK NOT HAVING A CELL PHONE IS A ROMANTIC NOTION...
PERHAPS...
BUT IT'S AN IDEAL AND I'M A IDEALIST. EVERYTHING OUT THERE IN THE WORLD WAS ONCE AN IDEAL OR A NOTION...
I'M NOT GOING TO WIN, BUT I'LL HOLD ON TO MY IDEAL TO THE END.

2/14/16
WHOOP! WHOOP! MEOW! MEOW!
THEY JUST MOVED.
YEAH. ASK NICELY AND THEY GIVE YOU GRIEF.
ACT CRAZY AND THEY GET OUT OF THE WAY.
2/15/16
IT'S BEEN MONTHS SINCE I'VE HAD MY DAY OFF NOT BE FILLED WITH THINGS I HAD TO DO.
ENDLESS CHORES.
I HARDLY KNEW WHAT TO DO WITH MYSELF.
RIDE? YES? NO? YES. WHAT BIKE?
SO I DEFAULTED TO "THE LISTS"...
PROJECTS! PROJECTS! PROJECTS!
2/16/16
HEY, YOU DON'T STINK TODAY!
THANKS I GUESS.
NO, I'M PAYING YOU A COMPLIMENT! NORMALLY YOU DO!
SOME COMPLIMENT.
WELL IT WAS BATH DAY TODAY...

2/17/16

ALONE TIME HAS BEEN GOOD FORE ME. I LIKE BEING ALONE MORE AND MORE.
I KNOW IT'S ME, I FIND MY FRIENDS TO OFTEN BE ANNOYING, AGGRAVATING OR WEAK.
I CAN'T
AND I'M OK WITH THAT FOR NOW.
WHAT NEXT?

2/18/16

AT TIMES THE IDEA OF SOMETHING IS BETTER THEN THE ACTUALITY OF A THING.
I CAN THINK OF A THING THAT COULD HAPPEN AND HOW GOOD IT COULD BE.
KNOWING THAT IT WILL NOT HAPPEN AND IF IT DID IT COULD NEVER LIVE UP TO THE FANTASY. SAD IN A WAY

2/19/16

I THINK IF PUT TO TASK MOST PEOPLE WOULD NOT BE ABLE TO DETAIL WHAT THEY REALLY STAND FOR.
UH.
WE LIKE TO THINK THAT WE HOLD OURSELVES UP TO HIGH IDEALS
I STAND FOR TRUTH.
BUT IN REALITY MOST OF US ARE JUST NOT THAT STRONG.
IS THAT YOURS THEN?
UH-NO

2/20/16
EVERYDAY I HAVE TO FORCE MYSELF TO DO THINGS.
BEFORE YOU REST, STRIP 5 BIKES.
INSIDE ME IS A LAZY SLUG. MOST PEOPLE GIVE INTO THE SLUG. THE SLUG SAYS WHAT YOU WANT TO HEAR.
JUST RELAX
WELL, FUCK THAT SHIT.
SQUISH!
2/21/16
KNOCK KNOCK!
?
WE'RE OFFERING THIS MAGAZINE.
WATCH TOWER
I'M NOT INTO MIND CONTROL.
OH.
WATCH TOWER
2/23/16
KNOCK. KNOCK.
?
HEY!
HEY YOU'RE BACK.
DID YOU MISS ME?
UH...NO..
I KNOW
I'M SORRY, I DON'T MISS ANYONE.

2/23/16
INTO THE DARK.
NO MOTOR CYCLES
END
THERE ARE LITTLE SPOTS ALL OVER THE VALLEY WHERE YOU CAN DUCK INTO THE WOODS. AT NIGHT THEY TAKE A DIFFERENT TONE.
AND WE ROLL PAST COUNTLESS HOUSES WITH PEOPLE PLANTED IN FRONT OF THIER TV'S, WE FEEL ALL THE MORE ALIVE.
HAHAHAHAHA
2/24/16
LONG AGO WE ENTERED A CULTURE OF SITTING. SITTING IN AN AIR CONDITIONED HOUSE TO DRIVE AN AIR CONDITIONED CAR TO WORK IN AN AIR CONDITIONED OFFICE, ALWAYS SITTING.
NOW I SEE PEOPLE ALL AROUND ME WHO HAVE RUINED THIER BODIES, THEY HAVE BECOME WEAK AND LOST THIER WAY, IT'S SAD.
WHEN YOU'RE A KID YOU RUN AND PLAY ALL DAY, WHEN DO WE FORGET? THATS THE HARD PART — NOT FORGETTING.
2/25/16
WATCHING TV, YOUR BRAIN IS TURNING TO MUSH.
NO. I'M LEARNING THINGS.
NO, YOU'RE GETTING INFORMATION, NOT KNOWLEDGE. YOU HAVE SEEN SOMETHING DONE BUT CANNOT DO IT.
THERE'S A DIFFERENCE YOU KNOW.

2/26/16
JUST IN CASE...
CHAIN
I WAS GOING RIDING WITH A FRIEND BUT NEEDED TO BRING A PART INTO WORK SO TO COVER MY BASES I TOOK IT WITH ME. SURE ENOUGH, WE HAD PROBLEMS.
MY TIRE IS ROACHED.
SO I GOT DROPPED OFF AT WORK WITH MINUTES TO SPARE. BUT I DID MY JOB WITH NO EXCUSES - THAT'S WHAT MATTERS.
ALL BASES COVERED.
2/27/16
BICYCLES FROM 6:30 AM TILL 9 PM - BEGIN!
WELD. WELD. WELD.
WORK. WORK. WORK.
BE RIGHT WITH YOU!
RING RI
RING
RING
BUILD BUILD AND THEN WELD WELD WELD. END THE DAY WITH A BIKE MAGAZINE!
LOOKING GOOD!
1/3 INTO THE RIDE MY AXEL SNAPPED.
WITH THE REAR WHEEL RUBBING ON THE FRAME, I DID THE REST OF THE RIDE. IT WAS LIKE RIDING WITH THE BRAKES ON THE WHOLE TIME.
UH. UH. UH.
BUT I FINISHED.

TIME SMACKS YOU UPSIDE THE HEAD AND YOU DON'T KNOW WHICH WAY IS UP.
LONG IS SHORT, SHORT IS LONG WE CAN'T COMPUTE.
IT'S BEEN FOREVER.
REALLY?
NO, ONLY TWO WEEKS.
YEAH.
BUT IN THE END, USE YOUR TIME WELL AS NO MATTER WHAT, WE ALL RUN OUT.
JUST SAY THIS BIKE IS 300 DOLLARS.
NO
WHY?
WELL, IT'S NOT SO I WOULD BE UNTRUE.
BUT EVERYONE LIES YOU KNOW.
NO. NOT EVERYONE. BUT I DON'T CARE WHAT PEOPLE DO, I HAVE TO LIVE WITH MYSELF.
I'M COMMING FROM FAR AWAY SO CAN I JUST WAIT FOR IT, WILL YOU BE BUSY?
I HAVE NO WAY TO KNOW THAT. YOU WANT ME TO GIVE YOU AN ASURANCE OF HOW THE FUTURE WILL BE. THERE'S NO WAY TO DO THAT.
IT NEVER ENDS.

3/3/16
OH THAT PUNK MUSIC IS TERRIBLE. I'VE NEVER HEARD SUCH AWFUL SOUNDS.
OK.
NOW JIMI HENDRIX.
OH, HE BLOWS! I'M GLAD HE'S DEAD.
HOW CAN YOU SAY THAT!?
HEY MAN, YOU JUST TRASHED MUSIC I LOVE AND THAT'S FINE - YOU CAN. BUT YOU CAN'T TAKE SOMEONE NOT AGREEING WITH YOU - TOO BAD.
3/4/16
I BROUGHT COFFEE...
LATER...
GRANT. THAT COFFEE WAS SO STRONG! THERE'S A DEATH CAMP COMING OUT OF MY BUTT!
STILL, FARTS NEVER STOP BEING FUNNY.
DISGUSTING!
3/5/16
ONCE EVERY COUPLE OF YEARS I GET TRICKED INTO GOING OUT.
IT'S LIKE EATING BAD FOOD YOU FORGOT WHY YOU HATED IT.
NOW YOU REMEMBER.
READY?
OH YEAH.

2/6/16
ONCE I LAYED IT OUT I KNEW.
I WAS GOING TO BUILD A TRACK IN MY YARD, AND THEN HOST A PARTY FOR IT.
DETH
MOTO
AND IT'S GOING TO BE RAD.
IDEAS!
2/7/16
NO RAIN! I CAN GO HIT THE TRAIL..
KABOOM!
WOOSH!
OR NOT.
2/8/16
WHAT DID YOU DO TODAY?
I MADE A BMX TRACK IN MY YARD.
WHAT? HOW?
HERE I'LL DRAW IT.
IT LOOKS LIKE A DICK.
I DOES. DAMN.

3/9/16

DO THE WORK. THE WORK IS GOOD. LOVE THE WORK AND THE WORK WILL LOVE YOU BACK.

THE WORK GIVES YOU EVERYTHING YOU NEED: MONEY, PURPOSE, A SENSE OF ACCOMPLISHMENT, DRIVE. GOALS.

MORE. MORE.

GREASE

DO THE WORK WELL AND YOU LIVE WELL. SLACKERS JUST GET MORE SLACK, THEY DON'T KNOW WHAT THEY ARE MISSING OUT ON.

EVERYTHING.

3/10/16

I'M JUST A GIRL

FUCKN' NO DOUBT! YUCK!

LET'S TRY THIS STATION...

FIDLE FIDLE.

CAUGHT IN A SPIDER WEB...

NOT WINNING.

THAT INTERNET CRAP AGAIN...

HERE WO GO AGAIN.

MY INTERACTIONS WITH PEOPLE IN PERSON ARE 99.9% GOOD. POSITIVE.

HIGH YA!

ON THE WEB, ALL YOU GET IS SNIPES FROM PEOPLE AND NEGATIVITY, IT'S LAME.

NO ESCAPE.

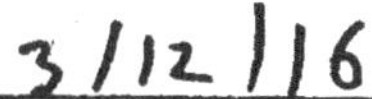

3/12/16

ADVENTURE IS FOR THE FEW.

EVERYONE SAYS THEY WANT ADVENTURE BUT WE KNOW THE TRUTH.

THIS RIDE IS SCARY.

MOST PEOPLE WOULD RATHER BE SAFE.

WELL, GO HOME THEN.

3/13/16

THE FORMULA FOR FUN:

A MOUNTIAN TOP.

16" KIDS BIKES.

3 IDIOTS.

FULL MOTORCYCLE GEAR.

3/14/15

OTHER PEOPLE VEX ME AT TIMES. I FEEL SO SELFISH BECAUSE I DONT WANT TO DEAL WITH LAME CRAP FROM OTHERS.

NO CRAP.

COULD I LIVE ON AN ISLAND, HAVING MY NEEDS MET, BE HAPPY?

BEING LONELY HAS BEEN A LIFE LONG CONDITION FOR ME SO PERHAPS IT WOULD NOT BE A BIG LEAP.

3/15/16
I NEED TO BE LEFT ALONE TO DO THE WORK.
THINGS WOULD GO WAY SMOOTHER IF I CAN JUST GET LEFT ALONE.
BUT IT SELDOM HAPPENS.
BAROOO!

3/16/15
EVERY DAY I LOOK FORWARD TO WHAT I GET TO DO. IN THIS REGARD LIFE IS VERY GOOD.
I HOLD ON TO SIMPLE THINGS LIKE A CUP OF COFFEE, A TRAIL RIDE, DOING A SMALL PROJECT. THESE THINGS GIVE ME BALANCE, PERSPECTIVE, JOY.
I VALUE THESE THINGS BECAUSE ONE DAY THEY, LIKE EVERYTHING ELSE WILL BE GONE.

3/17/15
LOOK! THERE'S GINA!
DON'T CARE.
WHO'S GINA?
ANOTHER ONE OF NATILE'S PIPE DREAMS.
Click

3/18/16

WORK ALL DAY AND SO MUCH MORE TO DO. FINDING TIME TO DO IT ALL IS THE CHALLENGE.
NOT WHAT. BUT WHAT NEXT?
I SEE PEOPLE STRIVE TO BE AT A POINT WHERE THEY HAVE TO DO NOTHING.
IS THAT LIVING? I'LL TAKE TOIL OVER NOT KNOWING WHAT TO DO WITH ONES SELF ANY DAY.
TIME TO DIG!
3/19/16
RIDE?
YEAH FOR SURE.
YEAH.
PICK ME UP?
WHEN?
NOT 7?
7:30?
NO.
NEED YOUR BEAUTY SLEEP?
WELL ANY EARLIER AND I'LL JUST GO TO WORK.
WELL TO HELL WITH THAT!
3/20/16
I REBUILT THE STEERING IN MY VAN TODAY.
OK. 17, 18, 19, 20, 21, 22, 23 TURNS.
IT WAS NOT HARD, I'VE NEVER DONE IT BEFORE BUT IT ONLY TOOK 1 1/2 HOURS. THE OLD ONES WERE 50 YEARS OLD.
THE IMPORTANT THING IS I DID IT MYSELF.
VAROOM!

3/21/16
ENDLESS CHORES.
1 DOWN, 37 TO GO...
PLAY HARD, ALWAYS
SORE.
BUT IN THE END I'LL ALWAYS ASK FOR..
MORE.
2/22/16
LOOK AT THAT FAT BITCH THERE..
PSYCHIC READER
I SEE IN YOUR FUTURE... ANOTHER ICE CREAM SANDWICH!
OH MAN YOU'RE MEAN!
REALLY! 8 BILLION PEOPLE IN THIS WORLD AND I HAVE TO HOLD ALL THIER HANDS?!
2/23/16
ANYTHING NEW?
OH YES.
I FEEL SORT OF BAD FOR PEOPLE WHO DON'T STRIVE FOR NEW THINGS. NEW GOALS, NEW IDEAS, THEY'VE CHEATED THEMSELVES.
AND THEN..
I THINK ANYONE COULD LAYER MANY INTERESTS, PROJECTS, GOALS, IDEAS ETC. BUT THEY DON'T.
OH YEAH' THERE WAS THIS THING.

3/24/16
DID I BREAK THE RULES? I'M SUPER HARD ON MYSELF.
THE RULES!
HER
SOMEONE GAVE ME THIER PHONE # AT WORK. IT WAS SOME FLIMSY PRETEXT ABOUT A BIKE. I THINK THAT'S NOT THE REAL REASON.
!
MY #
WHILE I'D NEVER ASK ANYONE OUT AT WORK, THEY CAN. SO I KEPT IT ABOUT THE BIKE EVEN THOUGH I DOUBT IT'S THE REAL REASON.
LET'S JUST KEEP IT LEGIT.
3/25/16
IN THE END ALL YOU HAVE IS YOUR CHOICES AND HOW THEY SHAPED YOU.
HIC!
IT'S SO HARD FOR US TO SEE WHERE THE ROAD OF LIFE LEADS. WE MOSTLY WIND UP IN A PLACE NOT EVER SEEING HOW WE GET THERE.
I'M.. HERE?
ONE EYE ON THE ROAD, ONE ON THE HORIZON AND ONE'S HEART TO THE STARS - THE ONLY WAY TO TRAVEL.
3/26/16
IN A SEA OF HUMANITY, CONNECTIVITY IS EVER MORE RARE.
SO MANY PEOPLE IN THE SAME PLACE YOU'D THINK WE WOULD HAVE EASY CONNECTIONS BUT IN THIS SEA, WE OFTEN DRIFT ALONE.
SO WHEN YOU DO FIND SOMEONE THAT YOU CAN CONNECT WITH IT IS A RARE THING INDEED
AHOY!

3/27/16
3 HOURS OF SLEEP IS JUST NOT ENOUGH.
OH BUT IT WAS SO WORTH IT THOUGH. MAGICAL HOURS SPENT NOT SLEEPING GETTING A LITTLE CLOSENESS.
SLEEP YOU CAN CATCH UP ON, CONNECTIVITY WITH OTHERS IS VERY FINITE.
Z
3/28/16
I DON'T LIKE DEALING WITH PEOPLE'S DAMAGE OR MISTAKES - IS THAT FAIR? I DON'T KNOW.
NO WAY MAN.
EVERYONE HAS PROBLEMS, WE CAN TRY AND SOLVE THEM. BUT WHEN A NEW PROBLEM OCCURS JUST AS SOON AS THE OLD ONE IS FIXED.
IT'S CALLED BEING AN ADULT.
IT'S BEST TO PUT YOUR FOOT DOWN.
TIME TO CATCH UP WITH THE REST OF US.
3/29/16
WELL THERE WENT 12,440...
IRS
TAXED SO MUCH THIS YEAR. I'VE DONE SO GOOD KEEPING MY OVERHEAD IN CHECK, RUNNING MY BUSINESS VERY WELL.
HATE PHONE. HATE.
HELLO!
THE IRS OF COURSE REWARDS YOU FOR NOT BEING A FUCK UP BY TAKING MORE.
BLAST.

3/30/16
HEY IT'S LARRY THE TALL BLACK GUY, DID I LEAVE A BIKE THERE?
LARRY? YEAH I THINK YOU DID... WHAT TWO, THREE YEARS AGO?
DIDN'T YOU GO TO AFRICA?
YEAH, THAT WAS...
2-3 YEARS AGO!
WELL SHIT MAN, I THOUGHT YOU WERE DEAD!
OH- WELL.. DAMN.
HA HA HA HA HA HA HA HA
3/2/16
GO TO BED STUPID.
REST HAS BEEN HARD TO GET. I ALWAYS WANT TO DO MORE BUT MORE CAN TIP OVER INTO "TOO MUCH". THEN NOTHING GETS DONE.
SOUP. SLEEP. CAN'T GET SICK.
RECOVERY, BEING THE CHANCE TO BEGIN AGAIN ANEW SHOULD NOT BE PASSED UP.
WAK! WAK! WAK!

4/2-16
HERE I GO AGAIN, MAKING A GIFT FOR MY VERY TEMPORY LADY.
I GUESS I'M THE MOST DIE-HARD ROMANTIC TO KEEP DOING THIS IN HOPES THAT SOME DAY...
I MADE THIS FOR YOU!
...ONE WILL STICK AROUND.
HELLO?
4/3/16
OH, IT'S A GOOD LIFE. I JUST LIKE TO NOTE WHEN FOR A MOMENT, THINGS ARE IN A GOOD PLACE.
DIRT
TODAY I WORKED FROM 6 AM TILL 5 PM WITH NO BRAKES. I KNOW NOW IT'S THE KEY TO GET WHERE I NEED TO GO.
ALL DAY I MADE PEOPLE HAPPY AND THAT'S THE KINGDOM THAT I NOW HOLD THE KEY TO.
4/4/16
I WISH I HAD MET YOU SOONER.
YEAH.
ME TOO.

4/5/16
MAN, MY PANTS ARE FALLING DOWN.
HEY MAN, AFRICA CALLED, THEY WANT THIER DIET BACK.
HA.
4/6/16
I HAD TO TAKE TWO DAYS OFF THE BIKE AND OF COURSE I THOUGHT I'D BE SLOW.
BUT THE REST MADE ALL THE DIFFERENCE, I CLIMBED LIKE A GAZZLE.
ON RARE OCCASSIONS, A CHANGE TO COME BACK FRESH IS VITAL.
4/7/16
HOW OLD ARE YOU? 45?
44.
HOW COME YOU DON'T HAVE ANY WRINKLES?
?
OH WELL, I'M 12. IN HERE.
!

4/8/16
STUPID RAIN.
GRR
PEOPLE ARE QUICK TO SAY WE NEED THE RAIN - WE MAY BUT I LIVE IN A DESERT FOR A REASON.
LOOKS LIKE NO RIDE.
I NEED THE SUNSHINE AND THE TRAIL - WITHOUT THEM I'M ONLY 1/2 A MAN.
THAT'S 2 DAYS IN A ROW NOW!
4/9/16
ALL I HAVE TO DO IS SAY IT RIGHT?
BUT IT HAS TO BE TRUE. DO I LOVE HER? IS IT TOO SOON? IT IS ALL I REALLY WANT OUT OF LIFE.
SO WHY NOT GIVE IN?
4/10/16
OH HERE I GO...
WRRRRRRRR
I MADE A RING. I JUST FEEL THATS ITS REAL. IS THERE A TIME TABLE I SHOULD ADHERE TO? IT IS NOT ABOUT ANYONE ELSE.
WILL LOVE PROPEL ME FORWARD? AS LONG AS I LET IT I THINK IT WILL.

4/11/16
HOW'S THE HUMMUS?
LET'S GO TO THE ROOF TOP.
WATERY BUT GOOD!
AS WE WENT OUT WE WERE FACED WITH A DOWN POUR OF RAIN. WE HIDE UNDER THE TREE, EATING AND LAUGHING.
IN YOU GO!
THUNDER CLAPPED OVER HEAD AND FOR A TIME LIGHTNING STRUCK FOR TWO SOULS IN THE LAND OF THE LOST.
4/13/16
9, 10, 11, 12! DO WE HAVE FIREWORKS?
WE HAVE A RULE, 12 PEOPLE AND FIREWORKS MEANS WE GET TO GO TO JOE PEEPS
SSSSSS
ONCE A YEAR THINGS ALIGN SO WHEN IT DOES, IT'S MEMORABLE.
HA HA HA HA HA HA
4/15/16
WE'RE GOING TO THE TOP. COOL?
SURE.
HEY. I LOVE YOU.
YEAH?
I LOVE YOU! LOTS.

AND SO IT ENDS. SO FAST THINGS ARE OVER. I KNEW. SHE WAS MOVING AWAY WHEN I MET HER.

3:45 AM.

I'VE NEVER LOVED SOMEONE SO HARD AND SO FAST IN MY LIFE. SHE FELT THE SAME. A HARD GOODBY FOR NOW.

WILL LOVE BRING US BACK TOGETHER? I'D SAY IT'S NOT SO STRONG AS REALITY THAT IS.

4/15/16

WELL IT'S HARD NOT TO MOPE. I DID GOOD. NO TEARS. THAT'S HUGE FOR ME. I'M A CRYER.

BUT FOR ONCE I FEEL LIKE I WON'T KEEP CRYING ONCE I START. THE SADNESS INSIDE ME THAT I KEPT IN IS NOT THERE SO MUCH ANYMORE.

I THINK I MADE PEACE WITH MY SADNESS OVER TIME AND IN DOING SO, I WAS ABLE TO LET IT GO.

4/16/16

I NEEDED A SHED.

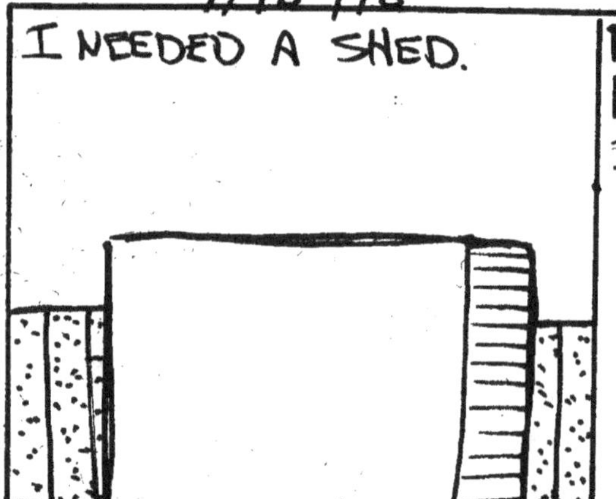

BUT I CAN'T ASK FOR HELP SO I MAKE IT INTO A PARTY.

THIS WAY I CAN GIVE AND GET ALL AT ONCE.

4/17/16
AFTER GETTING THE CRAP BEATEN OUT OF ME AND THEN RIDING TODAY. SORE. BUT I. JUST. FEEL. GOOD.
I MISS MY GIRL SO BAD THAT I'M IN PAIN TOO, THOUGH I KNOW SHE LOVES ME.
JUST KNOWING THAT AND SEEING HOW MY FRIENDS JUST MADE ME FEEL SO GOOD ABOUT BEING ME. I CAN SMILE BECAUSE I GOT LOVE IN MY LIFE AND THATS A GOOD THING.
4/18/16
I'LL MAKE A PROTOTYPE OUT OF WOOD. THIS WILL BE COOL.
FINALLY GOT IT DONE. LET'S GET A QUOTE.
$250.00
THAT'S WAY MORE THAN I THOUGHT.
OH WELL.
MILL
4/19/16
DAVE! YOU MADE IT!
YEAH MAN I DON'T NEED TO GO 30 MILES AN HOUR YOU KNOW.
OK.
IT'S NOT LIKE I NEED TO GET UP AT 8 IN THE MORNING, I JUST GO MY OWN PACE.

4/20/16
MAN, IF YOU RAN FOR OFFICE, I'D VOTE FOR YOU IN A MINUTE!
REALLY? WHY?
YOU JUST TELL THINGS LIKE THEY ARE, IT'S SO RARE AND REFRESHING. THERE NEEDS TO BE MORE PEOPLE LIKE YOU!
WELL, GOOD LUCK WITH THAT.
4/21/16
MY INNER DIALOG JUST BEAT THE LIVING CRAP OUT OF ME, IT WAS HARD NOT TO START BAWLING LIKE A BABY.
SNIFF
TONIGHT WAS TRAIL RIDE NIGHT. ONCE ON MY BIKE I COULD GET MYSELF BACK TO GROUND. BICYCLES ONCE AGAIN HAVE SAVED ME.
SOMETIMES THEY GIVE YOU A THROW TO KEEP YOU ON YOUR TOES BUT BIKES GIVE LOVE TO ANY WHO CHOOSE TO RIDE THEM.
4/22/16
TONIGHT I SLEEP GOOD.
WHY? WELL I GUESS I JUST MADE PEACE WITH THE THINGS THAT ASAIL MY MIND. I'M FLAWED BUT DOING THE BEST I CAN.
SO I'LL SLEEP GOOD KNOWING THAT TOMORROW I'LL BE JUST A LITTLE BETTER THAN THE PERSON GOING TO SLEEP TODAY.
Z

4/23/16
Look, a minibike!
Oh man, the look on your face was priceless! Like you just saw someone who raped you!
It was that obvious?
Oh man.
Oh yeah.
4/24/16
Shit.
What do I do? For a moment I was on the fence but I own up to my mistakes.
Hey man, I hit your car with my bike.
Either way, the choice is more important than the outcome.
Oh— don't worry about it.
4/25/16
1000 zines to staple. I was going to do it in a coffee house but then decided to just do it at home.
I realized that while I'd work faster not at home I was also doing it for attention.
What are you doing?
It is better to just do things to do them for thier own sake than to have an expectation of a reward.

4/26/16
INTO THE NIGHT.
OVER HILLS AROUND SMALL MAN MADE LAKES FOR RICH PEOPLE WE RODE.
WE'RE ALIVE FOR BUT A MOMENT BUT IF WE CHOOSE TO LIVE THE DURATION FEELS LONGER..
RAD!
4/27/16
SO I WENT ANYWAY.
WHAT ELSE AM I TO IN THIS LIFE BUT STRIVE AND DRIVE, SEEK AND DO? I CAN SIT HOME LIKE OTHERS WAITING.
BUT ANSWERS DO NOT KNOCK ON YOUR DOOR, THEY MUST BE SOUGHT OUT.
4/28/16
KNOCK KNOCK
I'M HERE TO SERVE NATAILE D-SOME PAPERS.
OH..UH SHE DOES NOT LIVE HERE.
CAN I PUT MY PANTS ON? I'M SPORTING SOME MORNING WOOD.
HEH.

4/29/16

HOW ARE YOUR COMICS GOING?
HUN? YEAH, NEVER ENDING.
DO YOU LET PEOPLE SEE THEM?
IF THEY WANT BUT THEY HAVE NO EXTRINSIC VALUE.
WHAT?
SEE THIS 50 DOLLAR BILL? IT HAS VALUE TO OTHERS, EXTRINSIC VALUE. MY IDEAS DO NOT.
BANK
BANK
ANOTHER NOTCH IN MY BELT.
I HAD TO. MY PANTS WERE FALLING DOWN. I'VE NEVER BEEN THIS SKINNY.
SWIMMING IN A MED T SHIRT.
I GUESS IT'S A GOOD THING, I DON'T LOOK LIKE I'M STARVING JUST LIKE I'M STILL A KID. (WITH GREY HAIR)
HAVE YOU LOST MORE WEIGHT?
I THINK SO.
I LOVE YOUR LIFE.
REALLY?
WELL, YOU'RE ONLY SEEING AN ASPECT.
GREASE
NO, IT'S YOUR ENERGY. I CAN FEEL IT.
OH.

5/2/16
THE CARPET NEEDED TO GO. IT WAS NASTY 16 YEARS AGO WHEN I MOVED IN.
GRRR!
I USED A SCREWDRIVER, HAMMER, CHISSEL, GRINDER, SHOVEL, WET/DRY VAC, KITCHEN KNIFE, MOP BROOM + PLYERS + ABOUT 7 HOURS TO GET THAT NASTY CARPET OUT.
I'M FULL OF DUST AND SORE AS HELL BUT I WON.
WHAT A CHORE!
YOU'RE THE SAME AGE AS MY SON, 33, 34?
NO MAN. I'M ALMOST 45.
THAT'S AMAZING! I HAD NO IDEA YOU WERE THAT OLD.
I AM.
WELL, MY HAT'S OFF TO YOU. WHAT EVER YOU'RE DOING IT'S IMPRESSIVE.
HEH. THANKS.
HEY!
HEY. I HAD A QUESTION FOR YOU.
THE OTHER DAY YOU POKED YOUR HEAD IN AND ASKED IF I WAS OK. HOW DID YOU KNOW SOMETHING WAS WRONG?
I JUST DID. SOMETIMES I JUST KNOW.
IT'S A WIERD WACKY WORLD THANK GOD FOR THAT!
HEH.

5/5/16
EDDIE GOT IN A MOTORCYCLE ACCIDENT!
WE NEED TO GO SEE HIM.
NEXT WEEK!
THIS VAN IS SO NOISY!!
BUB BUB BUB BUB
MAN, I'M JUST THRILLED TO BE ALIVE AND I'M NOT LOSING MY LEG!
5/6/16
IT'S 5:30 AM. I'M AWAKE, MAY AS WELL GET UP.
IT'S HARD TO SEE PAST THE NOW WHEN NOW IS A WARM BED. BUT I KNOW THE TRUTH.
COLD!
THE TRUTH IS OUT IN THE HILLS WITH NATURE'S BRUSH STROKES IN HUES OF GREYS & PURPLES TO WARM MY HEART & SPIRITS. TO BE AWAKE.
RAD!
5/7/16
MAN, I'M SO BEAT BUT I CAN'T JUST SIT HERE LIKE A SLUG. WHAT TO DO...
HERE I COME TO THE RESCUE!
COFFEE!
OH SLEET NECTER OF THE GODS TO GUIDE ME TO PURPOSE ONCE AGAIN...

5/8/16
IS IT BAD? I JUST DON'T CARE THAT MUCH WHAT OTHER PEOPLE DO.
BLAH.
WETHER YOU'RE HAPPY OR SAD, ARE CONTENTED OR FULFILLED IN LIFE, THAT'S ON YOU
ALL I CAN DO IS FOCUS ON THOSE THINGS FOR ME - NO ONE CAN MAKE CHANGE EXCEPT ONE'S SELF.
5/9/16
OH HOW I HATE MY DRAWINGS...
EVERYTIME I LOOK AT THEM THEY LOOK AWFUL TO ME.
SO BAD.
I WISH I COULD MAKE MY HAND DO WHAT MY MIND IS SEEING BUT IT DOES NOT WORK THAT WAY.
5/10/16
HOLD ON PLEASE, I NEED TO FINISH UP WITH HER BEFORE I CAN HELP YOU!
THAT'S A PROBLEM OF ABUNDANCE.
I GUESS THAT'S A GOOD THING.

5/11/16
I NEED IT NOW.
CAN'T. I HAVE 4 BIKES AHEAD OF YOU, YOU'LL NEED TO WAIT YOUR TURN.
I CAME ALL THE WAY FROM STUDIO CITY.
SO I DON'T CARE IF YOU CAME FROM MARS. YOU HAVE TO WAIT YOUR TURN.
HOW OLD ARE YOU?
WELL TIME TO GROW UP THEN.
82.
5/12/16
NO MAN THAT PICTURE OF THE EARTH IS ALL CGI, WE DON'T REALLY KNOW. HAVE YOU SEEN NASAS SYMBOL? IT'S THE FORKED TONGUE!
OK.
ALSO THE EARTH IS NOT A ROUND AS THEY SAY IT IS, THE SUN IS SMALLER+CLOSER, THERE'S MATH TO PROVE ALL THIS!
REALLY.
IT'S A LOT TO SWALLOW ALL AT ONCE BUT IT MAKES ME WONDER.
5/13/16
POOR VAN. I LOADED IT OUT AND THEY TOWED IT BACK. SOMETIMES I WONDER WHY I KEEP DOING THIS.
WELL I JUST WENT TO IT, TRYING BATTERIES AND THEN HITTING THE TEST LIGHT, CHECKING EACH CONNECTION.
HMM.
AFTER A COUPLE HOURS SURE ENOUGH, I FIGURED IT OUT.
VAROOM!!

5/14/16
OH HOW I NEED TO PUT THIS DAY BEHIND ME. I HATE EVERYONE RIGHT NOW.
SNIFF.
I PUT SO MUCH TIME AND ENERGY INTO THINGS AND PEOPLE AND THEY FAIL YOU OVER AND OVER.
WHAT DO YOU MEAN YOU FORGOT?
I'M TRYING HARD NOT TO BECOME SOUR LIKE EVERYONE ELSE BUT RIGHT NOW, IT'S HARD.
5/15/16
I DON'T GET PEOPLE, WHY THEY ARE SO GRUMPY ALL THE TIME.
YEAH.
I THINK WE'RE LIKE THAT NORMALLY, AS AMERICANS. WE HAVE TO WORK AT NOT BEING GRUMPY.
I KNOW. FOR SURE I DID.
I WANT TO TRY AND DRIVE.
ARE YOU SURE DAD? WELL LETS GO SOME PLACE SAFE TO TRY.
CAN YOU MOVE YOUR FOOT OVER FROM THE GAS TO THE BRAKE?
NO. BUT I'LL JUST USE BOTH FEET LIKE I ALWAYS DID.
OH! WELL I NEVER KNEW THAT ABOUT YOU.

2/17/16

DO YOU HAVE THIS 24 x 3 TIRE?
YEAH, IT'S 25.00

WELL, I'M SENDING A GUY OVER THERE TELL HIM IT'S 30.00.
THAT PUTS ME IN A POSITION.

LOOK, IT'S 25.00 THEN IT'S 25. WHAT YOU WANT ME TO DO I CAN'T. NOT FOR THEM, BUT FOR ME. I CAN'T DO THAT.
OH.

2/18/16

I NEED IT NOW.
CAN'T. I HAVE 3 BIKES AHEAD OF YOU.
HOW LONG?
DON'T KNOW.

YOU'RE MAKING ME LATE.
NO, I'M NOT. YOU HAVE TO WAIT YOUR TURN.
I'VE BEEN COMING IN HERE FOR 10 YEARS.

YEAH, AND I'VE BEEN TELLING PEOPLE THEY HAVE TO WAIT THIER TURN FOR 12 YEARS.

IT IS SO HARD NOT TO TAKE YOUR TRASH AROUND WITH YOU.

LOTS OF PEOPLE CAN'T NOT LEAVE IT AT HOME, NOT DOING THAT RUINS EVERYTHING AROUND YOU.

I TRY HARD TO LEAVE THAT CRAP AT HOME.

5/20/16
OH THE MOST TERRIFING ACT! IT PREYS UPON MY MIND.
CAN I CHANGE AN IDEA THAT I'VE HELD ON TO FOR SO LONG, SO HARD? SHOULD I? HOW DO I KNOW IF I'M WRONG TO DO SO?
I ONLY KNOW IF I TRY, BUT IF I DO THERE'S NO GOING BACK.
DOOM EITHER WAY.
5/21/16
OH HOW LOVE ESCAPES ME AGAIN AND AGAIN. I DON'T KNOW WHY.
I'VE TRIED SO HARD TO FIND SOMEONE TO LOVE AND IT NEVER LASTS. JUST WHEN I THINK I'VE GOT A HANDLE ON IT, LOVE SLIPS THROUGH MY FINGERS.
AM I DESTEND TO WALK THROUGH THIS LIFE ALONE? WHAT IS MY CHARACTER DEFECT? OH YEAH....
I'M REAL.
5/22/16
HEY WHAT'S THAT?
I HAVE FOOD FOR YOU.
WOW! THANKS! WHAT DID I DO TO DESERVE THIS?
NOTHING.
YOU'RE MY FRIEND.

5/23/16
SPENDING SO MUCH TIME ON A FLYER, I DID NOT LIKE THE OLD ONE SO I'M MAKING A NEW ONE.
WHY? WELL I FEEL THAT I HAVE TO GIVE EVERYTHING MY ALL. EVERYTHING, EVERY PERSON ALL THE TIME MY ALL.
SO IN THE END I KNOW I DID MY BEST IN EVERYWAY AND CAN'T FEEL LIKE ANYONE OR ANY THING WAS WASTED BY MY ACTIONS.
5/24/16
SO MUCH STUFF, I COULD GET BY WITH LESS.
IT'S HARD TO KNOW IF ANOTHER THING BRINGS YOU CLOSER TO HAVING MORE COOL STUFF.
OR YOUR STUFF JUST WINDS UP OWNING YOU.
WHERE DO I PUT IT?
5/25/16
SNAP!
WELL THAT'S A NEW ONE...
ONE RIDE CUT SHORT AT LEAST I DO THIS ALL THE TIME SO I DON'T FEEL CHEATED.

5/26/16
CAN YOU TAKE THE CASSETTE OFF THIS RIM? IT'S SUPER STUCK.
SURE.
MOMENTS LATER...
WHA?!
HERE YOU GO!
HOW DID YOU DO THAT?
OH, I TOOK IT TO THE GUN SHOW!
5/27/16
!
I HAVE NO PROBLEM WITH CRITTERS OUTSIDE.
LET'S GET THE TRAP.
BUT IN MY HOUSE, I'M NOT TAKING ON BOARDERS.
PEANUT BUTTER "MOUSE CRACK"
5/28/16
I DON'T KNOW IF I'LL BE BUSY IF YOU GET HERE. I DON'T KNOW HOW LONG IT WILL TAKE.
YOU MEAN THAT GUY IS MAD AT YOU BECAUSE YOU CAN'T SEE INTO THE FUTURE?
MORE OR LESS. YEAH I GET THAT ONE EVERY DAY.

5/29/16
MY DAD SAID HE'D RATHER HAVE WEALTH AND MISERY THEN BE POOR + HAPPY.
NOT ME
ALL MONEY DOES IS BUY YOU COMFORT, NOTHING MORE.
I'D TRADE THAT FOR LOVE AND PEACE OF MIND ANY OLD DAY.
NOT ME.
5/30/16
3 MOUNTIAN PEAKS, 60+ MILES AND 7000 FEET OF ELEVATION.
I'VE NEVER ORGANIZED A ROAD RIDE BEFORE. I FIGURED I'D BE RIDING ALONE OR WITH ONE PERSON. WE HAD 18 STARTERS.
AT THE END, WE DID IT. SOME FINISHED, SOME NOT BUT ALL KNOWING THEY DID THEIR BEST.
RIDE COMPLETED BUTTON
5/31/16
GET UP I GUESS..
OH, SO SORE FROM YESTERDAY..
OK..SLOWLY...TO... THE... COFFEE... POT...

6/1/16
SO?
YEAH I GOT DUMPED FOR JESUS.
THAT'S SO INTOLERANT.
YEAH, IT IS I KNOW.
JUST LIKE THE REST THOUGH, THEY ALL COME BACK TO YOU 18 MONTHS LATER.
I DON'T GET IT.
WHAT?
WHY IT HAS TO BE SO POINTLESSLY DIFFICULT?
6/2/16
USING OLD ROAD BIKE FRAMES, I MADE A "NEW" BIKE FOR COASTER BRAKE OFF ROAD RIDING. I WANTED A LIGHTER BIKE AND WANTED TO MAKE IT MYSELF.
IT RODE LIKE A DREAM. I COULD NEVER GET ANY THING LIKE IT BY SPENDING MONEY. I WAS SO HAPPY WITH THE RESULT.
SICK!
THE BEST IS I MADE IT MYSELF AND ONLY SPENT $3.00 ON A NEW CHAIN (WHOLESALE OF COURSE)
6/3/16
NICE TO SEE SOMEONE SITTING WITH NO WIRES ATTACHED.
?
OH YEAH, I'M AGAINST WIRES.
NO CELL PHONE?
NO.
THAT'S SO GOOD.
?

6/4/16
ABAST YE!
WATER BALOON
LATER.
YOU GUYS DRESSED UP LIKE PIRATES AND BATTLED IN THE LAKE AT THE PARK?!
YES.
YES.
HOW?! THERE'S NO WAY THAT CAN BE LEGAL!
HEH.
HEH.
6/5/16
WELL MOM, THERE'S SO MUCH ABOUT WHAT DRIVES ME THAT YOU HAVE NEVER SEEN.
LIKE THAT GARBAGE DISPOSAL. I WOULD HELP ANYONE IN MY LIFE LIKE I HELPED YOU WITH THAT. MY ALL AT ALL TIMES.
IT'S ALL I HAVE REALLY.
6/6/16
WHERE DO WE GO WHEN WE SLEEP? ANOTHER WORLD? OR A LAND WITH ONLY ONE TRUE OCCUPANT?
WHAT IF OUR WAKING LIFE IS REALLY THE DREAM AND THE DREAM IS THE REAL LIFE? BOTH WORLDS COUNT. I'VE SEEN THINGS IN DREAMS THAT CAME TRUE.
WHAT THE?
SLEEP IS IMPORTANT THOUGH. WITHOUT SLEEP, FOOD OR WATER LACK OF SLEEP KILLS YOU FIRST. SO DO IT WELL!

6/7/16
HERE'S SOME STEW I MADE FROM MY OWN GARDEN. CABBAGES, CALIFLOUR & BROCOLLI!
FOR ME?
LOTS O' CABBAGE! GOOD!
HOW WAS IT?
SO GOOD! I'VE BEEN FARTING UP A STORM ALL DAY!
6/8/16
ONE DAY I HOPE FOR HUMANITY TO STOP SUCKING SO BAD BUT IT WON'T EVER HAPPEN.
THE MORE ENCOUNTERS I HAVE WITH PEOPLE, THE MORE I SEE THAT WE ARE DOOMED.
WHAT DO YOU MEAN I HAVE TO!? WAIT MY TURN..
YEAH.
WHILE I CAN CHOOSE TO RISE ABOVE, I FEAR MOST PEOPLE CAN'T
THAT CAVE IS SOUNDING REALLY GOOD NOW.
6/9/16
SLAM!
KEYS?
HOW COULD I LOCK MYSELF OUT? WELL I DID.
WHO'S SMARTER, ME OR THE DOOR?
WELL SO MUCH FOR SECURITY, IN 10 MINUTES I WAS IN MY PLACE.
ANY ONE CAN BREAK IN HERE.

6/10/16

STRESS IS A KILLER. AT TIMES I FEEL LIKE A BALLOON STRETCHED TO IT'S LIMIT.

IN MY LIFE'S JOURNEY I'M LOOKING FOR THE KEY TO LET THE PRESSURE OUT, TO NOT STRESS.

THUS FAR IT HAS BEEN A CONSTANT CHASE TO THE HORIZON TO SURMOUNT, ONLY TO FIND ANOTHER ONE DAY I HOPE IT WILL END.

IT'S REAL SIMPLE. YOU GET ONE ITERATION, ONE PASS THROUGH THIS LIFE NO MATTER WHAT YOU BELIEVE.

SO LIVE WELL AND NEVER FORGET TO PLAY, DO AS MUCH AS YOU CAN AS OFTEN AS YOU CAN,

FOR SOON ENOUGH IT WILL BE OVER.

6/12/16

ANOTHER WEEK HAS GONE BY, HOW FAST THE TIME TICKS OFF.

MY LIFE BEING PAST THE 1/2 WAY POINT I'VE DONE SO MUCH BUT FEEL LIKE I'VE DONE SO LITTLE.
TO DO

I GUESS IT'S A GOOD THING TO FEEL THAT WAY INSTEAD OF HAVING THE SENSE OF TIME DRAGGING BY.

6/13/16
IDEAS COME AND GO SO QUICKLY, IT'S HARD TO HOLD ON TO ONE.
!
AND THE IDEA THAT I'LL WALK THE EARTH ALONE IS ONE THAT I SEEM TO KEEP COMING BACK TO.
BUT I'M NOT READY TO GIVE UP ON MYSELF YET.
6/14/16
LOOK MAN, I HAVE NO MONEY. NONE CAN YOU FRONT ME?
UH
IT'S 12
YEAH.
I'LL GET IT TO YOU I SWEAR!
IF YOU DON'T, GETTING YOU OUT OF MY LIFE FOREVER FOR A SMALL SUM LIKE THAT, IS A BARGAIN!
6/15/16
MAN, YOU GOT SOME SERIOUS INTEGRITY. THATS SOMETHING, THAT IS ADMIRABLE
OK?
YOU GOT MORE INTEGRITY THAN THE COPS.
HEH.
WELL, THAT DOES NOT TAKE MUCH, TO BE BETTER THAN THEM.
!

6/16/16
WHAT CAN I REALLY EXPECT?
WHEN SOMEONE LIES TO ME OR FAILS ME IN A WAY I DEEM TO BE NOT ACCEPTABLE, THAT'S IT. I GET THEM OUT OF MY LIFE.
WE'RE DONE THEN.
I WON'T WASTE TIME ON THE BAD ONES. I'D RATHER BE ALONE THAN SURROUND MYSELF WITH MORAL WEAKLINGS.
6/17/16
MMM. MMM. MMM. MMM. MMM. MMM.
WADA THINK? IT'S MY IMPRESSION OF A CELL PHONE ON VIBRATE!
PRETTY GOOD.
6/18/16
LOOK MAN, WISDOM IS NOT TRANSFERABLE. YOU HAVE TO FIGURE OUT THINGS FOR YOURSELF.
ALL OF HUMAN HISTORY YOU'D THINK WE CAN LOOK BACK A BEGIN ANEW WITHOUT ALL THE MISTAKES WE'VE MADE IN THE PAST. BUT NO! WE NEVER LEARN.
AND WE NEVER WILL.

6/19/16
HOW WAS THE RIDE?
OH, WE HAD AN ADVENTURE!
WE GOT YELLED AT BY SOME GAS CO. SHRUB. SO WE SPLIT UP.
EXCEPT ME, I WAS HIDING IN THE BUSHES!
6/20/16
TOO MUCH COFFEE, HEAT WAVE AND STUPID INTERNET. DOWN THE RABBIT HOLE I GO.
DREDGING UP PEOPLE FROM THE PAST. OLD LOVES, OLD FRIENDS, NOT SURE IF I SHOULD.
OH WOW. HE LOOKS AWFUL.
I THINK AT TIMES I JUST FEEL LIKE I'VE LOST TOUCH WITH EVERYONE AND EVERYTHING.
IT'S A LONELY WORLD.
6/21/16
LITTLE SPECS OF LIGHT UPON THE MOUNTIAN.
WE RODE THROUGH THE NIGHT UP ONE OF THE STEEPEST HILLS THEN OVER THE SPINE OF THE RANGE.
AFTER SUCH A RIDE, THE REWARD WAS ALL THE SWEETER.

6/22/16
I GUESS MY PROBLEM IS I'M LOVE STARVED.
- GIRGLE...
EVERYTHING ELSE I HAVE IN ABUNDANCE, LOVE HAS ALWAYS BEEN HARD TO FIND.
NOPE.
GOING TO BED HUNGRY NIGHT AFTER NIGHT MAKES ONE LEARY IN THE MORNING.
STOP IT.
6/23/16
ALL THE POWER TO CONNECT WITH OTHERS AND THERE'S NO CONNECTION.
WRR WRR WRR
IN A SEA OF HUMANITY WE ALL DRIFT ALONE. CONNECTIONS WITH OTHERS IS NO LONGER REAL BUT THROUGH PROXY. WE DISCONNECT AND CALL IT "SOCIAL."
CLICK CLICK
TECHNOLOGY DOES NOT IMPROVE THE QUALITY OF OUR LIVES, IT ONLY MAKES MAN'S INHUMANITY TO MAN ALL THE GREATER STILL.
6/24/16
I GOT TO BE UP AT 5:30 IN THE AM. ADULT STUFF.
DON'T YOU HATE THAT?
NAH, NOT REALLY. I NEVER FORGET TO PLAY. I DO MORE THAN MOST.
I PLAY A LOT.
THAT'S GOOD.

6/25/16
ALL DAY LONG THE DREAD HUNG OVER ME AT WORK. I HAD TO TRY SO HARD TO KEEP IT IN.
SNIFF...
AS I PEDALED HOME I KNEW DOOM WAS A PHONE CALL AWAY.
-SNIFF-
AND IT WAS.
DAD DIED.
6/26/16
I SO JUST WANTED TO BE ALONE BUT I WENT OVER TO MY PARENTS HOUSE ANYWAY.
DOING THE RIGHT THING EVEN WHEN IT'S THE LAST THING YOU WANT TO DO IS THE HARDEST THING YOU CAN DO.
HEY.
BUT IT'S THE ONLY THING YOU CAN DO.
YOU ARE SO DIRTY! I'M GLAD YOU CAME!
ME TOO
6/27/16
STAYING MOTIVATED IS A BEAR.
FIGHTING EVERY URGE TO JUST LAY DOWN AND QUIT, IT IS EVER PRESENT.
BUT THEN I'D BE LIKE EVERYONE ELSE.
OH YEAH, I FORGOT ABOUT THAT PART.

DO YOU HAVE A FAVORITE PHILOPHER?
I SORT OF HAVE MY OWN IDEAS.
YEAH?
WELL, PERCEPTION IS ALWAYS FLAWED SO IF THAT IS TRUE THAN TRUTH IS NOT REAL.
OH.
OK?
A LETTER WITH NO RETURN ADDRESS. NO LETTER INSIDE JUST A PHOTO COPY OF SOME BIBLE QUOTES.
OK?
WHO? AND WHY? JUST ANOTHER ONE OF MY WEIRD MOMENTS.
F'ING WEIRDO.
IN THERE.
WE WENT IN A TUNNEL FOR OVER A MILE IN THE COOL DARK.
ALL THESE YEARS I HAVE DREAMED OF A TUNNEL I COULD RIDE MY BIKE THROUGH AND IT WAS THERE ALL ALONG.

7/1/16
SOME ONE STOLE MY BACK PACK!
I LOOKED ALL OVER FOR IT, ONLY AFTER SOME TIME HAD PASSED I REALIZED I WAS THINKING OF THE DAY BEFORE.
OH MY!
SELDOM DO I FORGET THINGS OR NOT KEEP MY MIND IN ORDER SO SUCH MOMENTS CREATE A LITTLE WORRY FOR ME.
!
7/2/16
I NEED TO PULL OUT THE BIKES SO COULD YOU MOVE OVER FOR A FEW MINUTES?
OH! I GUESS I'M IN THE WAY HUH?!
YEAH, YOU ARE.
7/3/16
YEP - IT'S STOLEN
THAT SUCKS!
YEAH, OH WELL. I SHOULD LEARN NOT TO LEAVE STUFF IN MY TRUCK.
I HAVE OTHER THINGS THAT WEIGH ON MY MIND MORE THOUGH.

LET'S MOVE THE CARS.
I CAN MOVE MY CAR.
WUB WUB WUB WUB WUB
NO. IT'S TWO POINTS.
1. A PLACE TO PARK.
AND 2. I GET TO PISS OFF MY ASSHOLE NEIGHBOR.
I KNOW. LAUGH IT UP. IT'S GOOD FOR YOU.
I KNOW.
I LOVE TO LAUGH. I THINK WE CAN USE MORE OF IT.
WHEN DID EVERYONE GET SO DAMN SERIOUS?
SO...
FLIPPERS!
DO YOU THINK WE CAN MEND THEM WITH A BICYCLE TUBE?
I DUNNO...
...BUT YOU JUST MADE MY DAY!

7/7/16

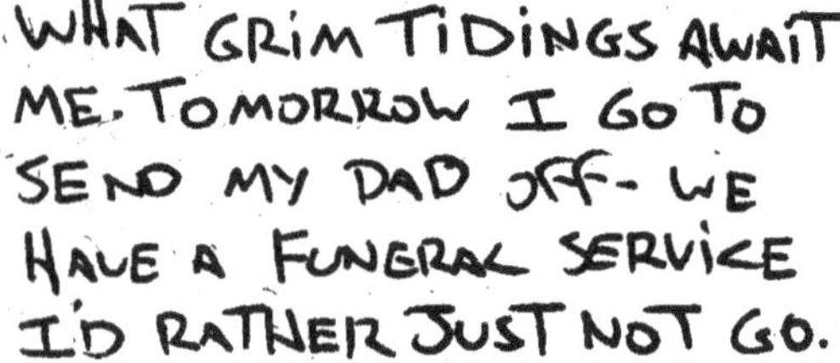

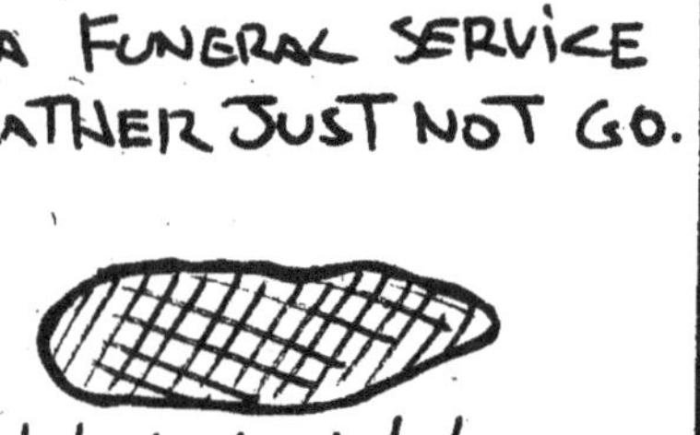

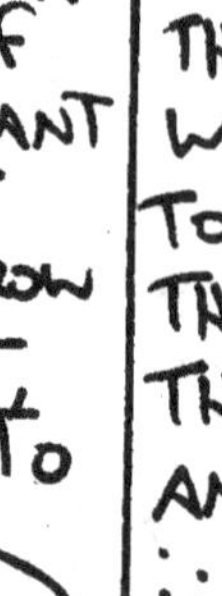

7/8/16

7/9/16

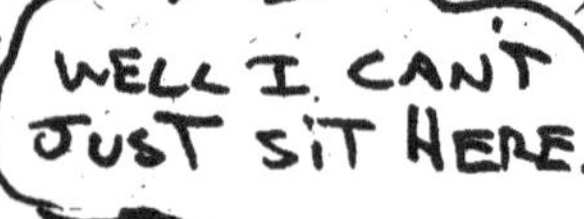

7/10/16
OH MAN!
MY SHOE LACE GOT STUCK IN MY CRANK JUST AS I WORKED MY WAY INTO FIRST PLACE AND QUICKLY LOST IT.
GASP! WHEEZE!
I JUST KEPT PEDALING UNTIL IT SNAPPED. THAT'S WHAT I NEEDED TO PUSH ON FOR THE WIN.
I'M BEAT.
7/11/16
WHAT DID I DO TODAY? I ROOFED A SHED. MAILED OUT A PAIR OF BARS I SOLD. A SEAT POST & A BIKE! COOL.
WRRRRR
I WELDED A BMX SIDE-HACK AND FIXED TWO OTHERS. SWAPED OUT THE A-ARM ON MY VAN W/ A FRIEND. READ. MADE 40 HAND-MADE ENVELOPES.
PRINTED FLYERS, LAUGHED. ORGANIZED SOME BIKE JUNK. UPDATED MY EVENTS ON THE WEB. PLANTED SOME ICE PLANT IN POTS. I FECT LIKE IT WAS NOT ENOUGH AND FECT ALONE WHICH IS A BUMMER.
WELL, IT'S A START.
7/12/16
YOU GOT THESE FOR US?
YEAH.
TEENAGE MUTANT NINJA TURTLES
WE DID THE NINJA TURTLE RIDE THROUGH A TUNNEL 1½ MILES LONG.
AND OF COURSE AT THE END WE HAD PIZZA.

SO MUCH RUNS THROUGH OUR HEADS... IT IS SCARY WHEN YOU THINK OF IT.
WHY?
DO THAT NEXT.
WORRY
WHAT DID I FORGET?
FIX VAN
LONELY
SO MUCH TO DO.
MAKE TROPHIES
HUNGRY
TIRED
THINGS HURT.
GET FOOD
I HAVE A GOOD REASON. ON THE LIST.
TRY AND RELAX
OUR MODERN WORLD IS POISON. MORE TOYS, TECH, THINGS, STUFF, MONEY ETC. FAILS TIME AND TIME AGAIN TO EASE OUR TROUBLED THOUGHTS.
A MOMENTS PEACE...
PERHAPS ITS TOO LATE TO TURN BACK.
...WOULD BE NICE.
BA DA BA DA DA DA
HOW ARE YOUR HANDS?
OH! THEY HURT!
LOVE THE VAN.
YEAH I GET LOTS OF PROPS
FROM OLD DUDES
YEAH.
NOT FROM THE LADIES THOUGH.
REALLY? I DO IN MINE.
YEAH MAN, YOU GOT ALL THAT HAIR, YOU GOT GAME.
NO WAY. THE ONLY GAME I HAVE IS SORRY, TROUBLE, AND UNO.

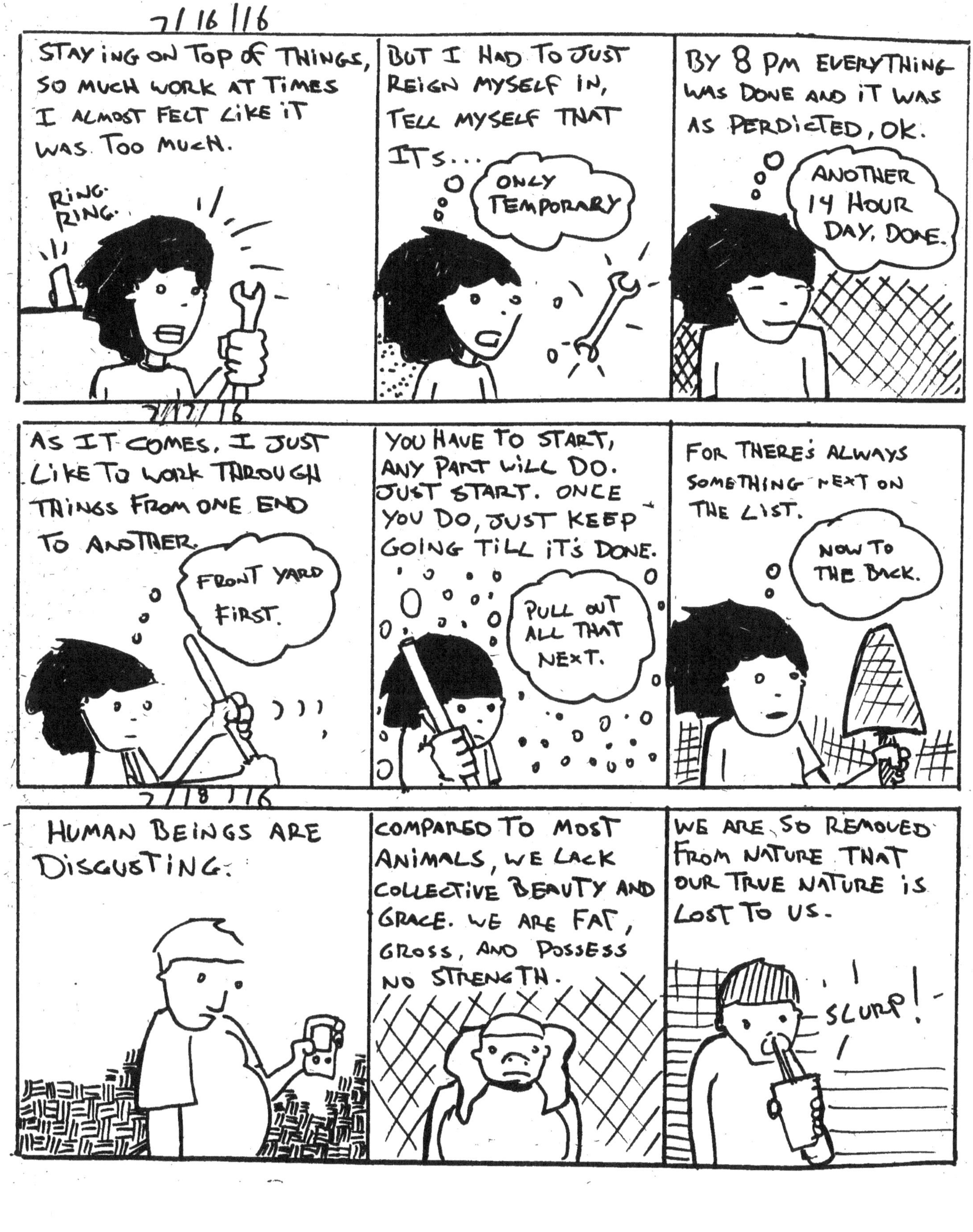

Panel 1: STAYING ON TOP OF THINGS, SO MUCH WORK AT TIMES I ALMOST FELT LIKE IT WAS. TOO MUCH.

Panel 2: BUT I HAD TO JUST REIGN MYSELF IN, TELL MYSELF THAT ITS...

Panel 3: BY 8 PM EVERYTHING WAS DONE AND IT WAS AS PERDICTED, OK.

7/17/16

Panel 4: AS IT COMES, I JUST LIKE TO WORK THROUGH THINGS FROM ONE END TO ANOTHER.

Panel 5: YOU HAVE TO START, ANY PART WILL DO. JUST START. ONCE YOU DO, JUST KEEP GOING TILL IT'S DONE.

Panel 6: FOR THERE'S ALWAYS SOMETHING NEXT ON THE LIST.

7/18/16

Panel 7: HUMAN BEINGS ARE DISGUSTING.

Panel 8: COMPARED TO MOST ANIMALS, WE LACK COLLECTIVE BEAUTY AND GRACE. WE ARE FAT, GROSS, AND POSSESS NO STRENGTH.

Panel 9: WE ARE SO REMOVED FROM NATURE THAT OUR TRUE NATURE IS LOST TO US.

7/19/16

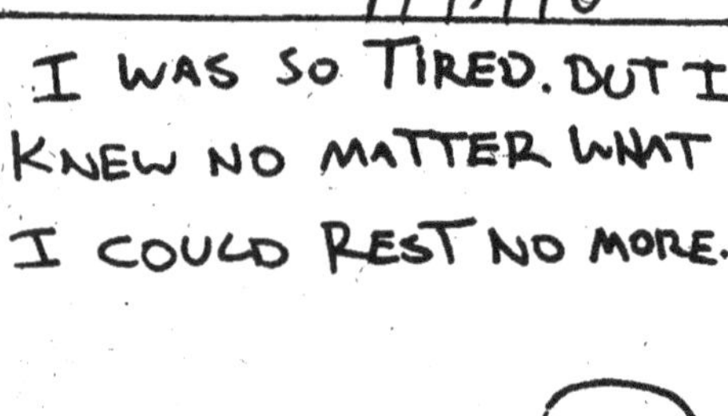
I WAS SO TIRED. BUT I KNEW NO MATTER WHAT I COULD REST NO MORE.
OH.

I COULD FEEL THE HEAT AND HARD RIDING SAPPING THE WILL TO MOVE FROM ME.
GET UP!

YOUR BODY LIES TO YOU ALL THE TIME. BE CAREFUL OF WHAT YOU CHOOSE TO LISTEN TO.
NO MATTER WHAT, RIDE TOMORROW.

7/20/16

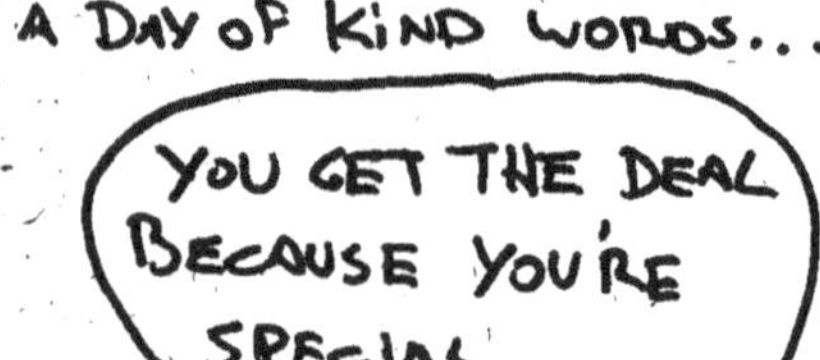
A DAY OF KIND WORDS....

YOU GET THE DEAL BECAUSE YOU'RE SPECIAL.
!

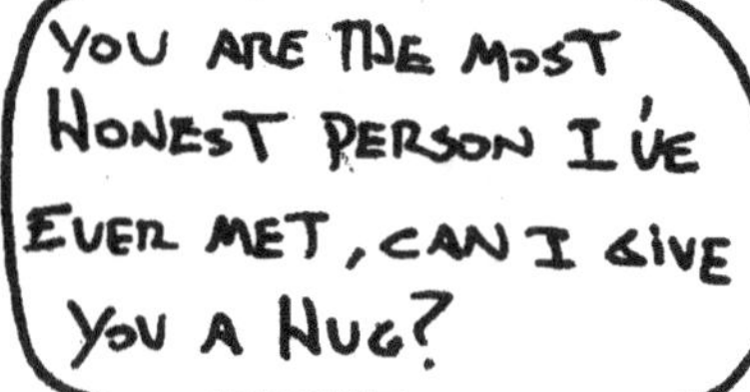

YOU ARE THE MOST HONEST PERSON I'VE EVER MET, CAN I GIVE YOU A HUG?
UM... OK.

NICE WHEEL STAND BRO!

7/21/16

WE ALL FEEL LIKE WE ARE STRONG, AND WHEN THE TIME IS THERE, DO THE RIGHT THING.
S

HOWEVER WHEN FACED WITH A REAL ISSUE MOST OF US, NEAR ALL OF US FALTER.
HELP!

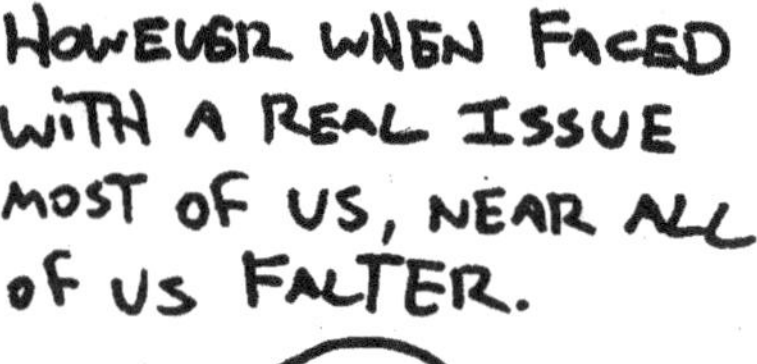
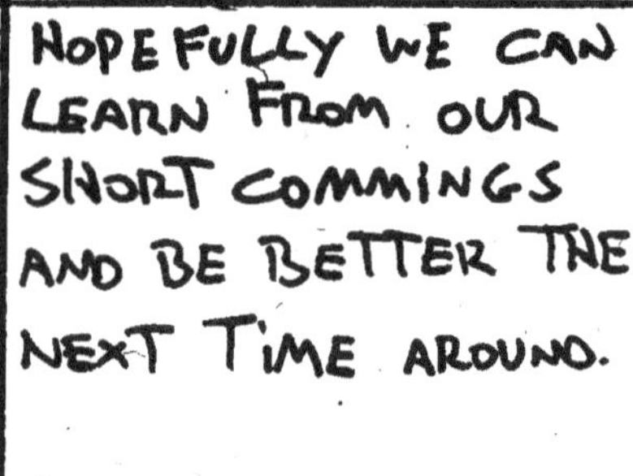

HOPEFULLY WE CAN LEARN FROM OUR SHORT COMMINGS AND BE BETTER THE NEXT TIME AROUND.

7/22/16
LOOKING AT MY FAN, LIKE MANY THINGS I HAVE NO IDEA AS TO HOW IT GOT HERE.
SOME THINGS YOU NEVER HAVE TO PAY FOR, THEY JUST COME TO YOU. LIKE HAMMERS, I MUST HAVE A DOZEN OF THEM; NEVER BOUGHT ONE IN MY LIFE.
JUST LIKE PEOPLE, STUFF JUST FLOWS IN AND OUT AND WHY, WHO KNOWS?
7/23/16
GOOD RIDE!
YEAH! BOB YOU'RE A BEAST!
OH, I'M PRETTY SLOW.
FOR YOUR AGE? I DON'T THINK SO.
67
I KNOW GUYS 20 YEARS YOUNGER THAN YOU THAT CAN'T KEEP UP.
7/24/16
HOW DO YOU BEAT THE HEAT?
OH THAT. WELL, I DON'T.
I JUST MELT.

7/25/16
STUCK IN TRAFFIC.
IT'S OK THOUGH. I SELDOM DO IT. I FEEL BAD FOR PEOPLE THAT THIS IS A HUGE PART OF THIER LIVES.
I WOULD NEVER SEE DOING THAT TO MYSELF AS NORMAL. IT'S A TINY DEATH EVERY MILE.
Boo.
7/26/16
SANDWICHES?
CHOMP. GOBBLE.
DID YOU EAT BOTH? ONE WAS FOR ME!
YOU DIDN'T SAY ANYTHING.
7/27/16
IF YOU CAN'T KEEP A PROMISE TO YOURSELF, WHAT GOOD ARE YOU TO ANYONE?
I KNOW I SAID NO MORE BUT...
THE WORLD WILL BE AS IT IS UNTIL PEOPLE MASTER THEMSELVES. YOU HAVE TO START WITH YOU.
I GUESS SINCE THAT WON'T EVER HAPPEN, WE AS A SPECIES ARE DOOMED.

7/28/16
HOW LONG HAVE YOU KNOWN HIM?
SINCE THE 1980's
THAT LONG? WOW!
YEAH, WHEN WE ALL HAD HAIR OR HAIR THE SAME COLOR.
I FORGOT YOU ARE WAY OLDER THAN YOU LOOK.
YEAH.
7/29/16
ONE STEP CLOSER TO FINISHING A LONG PROJECT.
CLICK CLICK CLICK
IT'S GOOD TO FINISH HARD THINGS.
I NEED THE NEXT DRAWING.
YOU CAN LOOK BACK AND SAY...
WE DID IT.
7/30/16
AS TIME MARCHES ON I FEEL LESS AND LESS INVOLVED WITH HUMANS.
THINGS SEEM SIMPLE TO ME. ANY PROBLEMS I HAVE ARE 99% IN MY HEAD. I DO, OTHERS TALK IN THIS I AM ALONE, IT'S OK.
CONNECTIVITY HAS ALWAYS LEAKED ME BUT NOW AT THIS MOMENT IT FEELS LIKE TAKING A WARM SWEATER OFF ON A HOT DAY, IT FEELS RIGHT TO LET IT GO.
WHO NEEDS UNO?

7/31/16
WELL, WHAT DID YOU EXPECT?
HMM.
I DON'T THINK ONE CAN TIE THEIR HAPPINESS TO ANOTHER PERSON.
IT HAS TO COME FROM WITHIN.
HMM.
I WATCHED THAT SHOW YOU TOLD ME TO CHECK OUT. NOT SO GOOD.
REALLY?
I JUST FEEL LIKE THERE ARE SO MANY THINGS THAT NEED MY TIME I SHOULD BE DOING.
I GET IT, IF YOU'RE GOING TO WASTE TIME ON T.V, IT HAS TO BE EXCELLENT T.V.
YEAH.
8/2/16
WE RODE OVER TO HOLLYWOOD FROM THE SFV.
TO A MAGICAL PLACE CALLED OKI DOG.
OKI DO
WHERE WE WERE REWARDED FOR OUR HARD JOURNEY WITH FOOD FROM THE GODS.
CHILI
2 HOT DOGS
PASTRAMI
CHEESE
IN A TORTILLIA

8/3/16
ARE YOU OK?
NO... I'M INJURED.. SOME ONE..BLUBREL DEG MESSS....
IT WAS WIERD. I JUST LEFT HIM THERE, I WAS TOO BUSY TO DO ANYTHING ABOUT IT.
HOPE HE'S OK, AND DID NOT PUKE IN MY BATHROOM.
LATER HE WALKED OUT.
SORRY ABOUT THAT.
8/4/16
A NEW FRONTIER...
SQUISH SQUISH
I DID LAUNDRY. I DO IT NOT TOO MUCH BUT TODAY WAS DIFFERENT. TODAY I SEPERATED MY WHITES.
BLEACH
THE FIRST TIME EVER.
IT LOOKS CLEAN FOR ONCE.
8/5/16
TALKING ABOUT IT ONLY MAKES IT TAKE LONGER.
I HATE TALKING, TALKING IS A WASTE OF TIME. TALKING IS BULLSHIT.
SHUT UP. SHUT UP. SHUT UP. SHUT UP. SHUT UP. SHUT UP.
JUST SHUT UP.

8/6/16
WHAT IS THERE TO WORRY ABOUT? I WORRY ABOUT WORRY.
I THINK STRESS WILL KILL ME AT SOME POINT. MY MIND SELDOM AT EASE.
TO LET GO. A GREAT IDEA. IF ONLY I HAD THE KEY TO UNLOCK THE WAY TO INNER PEACE, THAT WOULD BE GRAND.
8/7/16
YOU MADE IT!
HUF HUF HUF
OH MAN, THAT WAS HARD.
SURE.
YOU'LL GET IT BACK I KNOW.
UG. YOU DON'T EVEN LOOK TIRED!
I FEEL GOOD.
BUT HUNGRY.
8/8/16
HELLO
HEY.
ITS SO ODD HOW EVERYWHERE I GO PEOPLE KNOW ME.
HI.
HEY.
I DON'T LET IT GO TO MY HEAD THOUGH NEVER WOULD HAVE THOUGHT THAT I'D BE KNOWN BUT I AM.
STRANGE BUT GOOD.

8/9/16
HANGING WITH FRIENDS HAS BEEN SO GOOD LATLEY. WELL, IT FEELS RIGHT.
WE FORGET THAT OFTEN TIMES THE BEST THINGS ARE RIGHT IN FRONT OF US.
MEOW! MEOW!
BECAUSE WE'RE SO BUSY LOOKING AT WHAT LIES AHEAD.
HA HA HA HA
8/10/16
HUNGRY.
ALL DAY I KNEW WITH ALL THE ACTIVITY I WAS NOT EATING ENOUGH. I COULDN'T THINK STRAIGHT AT ALL.
WHERE I FILLED MY BELLY I LOST HUNGER AND THE WILL FOR THE DAY TO HOLD OUT TILL TOMMOROW.
WEAK.
8/11/16
WHAT A PETTY DICK HEAD!
OFTEN, I SEE HOW PEOPLE ACT AND I JUST SEE HOW THE MODERN WORLD IS A FAILURE.
HOW LAME CAN YOU BE?
IT WILL FAIL BECAUSE HUMANS HAVE GAINED NO WISDOM FROM THE PAST.
OH WELL

8/12/16
OH. HE GAVE ME THE PESANT WAVE OFF.
I LOVE WHEN PEOPLE GET MAD AT ME. BECAUSE I WONT GIVE THEM SPECIAL TREATMENT.
OH MAN.
IT MUST BE HARD GOING THROUGH LIFE THINKING YOU'RE MORE IMPORTANT THAN ANY ONE ELSE.
8/13/16
SANDING AND SANDING. SO MANY PARTS TO PREP.
NEARLY EVERY DAY I DID 5 OR 10 AND THEN I WAS DONE. IT WAS A TASK.
HUM. HUM.
MOST DAYS THOUGH I'D RATHER MESS WITH A MACHINE OR MAKE A PART THAN TALK.
8/14/16
UP AT 5:30 AM AND WE RACED. SO HARD BECAUSE I RODE IT THE NIGHT BEFORE TO MARK THE COURSE.
WORKED ALL DAY AND IT WAS A FULL HOUSE I WAS TURNING WRENCHES TILL THE VERY END.
THEN TRUCKED HOME A LOAD OF BIKE PARTS. UNLOADED MY VAN OF BIKES ETC. BY 8:30 OR SO. I WAS FINALLY DONE. YOU KNOW, I WOULDN'T HAVE IT ANY OTHER WAY.
OK. ENOUGH.

8/15/16

ALL RELATIONSHIPS ARE LIKE A JOB. YOU CROSS THE LINE, YOU GET FIRED. IT'S THAT SIMPLE.
I WASH MY HANDS OF YOU.

IT USED TO BOTHER ME BUT NOW WHEN IT HAPPENS LIKE A FLICK OF A SWITCH, I JUST TURN IT OFF.
ON
OFF

BECAUSE YOU SHOULD NEVER WASTE TIME ON THE BAD ONES.
HO HUM OH WELL...

A DEAD SQUIRREL!

I DON'T KNOW ABOUT YOU GUYS BUT I JUST BUNNY HOPPED A DEAD SQUIRREL!

PEOPLE WANT TO GET A HOLD OF ME AND JUST-NO. I COULDNT EVEN WORK UP THE DRIVE TO RETURN A PHONE CALL.
NAH.

AFTER BEING FORCED OVER AND OVER AGAIN TO TALK TO PEOPLE ALL DAY, I JUST WANT ALONENESS AND SILENCE. SILENCE MOST OF ALL.
I CAN'T HEAR YOU.

WHEN MY FACE HURTS I KNOW I'VE HAD TOO MUCH CRAP. I JUST NEED TO HIDE FOR A DAY AND IT WILL BE OK.
NO TALKING.

8/18/16
IT IS A CONSTANT SELF-REMINDER: NEVER FORGET TO VALUE WHAT YOU HAVE.
THIS IS GOOD.
LOOKING PAST WHAT YOU HAVE IS A SURE FIRE WAY TO FORGET THAT IT IS THERE.
THE GOOD STUFF
WHAT MAY BE
WHEN I'M HAVING A ROUGH TIME I TAKE A MOMENT TO REMEMBER.
WELL, IT COULD BE WAY WORSE.
8/19/16
JUST FINISH IT.
SO MANY GOOD IDEAS DIE ON THE VINE...
NO.. NOT.. YET..
BECAUSE THEY'RE WAITING TO BLOSSOM INTO SOMETHING GREAT.
IS IT DONE?
UM NO.
8/20/16
I HAVE NOT TRAIL RODE IN NEAR A WEEK, I WAS TOO TORE UP FROM THE LAST MONTH AND 1/2
MY LEGS HURT.
I HATE RESTING, I FEEL LIKE A QUITTER.
WHO CARES IF YOU HURT! JUST GO!
BUT BETTER TO QUIT FOR A SMALL TIME THAN TO HAVE YOUR BODY QUIT ON YOU.
I FEEL GOOD NOW.

8/24/16
IT'S 8.
HE'S LATE. LETS GO.
LATER:
WE HAD A FLAT
WE GOT THERE AT 8:04.
SO, YOU WERE LATE THEN.
8/22/16
I DON'T WANT TO TALK ABOUT OR CRITISIZE OTHER PEOPLE, IT'S LOW THINKING.
ANY LOOK AT ONES SELF WOULD SEE A NEED TO CLEAN ONES HOUSE FIRST BEFORE LOOKING AT OTHERS.
IF YOU SPENT 1/2 THAT ENERGY SPENT ON OTHERS ON YOUR SELF PERHAPS YOU'D BE SOMEWHERE.
8/23/16
GOT YOU!
CRUNCH!
HMM
WHAT? NO WAY! I SQUISHED YOU!

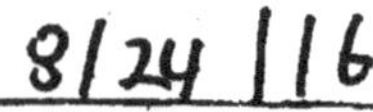
8/24/16

I'M PAST THE ½ WAY POINT IN MY LIFE AND AS TIME HAS GONE ON I FEEL MORE CONNECTED AND AT EASE WITH MY WORK.

BEFORE WORK I WORKED ON WORK AND AFTER WORK I WORKED SOME MORE.

I LOOK FORWARD TO LONG DAYS OF THINGS DONE AND WORK FINISHED. PRODUCTIVITY AT THE CORE OF MY BEING, AND OTHER PEOPLE? WELL LESS SO.

8/25/16

THAT'S THE LAST OF THEM.
B22
22

WELL THAT'S ONE STEP, POLISHING IS NEXT.

I COULD JUST MAKE STUFF ALL DAY, IT'S SO COOL.

8/26/16

ONE THING THAT ALWAYS MAKES ME HAPPY IS FIGURING OUT HOW TO DO SOMETHING BETTER.
NOW THAT I HAVE A BIKE TRAILER

IT MEANS THAT I CAN DO MORE, SAVE TIME AND BE ON TOP OF THINGS BETTER.
I CAN HAUL I BIKE IN AS I NEED THEM INSTEAD OF WAITING TO HAVE A LOT TO USE MY TRUCK.

IT ALSO MEANS I'VE IMPROVED ON MYSELF
THIS OPENS UP SO MUCH GOOD STUFF!

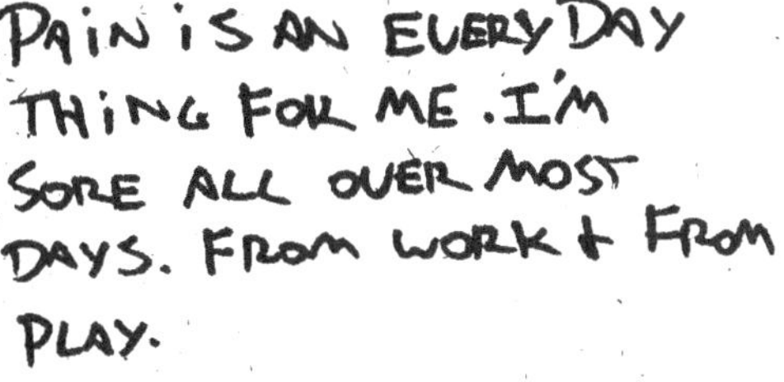

PAIN IS A BASELINE. LEGS HURT? RIDE MORE. HANDS HURT? YOU'RE DOING A LOT. AN INDICATOR THAT I'M IN THE RIGHT DIRECTION.

8/30/16
WHAT?
THERE'S A DEAD BODY IN YOUR YARD.
SO I LOOKED OUTSIDE AND SAW THE WHOLE STREET HAD BEEN BLOCKED OFF.
POLICE LINE DO NOT CR
SOMEONE HAD BEEN SHOT DOWN THE STREET.
FUNNY. SOUNDED LIKE FIRE WORKS.
8/31/16
I DON'T WANT TO BE ONE OF THOSE PEOPLE THAT MAKES EXCUSES INSTEAD OF DOING THINGS.
I OVER SLEPT.
ON OCCASSION I DO AND WHEN I DO I JUST GET SO MAD AT MYSELF.
THE WORLD IS FULL OF LOSERS LIKE THAT I WON'T DO THAT AGAIN.
JUST KEEP GOING AND KEEP IN MIND WHEN YOU MAKE AN EXCUSE TO NOT DO SOMETHING IT'S YOU WHO LOSES OUT THE MOST.
9/1/16
OH CRAP.
THAT'S ANOTHER X-GIRL FRIEND THAT'S CONNECTED TO ME VIA THE WEB, SOME HOW. I THINK THAT MAKES 4 OR 5 THAT I KNOW OF.
NO ESCAPE
THERE COULD BE EVEN MORE OUT THERE THAT AREN'T MAKING THEM SELVES KNOWN.
MANY WANT TO KEEP IN TOUCH BUT NOT STICK AROUND.

HOW I'VE BEEN IN A WIERD MOOD.
I THINK SOMETIMES YOU'RE JUST DOWN FOR NO REASON.
MADE MAD CASH THIS MONTH, SO WHAT.
I THINK AS LONG AS I'M AWARE OF IT AND KNOW IT WILL PASS I'LL BE FINE.
9/3/16
IT'S BEEN GOING ON FOR A WHILE.
I JUST DON'T WANT TO TALK TO ANYONE.
I THINK IT STEMS FROM WORK HAVING TO TALK TO PEOPLE ALL DAY WETHER OR NOT YOU WANT TO.
RING RING RING
Hi.
AT THE END OF THE DAY I CRAVE ONLY TWO THINGS...
SOLITUDE & SILENCE.
9/4/16
I'M LOOKING FOR PAUL.
RIGHT HERE.
YOU OLD MAN. I DIDN'T EVEN RECONIZE YOU, IT'S RALPH.
RALPH? WHA...
YOU'RE SO THIN! HAHA HA HA HO!
I FEEL LUCKY BECAUSE LOVE IS THE MOST POTENT FORCE IN MY LIFE.

9/5/16
AFTER YEARS OF THINKING ABOUT IT, I GOT IT OFF THE GROUND.
45 MILES ON CRUISERS ON THE TOP OF A MOUNTIAN - DIRT + ROAD. 20 + STARTED ONLY 1/2 FINISHED.
UNCRAMP LEGS!
HOPEFULLY WE'LL DO MORE BAD ASS RIDES. I KNOW I WILL.
TIME FOR HOT DOGS!
9/6/16
DO YOU HAVE A ADULT TRIKE?
I DO. IT'S 250.
CAN YOU HELP ME GET IT TO MY CAR?
SURE.
OK. I'LL TAKE IT.
COOL.
OH, IT'S SO NICE WHEN THEY ARE EASY LIKE THAT.
9/7/16
HEY! HOW'S IT GOING?
OH.
YOU KNOW.
LIVING LIFES ADVENTURE.

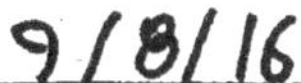

Row 1, Panel 1:

Row 1, Panel 2:

Row 1, Panel 3:

Row 2, Panel 1:

Row 2, Panel 2:

Row 2, Panel 3:

Row 3, Panel 1:

Row 3, Panel 2:

Row 3, Panel 3:

9/11/16
A DAY SPENT DOING THE WORK. UP AT 5:30 DID AN EVENT AND GOT DONE AT 5 PM.
OK, ON TO THE NEXT THING.
THEN WENT TO A GATHERING OF BIKE SHOP OWNERS & WORKERS TO TALK ABOUT WORK.
DO SOMETHING YOU LOVE AND YOU WILL WORK ALL THE TIME, BUT YOU WON'T MIND IT SO MUCH.
10 PM HOME. THAT'S A DAY!
9/12/16
I'M WILLING TO PUT THE TIME IN IF YOU ARE...
THAT'S THE DEAL. KEEP WORKING ON IT AND EVENTUALLY, YOU ARE DONE.
FOR MOST PEOPLE, THAT'S THE HARD PART.
9/13/16
PEOPLE TRY AND HUSTLE ME ALL THE TIME.
25.
AND THIS?
20.
SO 40 THEN.
NO.
I'M SURE THEY PULL THAT CRAP EVERYWHERE THEY GO.
25 + 20 ARE 45.
BUT I AM SELDOM IF EVER, FOOLED.
SO HOW MUCH?
I ALREADY SAID THAT.

9/14/16
HEY!
OH! HELLO.
I FINISHED THAT PICTURE WE WERE TALKING ABOUT. IT'S BEEN IN MY LOCKER FOR A WHILE. I HAVE NOT SEEN YOU!
LOCKER?
SEE YOU!
LOCKER? OH SHIT THIS GIRL IS IN HIGH SCHOOL!
9/15/16
WHAT? YOU DON'T HAVE A TV?!
NOT FOR 25 YEARS.
LOOK AT IT LIKE THIS: WHEN YOU'RE AT THE END OF YOUR DAYS YOU REGRET NOT TAKING ENOUGH RISKS OR LOVING SOMEONE ENOUGH.
BUT DO YOU HAVE REGRET ABOUT NOT CATCHING UP ON YOUR MORK & MINDY RE-RUNS? NO, YOU DON'T.
9/16/16
SO MANY THINGS AT ONCE AND IT JUST SCRAMBLES YOUR MIND.
I TRY TO HAVE A SIMPLE LIFE BUT IT IS ANYTHING BUT.
WHAT NOW FUCKING INTERNET FIX IT TOO MUCH TO DO TIRED CAN'T SLEEP WHAT?
HOWEVER IF IT WERE DIFFERENT I'D BE BORED TO DEATH.
NOW WHAT DO I DO?

9/17/16
RIDE?
7:30, RIDE AT 8.
YEAH.
NO, WE LEAVE AT 7:30 ANY LATER IS TOO LATE.
YOU CAN SLEEP SOME OTHER TIME.
9/18/16
ANOTHER CUP, YOU'LL BE AMPED.
IT'S A FREE REFILL.
THE OTHER PLACE I GO RAISED THIER PRICES SO I GET A SMALL IN A LARGE CUP. A REFILL IS A DOLLAR SO THATS $1.50 EACH CUP.
I DO THINGS LIKE THAT ALL DAY, THATS WHY I'M A THOUSANDAIRE!
HA!
9/19/16
SITTING AROUND WAITING FOR THINGS TO HAPPEN THAT DON'T HAPPEN SUCKS.
I THINK LOTS OF PEOPLE JUST WAIT AROUND FOR THINGS TO HAPPEN. BUT NOT ME, I GO MAKE THINGS HAPPEN.
SO WHEN I CAN'T, I DIE A LITTLE INSIDE.
THIS BLOWS.

9/20/16
THE TRUCK!
AFTER YEARS OF TRYING I FINALLY HAVE THE TIRES I WANTED TO MAKE.
ONLY 99 MORE TO GO.
67 CDS
LOADS OF TIRES.
THAT'S A LOT OF TIRES!
9/21
ALL THE WORRY ABOUT WHAT COULD GO WRONG AND...
THESE ARE BETTER THAN I EXPECTED!
WHEN I GOT TO LOOK AT THEM CLOSELY AND SAW MY HARD WORK MATERIALIZE INTO THE REAL, I WAS ELATED!
AT LONG LAST!
WAVES OF HAPPINESS AND CONTENTMENT WASH OVER ME AND I WAS FURFILLED.
HUM HUM HUM HUM HUM HUM HUM HUM HU HU HU
9/22/16
ANY LADIES?
NAH.
SOME DAYS I'M RACKED WITH TERRIBLE LONELYNESS AND OTHERS I FEEL LIKE I DON'T HAVE TIME FOR EVEN A CAT.
PERHAPS I THINK I NEED IT MORE THAN I REALLY DO.
HUM

9/23/16
EVERY DAY ONE TRIES TO GET WHAT THEY THINK THEY NEED. IT IS A CONSTANT SEARCH.
ARE WE THERE YET? DO YOU ACHIEVE SOME SENSE OF BALANCE?
I THINK A VITAL COMPONENT THAT PEOPLE OFTEN MISS IS TO LOOK AT ONE'S SELF TOO.
OH.
9/24/16
TODAY I LOST THE BATTLE WITH MYSELF.
I ALLOWED STRESS TO TAINT MY WHOLE DAY. I LOST A DAY OF ENJOYMENT AND PURPOSE FOR POINTLESS WORRY.
WHILE BEING AWARE OF IT IS ONE THING, DOING SOMETHING ABOUT IT, WELL THAT'S A DIFFERENT STORY.
9/25/16
HOW'S LIFE?
YEAH?
CAN'T COMPLAIN. YOU?
TRY BEING A BLACK MAN IN LA...
FUCK THAT.
HA HA HA HA!
I'LL TAKE WHITE PLEASE.

9/26/16
THERE'S THIS DOWN HILL DROP I WANT TO TRY, YOU WANT TO GIVE IT A GO?
SURE.
IT LOOKS SO INTIMIDATING FROM UP TOP.
I'LL GO FIRST
WOOOT!
OK. FUCK YOU.
9/27/16
BATTLE AFTER BATTLE. PEOPLE ARE SO HARD TO DEAL WITH SOMETIMES.
I DON'T KNOW HOW LONG IT'S GOING TO TAKE.
I FEEL LESS AND LESS CONNECTED TO PEOPLE. THEY VEX ME. I CAN SEE MY SELF NOT WANTING ANY CONTACT.
...
PERHAPS IT IS JUST A PHASE. WELL, I HOPE SO.
THAT SHACK OUT IN NOWHERE IS SOUNDING GOOD RIGHT NOW.
9/28/16
A LITTLE REMINDER: WHEN STRESSED, JUST GO RIDE.
UP IN THE MOUNTIANS AS THE SUN PEAKS OVER HEAD AND YOU BASK IN THE LIGHT OF A NEW DAY.
GLOWBULB.
COFFEE HELPS TOO.
OH YEAH.

9/29/16
I'M SO STUPID. I DID IT AGAIN, JUST WORRIED MYSELF SICK.
I'VE BEEN SO STRESSED OUT ABOUT MY BICYCLE TIRE VENTURE... SURE ENOUGH I GAVE MYSELF A STOMACH ACHE OVER IT.
DAMN.
AND OF COURSE, ALL FOR NOTHING.
DAMN!
SOLD! SOLD! SOLD!
9/30/16
I WISH I COULD DRAW.
YOU CAN.
I HATE MY DRAWINGS. I HAVE NO NATURAL TALLENT, NO REAL SKILL BUT I KEPT AT IT. 1000's UPON 1000's OF ITERATIONS.
BUT AT SOME POINT IN THE NOT TOO DISTANT PAST, I STARTED AT ZERO LIKE EVERYONE ELSE.
10
GOOD TO SEE YOU!
ANH... A TRIP DOWN MEMORY LANE...
YOU DID THAT!
I DID.
WOLFPAK HUSTLE
ONCE IN A GREAT WHILE IT'S A NICE PLACE TO VISIT.
BUT NEVER TO STAY.

10/2/16
I NEED A CIRCULAR/BELT SANDER.
YOU DO?
I HAVE ONE.
YOU HAVE THAT WORK STAND, I'LL TRADE YOU...
YES!
THE BARTER SYSTEM STILL ALIVE AND WELL!
10/3/16
WHEN YOUR NEEDS ARE NOT BEING MET, NOT MUCH ELSE MATTERS.
FOOD SLEEP FOOD SLEEP FOOD SLEEP FOOD SLEEP FOOD
I RUN ON FUMES ALL THE TIME SO IT IS EASY TO GO PAST THE POINT WHEN I CAN FUNCTION...
IF I DON'T EAT NOW, I'M DONE FOR.
SOME NEEDS JUST LEAVE A NAGGING REMINDER THAT YOU ARE LACKING.
I'M LOVE STARVED TOO.
10/4/16
EVERYONE DOES THAT WHEN I SAY I DON'T HAVE A CELL PHONE.
THEY TRY AND JUSTIFY HAVING ONE BUT THEY FEEL ASHAMED OR EMBARESED.
LIKE YOU'VE DONE SOMETHING AWFUL IT'S JUST A CHOICE.

10/5/16
CHOP CHOP CHOP
BERMS LOOKING GOOD.
YUP.
AND FOR THOSE UNWILLING TO PUT FORTH THE EFFORT: NOTHING.
RAD!
10/6/16
SHAWN'S GOING TO RIDE WITH US TONIGHT.
YEAH RIGHT.
I SAW HIM, HE'S WEARING SHORTS!
WHATEVER MAN, UNDERWEAR DOESN'T COUNT.
10/7/16
I WAS JUST LISTENING TO DRI THE OTHER DAY!
THAT'S SO COOL YOU LIKE THE SAME MUSIC AS ME!
DRI
IT WAS. BUT ME MAKE A MOVE? AT WORK? NO WAY. BEING PRINCIPLED HAS GOTTEN ME A LOT IN THIS WORLD.
WANT TO, BUT NO. IT WOULD NOT BE RIGHT.
SOMETIMES YOU LOSE THINGS TOO WHILE GAINING THE WILL NOT TO DO A THING.
OK. BYE.

10/8/16
THE BASICS ARE SO HARD TO GET SOMETIMES.
FOOD. SLEEP. FOOD. SLE FOOD. SLEEP. FOOD. SLEEP. FO EEP. FOOD. SLEEP. FOOD. SLE OD. SL FOOD. SLEEP. FOOD SLEEP. FOOD. SLE FOOD. SLEE EP. FOOD. SL FOOD EP. FOOD. SL SLE OD. SLEEP. FO EEP. OOD
I'M OFTEN LACKING IN BOTH.
I'D SLEEP IF I WAS NOT SO HUNGRY.
SO WILL PIGING OUT AND GOING TO BED EARLY FIX THINGS? PERHAPS FOR A DAY SOME BALANCE IS RESTORED.
10/9/16
OK. HERE'S MY LITTLE QUIET PLACE. SEE?
IT'S THE ONLY MOMENT TODAY WHER YOU'LL HAVE NO NOISE.
THAT'S TRUE.
10/10/16
A DAY FILLED WITH BIG STEPS IN BIG PROJECTS FINISHED. THINGS MOVING ON SO.
OK. FINAL FORMAT TIME.
YEP.
NO MATTER HOW MUCH I DO, I NEVER FEEL LIKE I DID ALL I COULD.
IF I'D ONLY GOT A LITTLE MORE DONE.
OTHERS WOULD BURN TRYING TO DO ½ MY DAILY TOIL BUT I'M WORKING FOR THE HARDEST SLAVE DRIVER EVER.
ME.

10/11/16
A LIFE WITHOUT DISTRACTIONS IS A LONG ONE.
KEEPING EVERY HOUR FILLED WITHOUT THINGS LIKE TV OR MOVIES YOU HAVE VAST STRETCHES OF TIME TO FILL EACH DAY.
HUM... PROJECT # 512 IS NEXT.
AND I HIGHLY RECCOMEND THAT YOU DO.
37 MORE BOOK TO GO.
10/12/16
OK - LAP 2 OF THE TIME TRIAL!
RAD!
GO PAUL! YOU'RE RAILING IT!
OOF!
10/15/16
SO I RODE ANYWAY.
I WAS SO TIRED AND SORE FROM YESTERDAY BUT I RODE ANYWAY I DID SO GOOD, GOT UP THINGS THAT ARE HARD TO DO.
HUF. HUF. HUF.
BECAUSE ONE DAY I WON'T BE ABLE TO RIDE LIKE I DO NOW SO I DON'T WANT TO PASS UP A CHANCE.

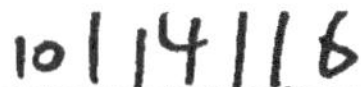

10/14/16
WHAT A WEIRD MOOD. THERES NOTHING LIKE FAMILY TO PUT ONE IN A STATE FOR NO GOOD REASON.
I WONDER THOUGH, IF NOT RELATED TO THEM WOULD I WANT THEM IN MY LIFE?
THEY ARE AT BEST ANNOYING.
I DON'T WANT TO FEEL THIS WAY, BUT I DO.
HONESTLY, I DON'T REALLY LIKE THEM AS PEOPLE.
10/15/16
AH THE WORK!
DAY BEGUN AT 5:30 AM AND NOW AT 11:30 PM IT IS TIME FOR REST. I DID SO MUCH, SO MANY DIFFERENT TASKS TODAY. I AM FILLED WITH A SENSE OF ACHIEVEMENT.
I CAN SPEND ALL DAY DOING MANY TIMES OVER WHAT OTHERS CAN DO IN A DAY. DAY IN AND DAY OUT THE WORK NEVER PUSHES BACK, JUST FORWARD.
I TRY AND BE KIND TO PEOPLE BECAUSE I THINK EVERYONE IS FIGHTING A HARD BATTLE.
HERE YOU GO. LET ME HELP YOU!
BUT I DON'T CARE TO BE UNDERSTOOD ANYMORE.
HAS ANYONE TOLD YOU YOU'RE VERY DIFFERENT?
YEAH.
NO JUSTIFICATION OR EXPLAINATION, JUST DETERMINATION.
IT ONLY NEEDS TO MAKE SENSE TO ME.

10/17/16.
HOW'S IT GOING?
OH..
WELL-GOOD..WELL I HAVE ALL MY LIMBS...
OH IT'S LIKE THAT HUH?
YEAH.
10/18/16
THE INTERNET IS SORT OF CREEPY.
?
I'M WATCHED, I HAVE "FOLLOWERS". I KNOW A FEW (4 OR 5) EX-GIRL FRIENDS ARE LOOKING AT WHAT I'M UP TO, THAT I KNOW OF.
DO I WANT TO KNOW WHAT THEY ARE THINKING? I DOUBT I'D BE OK WITH THE REASON.
OH MAN.
10/19/16
I HAVE THESE OLD BIKES, YOU WANT THEM?
SURE
WELL, THEY NEED WORK. FLATS ETC.
THAT'S FINE.
I'M NOT GOING TO COMPLAIN ABOUT FREE BIKES!

10/20/16
C'MON' IT'S ONLY 5 BUCKS LESS.
NO. IT'S NOT.
C'MON MAN. 5 BUCKS LESS, FOR ME MAN. 5 BUCKS, JUST 5 BUCKS, 5 BUCKS, 5 BUCKS. 5 BUCKS TIMES 1000'S OF PEOPLE MEANS 10'S OF 1000'S OF DOLLARS.
MEANS NO MORE SHOP. SO NO LESS. KEEP WALKING.
10/21/16
WE CAN NEVER GO BACK.
NOT LIKE IT USED TO BE.
IT NEVER IS.
WE MUST LOOK FORWARD.
I'M LIVING FOR THE NOW AND WHAT MAY BE...
OR BE DOOMED TO BE STUCK IN WHAT WE CAN'T CHANGE INSTEAD OF WHAT WE CAN.
BUT WHAT WAS IS NO LONGER.
10/22/16
IN SOME THINGS, NO MATTER WHAT, I FAIL.
I LOVE YOU.
I GUESS IT IS NOT SUPPOSED TO MAKE SENSE AT THIS POINT. REGARDLESS, I'M LEARNING TO BE HAPPY WHILE EMBRACING THE IDEA.
HUM HUM HUM
IT'S NOT GIVING UP ON AN IDEA SO MUCH AS MAKING FIT WHAT YOU HAVE.

10/23/16
GO OUT OR VEG OUT. TO DENNY'S, MY OLD HAUNT OF DAYS OF YOR.
DENNY'S
WE STILL SUCK.
NOW, THE COFFEE IS BAD AND MUST BE DEALT WITH JUST SO OR THE BALANCE IS OFF.
YOU MUST GUARD IT AGAINST A CORRUPTIVE REFIL.
NOT YET.
10/24/16
A LITTLE RELAXATION ON THE TRAIL WAS JUST WHAT I NEEDED.
I LOVE JUST STARING AT THE SKY. THE LAST BLUE IS SUCH A BEAUTIFUL THING TO ME.
I CLOSED MY EYES AND SAW THE RED INSIDE OF MY EYELIDS AND A STRANGE VIEW OF RED PARTICLES RUSHING TO A VOID
10/25/16
IT'S ONLY A COUPLE MINUTES LATE.
LATE IS LATE.
YOU WAIT 5 MINUTES FOR ONE LATE BOZO THEN ANOTHER 5 FOR ANOTHER THEN WHAT? HOW ABOUT SHOWING UP ON TIME.
IT ONLY TAKES ONE HOLE TO SINK A SHIP.

10/26/16

SOMETIMES YOU LOSE THE BATTLE WITH ONESELF.

I DEAL WITH DICK-HEADS ALL DAY AND I LET THEM GET TO ME. AS SUCH I WAS OFF KILTER.

SO NEXT TIME I CAN ENGAGE IN THE NEXT BATTLE SMARTER.

10/27/16

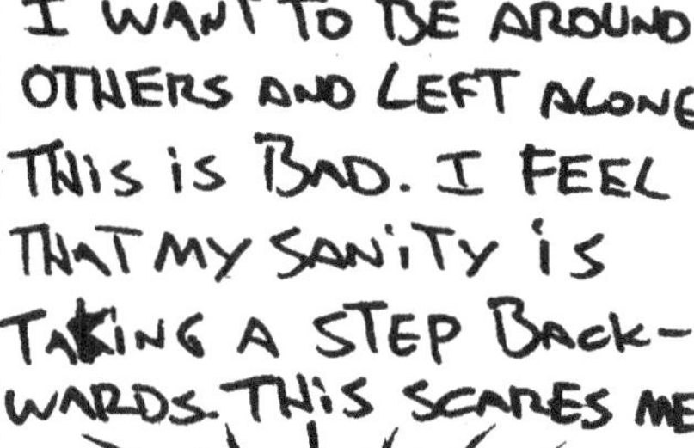

I TRIED TO STAVE OFF A SENSE OF DREAD WITH BUSYING MYSELF WITH VARIOUS TASKS BUT ONCE THE WELDER COOLED IT CAME CREEPING BACK.

I WANT TO BE AROUND OTHERS AND LEFT ALONE. THIS IS BAD. I FEEL THAT MY SANITY IS TAKING A STEP BACK-WARDS. THIS SCARES ME.

I KNOW FROM MY VAST EXPERIENCE IN REALMS OF A HAPPINESS DOWNTURN TO JUST HOLD ON TIGHT AND WEATHER THE STORM.

10/28/16

AND LIKE THAT IT WAS GONE.

I THINK TOO MANY DING DONGS AT WORK WAS BUMMING ME OUT BUT THINGS JUST MOVED ALONG. NOT HAVING TO TALK MUCH HELPED TOO.

EVERY DAY I HAVE SOME NEW THING TO DEAL WITH SO I'M IN CONTROL OR IT IS BUT IN THE END IT'S MY CHOICE.

10/29/16
I DREADED THE DAY IT COULD HAPPEN, AND IT DID.
OH CRAP.
THE VERY FEW THAT I'VE LOVED IN LIFE, I DON'T GIVE MY HEART OUT WILLY NILLY. SO, WHEN I DO IT IS FOR EVER EVEN WHEN THEY ARE GONE. KNOWING THAT LOVE DESTROYS
SAYING IT ANY WAY.
I LOVE YOU.
FEAR
SO WHEN ONE REACHES OUT OF THE VOID TO ME IT EVOKES A STRONG EMOTION.
I DON'T KNOW IF UPSET IS THE RIGHT WORD.
10/30/16
I WROTE BACK. STUPID. VERY STUPID. LOVE IS MY DRUG THOUGH. IT MAKES ME DO STUPID THINGS.
I SHOULD SO NOT BE DOING THIS RIGHT NOW.
TICKY TACK.
I KNOW WORDS ARE SO WORTHLESS, THEY FAIL YOU TIME & TIME AGAIN. YOU CAN'T REALLY ARTICULATE WHAT YOU FEEL.
OH HOW I MISS YOU.
WELL THE SADNESS, THAT ALWAYS DOES ITS JOB.
10/31
A FREAK OUT...
THAT'S BULLSHIT.
IF THAT'S WHO YOU ARE THEN YOU'RE JUST KEEPING IT IN CHECK. WHAT HAPPENS WHEN YOU HAVE A BIG FREAKOUT, MELTDOWN EXPLOSION AT WORK?
YOU GET FIRED. AND YOU CAN GET FIRED FROM LIFE TOO...

11/1/16
YOU KNOW MAN, WHEN YOU'RE IN THE BACK AND YOU FINALLY CATCH UP AND THE GUY IN FRONT IS SUPER ANTSY AND JUST TAKES OFF!
YEAH?
DON'T YOU SAY IT! FUCK YOU...
SO
DON'T BE THAT LAST GUY THEN, TRY HARDER.
11/2/16
1.10 FOR A REFILL? SINCE WHEN?
SINCE TODAY.
WELL IT'S TOO MUCH NOW, I DON'T THINK I'LL BE COMING BACK.
OH, YOU'RE JUST SAYING THAT.
YOU DON'T KNOW ME THOUGH.
11/3/16
IT'S HOPELESS IS IT NOT? IT IS, AND THE SHEER ENORMITY OF THE MATH IS OVERWHELMING.
WHY BOTHER?
4 BILLION WOMEN ON THIS PLANET AND FINDING ONE HAS BECOME THE CRUELEST JOKE, THE NEVER-ENDING KICK-IN-THE-PANTS.
OUCH.
IS IT THE COLD EQUATION THE BETTER I AM AT LIFE THE LESS I HAVE IN COMMON WITH OTHERS.

11/4/16
BACK IN TIME: AGE 11. LOCATION: UPSTAIRS BATHROOM.
AVOIDING ANOTHER HAIRCUT.
IT WAS A PIVIOTARL MOMENT AT THAT YOUNG AGE I DECIDED THAT THERE WAS NO GOD.
THERE IS NO GOD.
AND SO IT WAS.
I'M NOT GOING TO DEVOTE ANY THOUGHT TO IT.
11/5/16
I THINK I JUST NEED TO STOP BEING SUCH A HERMIT.
LIGHTS OUT HIDING IN BACK.
I LIKE BEING A HERMIT, I DO. AT THE SAME TIME I AM WRACKED WITH LONELYNESS OFTEN. ALSO, I DON'T LIKE TALKING MUCH OR BULLSHIT SO THAT MAKES ME LESS THAN 1% OF THE POPULATION.
GO OUT? OR HIDE OUT?
I USED TO BE MORE OF A SOCIAL CREATURE BUT I'M NOT SURE WHEN I WENT OFF THE RAILS NOR HOW TO GET BACK ON.
BUMPY.
11/6/16
WHAT A GREAT DAY..
AHAH AH AH
HUF HUF HUF HUF
3
I WON. NOT BECAUSE I WON A RACE. (I DID THOUGH) I WON BECAUSE I HELPED LOTS OF PEOPLE AND MADE THEM HAPPY.
SO, FOR A SCANT FEW, I MATTER SO THE EFFORT IS WORTH IT.

11/7/16

11/8/16

11/9/16

11/10/16
I LIKE TO THINK THAT DOING GOOD HAS THE REWARD BUILT IN TO IT; YOU NEED NOTHING MORE.
YOU DROPPED YOUR WALLET.
I DON'T THINK YOU SHOULD DO THINGS WITH AN EXPECTATION OF A REWARD. LIKE KARMA THE IDEA THAT YOU WILL GET A REWARD NULLIFIES THE GOOD ACT. THAT'S B.S.
WHAT GOES AROUND, COMES AROUND.
BUT WHEN YOU DO, ON THE RARE OCCASION, GET ONE. WELL, IT'S GOLDEN.
I DON'T HAVE A CELL PHONE...
WHAT? HOW CAN YOU NOT?
HOW? I JUST DON'T. LIFE EXISTED BEFORE, YOU KNOW.
YOU JUST DO WHAT PEOPLE HAVE DONE FOR 1000's OF YEARS, YOU MAKE PLANS AND YOU KEEP THEM.
OH
11/12/16
WHY DO WE DELVE IN THE PAST? I WONDER WHY I KEEP LOOKING BACK.
THE PAST IS CORRUPT THOUGH, WHAT YOU SEE IS NOT TRUE. WHAT YOU FEEL ABOUT IT IS THUS FALSE.
I WONDER IF...
THINKING YOU CAN TRANSPORT THE PAST TO THE NOW AND IT WILL FIX THINGS IS A FALSE NOTION AS WELL. BEST TO MOVE FORWARD.
LET'S JUST KEEP MOVING...

11/13/16
OH, I LOVE YOU!
THAT WAS EASY.
A FEW MINUTES GO BY...
AREN'T YOU ATOMIC CYCLES?
YEAH?
ONLY ME!
YOU ARE COUGAR BAIT!
HA HA HA HA HA HA HA HA
!
11/14/16
ENDLESS SIRENS...
OOWOOWOO WOO WOOW WOO WOO WOO WOO WOO
I WONDER THOUGH IS THERE THAT MUCH CRIME...
WOOWOOWOO WOO WOO WOO WOO WOO WOO WO OWOO WOO W OOWOO WOO WOO WOO WOO WOO WOO WOO WOO WOO WOO WOO WOO OWOO WOOW
OR IS IT JUST FOR SHOW?
HMM...
WOOWOO WOO WOO W WOO WOO WOO W WOO WOO WOO OWOO WOO WO OWOO WOO WO WOO WOO WO OOWOOWOOWO WOO WOO WOOW
11/15/16
SO MUCH WATER.
YEAH.
SO VAST. WE ARE SO SMALL IN THE WORLD.
WE'RE HERE SUCH A SMALL AMOUNT OF TIME...
...I KNOW. A SPEC IN TIME.
MAKE THE MOST OF IT.
HERE. I MADE A DICK OUT OF THE SAND.
HE HE HE HE HE HE HE HE HE HE

11/16/16
HE DIDN'T MAKE IT.
SO? WE STILL HAD FUN.
SHOW UP OR DON'T. JUST SAY YOU DON'T WANT TO. INSTEAD OF MAKING EXCUSES WHY YOU COULDN'T. IT'S JUST BULLSHIT.
I MEAN I'M GOING TO ENJOY MYSELF. I CAN'T MAKE PEOPLE DO THE SAME.
11/17/16
OH SWEET SPACE HEATER!
I DON'T LIKE TOO MUCH COMFORT - I THINK IT MAKES YOU WEAK IN SO MANY WAYS.
IT'S COLD!
SO?
BUT AFTER A LONG DAY AS THEY ALL ARE - A LITTLE WARMTH IF NOT GOTTEN BY ANOTHER A MACHINE IS OK FOR THE JOB TOO...
WRRRR...
11/18/16
HEY. ARE YOU OUT OF YOUR AREA?
...
THERE ARE MOUNTIANS TO RIDE.
HA HA OK!

11/19/16

OK THAT'S IT!

Click!

SO GOOD. JUST FINISHED #50 OF OUR ZINE. 16 YEARS NOW AND WE KEEP GOING.

HM HMM HMM

SHOULD I STILL BE MAKING PUNK-ROCK ZINES AT 45? WELL IT STILL FEELS RIGHT, SO YES.

WHAT'S NEXT?

AAAA!

SO MUCH MUD CAKED UP ON OUR TIRES WE HAD TO PEDAL DOWN HILL AND PUSH ALOT.

MUD CASING

ACTUAL TIRE

BUT WE FINISHED.

IT'S YOUR MOTHER IF YOU WANT TO TALK.

WELL I DON'T. I DON'T WANT TO DO ANY HARM EITHER. I WRESTLE WITH FAMILY BAGAGE AND MY STERN MORAL CODE I FORCE UPON MYSELF.

? ? ? ? ? ? ? ?

EVERYTHING HAS VALUE, EVEN FAMILIAL TIES HAVE A COST/BENIFIT EQUATION. FOR NOW AT LEAST, I'M AT A NEGATIVE BALANCE.

11/22/16
YEAH IT RAINED SO THERE WAS ONLY 20 CARS SO WE GOT RIGHT NEXT TO THE TRAIL...
YEAH. THAT'S REAL IMPORTANT WHEN YOU GO TO EXERCISE TO GET AS CLOSE TO THE EXERCISE AS POSSIBLE
IT'S FUNNY DAMIT.
11/23/16
!
OK. THAT GUY HAD AT LEAST 10 GRAND AND HE GAVE IT TO THAT GUY OVER THERE.
SOUPS GOOD THOUGH.
11/24/16
PLANS DASHED DUE TO A COLD. I DID WHAT MOST PEOPLE DO ON A DAY OFF. NOTHING.
WHAT A DRAG.
I SAT.
MY BUTT IS SORE.
AND WASTED TIME ON THE INTERNET.
OH. KILL ME NOW.

11/25/16

I LOOK AT ONE'S MENTAL ENERGY LIKE FUEL: YOU ONLY HAVE SO MUCH A DAY YOU CAN USE.

SO IF YOU WASTE IT ON PETTY GOSSIP AND OTHER BULLSHIT WHEN YOU REALLY NEED IT, YOU'RE OUT OF GAS

KEEP ONE'S MENTAL EYE ON THE ROAD AND YOU'LL HAVE PLENTY TO WORK WITH.

11/26/16

I WANTED TO BUT GETTING WELL WAS MORE IMPORTANT THAN MEETING A GIRL. TIMING COULD NOT BE WORSE.

I'M OK WITH THINGS NOT WORKING OUT AS I'M USED TO IT.

11/27

I REALLY HATE EATING OUT. IT'S SUCH A RIP OFF.

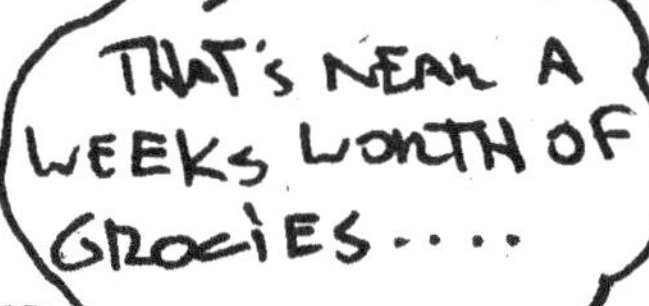

SOMETIMES BEING WITH YOUR FRIENDS MAKES IT WORTH IT. SOMETIMES.

11/28/16
SO, WHAT DID YOU THINK OF GINA?
OH MEOW MEOW
WHAT DOES THAT MEAN?
OH. GOOD VERY GOOD.
11/28/16
IN THE 40'S TONIGHT. I WAITED IN THE COLD THINKING THAT NO ONE WOULD SHOW FOR THE RIDE.
BUT SURE ENOUGH PEOPLE SHOWED UP.
WHAT CAN I SAY? I'M BLESSED WITH GREAT FRIENDS.
YEAH.
COLD!
11/30/16
THIS YEAR BLAZED BY SO FAST. WAS IT GOOD? SO FAR, I'D SAY IT WAS A YEAR OF UPS AND DOWNS— SO FAR—.
BUT I REALIZED THAT WE'RE HERE FOR SUCH A SHORT AMOUNT OF TIME SO THINGS BOTHER ME LESS & LESS.
OH WELL..
CAN MY INNER PEACE SPREAD OUT TO MY SURROUNDINGS? I HOPE SO..

12/1/16
MY SPACE HEATER IS TALKING TO ME.
...
I SWEAR I HEAR VOICES OR MUSIC? IT IS ALL METAL AND THUS COULD BE PICKING UP A RADIO SIGNAL.
...
?
I'M NOT CRAZY. THE ONE IN MY BEDROOM IS NOT SPEAKING TO ME, IT JUST KEEPS ME WARM.
12/2/16
NINJA BATTLE
HA!
OOF!
HA!
AG!
12/3/16
NO, YOU'RE A ROCK STAR!
URMM
I AM NOT. I WISH PEOPLE WOULD NOT ELEVATE ME SO. I DO NOTHING BUT TRY, ANYONE CAN DO THAT.
NOT REALLY.
ONE DAY I'LL BE GONE AND EVERYTHING I'VE DONE AND MADE WILL BE GONE TO. SO...
IT'S NO BIG DEAL.

12/4/16

12/5/16

12/6/16

12/7/16

RELY ON THYSELF.

I LEARNED THAT LONG AGO. NO ONE WILL LOVE YOU AS MUCH AS YOU DO, OR WORK AS HARD OR RESPECT YOU AS YOU CAN FOR YOURSELF.

NO ONE CAN YOU RELY UPON OR TRUST OR COUNT ON MORE THAN YOURSELF. YOU ARE YOUR ONE BEST FRIEND AND ALLY. NEVER FORGET THAT.

12/8/16

SLOWNESS BEGETS MORE SLOWNESS.

IT'S SLOW AT WORK LIKE IT IS ALWAYS THIS TIME OF YEAR. AND WHEN I GOT HOME I JUST SAT AROUND - DID SO LITTLE - WHAT A SLOB.

I NEED TO SEE THE SLOW TIME AS A TIME TO DO MORE THAT I WANT TO THAN LESS OVERALL

12/9/16

ALL THESE PEOPLE AND IT IS SO GRIM. SO MANY FACES. TIRED. POOR. STARVING FOR FOOD, FOR LOVE - THE MODERN WORLD IS A LONELY PLACE.

SPACING IS NEVER RIGHT. OUR CULTURE BREEDS INTERNAL DISSATIFICATION. EVERYONE IS TOO CLOSE. TOO FAR.

BETWEEN WALLS, FENCES AND GATES BOTH REAL AND ELETRONIC. WE STAND CLOSE BUT FAR AWAY AS WELL.

12/10/16
NO.
HERE.
HERE?
ARE YOU SURE?
3RD TIME AROUND THE BLOCK...
LEFT.
LEFT?
SURE?
RIGHT?
NO.
RIGHT
NO.
LEFT.
OK. THAT'S ENOUGH. YOU CAN RIDE HOME FROM HERE.
12/11/16
?
GINA'S PHONE NUMBER DID SHE PUT IT HERE?
WELL, IT WAS A NICE TREAT HOW EVER IT GOT THERE.
I'LL KEEP THAT.
12/12/16
RING RING RING RI
RING RING RING
YOU WANT TO GET THAT?
NO. I'M TALKING TO YOU.
RING RING RING RING.

12/13/16
ARE YOU DOING CHRISTMAS?
YOU MEAN A PAGAN HOLIDAY UNDER A CHRISTIAN HOLIDAY UNDER A CAPITALIST HOLIDAY?
FUCK NO.
12/14/16
I WAS UP TO 5 SHOWERS A DAY!
THAT'S CRAZY!
WHEN I WENT TO DO SOMETHING ELSE, I'D TAKE A SHOWER.
NO ONE GET'S THAT DIRTY, I'M FILTHY, AND I SKIP DAYS. NO ONE NEEDS TO EVERDAY.
12/15/16
FUCKING HUMANS.
HA HA HA HA HA HA HA HA HA HA HA HA HA HA HA HA HA A HA HA HA HA HA HA HA HA HA HA HA HA HA HA
ALL THESE PEOPLE WITH THEIR IDEAS AND OPINIONS AND PET THEORIES...WHAT A JOKE.
HE HE HE HE
THE MOMENT YOU THINK YOU'VE GOT IT ALL FIGURED OUT IS THE MOMENT YOU DON'T HAVE A CLUE.
OH SHUT UP!

12/16/16

LET'S HAVE SOME FUN.
PIZZA!

LET'S ENJOY THE MOMENT WHILE WE CAN FOR BY ITS NATURE, A MOMENT IS HERE AND THEN GONE AGAIN.

NO MOMENT CAN BE RE-CREATED NOR HELD ON TO IN PERFECT CLARITY.

12/17/16

AH-THOSE MOMENTS OF BALANCE ARE SO RARE.
Debt

I THINK PEOPLE MISS THEM BECAUSE THEY ARE FOCUSED ON ONE THING THAT IS NOT IN HARMONY.

BUT WHEN EVERYTHING ELSE IS SO FINE-TUNED THAT ONE THING GETS DROWNED OUT IN THE NOISE.
HMM
HMM
HMM
HMM

12/18/16

CAN'T WAIT TO GET TO BED AT TIMES.

IT'S TOO COLD, WINDY, & DARK OUTSIDE TO DO ANYTHING. I SHOULD PUSH MYSELF MORE TO BE MORE PRODUCTIVE.

BUT NOT TONIGHT.

12/19/16

THE EARTH.

I WATCHED A LIVE STREAM FROM THE SPACE STATION OF THE PLANET TODAY. IT EVOKED SUCH STRONG EMOTION.

SNIFF.

ON THE OUTSIDE IT LOOKS SO PEACEFUL BUT KNOWING THAT WILL NEVER BE THE CASE ON THE SURFACE, WELL IT'S SAD.

12/20/16

ANOTHER BIKE STOLEN!

LIKE LOST LOVES I'LL LIE AWAKE AT NIGHT DREAMING OF MY BIKES

AND LIKE A LOST LOVE, THEY WILL NEVER RETURN...

BLAST.

12/21/16

LET'S PARTY!

NAA...

NOT TONIGHT FELLAS.

12/22/16
I READ YOUR ARTICLE AND THEN I DELETED MY FACEBOOK PAGE.
REALLY?
IT GAVE ME GOOSE PIMPLES!
I USUALLY HATE WHAT I WROTE ONCE I GO BACK TO LOOK AT IT AGAIN, BUT FOR ONCE, IT DID SOME GOOD.
12/23/16
HERE THEY ARE!
3 + YEARS OF WORK IS FINALLY AT AN END.
IT LOOKS GREAT!
THERE'S NOTHING LIKE SEEING THE LIGHT AT THE END OF THE TUNNEL.
NOW LET'S SEE IF WE CAN SELL THESE PUPPIES!
12/24/16
FIVE ALREADY.
I'VE NEVER HAD ANYTHING I'VE DONE GET SNATCHED UP SO QUICK.
THAT'S AMAZING!
I COULD GET USED TO THIS FEELING.
WINNING!

12/28/16
WE'RE CROSSING THIS DRIDGE! IT'S HUGE!
12/29/16
!
FUNDS RECIEVED!
WELL JUST LIKE THAT, I'M GOING TO BE A HOME OWNER. IT'S NOT THAT I'VE NOT WORKED HARD TO GET THINGS.
IT'S REALLY HAPPENING!
IT IS THAT I'VE KEPT MY INTEGRITY AND IN DOING SO, I'VE BEEN VALIDATED.
12/30/16
I NEVER LIKED DOING YARD WORK ALL THAT MUCH, LIKE RAKING LEAVES.
BUT NOW THEY ARE MY TREES, MY LEAVES ON MY LAWN. WELL, THAT CHANGES THINGS RIGHT?

12/31/16

EVERYONE WANTS TO PUT THIS YEAR BEHIND THEM BUT IT MEANS NOTHING THE DATES ARE MAN-MADE.

ONE SHOULD EVOKE CHANGE WHEN IT IS NEEDED. THE TIME, LIKE ALL TIMES, IS NOW.

IF YOU LACK RESOLVE ON ALL DAYS, ONE MORE DAY WON'T MAKE A DIFFERENCE.

1/1/17

WHEN ASKED WHAT IT WOULD TAKE TO BE HAPPY MANY GO TOWARDS OBJECTS.

SOME GO TOWARDS LOVE.

BUT I THINK I JUST WANT TO BE HAPPY WITH WHAT EVER I HAVE AND WHOMEVER I'M WITH AT ALL TIMES.

1/2/17

A WHOLE WEEK OFF IS AT AN END.

I'M SO USED TO NOT HAVING A LOT OF TIME THAT A WEEK FELT LONG.

WHEN YOU LOOK FORWARD TO DOING YARD WORK TO FILL THE TIME, IT'S TIME TO GO BACK.

1/3/17
SO I GOT THIS PLAN, YOU HEARD OF ATLANTIS?
YEAH. THE UNDER WATER CITY.
SO I'M GOING TO BUY LAND AT THE BOTTOM OF THE OCEAN AND BUILD A CITY THEN I'LL BE DEALING WITH DONALD TRUMP DIRECTLY
I'LL BE INVITING YOU TOO...
WHEN YOU BUILD THE DOME, LET ME KNOW.
1/4/17
THE 2 SPEED DOES NOT WORK.
LETS LOOK AT IT.
USING MY BICYCLE WIZARDRY, I WAS ABLE TO SEE HOW IT WENT TOGETHER...
...AND FIX IT.
I LEARNED SOMETHING NEW TODAY!
1/5/17
I WISH I COULD STOP WORRING ABOUT THINGS.
I WISH I WAS NOT SO SHY, I WAS MORE OUT GOING.
I WISH WHEN I SAW OTHERS I DID NOT FEEL LIKE I HAD NOTHING IN COMMON.

6/17
ARE YOU GOING TO SEE THE NEW STAR WARS MOVIE?
NO
WHEN THE FIRST NEW ONE CAME OUT IT SUCKED SO BAD I SWORE AN OATH TO NEVER WATCH ANOTHER.
OH YOU AND YOUR MORAL UPRIGHTNESS!
SOMEONE HAS TO BE.
DELETE
IT HAD TO HAPPEN- IT HAS NOT BEEN WORKING, STUPID INTERNET DATING.
ONCE I MADE THE CHOICE IT WAS EASY TO PUT IT BEHIND ME.
JUST LIVE.
8/18
SOME ADVENTURE.
15
TAKING CARE OF BUSINESS
THANKS!
NO PROBLEM.
THE REWARD FOR A DAY WELL SPENT, IS GOING TO SLEEP WITH A CLEAR HEAD.
A RARE MOMENT.

1/9/17
WELL DIGGING A HOLE IN MY ROOM WAS NOT WHAT I WANTED TO DO...
BUT IT'S MY DEAL NOW TO FIX THE PLACE UP. I'D FEEL LAME IF I PAID SOMEONE TO DIG A HOLE.
THE PIPE!
CLUNK!
I'M SORE AS HELL BUT NO ONE CAN SAY I'M LAZY.
1/10/17
WELL, IT'S NOT RAINING I HOPE THEY SHOW UP.
THEY ARE SHOWING UP.
GOOD FRIENDS ARE HARD TO BEAT.
1/11/17
I'M GOING TO TRY AND GET OUT MORE.
BREAK UP MY ROUTINES SO I DON'T RUT OUT OR HERMIT OUT.
BUT NOT YET! NOT TODAY. NO...

1/12/17
COOL!
GETTING OUT OF MY NORMAL ROUTINE WAS GREAT. JUST TO BREAK IT UP A SMALL AMOUNT.
NICE TEA.
AND IN DOING SO PERSPECTIVE IS CHANGED.
THAT WAS GOOD!
1/13/17
I GOT THE DRAIN DONE BUT THERE'S ANOTHER LEAK.
OK. SO, DIG?
YEAH.
YOU CAN USE THE TOILET NOW THOUGH.
I CAN!?
OH HAPPY DAY!
1/14/17
CAN I SPEAK TO PAUL?
SOLICITOR
ARE YOU HOLDING A PIECE OF CHEESE?
NO?
WELL I CAN'T TALK TO YOU THEN.
?

1/15/17
GAINING 1st PLACE IN THE SECOND LAP.
OH SHIT!
I WAS GOING TO GIVE UP BUT MY PAL TOLD ME..
YOU'RE NOT A QUITTER!
SO I HUNG ON AND GOT 3RD W/ 1/2 A BAR BUT ALL TRY.
THIS IS TAKING HOURS
DRAW DRAW DRAW
WELDS ARE GETTING BETTER.
I TOLD MYSELF I'D BE PRODUCTIVE TODAY AND I WAS.
SO TIRED. JUST. DO...THIS...ONE... MORE...THING...
THAT IS IT THOUGH. JUST DO ONE MORE THING. MAKE THAT LITTLE EXTRA EFFORT EACH DAY.
OK DONE.
THEN I CAN REST A LITTLE EASIER KNOWING I GOT ALL I COULD OUT OF THE DAY.

1/18/17
WHAT'S THAT BOOK YOU'RE READING ABOUT?
ITS HOW WE ARE RUNNING OUT OF OIL AND IN THE SEARCH FOR MORE, THE U.S. DESTROYED RUSSIA, BY USING THE TALIBAN AND THEN ORCHESTRATED 9/11 TO CRACK OPEN THE MIDDLE EAST TO PLUNDER THEIR OIL
YOU ASKED.
1/19/17
YOU HAVE THAT SPOT WHERE YOU TOOK YOUR CAR TO?
OH YEAH CREATIVE AUTO. IT'S ON...
HE'S REAL HONEST. YOU HAVE TO PAY HIS PRICE BUT HE'S SUPER HONEST.
THAT'S FINE.
I WANT TO REWARD GOOD BEHAVIOR AND PUNISH THE BAD.
1/20/17
IN THE MIDDLE OF SOMETHING, WHEN YOU LEAST EXPECT IT.
YOU HAVE A GOLDEN MOMENT OF CLARITY! SOMETHING THAT HAS BEEN VEXING YOU IS SOLVED IN YOUR MIND.
THOSE LITTLE MOMENTS. HOW FEW AND PRECIOUS THEY ARE.

1/22/17
I HAVE PIZZA.
I MUST HAVE SOME.
I'M NOT ALLOWED TO REFUSE CHEESE.
IT'S AGAINST MY RELIGON.
1/23/17
OVER THE MOUNTAIN IN THE RAIN WE WENT. WIND NEARLY MADE ME STOP IN MY TRACKS SEVERAL TIMES...
I PUSHED AS HARD AS I COULD, I GOT A SOLID 2ND PLACE.
OW.
WET
COLD.
I KNOW I DID MY BEST BECAUSE MY BODY TOLD ME SO.
1/24/17
DRIVE EVEN IN THE MOST DRIVEN CAN LEAVE YOU.
SO MUCH TO DO AND NOT WANTING TO DO ANY OF IT WAS NOT A PLACE I LIKE TO BE.
WHAT TO DO?
FOR ME AT LEAST IS TO JUST START. TO START, PUTS YOU IN ANOTHER WORLD.
ZZZZ

1/24/17
IT'S FORTY FOUR DEGREES, ARE YOU COLD?
A LITTLE. IT'S NOT THAT COLD.
I AM WEARING 3 PAIRS OF SOCKS HOWEVER.
1/25/17
MAN THIS GUY ON A CRUISER PASSED BY ME ON THE TRAIL LIKE I WAS STANDING STILL!
WAS IT BLACK?
THAT WAS YOU?
HEH.
!
1/26/17
I'M LEARNING NOT TO TETHER MY HAPPINESS TO OTHER PEOPLE...
I'VE SPENT A LOT OF MY LIFE TRYING TO DO THAT VERY THING. THE REWARDS ARE FEW IF EVER.
CAN I BE ALONE ALL THE TIME AND BE HAPPY?
I CAN.

1/27/17
IT WILL NOT BE THE LAST SELFISH BRAT I HAVE TO DEAL WITH.
YOU MUST WAIT YOUR TURN.
ELBOW OF AUTHORITY
THE LAST DING DONG.
45.
45.
45.
45.
40?
42?
43?
44?
SO TRY NOT TO GET HUNG UP ON IT WHEN YOU DO...
HA HA
1/28/17
WHAT TO DO?
I WAS NOT GOING TO WASTE TIME ON THE WEB, LOOKING AT NOTHING. IT IS A HARD HABIT TO BREAK.
LET'S WORK ON THAT IDEA.
I JUST HAD TO TAP INTO MY IDEAS AND BY BED TIME I WAS 6 PAGES INTO A NEW CONCEPT. NOW THAT'S LIFE! GRAB IT WHERE YOU CAN.
1/29/17
HUF HUF HUF HUF HUF HUF
ROUND AND ROUND AND BY LAP 3 I WAS IN THE LEAD. USUALLY I DON'T PUSH HARD WHEN I DON'T SEE SOMEONE...
BUT THIS TIME I DID
1ST!
PEU!

1/30/17

I'VE TRIED FOR SO LONG TO BE STRONG BUT I JUST CAN'T TAKE IT ANY MORE. INSIDE, I'M FALLING APART.

I WISH I DID NOT FEEL LIKE I HAVE TO SELL MYSELF TO MY FAMILY, THAT THEY COULD LOVE ME FOR WHO I AM. THEY CAN'T.

HOW DOES IT MAKE YOU FEEL? MAD? JUST ALONE AND UNCONNECTED, STARVING FOR A LITTLE WARMTH.
SO COLD.

THE MORE I LET GO OF THINGS, THE BETTER I AM.

I PLAN FOR WHAT MAY COME NEXT BUT OVER TIME I'VE LEARNED NOT TO HANG ON TO AN IDEA SO TIGHT.
GRRR!

IT'S SOON GONE BEFORE YOU KNOW IT.
BAH!

GETTING THINGS DONE. IT. IS. SO... GOOD.

I CAN HAVE HOLES IN MY LIFE AND FILL THEM WITH THINGS TO DO. TASKS TO FINISH. I'M ADDICTED TO DOING THINGS. MY DRUG.
NOW... NEXT?

IT'S A GOOD FORM OF AFLICTION THOUGH.
OH YEAH.

2/2/17
CAN I PUSH?
CAN I GET UP EARLY, WORK ALL MORNING, GO TO "WORK" AND BUST ASS THEN HIT THE PROJECT LIST HARD AND HIT THE PILLOW WITH A SMILE ON MY FACE?
WELL.
YES, I CAN.
2/3/17
I DROVE BEHIND YOUR TRUCK, THE STICKERS WERE SO OFFENSIVE!
YEAH?
YOU SHOULD LOOK AT WHAT YOU HAVE ON THERE...
SO...
IS THIS THE PART WHERE I'M SUPOSED TO CARE?
2/4/17
THEY NEVER GET IT.
WE HAVE TO WAIT?
I RODE IT OVER HERE...
CAN YOU DO IT NOW?

2/5/17
I CAN'T BELIEVE THAT PEOPLE GO HOME AND WATCH T.V. ON PURPOSE.
Click.
I MEAN, ITS JUST SO BAD... I FEEL DUMBER NOW JUST 2 MINUTES IN.
Click.
OK. I'M OUT. I HAVE TO GO SPACKLE SOMETHING.
2/6/17
OK. BAG OF MONEY.
?
I TAKE SMALL BILLS AND PUT THEM IN BAGS THEN THE SMALL BAG INTO BIGGER BAGS THEN ONE BIG BAG. THE BAG WAS FULL.
1's & FIVES. SO MUCH FUCKING MONEY! MONEY DOES NOT MAKE YOU HAPPY BUT IT CAN'T HURT.
7,200.
WOW...
2/7/17
HERE YOU GO.
WHAT IS IT?
SOMEONE SENT ME A CARDBOARD DICK IN THE MAIL!

2/8/17
1/2 THE PEOPLE I TALK TO AT WORK WANT TO SELL - NOT BUY.
I DON'T BUY BIKES.
IT HAS GOTTEN WORSE. PEOPLE ARE BROKE, THEY HAVE NO MONEY.
IT'S 10.
I HAVE 3 BUCKS.
IT'S A HARD TRUTH.
I'M BROKE.
YEAH, WELL I DON'T WANT TO JOIN YOU.
2/9/17
OOF!
I CRASHED. I BROKE MY SEAT POST LATER BUT I RODE. OH HOW I NEEDED IT! THE BIKE FIXES SO MUCH.
ALL THIS RAIN AND BEING STUCK INSIDE HAS BEEN HARD. MY BIKE HEALS MY SOUL TIME & TIME AGAIN.
2/10/17
YOU KNOW HOW IT IS. MAN, THE WIFE SAYS I NEED TO GET RID OF A BIKE TO GET ANOTHER ONE.
ACTUALLY, I DON'T KNOW. I DO NOT.
I WOULD NEVER BE WITH SOMEONE WHO TRIED TO CURTAIL THINGS IN MY LIFE THAT MADE ME HAPPY.

2/11/17
LAST NIGHT.
I CAN'T DRINK ANY MORE COFFEE.
TOO MUCH COFFEE. NONE TOMORROW.
NEXT MORNING...
CAN'T. RESIST.
2/12/17
TODAY I MET SO MANY PEOPLE THAT I TOUCHED IN A POSITIVE WAY AND 1 I DID NOT.
THANKS!
OVER ALL I'M DOING GOOD. THE ONE, WELL DON'T STEAL BIKES AND YOU WON'T HAVE ANY PROBLEMS.
YEAH.
I WENT TO JAIL
NO LENSES ↓
EVEN HE GOT THE MESSAGE IN THE END.
REGARDLESS, YOU STOLE IT. YOU MADE THAT CHOICE.
OK THEN.
I DID.
2/13/17
OVER THE MOUNTAIN AND OVER THE MOUNTAIN. TWICE.
I'VE NEVER DONE TWO LAPS BEFORE ON MY SINGLE SPEED. 50+ MILES AND 1000's OF FEET OF CLIMBING IN AROUND 6 HOURS. NOT BAD.
HURTING
HUNGRY THIRSTY
I PLAN TO WORK UP TO 4 LAPS FOR 100 MILES. EITHER I'LL MAKE IT OR MY BODY WILL FALL APART, WE'LL SEE.
SUMMON THE BEAST.

2/14/17
I CAN'T GO TONIGHT.
NO BIGGIE.
KEEPING UP WITH YOUR ATONOMOUS LIFE-STYLE IS HARD.
I KNOW. BUT SOME ONE HAS TO DO IT.
2/15/17
WHAT IS THE KEY TO LIFE?
THERE'S NO ONE KEY.
ONE KEY OPENS ONE DOOR AND ANOTHER KEY OPENS ANOTHER ETC. NOT ONE WILL BE ALL THERE IS...
FEW HAVE ONE KEY AND FEWER STILL HAVE KEYS TO MANY ROOMS. MANY ROOMS, MANY KEYS. HOW MANY DOORS DO YOU HAVE KEYS TO?
2/16/17
I CAME BY THIS MORNING BUT YOU WERE NOT HERE.
YEAH?
I BROUGHT MEATBALL SOUP FOR YOU BUT I GOT HUNGRY.
YEAH?
SO I ATE IT.
HA!

21/17/17
SO I RODE TO WORK IN THE RAIN.
IT HAS BEEN RAINING LIKE CRAZY. BUT I JUST PUT ON MY RAIN COAT AND AWAY I GO.
REAL CYCLISTS ARE KNOWN TO GET WET.
21/18/17
SURE. LET'S RIDE THE FULL LOOP. IT'S 25 MILES.
UAH OK. HOW LONG?
IT'S SO PRETTY UP TOP. IT'S WORTH IT. 3 HOURS. LEAVE EARLY RIGHT? 7AM NO LATER.
EH...
OK. I CAN SLEEP WHEN I'M DEAD.
YEP.
21/19/17
IT'S NOT SO BAD.
25 MILES IN THE MOUNTAINS USED TO KILL ME, NOW IT'S JUST FUN.
OH BICYCLE, HOW YOU'VE DONE ME SO WELL ALL THESE YEARS.

2/20/17
I HATE THE SENSATION THAT FOR THE MOST PART, I AM ON AN ISLAND.
I WOULD LIKE TO BRIDGE THE GAP I FEEL BETWEEN MYSELF AND OTHERS.
PERHAPS ITS TOO LATE.
FUCK IT.
2/21/17
THE BEST THIS IS AN OUTSIDE SINK SO YOU DON'T GET DIRT IN THE HOUSE.
WHO ARE YOU TALKING TO?! YOU THINK I CARE ABOUT DIRT?
IT TOOK ME 45 YEARS NOT TO SLEEP IN A GREASE STAIN, HOW LONG ARE YOU GOING TO WAIT!?
2/22/17
I NEED TWO BIKE RIMS, JUST THE OUTSIDE.
OK?
I'M GOING TO MAKE A TREAD MILL FOR MY CAT.
OK?
SURE. WELL, THAT'S A NEW ONE

2/23/17
IT'S YOUR OPINION. YOU CAN'T HAVE A WRONG OPINION.
I DISAGREE! YOU CAN HAVE AN IGNORANT, ILL-INFORMED OPINION AND THAT IS WRONG! IGNORANT & ILL-INFORMED!
OK. THANK YOU FOR YOUR TIME SIR.
2/24/17
I MADE FOOD. DO YOU WANT TO COME OVER?
NAH I DON'T WANT TO GO OUT NOW.
OK.
SOMETIMES ITS JUST THE RIGHT THING TO DO IS TO STAY HOME BY YOURSELF.
2/25/17
THE DREAD CHAOS OF MY MIND ATTACKS ME.
I FEEL LIKE I'M LOSING ANOTHER SKIRMISH WITH MY SANITY.
I HATE WHEN I FEEL LIKE THIS BUT MORE OFTEN THAN NOT, I DO.

2/26/17
PHONE OFF THE HOOK!
COFFEE POT ON!
..AND A BOOK TO MAKE A GREAT NIGHT ALONE RAD.
2/27/17
10 BUCKS? NO WAY!
ROADS CLOSED. I'LL FIND ANOTHER WAY IN.
I MANUVERED AROUND PROBLEMS. IT IS EASY. GETTING AROUND MYSELF IS THE HARD PART.
OH MAN.
2/28/17
SO SLOW THIS MONTH I KNOW I MADE CRAP.
TAC TAC TAC TAC AC TAC TAC TAC TAC TAC TAC TAC TAC TA TAC TAC TAC TAC TAC TAC TAC TAC TAC TAC
FOR WINTER NOT BAD! SEE HOW SILLY I AM WORRING ABOUT NOTHING

3/1/17
TODAY I GOT HUGS, TIPS & SMILES AT WORK.
TAKE AN EXTRA 5
SO OFTEN DO YOU WONDER IF YOU'RE ON THE RIGHT PATH.
?
A FEW SIGNS HERE AND THERE THAT YOU ARE, HELP YOU ALONG THE WAY.
THANKS!
3/2/17
I DON'T GET THAT SHIT.
YOU SPEND YOUR WHOLE CHILDHOOD TRYING TO MAKE YOUR OWN CHOICES THEN WHEN YOU'RE FREE AT LAST YOU GET MARRIED AND HAVE TO, AS AN ADULT ASK PERMISSION TO DO THINGS.
FUCK THAT NOISE!
HEH.
3/3/17
I'VE BEEN WITH THIS SAME LADY FOR 20 YEARS AND I THINK SHE HAS HATED ME FOR TWENTY YEARS.
OH.
THAT'S A BUMMER.
YEAH. IT IS.
?

3/4/17
I CAN'T DO IT NOW, IT WOULD NOT BE FAIR
OH FAIRNESS, AM I YOUR ONLY WORSHIPER? SOMETIMES I FEEL LIKE I AM THE ONE PERSON ON THIS GLOBE THAT BELIEVES IN FAIRNESS.
I WILL HANG ON TO MY IDEALS TO THE END, EVEN IF IT MEANS I AM A STRANGER TO EVERYONE.
YOU COULD CHARGE HIM STORAGE.
NO. IT WOULD NOT BE FAIR.
3/5/17
ALL THE FUN ONE CAN HAVE AT THE PRICE, OF AN EFFORT.
3/6/17
TRADE FOR ONE OF MY PEANUT BUTTER SANDWICHES?
SURE.
LOOK AT THIS OUT HERE, SO PRETTY.
I COULD LAY OUT HERE FOREVER!

3/7/17
WE NEED TO MAKE THE RIDES HARD AGAIN. WE USED TO HAVE A FEARSOME REPUTATION BUT WE'VE RELIED UPON THAT AND GOTTEN SOFT AS A RESULT.
THERE'S NO ONE LEFT TO COUNT AGAINST. THE OTHER GROUPS ARE ALL GONE.
I MEAN, DOES A GLACIER FEEL A PEBBLE GETTING CRUSHED UNDERNEATH IT?
3/8/17
OH HOW ONES' FEELINGS ARE SO HARD TO CONTROL. HOW THEY ATTACK YOU OVER AND OVER AGAIN.
ONE CAN ONLY SET THEM ASIDE FOR A MOMENT BUT SOON THEY DEMAND ATTENTION.
GRRR...
BUT TO FEEL NOTHING? NEVER. WITH NO FEELING YOU LOSE YOUR HUMANITY.
HE'LL BE GONE SOON ENOUGH.
3/9/17
LET'S GO CRAZY AND DO THE YELLOW TIRES
YEAH YOU ONLY LIVE ONCE RIGHT? YOU MAY AS WELL GO CRAZY.
I THINK WE DON'T DO IT ENOUGH.
HMM.

3/10/17
YOU DO SO MUCH.
I WANT TO.
I WANT TO DO ALL I CAN ALL DAY, LOOK BACK AND SEE I DID A LOT. THE DAY WAS USED WELL.
ONE DAY I WON'T BE ABLE TO DO THIS, SO NOW IS THE TIME.
OH HI!
HI
LOOK UH.. I'M SORRY I FORGOT TO SHOW UP TO THE WAKE. I WANTED TO APOLOGISE.
OH! WE'RE HUMAN, IT'S OK.
I JUST DON'T WANT TO BE THAT GUY, YOU KNOW.
HAVE SOME BACON, THEY LEFT IT ON THE OTHER TABLE.
OH MAN
AND A COOKIE!
OH! SHE'S COMING BACK!
OOP! SHE JUST LOOKED AT US AND LEFT. WELL, SHE COULD SKIP A MEAL.
OUCH.

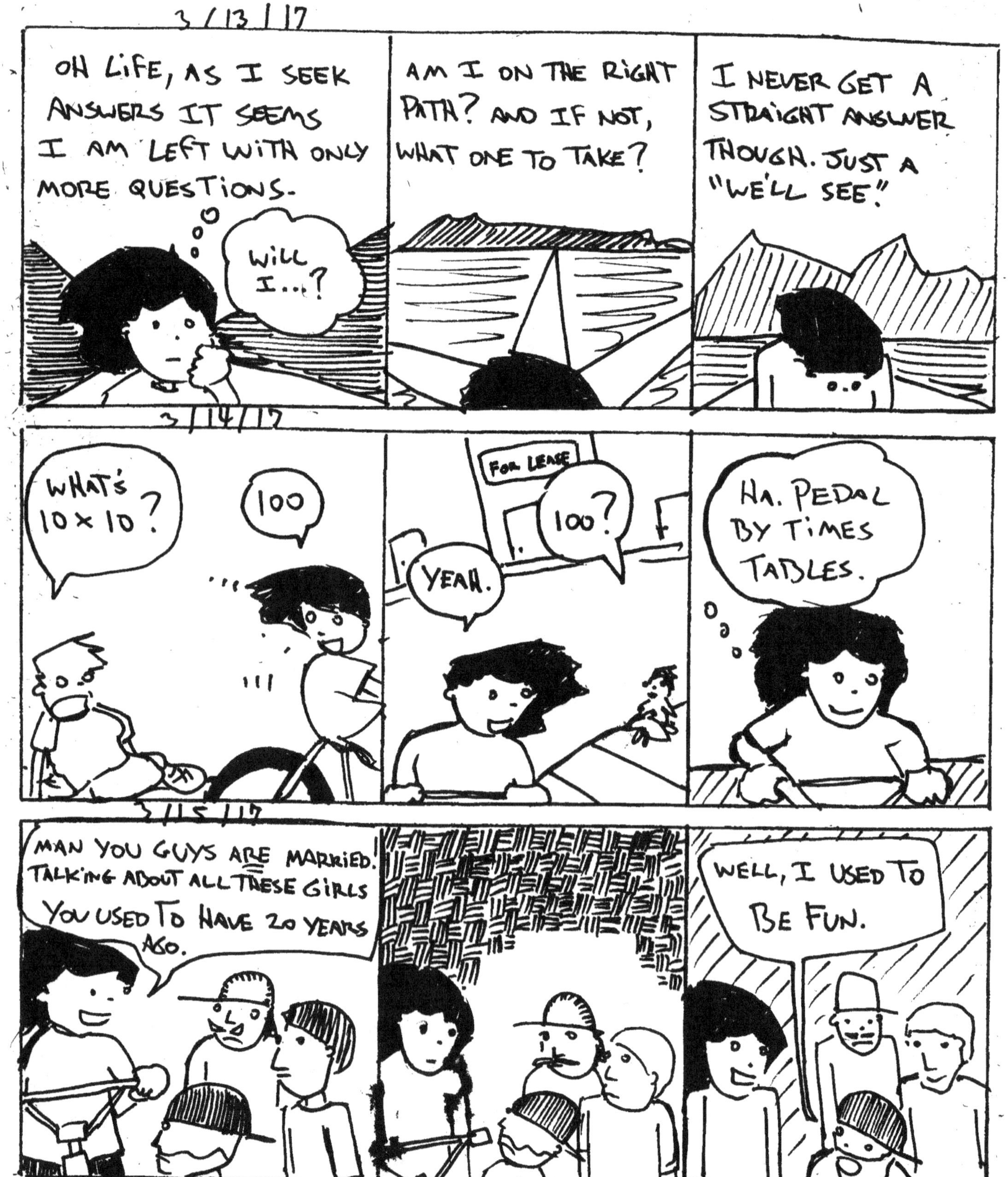

3/13/17
OH LIFE, AS I SEEK ANSWERS IT SEEMS I AM LEFT WITH ONLY MORE QUESTIONS.
WILL I...?
AM I ON THE RIGHT PATH? AND IF NOT, WHAT ONE TO TAKE?
I NEVER GET A STRAIGHT ANSWER THOUGH. JUST A "WE'LL SEE!"
3/14/17
WHAT'S 10 × 10?
100
100?
YEAH.
HA. PEDAL BY TIMES TABLES.
3/15/17
MAN YOU GUYS ARE MARRIED! TALKING ABOUT ALL THESE GIRLS YOU USED TO HAVE 20 YEARS AGO.
WELL, I USED TO BE FUN.

3/16/17
LOOK, IT GOES WAY DEEPER THAN THAT.
IF YOU'RE ALWAYS SHOOTING DOWN IDEAS INSTEAD OF SEEING SOLUTIONS...
EVENTUALLY YOU CAN'T SEE ANY SOLOUTIONS.
3/17/17
THERE IT IS, THE 70 DOLLAR TOOL!
NOTHING LIKE HAVING THE RIGHT TOOL FOR THE JOB.
WRRR
WRRR
WRRR
WRRR
ONCE YOU DO, YOU CAN'T GO BACK.
ONE SEAT POST IN!
3/18/19
DID YOU BRING THE FRAME?
OK LET'S DO IT.
YES.
OH SHIT! YOU ACTIVATED THE PAUL!
PROJECT MODE
YOU'RE GOING TO FINISH THAT NOW?
SURE, WHY NOT?

3/19/17
THAT'S SO EARLY! YOU KNOW SOME PEOPLE LIKE TO SLEEP!
YEAH, I'VE HEARD ABOUT THAT...
SLEEP SEEMS LIKE A NEAT IDEA.
3/20/17
I WORK SO HARD AT ALL I DO. I HAVE TRIED TO DO A LITTLE GOOD, TO BE GOOD. PERHAPS THAT PLAN IS THE CRUEL JOKE?
I FEEL LIKE IT IS. FOR NO MATTER WHAT I DO. I NEVER SEEM TO MEASURE UP. I AM ALWAYS FALLING SHORT.
OOF!
WILL I EVER BE GOOD ENOUGH FOR SOMEONE TO ACCEPT ME FOR WHO I AM?
3/2?/17
THINK ABOUT IT. PLAN AHEAD. 3 STEPS AHEAD. MAKE THE LISTS, GET SOMETHING DONE NOW. DON'T WASTE TIME.
DO MORE. HOW MANY PROJECTS? HOW MANY TASKS? WHAT NEEDS TO BE FINISHED NEXT? WHAT IS MORE IMPORTANT? IS THIS THE RIGHT WAY? SO MUCH UNRESOLVED.
LAY AWAKE AND WORRY. STRESS IS CONSTANT. DWELL UPON MISTAKES & LONELEYNESS. HOW TO SOLVE IT?

3/22/17
HOW CERTAIN UNCERTAIN IS.
I JUST DON'T KNOW.
ALL I CAN COUNT ON IS HOW FRAGILE THE THINGS I WORK FOR ARE NO MATTER WHAT I DO.
COULD BE THE LAST TIME.
AND UNDERNEATH, HOW FRAGILE I AM.
WHAT A BEATING LIFE IS SOMETIMES.
3/23/17
THIS SUCKS.
WELL LETS DO SOMETHING ABOUT IT NOW
LET'S PILE THESE UP LIKE SO
HERE'S ONE.
BETTER!
3/24/17
YOUR THOUGHTS PREY UPON YOUR MIND. GOOD ONES? JUST THE BAD.
IT'S A CYCLE OF BAD THOUGHTS THAT IS EASY TO SEE...
BAD THOUGHTS
THAT FEEDS MORE BAD THOUGHTS
LEADS TO BAD BEHAVIOR
...BUT HARD TO GET AWAY FROM.
ONE DAY.

3/25/17
THEN I...
YOU TOLD ME ALREADY.
OH.
OH WHEN YOU RUN OUT OF STORIES, IT'S A SHAME. THAT MEANS YOU'RE NOT MAKING NEW ONES.
I TOLD YOU ALREADY?
IN A WAY YOU'RE ALREADY DEAD.
YEAH. LIKE 3 TIMES ALREADY.
3/26/17
WHAT A VIEW.
IT'S 7 MILES UP.
IT WAS?
BUT WORTH IT.
3/27/17
OH HOW PLEASED WITH MY SELF I AM AS I GOT SO MANY THINGS DONE I'VE BEEN JUST THINKING ABOUT DOING.
THAT TOOK ALL DAY.
IT DID. BUT A DAY FILLED WITH ADVENTURE, PROGRESS. FULFILLMENT, A SENSE OF ACHIEVMENT ETS.
TIRED.
THAT'S A DAY IN A LIFE WORTH LIVING.

3/28/17
IT'S ALMOST TANK-TOP WEATHER.
I CAN'T WEAR ANY SLEEVELESS SHIRTS..
WHY?
BECAUSE ADVERTISING YOU HAVE MUSCLES MAKES YOU A DOUCHE.
OOH!
3/29/17
LET'S TRY OATMEAL WITH PEANUT BUTTER AND A LITTLE SUGAR.
!
IT'S MAGICAL!
3/30/17
I WOULDN'T COME HERE IF YOU WER'NT HONEST & FAIR LIKE YOU ARE!
I DON'T GO ANY WHERE ELSE.
SOME TIMES I FORGET THAT I HAVE VALUE TO OTHERS.

3/31/17
SOMETIMES THERE IS NOT ENOUGH TO GO AROUND.
YOU GET SPREAD TOO THIN TO HAVE A TASTE TO BE EFFECTUAL.
THIS IS WHEN I FEEL MOST ALONE.
FOR ALL THE THINGS I CAN GET IN LIFE COME TO ME, HUMAN INTERACTION IS NOT ONE OF THEM.
I COULD NOT COUNT ON ONE FINGER A PERSON THAT DOES NOT SWIM IN MODAL AMBIGUITY.
JUST LIE.
I CAN'T
I DON'T FEEL LIKE I'M BETTER BY NOT LETTING MYSELF SLIP. JUST AN ACCUTE ALONE-NESS LIKE A DAGGER IN MY HEART.
4/2/17
HAVE WE BECOME TOO ACCEPTING OF FAILURE? OF NOT TRYING HARD ENOUGH?
YOU'RE LATE AGAIN.
WHILE MANY ARE QUICK TO PLAY THE EXCUSE CARD, I FOLD MY HAND.
I'M PLAYING WITH A DIFFERENT DECK.
DECK OF SOLUTIONS

4/3/17
YOU SEEM VERY WISE
MAYBE.
BUT IN MY MIND NO. MOST DAYS I FEEL LIKE A FOOL. JUST DOING THINGS TO NOT LOOK AT ONES SELF.
NEXT THING?
I MAY NOT FIND SOMETHING I LIKE.
4/4/17
LOOK. JAG IS ON HIS PHONE.
I'LL CALL HIM.
HUH?
HEY DICKHEAD.
GET OFF YOUR PHONE.
4/5/17
I DON'T NEED THAT CELL PHONE CALL ME WHEN YOU GET THERE CRAP.
YEAH I TALK TO YOU LAST WEEK AND HERE I AM...
YES. YOU MAKE PLANS AND YOU KEEP THEM.

FOR A FEW DAYS NOW MY PHONE AT WORK HAS NOT RUNG MUCH. IT WAS QUIET WHICH I LIKED BUT ODD TOO, BECAUSE IT RINGS ALL DAY.
RING RING
I HATE PHONES. HOWEVER I NEED IT AT WORK SO I LOOKED AT IT.
HMM.
ROBOT SELLING THING TIME WASTING MACHINE
WELL IT WORKS NOW.

I LET THIS KID SHARE MY TABLE HE WAS TRYING TO SALVAGE SOMETHING WITH HIS GIRL FRIEND. HE WAS FAILING. BADLY.
HUH HUH HUH AUH

AT SOME POINT HE WAS HUNCHED OVER AND SOBBING. MY EMPATHY GENE BEING TOO BIG, I JUST LOOKED AT HIM, FEELING HIS SENSE OF HELPLESSNESS COMPLETLY.

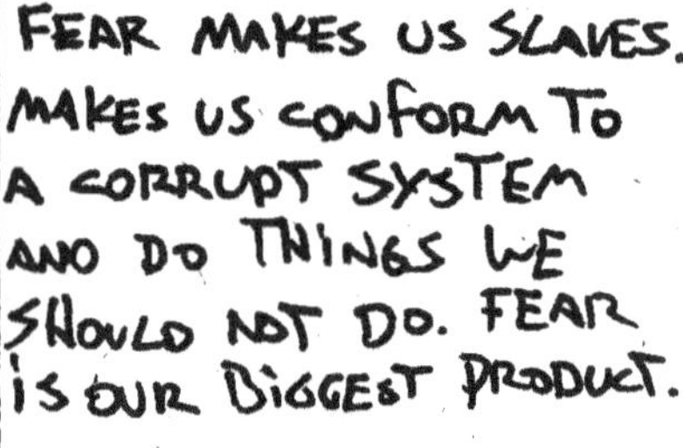

I GUESS IT TOUCHED A NERVE BECAUSE I'VE BEEN HIM SO MANY TIMES. POWERLESS TO HELP HIM I WAS RELIVED WHEN HE LEFT.
SNIFF

WHAT IS THE DRIVING FORCE IN OUR WORLD? LOVE? HATE? GREED? I THINK IT IS FEAR.

FEAR OF WHAT IS AND WHAT MAY BE FEAR OF WHAT WILL HAPPEN AND NEVER KNOWING WHY. LIFE SELDOM MAKES SENSE.
I'M LEAVING.

FEAR MAKES US SLAVES. MAKES US CONFORM TO A CORRUPT SYSTEM AND DO THINGS WE SHOULD NOT DO. FEAR IS OUR BIGGEST PRODUCT.
BUY
BUY
BUY

4/9/17
NO TRESPASSING THIS MEANS BIKES & HIKERS
WHAT IS THIS BULL- SHIT?
WHERE'S JACK?
I KNOW.
LATER..
WHERE WERE YOU? DID YOU TRASH THAT SIGN?
I PLEAD THE 5TH.
4/10/17
AFTER TRYING OVER AND OVER AGAIN I GOT A CAT.
HIS NAME IS MORRIS AND HE LIKES TO HIDE UNDER MY BED, BUT ALSO LIKES TO BE PETTED.
Prr Prr Prrr
JUST HAVING HIM HERE HAS PUT ME AT EASE. SHOULD HAVE DONE IT LONG AGO.
MRWW?
4/11/17
MORRIS!
GONE. I DAY. I CAN'T EVEN KEEP A CAT LET ALONE ANOTHER PERSON.
I CAN'T KEEP GOING ON LIKE THIS.

4/12/17
I'M NOT IN THE PERFECT PERSONS CLUB.
I'M NOT. THE DIFFERENCE IS I LOOK AT MYSELF AND SEE WEAK AREAS.
I CAN DO THAT BETTER.
AND AM HUMBLE ENOUGH TO SEE THAT I NEED TO CHANGE.
AND I WILL
4/13/17
THANKS!
NO PROBLEM.
I HAD A GOOD DAY AT WORK, IT IS WHERE I SHINE. I WENT HOME GREASY, TIRED BUT A SMILE, IT WAS THERE.
IT IS EASY TO FORGET THE GOOD THINGS YOU HAVE WORKED SO HARD FOR BUT DID FORGET BECAUSE YOU'VE GOTTEN USED TO THE GOOD.
4/14/17
UNFINISHED BUSINESS HAUNTS ME AT ALL TIMES.
BOO
IT IS A BLESSING AND A CURSE. I FINISH NEAR EVERY THING I DO.
..AND DONE.
BUT I'LL NEVER BE FREE FROM TASKS.
AND NEXT?

4/18/17
YOU WILL ALWAYS HAVE TIMES WHEN PEOPLE IRK YOU OR MAKE YOU MAD.
GRRRR.
BUT THEN THEY OWN UP TO SOMETHING THEY DID SOMETIMES TOO.
I KNOW I WAS OUT OF SORTS.
AND PATCHING THINGS UP, WELL IT'S A GREAT FEELING.
IT'S OK.
4/19/17
THE INSTINCT TO SURVIVE IS THERE, BUT TO LIVE?
WE FORGET SO EASY. ONE HAS TO BE HYPER-VIGILANT TO BE ALIVE FOR LIFE.
MOVIE?
NO. MOONLIGHT HIKE.
IF YOU FAIL TO DO SO, IT WILL PASS YOU BY.
4/20/17
A WHOLE BOX OF SALTINES, ON A UPSET STOMACH, THEY DO WONDERS.
CRACKERS
WATCH ME EAT 3/4 OF THEM IN A DAY. HARD. FLAVORLESS THAT TURN TO MUSH.
NOM NOM
TOMORROW, IF I'M LUCKY, I GET TO TAKE A SALTINE.
DELICIOUS.
CRUNCH.

4/21/17

I CAN'T REMEMBER BEING THIS TIRED.

MY WHOLE BODY IS SORE. I HAVE NOT EATEN ENOUGH. I HAVE TO WORK TOO HARD. REST DOES NOT COME EASY.

BUT I MUST GO ON... THERE IS NO OTHER WAY.

4/22/17

OH MAGIC ELIXIR TO THE RESCUE!

AFTER TWO DAYS W/O COFFEE IT WAS SUCH A TREAT. AFTER 1/2 A CUP THE VEIL OF PAIN & UNCERTIANTY LEFT

CAN SOMETHING LIKE COFFEE BE A PART OF YOU? I GUESS IT CAN.

4/23/17

ONCE AGAIN ON THE SOLO PATH.

I HAVE SO LITTLE FREE TIME, JUST A FEW HOURS HERE AND THERE SO I CAN'T WAIT FOR OTHERS MUCH.

NOR DO I WANT TO.
JUST ME, MY BIKE AND THE SUNRISE.

4/24/17
IN YOUR MIND YOU TURN A CORNER AND YOU'RE IN A DARK PLACE FOR NO GOOD REASON.
I GATHER NEAR EVERYONE HAS THESE SPACES. I KNOW THEY FILL MY MINDSCAPE. I WISH THEY DID NOT.
CAN'T SEE.
I JUST KEEP TELLING MYSELF THAT THE DARK IS A TEMPORARY SPACE BETWEEN LIGHT PLACES.
I SEE LIGHT!
4/25/17
NICE TO SEE YOU
YOU TO
I REALIZED TODAY THAT I LIVE FOR OTHERS. WHATEVER BLACK INTERNAL DIALOG I HAVE DOES NO GOOD. PEOPLE INTERACT WITH ME BECAUSE I CAN GIVE THEM THINGS THEY DON'T GET ANYWHERE ELSE.
ME.
GLAD I REALIZED IT.
4/26/17
COME HERE KITTY KITTY.
KITTY KITTY KITTY
FINALLY! SO GLAD.
PRRRRRRRRRRRRA

4/27/17
PRRRR
I THOUGHT I LOST MY KITTIES BUT I JUST KEPT PUTTING FOOD OUT AND MAKING THEM GET CLOSE.
MERU...
I'M NOT 100% YET BUT CLOSE ENOUGH TO FEEL SO GOOD ABOUT STICKING WITH IT TO WARM THEM TO ME.
4/28/17
THE WIND IS HOWLING. IN THE MOUNTIANS THE WHOLE PLACE RUMBLES.
BRRRRRR RRR RRR RRR RRR BRR
NATURE IS SO POWERFUL. WE ARE AT IT'S MERCY AT ALL TIMES.
WOOSH!!!!
HOW SOON WE FORGET.
4/29/17
OH SLEEP, TAKE ME NOW FOR I HAVE EARNED A NIGHTS REST.
I WAS TELLING SOME-ONE: I JUST WORK 1/2 THE DAY TO STAY ON TOP OF THINGS.
OH.
AT FIRST THEY DID NOT GET IT...
1/2 THE DAY, 12 HOURS.
OH!

4/30/17
JUST A LITTLE BIT MORE...
EVERY DAY I TELL MYSELF TO DO A LITTLE BIT MORE.
WRRRR
IT'S GOOD BECAUSE JUST A LITTLE BIT MORE OVER TIME ADDS UP TO A LOT.
1/2 WAY FINISHED.
5/1/17
AFTER MUCH MANUVERING I WOUND UP AT A PRISON TO SPEAK TO IMATES.
SO...
CLEAN SHIRT
AT FIRST I WAS A TAD NERVOUS. BUT I QUICKLY REALIZED THAT THERE WAS NOTHING TO WORRY ABOUT
ANOTHER THING TO KEEP IN MIND...
THEY WERE GLAD TO HAVE ME.
5/2/17
NO, YOU CAN'T HATE THAT...
DEER
FUCK THAT!
YOU DO NOT GET TO TELL ME WHAT I CAN OR CAN'T HATE! OR HOW MUCH!
I'LL HATE WHAT I WANT TO, WHEN I WANT TO SO GO STICK IT!

5/3/17
OH MAN, YOU ARE THE MOST HONEST GUY!
OH, THANK YOU!
I TRY TO BE HONEST, I DO. I LIKE TO THINK I AM. I MAY BE WRONG. BUT I DO TRY.
WELL, I TRY...
SO WHEN SOMEONE SEES HOW I AM, IT IS A GREAT FEELING.
5/4/17
SO THE DOCTOR SAID I'm OFF WORK FOR MY WRIST, FOR THE PAIN.
OH, REALLY?
I'M IN PAIN ALL THE TIME. MY HANDS GET SORE, MY ELBOW + KNEES. I PUSH MYSELF HARD BUT PAIN IS NORMAL FOR ME.
I THOUGHT THAT WAS JUST PART OF BEING ALIVE.
OH.
5/5/17
I WAS THINKING TODAY HOW I LOVE COFFEE SO MUCH.
FOR A FEW CENTS A CUP YOU GET A LOT. IT HAS BEEN MY ONLY VICE MY WHOLE LIFE TOO, I FIGURE ONE IS OK.
ONLY YOU.
I HAVE GIVEN IT UP AT TIMES AND DONE TOO MUCH AS WELL. BUT OVERALL IT HAS SERVED ME WELL.

5/6/17
YOU SHOULD BE HANGING OFF THE CHANDILIERS EVERY DAY! YOU OWN YOUR OWN BUSINESS...
I SHOULD. I'D LIKE TO. I THINK I'VE LET MY EXPERIENCES WITH OTHER PEOPLE CLOUD MY WORLD VIEW.
THAT'S WHAT HAPPENS WHEN YOU'RE SENSITIVE AND INTELLIGENT.
YOU MEAN GIVING A SHIT?
YEAH.
5/7/17
SO MUCH TO DO!
IT WAS. MY WORKLOAD IS INSANE. ALL MY HARD WORK IS PAYING OFF.
BE WITH YOU IN A MINUTE!
AT TIMES, TOO WELL.
I DON'T THINK I CAN KEEP THIS PACE UP.
5/8/17
I PUSHED MYSELF FAR TODAY. BUT AT SOME POINT MY DRIVE WENT OUT.
WOO!
I DON'T KNOW A SINGLE PERSON THAT COULD DO ALL I DID TODAY WITHOUT FALLING ON THIER FACE.
WUMP!
BUT I STILL FELT LIKE I WAS SLACKING OFF.
I SHOULD NOT FEEL LAZY, BUT I DO.

SOMETIMES I WONDER WHAT IS WRONG WITH ME. I SHOULD BE HAPPY ALL THE TIME BUT I AM NOT.
I HAVE MORE FREEDOM THAN MOST, LIVE BY MY OWN RULES, ANSWER TO FEW IF ANYONE. I GOT THERE BY BEING STRONG.
OPEN
BUT IN DOING SO, YOU'RE NOT LIKE OTHER PEOPLE AND THUS ALWAYS ON THE OUTS. I THINK THE SEPERATION IS WHAT IS THE WORST.

MET ONCE A YEAR AGO
TOM!
WOW! YOU HAVE A GOOD MEMORY!
YES. CURSED TO NEVER FORGET A THING.

I NEED THIS TUBE AND TIRE.
OK. I'LL NEED SOME TIME.
REALLY? HOW LONG? I SHOULD HAVE CALLED FIRST!
IT WOULD HAVE MADE NO DIFFERENCE.
PHONE CALLS DO NOT GUARANTEE THE FUTURE YOU KNOW.

5/12/17
I SPEND SO MUCH TIME TALKING AT WORK. WHEN I GET HOME I JUST WANT TO NOT SAY ANY- THING.
. . .
1/2 MY TIME AT WORK TALKING IS NOT ABOUT WORK, PEOPLE JUST LIKE TO COME IN AND VISIT WITH ME, I LISTEN.
SO THEN
OH
I GET THE IMPRESSION THAT NO ONE GETS HEARD ANY MORE SO SOMEONE LIKE ME IS HARD TO FIND.
I'M LISTENING.
5/13/17
I DON'T REALLY LIKE — STANDING AROUND DOING
BMX   MOTO TRACK
PARTIES. IN FACT NOTHING IS SO ANTI- INTO THE MIX AND
THE IDEA OF ME. BUT ADD A NOW YOU'VE GOT SOMETHING!
5/14/17
THANKS FOR LAST NIGHT, IT WAS FUN!
THAT'S ALL I NEED TO KEEP GOING.
WORTH ALL THE EFFORT.

5/14/17
SO SORE & TIRED. I REALY NEED TO EAT A HUGE MEAL...
...AND GO PASS OUT.
BUT THERE IS SO MUCH TO DO...
5/15/17
WHAT THE HELL, WHY THE SOMBER MOOD?
NO BEER.
WHAT? WHO ARE YOU GUYS?
5/16/17
OK. GOOD NIGHT.
PERHAPS A MEET UP WITH A GIRL? WE'LL SEE....
LET'S NOT GET OUR HOPES UP BUT IT WOULD BE NICE.

5/17/17
WE RODE ALL THE WAY ACROSS TOWN FOR A RIDE.
BUT WHEN WE GOT THERE...
WE'RE DOING A ROAD RIDE TONIGHT
OH.
THE GUILTY PARTY WAS DEALT WITH.
YOU SAID IT WAS A CRUISE!
5/18/17
MY LEGS ARE FRIED.
SHOULD I CUT MY RIDE SHORT? I AM OUT HERE TO ENJOY IT. I SHOULD NEVER CHEAT MYSELF.
GLAD I DID THE WHOLE THING...
A NIGHT ALONE: WHAT I NEEDED.
BZZT.
I HAVE PEOPLE OVER SEVERAL NIGHTS A WEEK. AT SOME POINT I JUST NEED TO DECOMPRESS FROM HUMAN CONTACT.
TOMORROW I CAN TAKE ANOTHER DOSE.
BAROOO!

5/21/17
STEVE HAS TICKETS TO THIS BAND - UM - LIVING COLOR.
FOR REAL?
ARE YOU SURE IT'S NOT A COVER BAND?
WHY DOES IT MATTER?
OH MAN, WHY SPEND ALL THAT TIME LEARNING TO PLAY AN INSTRUMENT JUST TO COPY SOMEONE ELSE'S MUSIC? I'D RATHER BURN ALL MY GEAR!
5/23/17
THE WHOLE TRAIL WAS OVERGROWN...
BUT I WENT ANYWAY. 17 MILES. 17 MILES OF PUSHING AND GETTING THWACKED IN THE FACE BY PLANTS
BUT I FINISHED.
5/23/17
WE'VE GONE SO FAR THIS RIDE IS TOO LONG.
REALLY? WHAT ARE YOU GOING TO LOSE? AN HOUR OF SLEEP?
IT'S A SMALL PRICE TO PAY FOR ADVENTURE!

5/25/17
I WONDER WHY I KEEP TETHERING MYSELF TO PEOPLE. THEY ALWAYS LET ME DOWN.
YOU FLAKED.
ISOLATION IS MY BEST FRIEND AT TIMES, IT NEVER LEAVES ME.
AND IT WILL BE THERE WITH NO PROMPTING.
HEY.
WAZZUP.
5/26/17
I KNEW I WAS GOING TO BE FLAKED UPON SO. I MADE BACK UP PLANS AND WENT OUT.
I HUNG OUT WITH SOME PEOPLE I KNEW AT AN EVENT. IT WAS MORE OR LESS "NORMAL".
YOU BROKE YOUR PELVIS?
YEAH.
THEN I WENT HOME AND WAS ME.
?
5/22/17
THE COMPLETE LACK OF ANYTHING REMARKABLE TODAY WOULD BE GOOD TO SOME, BUT TO ME IT'S NOT WHAT I STRIVE FOR.
HMM
I'M ADDICTED TO ADVENTURE AND ACHIEVEMENT. I NEED AN EVER-INCREASING DOSE TO BE SATISFIED.
NOT ENOUGH.
I REALIZED THAT I WILL NEVER BE PLEASED WITH THE CURRENT SUM OF MY EXPERIENCE AND OUTPUT
MORE.

5/22/17

MORE CALLS FROM THE PAST. I WRITE BACK, I MEAN IF THEY WERE NOT A DICK I CAN.

BUT I TAKE ALL EVIDENCE OF RELATIONSHIPS AND GET RID OF IT. I DID KEEP A COAT THOUGH, IT WAS TOO GOOD TO DISCARD.
GREAT COAT.

I SEE NO POINT IN HANGING ON TO THE PAST, IN DOING SO YOU CAN'T MOVE TOWARDS THE FUTURE.

WELL I DID IT AGAIN. I STARTED A PAGE AND THEN STARTED ANOTHER ONE.
ERASER #7?
SALT N' PEPPER HAIR

IT IS 2/26/24 NOW. AND I MUST SAY WHILE GETTING THESE COMICS READY FOR PRINT - I DO HAVE TO RE-LIVE MY LIFE SOME WHAT.
OH DAMN.

WHILE I'm 100% SURE I'VE NEVER MISSED A DAY, DATES DON'T STICK IN MY MIND.
WHAT'S THE DATE?
NO IDEA.

SOME OF THESE PAGES HAD MIXED MONTHS AND YEARS OR EVEN THE SAME EXACT SET OF DATES ON THEM.

I USED TO WORRY ABOUT KEEPING THE CHRONOLOGY IN ORDER AND VERY ORGANIZED ALL THE WHILE NOT SHARING THEM AS I HAD NO INTENTIONS TO.

BUT AT SOME POINT I REALIZED IT DOES NOT REALLY MATTER ALL THAT MUCH.

5/28/17

5/29/17

5/30/17

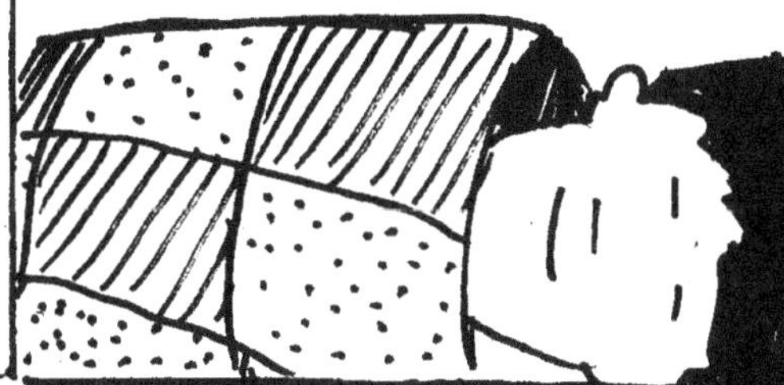

5/31/17
NO, I'M AGAINST YOU.
I AM. I'M AGAINST BLIND ACCEPTANCE, WHAT IS NORMAL, YOUR MORAL AMBIGUITY. THE PATH OF LEAST RESISTANCE.
AS IT LEADS TO NOWHERE.
I JUST WENT AHEAD AND DID IT ANYWAY.
GOING SLOW
RAN ACROSS TOWN THINKING I WOULD BE SPREADING TIME THIN.
RUNNING OUT OF TIME.
BUT FOR THE FEW THAT BUDGET TIME WELL, THERE'S ALWAYS SOME SPARE CHANGE.
6/2/17
I'M GOING TO THE STORE, I'LL BE GONE A WHILE.
HOW LONG IS THAT?
A WHILE IS A SHORT, UNKNOWN SPAN OF TIME.
NEH.

6/3/17
A GREAT DAY IT IS WHEN I CAN DEVOTE IT TO THE WORK.
7 AM
GET BIKES.
NO DAY IS BETTER THAN ONE SPENT GETTING THINGS DONE.
AND 16 HOURS LATER YOU KNOW YOU DID ALL YOU COULD.
OK FINISHED.
6/4/17
SO HARD TO DRAW, MY HANDS ARE BEAT UP BAD.
I FIGURE AT THE RATE I'M GOING I'LL BE IN PAIN ALL THE TIME.
HOPEFULLY I CAN STAVE IT OFF AS LONG AS I CAN.
I NEED YOU.
6/5/17
THE RULE OF TWICE.
IT WILL TAKE TWICE AS LONG TO SAND OR FILE SOMETHING AS YOU THINK IT SHOULD.
TAKING FOREVER.
AND TWICE AS LONG TO EXPLAIN SOMETHING AS IT SHOULD.
I TOLD YOU THAT ALREADY.

6/6/17
MAN, EVERYONE KNOWS YOU.
THEY DO?
BEING SUPER SHY AND INTROVERTED AS A CHILD I NEVER THOUGHT I'D HAVE SOME POPULARITY — NOW IT'S RIDICULOUS.
120 MILES FROM HOME
I KNOW YOU!
AT LEAST I'M KNOWN FOR SOMETHING GOOD.
OH, HELLO.
6/7/17
I LIKE YOUR HAIR.
OH. THANKS.
YOU MUST BE A GOOD PERSON, PEOPLE WITH ALL THEIR HAIR ARE.
LIKE HITLER AND STALIN?
BIKE REPAIR AND SHOOTING DOWN THEORIES!
6/8/17
I FELT SO LOW TODAY. I HATE THAT ABOUT MYSELF.
BUT LIKE ▮▮▮, I WENT ▮▮▮▮
▮▮▮ EVER IT ▮▮, IT WAS GONE.
BETTER.

6/9/17
IT DOES NOT MATTER.
WHAT I HAVE TO DO AND HOW HARD I WORK, NO ONE SEES THAT NOR CARES. SO, IT DOES NOT REALLY MATTER.
IN THE END, MY TOIL ONLY NEEDS TO MATTER TO ME.
AND IT DOES.
6/10/17
EVERY DAY SOMEONE, SOMEWHERE TRIES TO EXERT CONTROL OVER ME.
THAT'S A SHORT ANSWER? MAD?
I DON'T THINK I'M THAT SMART BUT I CAN SEE WHEN SOMEONE IS TRYING TO MANIPULATE ME.
OH THIS TRICK AGAIN.
I NEVER LET ON THAT I KNOW THOUGH, JUST MY LITTLE SECRET.
I SEE RIGHT THROUGH YOU.
6/11/17
YOU ARE THE MOST NATURALLY HIGH PERSON I'VE EVER MET.
I AM?
I WONDER HOW OTHERS PERCEIVE ME AND HOW I PERCEIVE MYSELF ARE SO FAR APART.
THEN WHY DO I FEEL SO AWFUL?
I'VE HAD MY WHOLE LIFE TO PRACTICE TRYING TO BE GOOD. MAYBE I'M THE ONE WHO'S WRONG?
HM

6/12/17
OK. GOOD FOR NOW.
DID MY 12 HOURS OF PRODUCTIVITY. THAT ALWAYS MAKES ME SMILE.
I CAN REST FOR 2 HOURS...
I'D HATE TO LOOK BACK AND FEEL LIKE I DID NOT DO WHAT I COULD.
...I COULD DO THAT THOUGH.
6/13/17
YOOOO!
TALKING TO CRACK- HEADS NOW.
NO. I'M GREETING MY PUBLIC.
YOU ROCK PAUL!
SEE?
6/14/17
FAN MAIL
GOT TWO LETTERS TODAY, FAN MAIL FOR THE ZINE.
IT'S NICE TO HAVE SOME POSITIVE FEEB BACK.
I'LL HAVE TO WRITE BACK

6/15/17
WELL I GUESS.
I CAN WANT TO BE ALONE AND FEEL VERY LONELY AT THE SAME TIME.
THAT'S NOT GOOD!
PERHAPS. IT IS HOW I FEEL.
6/16/17
HOW MY ALIENATION FROM OTHERS GRINDS ME.
EITHER I'M WIDE AWAKE OR I'M BLIND. I SEE WHAT OTHERS CAN'T OR I'M BLIND TO WHAT THEY CAN SEE. I DON'T KNOW.
AND PERHAPS AN ANSWER WOULD NOT SOLVE A THING.
6/17/17
HOW CAN I BE...
IN A PLACE WITH MILLIONS...
... AND BE SO ALONE?
ANOTHER NIGHT READING.

6/18/17
I AM A WEAK CREATURE.
I'D LIKE TO THINK I'M STRONG. TO SOME SURE, I AM. BUT ALL I SEE IS MY FAULTS.
WHY DID I DO THAT?
ALL I CAN DO IS TRY NOT TO REPEAT MYSELF.
PERHAPS NEXT TIME I'LL DO BETTER.
6/19/17
AS I WAS WAITING - SO TIRED FROM A HARD RIDE. I GOT TO DO A THING I LOVE THE MOST.
I LOVE TO JUST LAY THERE AND LOOK AT THE SKY. I COULD DO IT FOR HOURS.
FOR A TIME, I AM AT PEACE AND THAT IS A RARE THING.
6/20/17
UP AND OVER THE SPINE OF THE MOUNTAIN, WE GO.
UP ONE OF THE MOST STEEP ROADS...
RIDING WHERE NO ONE HAS DONE NOR WILL EVER DO...

6/21/17
OVER TIME I'VE GOTTEN TO A POINT WHERE IF I CAN'T STAND SOMEONE ANYMORE, I REALIZE THAT TRYING TO STOP THEM FROM SUCKING IS POINTLESS.
WHY BOTHER?
SUCH A HUGE WASTE OF TIME AND ENERGY TRYING TO GET SOMEONE TO NOT BE A WASTE OF SPACE.
DO YOU WANT TO GO OUT TO EAT?
SO YOU JUST STOP PUTTING ENERGY INTO IT, THAT'S ALL.
NO.
6/22/17
GO!
FUN EVERY TIME.
6/23/17
WE ALWAYS WANT TO BE SURE - DON'T WE? BUT WHAT CAN WE REALLY BE SURE OF?
AS MUCH AS WE TRY TO MAKE THINGS HAPPEN THE WAY WE'D LIKE THEM TO, IT SELDOM DOES.
I PLANNED THIS TRIP FOR US.
NOT GOING.
THE BEST YOU CAN HOPE FOR IS TO BE SURE OF YOURSELF.
OH? OK THEN, I'LL JUST GO BY MYSELF.
REALLY?
YEAH.

6/24/17
THAT'S SO WIERD. SHE LIKES YOU, SHE WON'T EVEN COME TO ME.
OH?
I DON'T KNOW WHY, I'M THE CAT WISPERER, THEY LIKE ME.
I HAVE SOME KIND OF CONNECTION WITH CATS.
PRRRRR
6/25/17
WITH ALL GOING ON PEOPLE ARE SO DISTRACTED, HOW DOES ONE STAY FOCUSED?
A LIFE WITH FEW DISTRACTIONS SEEMS TO BE A WAY..
NO TV
BUT I THINK PEOPLE WOULD RATHER BE DISTRACTED THAN NOT.
JUST AN HOUR..
6/26/17
AROUND THE ACTIVITY OF ZINE MAKING, WE CAN SPEND THE DAY TOGETHER.
CA-CHUNK
MOST PEOPLE WILL JUST HANG OUT AND DRINK BEER OR SOMETHING
I'M OUT OF STAPLES
AT THE END OF 8 HOURS, INSTEAD WE HAVE SOMETHING TO SHOW FOR IT.

6/27/17
THEN SHE SAID...
NO, THAT'S NOT WHAT SHE SAID.
I CAN TELL IT HOW I WANT!
OH, WHEN YOU KNOW YOU'RE NOT TELLING THE TRUTH? TELL IT RIGHT OR DON'T TELL IT AT ALL.
OH YOU RUINED IT!
GOOD.
6/28/17
SOMETIMES I WONDER IF I'M CUT OUT TO BE AROUND OTHERS...
ALL THEY DO IS LIE, TALK SHIT & DWELL IN NEGATIVE SPACES IT MAKES ME WANT TO INTERACT LESS & LESS.
I THINK WE COULD BE BETTER, WELL I KNOW I CAN. IT IS HARD TO SEE ANY OTHERS CAN'T.
6/29/17
WHEN I MEET SOMEONE I'M THINKING.
CUTE BUT...
I FIGURE IT DOES NOT TAKE LONG TO SEE WHAT THEY ARE UP TO...
OH.
GOT LAID OFF...
KID
AND WHEN THEY'D THINK IT IS OK TO MOVE IN WITH ME.
I GIVE THIS ONE THREE WEEKS...
MY X AND THEN...

AND THEN...
HA! HA! HA! HA! HA! HA! HA! HA!
I MADE SOMEONE LAUGH SO HARD TODAY, HE CRIED A LITTLE.
OH, YOU MADE MY DAY.
I WISH I COULD DWELL IN SUCH PLACES MORE OFTEN.
GLAD TO HEAR IT.
BUSY?
OH YEAH I LOVE WORKING HARD.
THAT IS THE THING — WORK. MY OWN WORK IS WHAT I CAN RELY UPON TIME AND TIME AGAIN.
YOUR BIKE IS READY.
KNOWING THE SIMPLE EQUATION THAT THE MORE I PUSH, THE MORE I GET. WELL, THAT KEEPS ME GOING.
THANK YOU!
YOU'RE WELCOME!
7/2/17
THE OIL LIGHT!
H
L
WE WERE SIDELINED FOR NOW. BUT WE CAN TRY TO RENEW OUR ADVENTURE TOMORROW WITH ANY LUCK.
AUTO PARTS STORE IS 7 MILES AWAY.
WE'LL DO WHAT WE SET OUT TO DO...

7/3/17
LET'S JUST WAIT UNTIL TOMORROW, WE CAN DO MORE THEN.
LA
YEAH.
SO WE SLEPT IN THE VAN.
LOVES
AND THE NEXT DAY WE GOT ON THE ROAD.
YES!
WE CAN USE THIS GUAGE INSTEAD OF THE SENSOR.
7/4/17
GOT TO THE RACE. I GOT 3RD IN MY CLASS!
AND WE BROKE DOWN AGAIN. THIS TIME WE GOT TOWED HOME.
REGARDLESS, WE HAD AN AWESOME ADVENTURE!
HOME!
7/5/17
YOU WANTED OATS, NATHAN SAID.
MEEEYOOORRR
I THOUGHT I TOLD HIM I HAD TWO. BUT ONCE SET IN MOTION, IT'S ON ME...
OH...
...TO OWN UP TO IT.
WHAT CHOICE DO I HAVE?
MEEEOOOORH

7/6/17
MEEEEEW
WHAT A CUTE KITTEN. HE WAS ALL OVER ME.
MY OTHER CATS THOUGH DID NOT LIKE OUR NEW GUEST.
MWRRRRR
?
7/7/17
I HAVE NO REAL NATURAL TALENT. EVERYTHING I'VE DONE, IT WAS THROUGH HARD WORK AND NOT LETTING GO
NOTHING HAS BEEN EASY AND I KNOW I'M ONLY REALLY GOOD AT ONE THING.
I LIKE YOUR DRAWINGS.
I'M GOOD AT BEING ME.
OH, WELL THANK YOU!
7/8/17
JAMMING WITH OTHERS WAS GOOD.
WE'LL SEE IF IT GOES BEYOND A FEW PRACTICES.
HOW'S IT GO AGAIN?
DRIVE OUT OF HOLLYWOOD I CAN DO WITHOUT.
WHAT THE FUCK?

2/9/17
THOSE GLOVES THERE...
THOSE ARE KIDS GLOVES, THEY WON'T FIT.
THEY... DON'T ...FIT.. UH!..
OK O.J.!
IT'S 90-100 DEGREES OUT SO WHAT DO I DO? I DRINK HOT COFFEE
AH SWEET NECTAR
I EAT HOT FOOD.
POTATOES + GARLIC, ANOTHER FINE 39¢ MEAL.
THEN 12+ HOURS OF METAL WORK + WELDING
OK. THAT'S ENOUGH.
10
10?! FOR DOTH?
I HAVE TO MAKE MONEY
NO.
7.
OK... HOW'S BIZ?
SLOW, ON ACCOUNT OF THE HEAT.
EVERY SHOP I GO TO IS SLOW...
YEAH AND THERE YOU ARE TRYING TO GRIND ME FOR 3 BUCKS.

7/12/17

WHO'S ON MY BED?

OK.

I GUESS YOU CAN STAY..

PURRR.

7/13/17

WHAT A MESS. I HAVE TOO MUCH GOING ON AND I CAN'T KEEP THINGS UP AND OUT OF THE WAY.

SOME DAYS I WISH MY LIFE WAS LESS CLUTTERED - I HAD MORE DOWN TIME.

NOW WHAT?

BUT THEN I'D BE BORING LIKE EVERY ONE ELSE.

WHATS NEW?

NUTHIN.

7/14/17

REMEMBER MY GIRLFRIEND?

YEAH

WELL, SHE DIED.

AS WE TALK - I CAN'T HELP MYSELF, I EMPATHISE..

I'M SORRY, IT MAKES ME SAD.

PEOPLE THAT SAY CARING IS WEAKNESS ARE FOOLS. CARING IS THE TRUEST FORM OF STRENGTH.

THANKS MAN, IT MATTERS.

7/12/17
WHO'S ON MY BED?
OK.
I GUESS YOU CAN STAY..
PRRRR.
7/13/17
WHAT A MESS. I HAVE TOO MUCH GOING ON AND I CAN'T KEEP THINGS UP AND OUT OF THE WAY.
SOME DAYS I WISH MY LIFE WAS LESS CLUTTERED- I HAD MORE DOWN TIME.
NOW WHAT?
BUT THEN I'D BE BORING LIKE EVERY ONE ELSE.
WHATS NEW?
NUTHIN.
7/14/17
REMEMBER MY GIRLFRIEND?
YEAH
WELL, SHE DIED.
AS WE TALK- I CAN'T HELP MYSELF, I EMPATHISE..
I'M SORRY, IT MAKES ME SAD.
PEOPLE THAT SAY CARING IS WEAKNESS ARE FOOLS. CARING IS THE TRUEST FORM OF STRENGTH.
THANKS MAN, IT MATTERS.

7/15/17
I HAVE 3 CATS NOW. IT'S COOL. THEY DON'T LIKE EACH OTHER BUT LIKE ME.
I'VE SORT OF DOWN-GRADED MY COMPANY TO FURY QUADRAPEDS.
PRRRRR
BECAUSE PEOPLE CAN BE SUCH A BUMMER.
I HAVE NO MONEY.
BUT...
IT'S 1 DOLLAR.
NO.
7/16/17
WE RACED SO HARD- WILL AND I BATTLED FOR THE END, LEAVING ALL OTHERS IN THE DUST.
EVEN THOUGH I GOT SECOND, I PUT THE HURT ON HIM.
THAT...WAS...HARD..
TIRED TOO, I WAS REWARDED WITH A SENSE OF ACCOMPLISHMENT
YEAH, I ALMOST HAD YOU.
7/17/17
SO MUCH BROKEN STUFF AND THINGS NEEDING DONE. THE DAY WAS FULL OF SET BACKS.
CLANG!
AH SHIT THE DRIVE SHAFT WENT OUT!
HOWEVER WE JUST KEPT PUSHING THROUGH THINGS.
WOOD FLOOR IS DONE.
SO, NOT GIVING UP IS WHERE IT'S AT FOR THE MOST PART.
I'LL FIGURE IT OUT.

2/18/17
OW! GAS IN THE EYES HURTS!
FIRE FIRE!
ALL THAT, BUT IN THE END, I GOT IT RUNNING AGAIN.
WUB WUB WUB WUB
2/19/17
I SEE THAT BIKE IS OF EXCELLENT CONSTRUCTION, MAY I TEST RIDE IT?
A DRESS
SURE, YOU GOT AN I.D.?
THIS IS WHAT I CARRY.
UH- A EL POLLO LOCO GIFT CARD AINT GOING TO DO IT MAN.
OH. OK
7/20/17
WHEN A GOOD BOOK IS OVER, IT'S A DRAG.
I WANT TO STAY IN THAT REALM FOREVER. REPLACING IT IS OFTEN HARD..
NOT TOO GOOD.
I'M NEVER ONE TO SAY...
IT WAS TOO LONG.

7/21/17
I KEEP TELLING MYSELF
I NEED TO GET OUT MORE.
BUT DO I? NO. I SPEND MORE AND MORE TIME ALONE.
I COULD GO OUT AND READ..
I SHOULD, BUT WILL I? NOT SURE.
NAH.
7/22/17
THERE'S A SHOW TONIGHT.
I HAVE TO GO MARK THE COURSE.
I DID NOT FEEL LIKE GOING OUT THERE AGAIN; A CHANCE TO GET OUT MORE IS SQUANDERED
SLEEPY.
I'LL HAVE TO DO SOMETHING THOUGH.
LONELY TOO.
RACE TIME
I JUST KEPT MY HEAD DOWN AND PUSHED.
TAKATAKA TAKATATA
OH A RATTLE SNAKE.
AND ALL THE PUSHING PAYED OFF.
THAT MAKES ME TIED FOR 1ST!
2ND!

7/24/17
REST DAY. I ONLY DID A NORMAL PERSONS DAILY TOIL TODAY.
YOU'RE GOING TO FIT ALL THESE BIKES IN YOUR VAN?
SURE.
THEN I VEGED OUT...
GAME OF THRONES NOT SO BAD.
AND ATE A WHOLE BOX OF COOKIES. NOT SO BAD.
ONE MORE..OH. FUCK IT.
7/25/17
PEOPLE ARE SLAVES TO THIER PHONES.
I SAW SO MANY PEOPLE WHO CARRIED IT AROUND LIKE A MONKEY THAT WON'T LET GO OF IT'S DICK.
..OOH.. .OHO.
IT'S LIKE A SORT OF MASS HYPNOSIS OR A NEW GOD. REGARDLESS ON THE OUTSIDE LOOKING IN, THEY ARE LOST.
7/26/17
6 AM TILL 9 PM — AND THERE'S STILL MORE TO DO.
I NEED TO SLEEP.
HOWEVER I DON'T SEE ANY WAY AROUND IT. THE WORK COMANDS IT.
BUT I HAVE TO DO THIS
FOR THOSE OF US WHO TRY, THERE IS ALWAYS MORE TO DO.
ONE MORE THING.

7/27/17
WE RODE FROM VAN NUYS ALL THE WAY AROUND DOGER STADIUM AND BACK. 40 MILES? 50? WE STARTED LATE AND FINISHED LATE. IT'S 1 AM NOW.
IT WAS WAY PAST MY BED TIME AND I WAS ALREADY TIRED AND HUNGRY. I RODE MOSTLY IN SILENCE.
HOWEVER I'M GLAD I DID IT. JUST TO ENRICH MY LIFE EXPERIENCE THAT MUCH MORE. IT WAS WORTH IT.
7/28/17
AFTER BEATING THE CRAP OUT OF MYSELF LAST NIGHT I RODE AGAIN AND IT WAS TOO MUCH.
I REALLY JUST WANTED TO REST BUT COULD NOT - WORK WAS WORK.
I KEEP PUSHING MY LIMITS - NEVER KNOWING HOW FAR OUT THEY ARE UNTIL IT'S TOO LATE.
OH MAN.
IT'S OK, I WAS STARING AT YOUR ASS.
OK. FUNNY. BUT WIERD.

7/30/17
YOU'RE A COOL DUDE. YOU'VE GOT A GOOD SPIRIT.
I DO?
IT WAS SO NICE TO HAVE SOMEONE JUST BE NICE TO ME AND SAY NICE THINGS. I NEEDED THE POSITIVITY BADLY.
ALL THE NEGATIVITY AND SHIT TALKING ALL THE TIME JUST BUMS ME OUT.
AT LEAST THERE IS ONE.
7/31/17
I DON'T WANT IT FOR FREE.
I DON'T WANT TO FEEL ENTITLED. NO ONE OWES ME ANYTHING. I'M AGAINST THE IDEA OF A "HOOK UP". I DON'T WANT A DISCOUNT.
HERE YOU GO.
PEOPLE'S TIME AND RESOURCES HAVE VALUE. TO EXPECT THINGS FOR FREE OR LESS JUST CHEAPENS YOU.
I'M GLAD TO PAY.
8/1/17
YOU KNOW WHAT I'VE BEEN LIKING A LOT?
WHAT?
JUST PUSHING MY SELF FURTHER THAN I WANT TO GO. NOT TO LISTEN TO MY BODY AND COVER MORE MILES.
REALLY!? NO SHIT!

8/2/17
PERHAPS IN THE END I'LL BE OK.
I WORRY SO MUCH ABOUT WHAT IS MISSING TO BE HAPPY THAT I'M FORGETING THE THINGS THAT GOT ME HERE.
ONE DAY, I'LL LOOK BACK, AND LAUGH AT HOW SILLY I WAS.
HA HA HA HA
8/3/17
MY OWN CURSE...
...IS TO PUSH A STONE UP A HILL, NOT TO HAVE IT ROLL DOWN AGAIN LIKE SYSPHUS BUT TO ROLL UP HILL AFTER HILL AFTER HILL.
I WILL NEVER FEEL LIKE I DID ENOUGH WITH MY TIME AND THUS NEVER BE SATISFIED WITH WHAT I DO.
DRAT.
8/4/17
OH THE HAPPY ROUTINE, SOMETIMES I FORGET I AM LUCKY TO HAVE ONE.
6AM RIDE..
MOST PEOPLE ARE JUST FORCED DOWN RUTS OF CAREER, MARRIGE, DEBT + STAGNATION TILL THEY DIE.
COFFEE + DRAW.
INSTEAD I HAVE HARD, BUT REWARDING ROADS TO TRAVEL UPON.
WORK. MAKE PEOPLE HAPPY. REPEAT.

8/5/17

!

CAN YOU TELL ME HOW TO FIX MY BIKE? I LIVE OUT HERE AGAIN.

THE DEVIL INCARNATE IS BACK IN TOWN. WHAT DO I DO? A SMART MAN WOULD SAY GO AWAY. HE WOULD.

BUT I'M NOT THAT SMART.

PERHAPS...

TAKi TiKA TiCKA

8/6/17

WHEN IS THE BIKE GOING TO BE DONE?

I DON'T KNOW. I AM WORKING ON IT NOW BUT YOU'RE MAKING ME STOP AND TALK ABOUT IT INSTEAD OF WORKING ON IT. YOU ARE MAKING YOUR BIKE TAKE LONGER TO FIX BY MAKING ME STOP.

OH.

DID YOU SEE THE ONE ABOUT THE ELEPHANT KILLING THE HUNTER?

NO.

THEY WERE IN SOME TREES AND THIS ELEPHANT GRABBED A HUNTER AND THREW HIM ON THE GROUND AND STOMPED ON HIM. DEAD.

I ALWAYS LOVE IT WHEN THE ANIMALS WIN ONE.

3/8/17
WE RODE OUR THE MOUNTIANS TO OKI DOG.
OKI DOG →
HOLLYWOOD
VAN NUYS →
IT WAS HARD BUT WE ALL DID IT.
THAT WAS HARD!
YEAH, BUT WHO ELSE CAN SAY THEY'VE DONE THAT? NO ONE.
8/9/17
HOW'S IT GOING?
FINE.
SOMETIMES IT'S NOT FINE. EVERYONE HAS THIER PROBLEMS SO WHY BOTHER?
SO LONELY IT HURTS.
IT'S ONE OF THOSE THINGS WHERE EVERYONE KNOWS THE TRUTH, BUT WON'T SAY SO.
...
8/10/17
OK. BEFORE YOU TRY AND RELAX TONIGHT, TRY AND FINISH SOMETHING.
SO I DID. I FINISHED SOMETHING.
AND IN DOING SO, DID MORE THAN MOST.

8/11/17
!
WHAT'S THAT?
BOX OF CHEERIOES I FOUND IN THE PLANTER.
YOU'RE NOT GOING TO EAT THAT?!
MUNCH MUNCH MUNCH MUNCH
8/12/17
YES! THAT LOOKS GOOD!
BZZZZZ
LOOKING GOOD, LET'S SEE HOW IT RIDES.
OH YEAH!
8/13/17
I WANT TO TRY IT OUT FIRST.
SURE.
CRASH! BANG!
!
YOU OK?
YEAH... SURE..
WELL YOU'RE A KNOWN QUANTITY BY NOW.
HE HE.

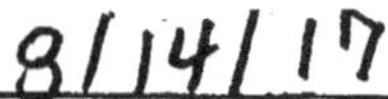

8/14/17
A GOOD DAY. REMINDER I GOT A LOT DONE. A BIG PROJECT PAST A BIG HURDLE.
LAST ONE.
THEN I JUST GOT TO HANG OUT AND READ WITH MY CATS. IT WAS PEACEFUL.
PRRRRR
SO I CAN REMIND MYSELF ABOUT THE GOOD TIMES, NOT JUST THE BAD ONES.
I CAN'T SEE THE PAGES CAT.
8/15/17
SOME DAYS YOUR FLOW NEVER COMES.
OOPS!
WHEN YOU HAVE GOOD FLOW, EVEN IF THINGS ARE SUPER BUSY YOU CAN KEEP A HANDLE ON THINGS.
BUT ON A NO-FLOW DAY EVERYTHING MOVES IN A JAGGED AKWARD PROGRESSION.
THIS IS TAKING WAY TOO LONG.
8/16/17
EVERY DAY I STRUGGLE TO BE RID OF SOME MENTAL BURDEN. SOME WORRY THAT I CARRY.
ONCE I FIGURE OUT HOW TO SHED THIS BURDEN...
ONLY TO HAVE ANOTHER ONE TO TAKE IT'S PLACE.
OOF!
KLUNK!

8/17/17
SOMETIMES I WONDER IF ALL THE THINKING I DO PAYS OFF.
I DO JUST SPEND TIME THINKING ABOUT THINGS. MAKING PLANS AND LOOKING AT MY ACTIONS.
OR SHOULD I JUST GIVE UP AND BE A NON-PRODUCER LIKE OTHERS? I WONDER IF HAPPINESS LIES AT THE END OF THAT CHOICE.
HMMM.
8/18/17
HOW DOOMED CAN I BE?
I SEE THIS GIRL THAT EXCITES ME SO. IT'S RARE BUT I DON'T DO ANYTHING ABOUT MY SECRET CRUSHES.
HA HA HA THAT'S FUNNY!
IN THE END I CAN'T DO MUCH ABOUT IT SO IT JUST HANGS OVER MY HEAD LIKE A CLOUD.
DRAT.
8/19/17
SOMETIMES I'M JUST NOT SURE.
I KEEP WONDERING HOW MY LIFE IS GOING TO TURN OUT...
FORGETING THAT I'M LIVING IT.
I HAD MISSED THAT VITAL POINT.

8/20/17
BZZZT!
OK, IT'S FIXED.
OH THANK YOU! THANK YOU! SO MUCH! NO ONE WOULD HELP ME BECAUSE I'M HOUSE-LESS.
AT THE VERY LEAST I CAN SAY I BUCKED A TREND.
BYE.
8/21/17
I HAD TO REALLY TEST MYSELF TODAY. WOULD I HAVE THE COURAGE TO DO WHAT I HAD TO?
AS I DROVE ALONG I WAS LOOKING FOR MY STOLEN BIKE AND AT THE SAME TIME, LOOKING INTO MYSELF FOR RESOLVE.
WELL AT LEAST I FOUND ONE.
I CAN.
8/22/17
I LOOK FOR SIMPLE SOLUTIONS IN LIFE. I THINK ABOUT WAYS TO MAKE MY LIFE EASIER.
THAT COULD WORK.
EVERY DAY IS A STEP TOWARDS THAT REFINEMENT.
STEP 1
STEP 2
STEP 3
ETC.
EXCEPT WHEN YOU ADD OTHER PEOPLE INTO THE EQUATION.
YOU DID WHAT?

8/23/17

WHY DON'T I GIVE YOU A 100 DOLLARS AND YOU FIX EVERYTHING?
UM

IT'S TOO MUCH. JUST LET ME TUNE IT UP AND I'LL CHARGE YOU WHAT I NORMALLY DO. THAT IS FAIR.

IT'S NOT GOING TO COST THAT MUCH.
OK.

8/24/17

I WENT OUT ON A DATE. IT HAS BEEN A YEAR AND ½ NOW SINCE I'VE BEEN WITH A GIRL.

IT WAS OK. I LIKED HER BUT NO SPARKS WERE FLYING. I'VE BEEN SO LONELY AND FUNNY I DID NOT FEEL DESPERATE AT ALL.

WELL SEE RIGHT? BUT THE STEP WAS IN THE RIGHT DIRECTION.
HMM.

8/25/17

AFTER GETTING SO MANY FLATS, I DECIDED TO TAKE GLOVES & A PUTTY KNIFE TO A SECTION COVERED IN THORNY PLANTS AND REMOVE THEM.

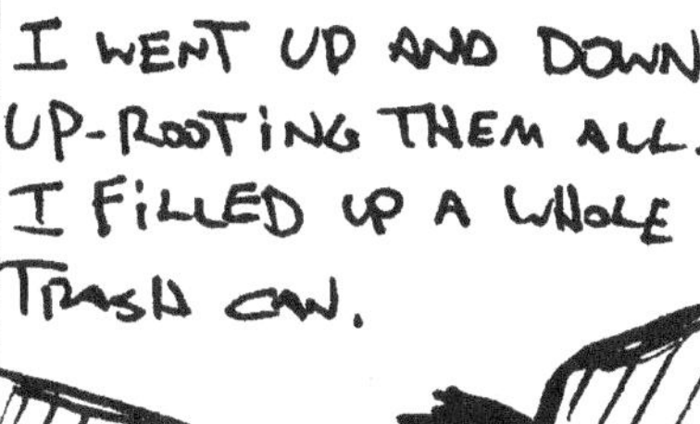

I WENT UP AND DOWN UP-ROOTING THEM ALL. I FILLED UP A WHOLE TRASH CAN.

ON THE WAY BACK, I WAS JUSTLY REWARDED WITH A FLAT TIRE.
REALLY?

8/26/17
I REALIZED TOO LATE.
I LEFT MY BIKE IN MY VAN!
BOB CAME TO THE RESCUE.
I'LL GO GET IT.
OK! THANKS!
OH YOU'RE TOO MUCH!
I'M SORRY I NEGELECTED YOU.
8/27/17
CLEANED IT!
CLEANED IT!
YOU GOT DOWN ALL THAT?
SURPRISED I DID!
8/28/17
A DEAD BEATLE. NO! IT'S STILL ALIVE!
STILL ALIVE!
WELL, NOT FOR LONG.

8/29/17

HOW FAR?
I DON'T KNOW.
LATER...
THIS VIEW!
AMAZING!
WHAT FUN WOULD IT BE IF YOU ALWAYS KNEW THE OUTCOME?
8/30/17
I LOOK AT HOW PEOPLE CLING TO AN IDENITY SO FIERCLY AND SEE WHATS MISSING.
I'M IRISH
TO ME, IT SEEMS LIKE PEOPLES DESIRE TO BELONG TO A GROUP, RACE, CREED, ETC. JUST PROVES THAT THEY HAVE TROUBLE ARTICULATING WHO THEY DO BELONG TO.
SO DESPERATE TO BELONG BECAUSE WE DON'T REALLY HAVE AN IDENITY.
?
8/31/17
IT IS 100° OUT NOW AND SUMMER IS AT AN END. SO TO SPEAK.
EVERY YEAR NOW FOR A WHILE THIS HAPPENS: SUMMER LETS US KNOW THAT IT'S NOT GONE FOR LONG. A LITTLE BURST OF HEAT TO REMIND YOU.
BEFORE YOU START GRUMBLING ABOUT THE COLD.
BRRR!

9/1/17
HE KNEW THAT ABOUT HER.
LIKE WHAT?
IT'S ALWAYS LIKE THAT.
PEOPLE PAINT THEM SELVES IN A CORNER AND ONLY FOUL WHILE HOLDING THE BRUSH.
EVERY ONE THINKS THEY ARE THE ONE THAT WILL BEAT THE ODDS. BUT IT NEVER WORKS OUT THAT WAY.
9/2/17
I WENT OUT — IT WAS FUNNY OR SAD.
ANOTHER SELFIE
IT'S GOOD TO GO OUT EVERY ONCE IN A WHILE...
ANOTHER SELFIE.
...TO REMIND YOURSELF AS TO WHY YOU STAY HOME.
HOME.
9/3/17
I THINK THE ONLY REAL DIFFERENCE BETWEEN ME AND MOST PEOPLE IS THAT I'M WILLING TO TRY.
I'LL GIVE IT A SHOT
MOST PEOPLE HAVE TALKED THEM SELVES OUT OF DOING A THING BEFORE THEY EVEN BEGIN.
I CAN'T DO IT.
HE'S RIGHT.
AND I'M FIGURING OUT WAYS TO MAKE IT HAPPEN.
I CAN.
RIGHT TOO.

9/4/17
45 MILES OF FUN.
OVER HILL AND MOUNTIAN WE RODE. OVER DIRT AND PAVE UP TO GREAT VIEWS TO SWEEPING DECENTS.
AND HAVING THE SHARED EXPERIENCE IS THE THING YOU KEEP THE LONGEST, THE THING THAT WILL ONLY GET BETTER WITH TIME.
9/5/17
IT'S 6. I'M GOING TO HANG OUT TILL RIDE TIME.
DON'T YOU STAY LATER?
TODAY? YEAH, TILL 6:30
BUT I'M DONE WORKING!
HEH.
9/6/17
I REALIZE HOW SMALL I AM. HOW I PUSH UPON THE WORLD AND IT DOES SO LITTLE OR NOTHING.
EVERYDAY, I DEAL WITH PEOPLE'S STUPID EGO. I SEE HOW FAKE IT IS. WHAT YOU THINK OF YOURSELF CAN CHANGE IN AN INSTANT.
I'M ONLY GIVING YOU THIS MUCH.
LIFE EXPERIENCE HAS MADE ME HUMBLE IN MOST WAYS. FOR ME, IT'S GOOD.

9/7/17
THE END OF THE DAY COMES EARLY FOR US SOMETIMES WHO TOIL LONG HOURS DAY IN AND DAY OUT.
REST IS IN SHORT SUPPLY. THE LISTS OF TASKS ARE LONG. EACH DAYS WORK MAKES AN 8 HOUR DAY SEEM LIKE A JOKE.
6 AM. GET GOING.
AN AWKWARD BALANCE PREVAILS MOST DAYS, ONLY WITH YEARS OF EXPERIENCE DOES IT COME.

9/8/17
WE CAN RESIST SO LITTLE. IN LIFE, WE INDULGE - IT IS OUR NATURE.
BUT TO SAY NO, YOU DON'T LOSE SOMETHING OR DENY YOURSELF SOMETHING.
CAKE?
OH..NO.
YOU GAIN THE WILL TO DO WHAT YOU NEED TO DO.

9/9/17
TALK IS CHEAP.
NO, IT IS EXPENSIVE.
HOW SO?
IF YOU BELIEVE THE TALK AND SPEND TIME AND RESOURCES TOWARDS A GOAL THAT THE OTHER PERSON IS JUST TALKING ABOUT - IT COSTS YOU.
I... I LIKE THAT.

9/10/17
THE BATTLE NOT TO BE A LAZY SLUG IS DAILY
I'M TIRED.
WHEN I GO HOME I FORCE MY SELF TO WORK FOR AROUND 2 HOURS AND FINISH SOMETHING.
WRRRRR.
THEN AND ONLY THEN CAN I STOP AND SORT OF ACT LIKE EVERYONE ELSE.
9/11/17
WHAT DAY IS IT? THE TWENTH?
IT'S 9/11
OH...OH!
OH! I FORGOT
OH... OH!
9/12/17
SOMETHING ABOUT GROWN MEN RIDING KIDS BIKES IN A BUNCH.
THE ENERGY WAS HIGH.
THE NIGHT-ELECTRIC.
WOOOO!

9/13/17
NO!
DO SOMETHING ELSE.
WAY BETTER.
9/14/17
MANS INHUMANITY TO MAN - HOW IT WILL NEVER END, AND HOW THAT BREAKS MY HEART.
NO NO. SO BAD.
I DON'T THINK HUMAN BEINGS HAVE COME VERY FAR AT ALL. WE ARE STILL SAVAGES. I CAN RISE ABOVE. I HAVE.
TERRIBLE
BUT CAN WE?
I'M NOT SO SURE.
9/15/17
5 AM RIDING IN DARKNESS IN THE MOUNTIANS, THE ONLY TIME WE CAN GO TOGETHER
WHEN YOU WANT TO DO SOMETHING, YOU MAKE THE TIME.
LOOK AT THE LIGHT!
NOT EXCUSES.
WHAT WE GET FOR GETTING OUT AND DOING IT.

9/16/17
WE HAVE THE FIGHT ON. COME OVER TONIGHT.
UM...OK.
I REALIZE THAT WHEN I'M WITH MY FRIENDS AND DOING "NORMAL" THINGS..
I JUST WANT TO GO HOME.
IT'S NOT OK THAT IT'S NOT OK.
9/17/17
MY NATURAL ELEMENT: ON A BIKE..
WHEN I RIDE, EVERY THING IS FINE. IT IS THE MOST VALUEABLE THING I CAN DO TO SAVE MYSELF FROM THIS WORLD.
THE BIKE IS TRUTH, IT NEVER LIES AND SHOWS ME WHEN I'M NOT RESPECTING IT. THE BIKE TAKES ME TO ALL REALMS I NEED TO TRAVEL AND MORE.
9/18/17
REJECTION IS THE NORM.
BEING TRUE TO YOUR SELF MEANS OTHERS WILL REJECT YOU THEY DON'T GET YOU AND DON'T WANT TO.
I AM?
YOU'RE WIERD!
BECAUSE THE TRUTH IS A MOTHERFUCKER
I'M NOT THE ONE THAT IS SO AFRAID TO BE THEMSELF THAT THEY FORGOT WHO THEY WERE.

9/22/17
THEN I CALLED HER A COPORATE LAP DOG!
OH!
THEY DON'T KNOW MY TENACITY, IF I COULD BOTTLE IT AND SELL IT I'D BE A MILLIONAIRE!
THE LID WOULD POP OFF!
YOU'RE A BIG HELP! THANK YOU, YOU DO A LOT!
I DON'T KNOW...
YOU DO! YOU'RE JUST BEING MODEST.
WELL, THERE'S ENOUGH EGO MANAICS OUT THERE...
I CHECK INTO IT, THAT HAS TO BE ILLEGAL..
OK COOL!
AHH..SET IT IN MOTION A BATTLE IS WHAT YOU DON'T WANT...
NEVER LAY DOWN YOUR SWORD.. BUT A BATTLE YOU HAVE!

9/25/17
TO BREAK ROUTINE. I HAVE TO FORCE MYSELF TO DO IT.
OK. I'LL GO.
SO I WENT TO WATCH A BLUES BAND. NOT MY KIND OF MUSIC BUT LIVE IT WAS COOL.
I SAW HOW HAPPY PEOPLE WERE AND WONDERED WHAT I WAS MISSING OUT ON.
HMM.

9/26/17
ALL MY FRIENDS ARE GETTING MARRIED NOW — IT'S JUST ME.
I KNOW. THEY HAVE ALL GONE AND LAYED DOWN THEIR SWORDS. YOU'RE GOING OUT ON YOUR SHIELD.
I'VE BEEN THERE. IT'S A LONELY PLACE TO BE BUT ALAS, A REAL ONE.

9/27/17
I WAS ON THE FENCE ABOUT GOING TO SOME CITY HALL MEETING BUT I WENT.
I LEARNED A LOT. AND I GOT SOME ISSUES CLOSER TO BEING SOLVED.
THIS IS THE GUY TO CALL.
BUT THE MAIN THING WAS I DECIDED TO DO SOMETHING ABOUT IT INSTEAD OF ROLL OVER.

9/29/17
GOOD CONVERSATIONS ARE SO FEW AND FAR BETWEEN.
MOST PEOPLE ARE FIXATED ON BUYING THINGS OR GOSSIP, THEY HAVE NO IDEAS AT ALL.
IT TELLS TIME IN 7 COUNTRIES
SO WHEN IT DOES HAPPEN, IT'S SPECIAL
NICE CHATTING WITH YOU.
9/30/17
I THINK I GOT A OLD MAN POINT TODAY.
HUH?
I DECIDED TO WEAR A FANNY PACK IN LIEU OF A BACKPACK ON MY BIKE.
IT'S WHEN YOU DON'T CARE ANYMORE, THAT'S WHEN IT HAPPENS.
9/31/17
I'D RATHER
MAKE UP SOMETHING FUN TO DO THAN SIT PASSIVELY TO BE ENTERTAINED.
OK. COURSE MARKED.
THERE'S NO MERIT IN WAITING FOR LIFE TO KNOCK ON YOUR DOOR - IT NEVER WILL.

10/1/17

PEOPLE LOOK AND SHAKE THIER HEADS. THEY LAUGH.
LEAN!

WE ARE NOT YOUNG BUT WE ARE. THERE BEING NO AGE LIMIT ON A GOOD TIME, WE NEVER FORGET.

TO PLAY IS TO LOVE. AND LOVE, WELL IT TRUMPS ALL THINGS.
HA HA HA HA HA HA HA HA HA HA HA HA

10/2/17

CANVASING MY AREA, I WENT FROM BUSINESS TO BUSINESS.
I OWN A SMALL BUSINESS TOO AND THE CITY IS TRYING TO FORCE US TO USE THIS NEW TRASH PROGRAM, IT'S A MONOPOLY.

POUNDING THE PAVEMENT IS HARD WORK AND MANY WERE UN-RECEPTIVE
WHAT? NO.

BUT SOME - THEY KNEW. SO IT WAS WORTH IT.
I'M SO GLAD YOU CAME!

10/3/17

EXTRA FUN TONIGHT.
ALL WAYS GOOD.

WELL WHAT ELSE COULD WE DO? I'D HATE TO HAVE A MUNDANE EXISTANCE.

ONE WHERE WE HAD NOTHING TO LOOK FORWARD TO...

10/4/17
THE PHONE RINGS LATE AT NIGHT. IT IS NEVER GOOD.
RING! RING!
?
AND IT WAS.
3 MESSAGES! THIS IS BAD.
VOIP?
BUT IT COULD HAVE BEEN WORSE...
P.J. GOT HIT BY A CAR BUT HE'LL BE OK.
SWEET RELIEF!
10/5/17
OH, HOW I MISS YOU.
IT IS FUNNY (OR SAD) THAT I GET REMINDED OF LOST LOVE AND LONELYNESS JUST FLOORS ME. IT IS MY CURSE.
I SEE WHY PEOPLE HAVE PETS NOW. THEY LOVE YOU WITHOUT JUDGEMENT.
PRRRRR
10/6/17
AFTER OVER A YEAR I GET TO GAME AGAIN.
IT WAS FUN — I FORGOT HOW MUCH I MISSED IT.
9 POINTS OF DAMAGE!
AND OF COURSE...
PIZZA!

10/7/17
DAMN PJ. YOU LOOK LIKE SHIT!
I KNOW.
THIS SUCKS MAN, I CAN'T DO ANYTHING, I'M GOING TO MISS OUT.
YEAH.
YOU'LL BE BACK SOON ENOUGH LIKE YOU WERE NEVER GONE.
FOR NOW.
YEAH.
10/8/17
WANT TO EAT? IT'S 9:30.
NO. TOO LATE...
...IT WILL GO STRAIGHT TO MY THIGHS.
HA!
I'M NOT THAT FUNNY. I TELL THE SAME 12 JOKES OVER AND OVER. I FIGURE WITH 8 BILLION PEOPLE, I HAVE A LOT OF PEOPLE TO MAKE LAUGH.
10/9/17
OH, THAT LOUD CHEWING SOUND WAS A' OPOSSUM.
CHOMP CHOMP CHOMP
YOU CATS ARE WORTHLESS COWARDS!!
RRRRROORWW!
GET OUT.
PUNT!

10 | 10 | 17
I SAW THAT GIRL IN THERE, I DID NOT SAY ANYTHING.
AS YOU SHOULD.
I WAS TEACHING HER HOW TO TAKE HER BIKE APART.
SO A LITTLE TRADE HUH?
NO, I'M NOT A CREEP LIKE YOU.
!
10 | 11 | 17
YOU LONG HAIR HIPPIE, YOU GET A HAIR-CUT YET?
NO.
IT'S JAMES, YOU DON'T RECOGNIZE MY VOICE.
SURE I DO. JAMES FISHER, IT'S BEEN 7-8 YEARS.
HELL, I'VE KNOWN YOU FOR A LONG TIME RIGHT? (32 YEARS)
HA HA.
10 | 12 | 17
IT DOESN'T MATTER, WE'VE BEEN HERE A SPECK IN TIME.
HUMANITY HAS BEEN AROUND WHAT 50-30,000 YEARS? HISTORY 11 THOUSAND AND THE EARTH IS 4 BILLION YEARS OLD?
A GRAIN OF SAND ON A BEACH, NOTHING.
DAMN.

10/13/17
EVERY DAY I TRY AND TAKE MY LOVE OF FUN AND PUSH IT OUT SOME.
I START WITH ME AND MOVE OUTWARDS TO OTHERS.
DO I POSSES ENOUGH RADIENCE TO EFFECT OTHERS? PERHAPS FOR A TIME.
10/14/17
DID YOU GO TAKE A CRAP YET?
THERE WAS A GUY IN THERE...
YOU DON'T KNOW WHAT IT'S LIKE WHEN YOU'RE OLD. YOU GOTT GO, YOU GOTTA GO! SO I TOOK A SHIT IN THE TRASH CAN.
YOU TOOK A SHIT IN THE JACK N' THE BOX TRASH CAN? YOU'RE AWESOME!
10/15
FUCK YOU I'M TAKING THIS
!
YOU STEAL FROM ME YOU PIECE OF SHIT!?
YES, I BEAT THE CRAP OUT OF A THIEF DRESSED LIKE A GIANT CHICKEN. I DON'T HAVE TO MAKE STUFF UP.
YOU DONE?
WUMP
WUMP
WUMP
WUMP
WUMP

10/16/17

THERE ARE SO MANY THINGS WRONG WITH THE WORLD, ONE DOES NOT HAVE TIME NOR ENERGY TO WORRY ABOUT IT ALL, LET ALONE ACT.

BUT WHAT YOU CAN DO IS CLEAN YOUR OWN HOUSE SO TO SPEAK. BE THE CHANGE THAT NEEDS TO HAPPEN BY FIRST DOING THAT WITH ONES SELF.

AND FROM THERE, MOVE OUTWARD.

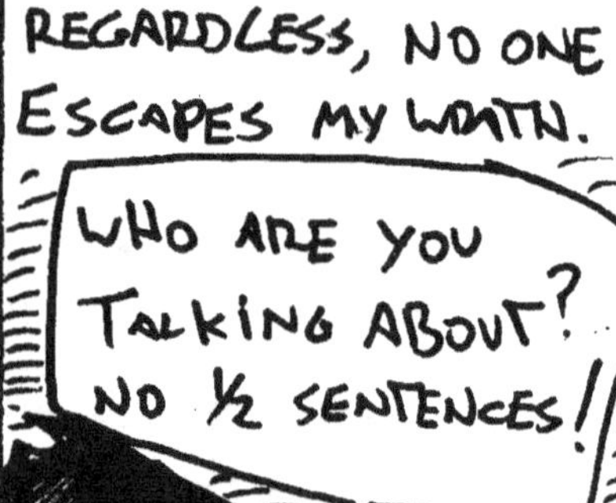

10/17/17

I DEMAND WHEN HAVING A CONVERSATION ONLY ONE THING:

I DON'T GET WHY IT IS SO HARD FOR PEOPLE TO SAY THINGS WITHOUT SLIDING INTO TRUNCATED CELL-PHONE ½ LANGUAGE.

REGARDLESS, NO ONE ESCAPES MY WRATH.

10/18/17

LATER:

10/19/17
6:30
OK. SEE YOU THEN.
AND NOTHING. NOT EVEN A CALL. I OFTEN WONDER HOW PEOPLE GET BY IN LIFE BY BEING FLAKY PIECES OF SHIT.
THEY DON'T.
10/20/17
BLACK OUT.
DO YOU HAVE CANDLES?
OH, IT'S NOT THE APOCALYPSE
OH. LIGHTS.
SORRY TO DISSAPOINT YOU, IT'S NOT THE END OF THE WORLD YET.
10/21/17
AFTER OVER A YEAR I AM PLAYING DUNGEONS + DRAGONS AGAIN.
OK ROLL TO HIT.
WE HAD TWO NEW PLAYERS AND IT WAS FUN, AND NEW AGAIN.
OK, YOUR TURN.
PIZZA
SO THERE'S NOTHING WRONG WITH THE GAME, JUST SOME TIMES THE PEOPLE YOU PLAY WITH
OK. 6 ZOMBIES DOWN. 4 TO GO!

10/20/17
UP
AND UP.
AND UP!
OK THATS ENOUGH.
10/23/17
OH, GOT A MOUSE HUN? GOOD JOB!
EEK
EEK
EEK
EEK
WELL, DON'T MAKE IT SUFFER TOO MUCH.
EEK
EEK
EEK
1/2 HOUR LATER...
OH CAT, YOUR CRUELTY KNOWS NO BOUNDS...
..EEE..
..EEEK...
..EEEK...
10/24/17
PENNY FOR YOUR THOUGHTS?
MUNCH. MUNCH. MUNCH.
HUH? OH I'M FINE. DOING GOOD.
REMEMBER THE GOOD TIMES

10/25/17
I GOT TWO FLATS. WHAT DO YOU THINK IT IS?
THEY ARE FLAT.
BOTH?
I CANNOT SEE WHAT IS WRONG ON THE PHONE.
BUT..
NOT ON THE PHONE, NOT ON THE PHONE, NOT ON THE PHONE.
REALLY?
10/26/17
LISTENING TO MY INTERNAL WISE-MAN HAS BEEN A LONG-FOUGHT BATTLE.
HMMM
I LIKE TO PLOUGH AHEAD BUT WHEN FLUMOXED AND ON HOURS 14 OF WORK...
I MEASURED BUT IT DOESN'T FIT.
...THE WISE MAN SAID..
I'M TOO TIRED TO THINK RIGHT. BEST REST ON IT.
10/27/17
THERE'S NOTHING LIKE TAKING AN IDEA AND MAKING IT MANIFEST IN THE FLESH.
MOST PEOPLE JUST TALK ABOUT WHAT THEY WANT TO DO.
I WANT TO MAKE A BICYCLE FORK.
BE THE FEW WHO TAKE THOSE WORDS AND DO.

10/28/17

INSTEAD OF WORKING AFTER WORK I WENT OVER TO MY FREINDS HOUSE AND ATE LOBSTER HE CAUGHT.
BEEN DECADES.

GETTING OUT OF MY ENVIROMENT WAS GOOD THOUGH. I COULD FEEL THE STRESS LEAVE MY TENSE FORM.

ONLY TO RETURN ONCE HOME.
HCP!

10/29/17

IT IS 5:45 AM - DARK WITH NO LIGHTS I CLIMB 1½ MILES UP THE TRAIL - SLOWLY.
IT THAT A ROCK OR A HOLE?

ONCE I GOT TO THE TOP, LIGHT WAS JUST PEAKING THROUGH. ALONE IN THE HILLS, THE DAWN GREETED ME.

MAGIC? PERHAPS FOR A TINY MOMENT, SURE WHY NOT?

10/30/17

GOT OFF TO A LATE START AND MY WHOLE DAY WAS FULL OF UPS AND DOWNS. STARTING EARLY IS THE WAY.
2 HOUR MEANS TRAFFIC, TRAFFIC!

GOT BEATIN' DOWN.
YOU'RE TRANSFERING ME AGAIN?

BUT ENDED ON A UP SWING.
SHEARED BOLT STUCK NO MORE!

10/31/17
I GOT SOME GREAT NEWS TODAY. A HUGE WORRY LIFTED OFF OF ME. I FLOATED.
STRESS JUST OOZED OUT OF ME.
CAN YOU PUT A DOLLAR AMOUNT ON PEACE OF MIND?
WORTH EVERYTHING ELSE YOU HAVE.
YOU'RE READING A BOOK ON A YOGI?
YEAH IT'S CRAP.
IT SHOULD BE SHELVED UNDER FICTION, HIS CLAIMS ARE OUTLANDISH.
BUT YOU'RE GOING TO FINISH IT.
WELL YEAH. I STARTED IT DIDN'T I?
11/2/17
HERE'S WHERE I DIFFER FROM EVERYONE ELSE:
THERE IS NO ENTITLEMENT. YOU DON'T DESERVE ANYTHING.
I DON'T THINK I'M OWED ANYTHING, NOTHING IS A GIVEN. GETTING WHAT YOU WANT VERY SELDOM, IF EVER HAPPENS.
LOST ANOTHER ONE.
I WILL STRIVE FOR AN OUTCOME BUT IF IT DID NOT COME ABOUT IT SHOULD COME AS NO SURPRISE.

11/3/17
CHANGE THINGS. NOT RIGHT. TOO LOW, DIFFERENT BARS, HIGHER STEM. NEW GRIPS. IS THE FRAME GOOD? SWAP SEAT. DO IT NOW.
YOU HAVE TO LEAVE IT. I HAVE OTHER PEOPLE WAITING ON ME, I CAN'T DO IT NOW.
OH!
OH WHITE PEOPLE, HOW I HATE THEE.
11/4/17
CRAP. I KNOW EVERY ONE!
11/5/17
AND IT ALL CAME TOGETHER.
BEST TURN OUT YET— FOR THE VINTAGE RIDE, 17 RIDERS.
DOING A LITTLE THING FOR A FEW, WELL IT'S WORTH IT.

11/6/17
I WONDER IF THIS WILL DO THE TRICK.
E Z O STRIP
OH WOW IT IS WORKING SO FAST!
WRRRR
NOTHING LIKE THE RIGHT TOOL FOR THE JOB.
9 BARS IN THE SAME TIME I DID ONE BEFORE. AWESOME!
11/7/17
WE GO IN THERE.
SEE? LOOK AT THE VIEW.
ADVENTURE IS IT'S OWN REWARD.
11/8/19
I LOOK FORWARD TO...
A WARM CUP OF COFFEE WHEN I GET UP.
OR SOME TIME OUT ON THE TRAIL AS THE SUN RISES.
AS LONG AS I CAN GET SOME TIME ALONE I CAN SORT OUT THINGS AND FOCUS ON BEING HAPPY.

11/9/17
TIME FOR PULL UPS.
!
IT WAS TOO FUNNY LOOKING SO NO PULL-UPS TODAY!
HE! HE! HE!
11/10/17
I'M SO GLAD TODAY THAT I KEPT IT UP AND GOT THINGS DONE AFTER WORK TODAY INSTEAD OF "RELAXED" WHICH IN MY WORLD IS THE SAME AS "WASTE TIME"
THE FACT IS, THERE IS NO TIME TO WASTE OR GIVE INTO FEELING TIRED. EVEN THEN, LOW ENERGY TASKS CAN BE DONE.
IT IS NOW WHAT I MUST DO TO RE-EVOKE MY PURPOSE.
SIMPLY DO.
5 AM WHY NOT GET UP?
5:00
SO I DID. A WHIRLWIND OF ACTIVITY ENSUED.
I DON'T GET PEOPLE THAT SLEEP IN, THERE'S SO MUCH LIFE TO BE LIVED.

11/12/17
GLARF.
GET THOSE DOUGHNUTS AWAY FROM ME! I CAN'T RESIST!
OH, NUMBER 3. SO HELP ME.
11/13/17
HOW EASILY OUR PERSPECTIVE CHANGES WITH ONE MINOR DETAIL.
LOOKS SO DIFFERENT.
I JUST RODE UP A TRAIL THAT I USUALLY RIDE DOWN. IT WAS LIKE ANOTHER WORLD.
AM I GOING THE RIGHT WAY?
IT WAS SO ODD THAT SUCH A SIMPLE THING COULD CHANGE YOUR WHOLE VIEW.
I CAN HARDLY BELIEVE IT IS THE SAME TRAIL.
11/14/17
YOU'RE GREAT TO TALK TO, REFRESHING.
I AM?
IT'S FUNNY, I GET THAT A LOT. I DON'T THINK I'M ALL THAT SMART. I'VE JUST BEEN SOBER ALL MY LIFE SO MY BRAIN IS NOT MUSH.
ALL I CAN SEE IS THE HALLOWNESS IN THINGS.
IF YOU SAY SO...

11/15/17
IT HIT ME SO HARD TODAY. ALL THE MUSCLES AND NEVER SAY DIE ATTITUDE I CONVEY.
GRRRR!
UNDERNEATH, I'M JUST A BOY. A SCARED AND LONELY BOY WHO'S NEVER HAD ANYONE LOVE OR ACCEPT HIM AS HE HAS OTHERS.
SNIFF
SO I RIDE ALONE.
11/16/17
I WISH I COULD MAKE MYSELF AS HAPPY AS I MAKE OTHERS.
YOU'RE THE WIZARD!
ALL DAY I DO SOME MENDING AND MAKE A SMILE APPEAR.
MRF.
I LOVE YOU MAN!
OH IF I WAS SO EASY, I WISH I WAS.
OOF!
11/17/17
THERE YOU ARE BEHIND THE TOILET AGAIN.
OH CAT, SUCH AN ETERNAL OPTOMIST...
THINKS ANOTHER MOUSE IS GOING TO COME OUT OF THAT HOLE.

IN THE ROADS OF LIFE WHICH DO YOU CHOOSE? THE EASY OR THE HARD?

THE PATH OF LEAST RESISTANCE MEANS YOU RESIST NOTHING THAT HAPPENS TO YOU.

WHILE THE HARD ROAD - THE ACT OF RESISTANCE MAKES YOU ALL THE STRONGER

11/19/17

I FORGET HOW SOME OF MY FREINDS AND I ARE SO APART IN TIME AND SPACE BUT OUR BOND TO EACH OTHER IS STRONG.

I MAY NOT SEE THEM MUCH OR TALK TO THEM MUCH BUT WHEN WE ARE AROUND EACH OTHER IT'S DIFFERENT.

YOU DID THAT?

YEAH.

I WILL ALWAYS COUNT MYSELF AS ONE OF THE LUCKY ONES FOR THIS REASON ALONE.

11/20/17

?

MEOW MEOW

WHAT IS IT MEOW? MEOW?

PRRRRR RRRR

11/21/17
THROUGHOUT THE NIGHT WE RODE TO OUR WOUNDED FREINDS HOUSE.
HE'D BEEN OUT OF ACTION SO WE WENT TO PAY HIM A VISIT.
HERE, A FRAME I MADE FOR YOU.
OH WOW.
THE BONDS OF FREINDSHIP CAN BE STRETCHED BUT SELDOM BROKEN.
11/22/17
FUN DERAILED.
STUPID COLD.
IT'S OK THOUGH. I KNOW IN TIME I'LL FORGET AND LOOK FORWARD TO THE NEXT FUN THING.
NINJA BATTLE.
WHEN YOU SOW THE SEEDS OF FUN THEY GROW ANEW AGAIN AND AGAIN.
11/23/17
BEING SICK IS THE ONLY TIME I WILL SIT AND WATCH A LOT OF VIDEOS ON THE WEB.
I SEE PEOPLE DO THIS ALL THE TIME.
I FEEL BAD FOR THEM. THEY ARE MISSING OUT ON REAL LIFE.
C'MON BODY KICK THIS THING.

11/24/17
YOU'RE A CAPITALIST!
URRR
YOU ARE! ONE OF THE BEST CAPITALISTS I KNOW!
OK.
ONE OF THE SMARTEST PEOPLE WITH MONEY I'VE EVER MET!
I GUESS I HAVE TO WEAR IT.
11/25/17
KA-CHUNK
WAS THAT A DATE OR? HMM? NOT SURE.
EITHER WAY, DOES NOT MATTER... FINE WITH THAT.
11/26/17
MY DOG DIED...
SORRY
SNIFF...
OK. COME HERE.
IT'S OK.
SOB SOB SOB SOB

11/27/17
SOMETIMES IT IS JUST NOT THAT GOOD.
SOMETIMES I JUST HAVE A BLAH DAY OR A (RARE) LAZY DAY. NOTHING REALLY COMES TO MIND.
I GUESS THAT'S OK THOUGH. I WOULD NOT VALUE THE GOOD ONES THAT STUCK OUT THEN.
11/28/17
THAT ZINE YOU DID WAS GOOD. THE BEST ONE YET.
REALLY?
YOUR WRITING IS GOOD, I'D AGREE WITH YOUR POINT - WHAT YOU SAID, YOU SAY IT WELL.
OH.
THAT IS A GREAT COMPLIMENT COMING FROM YOU, THANKS!
11/29/17
HERE YOU GO. WELL I WAS GOING TO TOSS IT, SO I CAN'T CHARGE YOU FOR IT.
HOW MUCH?
MAN. YOUR LIFE STYLE CHOICE IS AMAZING. YOU HAVE SOME INTEGRITY, HOW YOU DEAL WITH PEOPLE.
REALLY? IT JUST MAKES SENSE, THAT'S ALL ...

11/30/17
I'M UNSURE ABOUT SO MANY THINGS.
MY FEAR IS THAT I'LL NEVER BE AT EASE WITH WHERE I'M AT.
AND IN DOING SO LOSE OUT ON ENJOYING THE MOMENT.
SOMETHING IS MISSING, BUT WHAT?
12/1/17
I SEE YOU OUT HERE ALL THE TIME.
I LOVE SEEING YOU OUT HERE!
?
WELL.. THANK YOU?
12/3/19
I FEEL SO WIERD RIGHT NOW.
I'LL JUST NOT FEED INTO IT AND IT WILL PASS.
AND SURE ENOUGH, IT DID.

EVOKING LIFES PASSIONS IS A FULL-TIME OCCUPATION.
TO SEE LIFE AS A CHANCE TO GO OUT AND LIVE IT INSTEAD OF BEING A TOURIST.
NINJA BATTLE.
WHAT DID YOU DO?
THAT IS TO BE TRULY AWAKE.
I DON'T GET IT.
YOU NEVER WILL.
12/4/17
IT'S ONE THING I HATE IT IS SHOPPING. EVEN FOOD IS A CHORE.
FILLED WITH DREAD
AND LIKE MOST THINGS IT WAS WAY WORSE IN MY HEAD THAN REALITY.
3 PAIRS. THAT'S EASY.
GROSS
THEN I WONDER WHY I DO THAT.
THESE PANTS FIT ME FOR A CHANGE.
12/5/17
WRRRRRRWR
DAMN THAT RIDE WAS WINDY!
I KNOW.
TAP WATER
BUT LOOK HOW MANY PEOPLE SHOWED UP, WE HAVE A SOLID CREW.

12/6/17
ROUTINE HAS BEEN MY SAVIOR.
TOMORROW I DO X, Y, 2.
EVERY TIME I'VE BEEN OUT OF SORTS, ROUTINE HAS BEEN THE LIGHT AT THE END OF THE TUNNEL.
IT MAY NOT WORK FOR EVERYONE BUT IT WORKS FOR ME.
STAY ON THE TRACKS.
12/7/17
WHEN FACED WITH DOUBT I THINK OF THIS:
WHAT ELSE COULD I DO?
WHAT AN EMPTY LIFE SPENT GOING FROM PASSIVE ENTERTAINMENT TO PASSIVE ENTERTAINMENT
NETFLIX
HOW COULD I NOT WANT TO HELP THINGS ALONG OR FIX THINGS? OR MAKE PEOPLE HAPPY?
WELL, I CAN'T
12/8/17
RESIST.
MILK. NO COOKIES.
CRAP
TO STAY THIN AT MY AGE YOU HAVE TO WATCH WHAT YOU EAT. ALL THE TIME, THE BATTLE IS CONSTANT.
STAY STRONG.
AND I ALWAYS FEEL GOOD ABOUT NOT GIVING IN.

12/9/17
YOU'RE A GOOD PERSON PAUL.
WELL THANK YOU.
YOU ARE CAUSE YOU ARE WILLING TO CRY. MANY AREN'T
YEAH...
THOSE THAT DON'T ARE JUST CHEAPINING THEIR HUMAN EXPERIENCE.
12/10/17
OH LIFE - SOMETIMES YOUR ATTEMPTS TO MESS ME UP FAIL, I FEEL LIKE I GET ONE OVER ON YOU WHEN THAT HAPPENS.
#?!9#!
SEE THE THING THAT I FIGURED OUT IS THAT PEOPLE ARE NOT RATIONAL OR EVEN SANE MOST OF THE TIME.
OH...OK BYE!
!
SO I DON'T FALL INTO THE TRAP.
FUCK THAT.
RING. RING. RING.
12/11/17
LOOK, THE WAY I SEE IT, EVERYONE HAS THE POTENTIAL TO DO GREAT THINGS. SO I WANT THAT FOR MY FRIENDS...
...AND YOU HAVE MORE TALENT AND SKILL THAN NEAR EVERYONE I KNOW.
!
OH! WELL THANK YOU!

12/12/17
YEAH! PJ YOU'RE BACK!
YEAH.
WAS HIT BY A CAR.
I'M GLAD YOU'RE BACK.
ME TOO. THIS IS IT.
IT'S THE ONLY THING I WANT TO STAY UP FOR.
12/13/17
35 YR OLD PENCIL SHARPENER
WRRRR WRRRR
NICE AND SHARP.
OH DRAT.
SNAP!
12/14/17
I GO BEHIND THE GOODWILL AND SCAVANGE FREE BOOKS. SO MANY THROWN AWAY...
I READ THEM. SOME ARE GREAT, SOME NOT SO MUCH. I'VE READ BOOKS FROM THE 50's + 60's AND THEY WERE MEANT FOR TRUE INTELECTUALS.
GESTALT THEORY...
THEY ARE HARD TO READ, NOT MADE FOR THE PUBLIC OF TODAY, BUT I HAVE TO TRY ANYWAY...
THAT'S A LOT TO MAKE SENSE OF...

12/15/17

NOT A BIG CELEBRATION, JUST A JAR OF PEANUT BUTTER.

TODAY I SOLD ENOUGH BIKES TO GET BACK WHAT I PUT IN.

$41,975. THAT'S IT.

FOR INVESTMENTS— THAT IS STELLAR. AND I HAVE MUCH FURTHER TO GO.

WELL, I'M WINNING.

12/16/17

I WENT TO A PARTY AND....

COOKIES!

SO MANY HOME-MADE

COOKIES!

NOM NOM NOM

OK. ENOUGH. I GO HOME..

12/17/17

DO WE?

OH, HE HAD SO MUCH PROMISE.

BY NOW, I'VE SEEN SO MANY PEOPLE CRASH AND BURN.

AT THE START DOESN'T EVERYONE?

BUT IN THE END MOST DO NOTHING AT BEST AND MANY GO DOWN IN FLAMES. SO ISN'T THAT WHAT WE SHOULD REALLY EXPECT?

12/18/17
KA-CHUK KA-CHUK
THE FOUNDATION WAS DOWN EIGHT INCHES. IT'S BETTER NOW.
THE THING IS I DID IT MYSELF.
NOT PERFECT, BUT WAY BETTER THAN IT WAS!
12/19/17
IN THE NIGHT - THROUGH THE STREETS, AND THEN THE DIRT TO MOUNTIAN PATHS WE RODE. LITTLE SPECS OF LIGHT.
UP AND UP WE WENT AND THEN DOWN INTO THE DARK, OVER RUTS AND GRAVEL. THE NIGHT PLAYED TRICKS ON OUR MINDS...
HUH?
DID YOU SEE THAT?
NO ONE ELSE WAS UP THERE - BELOW, THE JEWELS OF THE CITY TWINKLED AT US. A TREASURE FOR US ALONE TO HARVEST.
12/20/17
YOU DO THINGS WITH HONOR, YOU KNOW THAT?
I DO?
IT'S FUNNY, BUT THAT IS WHAT I'VE LONGED TO HEAR AND WHAT I STRIVE FOR - HONOR. A CONCEPT, ONLY IN FANTASY NOVELS, CAN IT BE IN REAL LIFE?
WELL, THANK YOU!

12/21/17
BEEN MAKING ZINES FOR 17+ YEARS NOW. SO I JUST GET TO THE DEED.
6 AM, MAY AS WELL GO GET IT.
I FOLDED A STACK BEFORE WORK AND HIT THE REST AFTER WORK. 1000 COPIES.
KREASE FINGER
LIKE MANY THINGS, A LITTLE AT A TIME AND YOU GET RESULTS.
ONE DAY FOLD, STAPLE NEXT.
12/22/17
KA-CHUNK.
SPENT 5½ HOURS STAPLING ZINES. 1000 ZINES, 2 STAPLES. ON AND ON IT WENT.
THAT STACK IS NOT GETTING SMALLER
A WEEK FROM NOW I WON'T REMEMBER THE ORDEAL. MAKES ME WONDER WHAT ALL THE FUSS IS ABOUT.
DONE & DONE. NO BIG WHOOP.
12/23/17
ONE MORE DAY OF THIS FUCKING BULLSHIT.
ONE MORE DAY OF PHONY JOY, PHONY CHEER, PHONY BALONEY BROTHERHOOD. ALL FORCED, ALL FALSE.
MERRY XMAS!
HOW ABOUT BEING NICE TO PEOPLE ALL YEAR ROUND INSTEAD OF A FEW WEEKS?

12/24/17
OK.
CLOSED FOR Holiday
off FOR A WEEK - TO NEW ADVENTURES. NO PEOPLE. NO PHONE. NO INTERNET NO TALKING JUST ME-
NO LOVE - THE VAST CHASIM OF LONELYNESS OPENS WIDE AGAIN BENEATH ME. I GUESS I ONLY HAVE MYSELF TO BLAME.
12/25/17
YOU KNOW, I REALLY DON'T LIKE TRAVELING.
THE HIGH COST, LATE FLIGHTS, CRAMED SEATS, SCREAMING KIDS AND THE ENDLESS HURRY - UP AND WAIT.
I THINK I WILL ENJOY MY EXPERIENCE BUT GETTING THERE, I CAN DO WITHOUT.
13 HOURS LATER I'm HERE.
12/26/17
THERE WAS SO MUCH TO LOOK AT.
COOL!
DEALING WITH NORMAL PEOPLE - WELL I HAD TO. MANY BROUGHT LITTLE KIDS.
MAAAAA
I GUESS THE PARENTS WANT TO CULTURE THEIR CHILDREN BUT THE MESSAGE IS LOST ON THE SMALL ONES.
EXIDIT

12/27/17
THE NATURAL HISTORY MUSEUM WAS GEARED FOR KIDS. SO MANY PEOPLE. THE PRESS OF BODIES WAS A LOT TO DEAL WITH.
ALL I CAN SAY IS THE PARENTS - MOST OF THEM - LOOK STRESSED OUT & UNHAPPY.
POOR BASTARDS.
ONCE I GOT TO THE ART GALLERY - FAT SUBURBANITES WITH BROODS GAVE WAY TO FORIGN BORN FASHION PLATES.
BETTER I GUESS.
12/28/17
THERE WAS SO MUCH ART AT THE SMITHONIAN...
SO MUCH OF IT WAS SO SKILLFULY DONE - AND INTENSE. IT WOULD BE HARD FOR NEW ARTISTS TO CAPTURE THAT ENERGY. SOME MODERN ART IS LOST ON ME THOUGH.
?
IT DID MAKE ME FEEL LIKE MY CREATIVE EFFORTS HAVE BEEN SO VERY SMALL.
I NEED TO DO MORE.
12/29/17
YEAH PLANES!
THE PLANE & SPACE MUSEUM WAS SO COOL. I CAN SEE WHY IT IS OPEN 2 HOURS LONGER THAN THE OTHERS.
WW I ART
I STAYED ALL DAY FROM OPEN TO CLOSE TO TAKE IT ALL IN.
WELL I'M NOT GOING BACK AGAIN, FOOD CAN WAIT.

12/30/17
I JUST WANT TO BE ME.
ME IS I AND I IS ONE AND WE ALL KNOW ONE IS A LONELY NUMBER.
YOU SEEM SAD.
PERHAPS
I GUESS BEING ACCEPTEPED FUR NOT BEING ACCEPTEPED IS THE RIDDLE THAT NEEDS TO BE SOLVED.
12/31/17
PROJECTS PROJECTS PROJECTS
OH SAVE ME FROM MY WORST ENEMY.....
MYSELF.
BZZZZZZZZ!
ALRIGHT!
COFFEE
DOUGH NUT.
EVERY YEAR WE RIDE FROM THE SFV TO D.T. L.A. IT IS SUCH A FUN CRUISE.
BIKES CAN TAKE YOU PLACES & TAKE YOU PLACES. TODAY THEY LIFTED MY SPIRITS.

1/5/18
PEOPLE AGRAVATE ME SO MUCH. I AM SO SICK OF SELFISH BEHAVIOR.
BUT I KNOW THEY WILL NEVER CHANGE AND I WILL NEVER WIN.
SO BEING UPSET, I ONLY HURT MYSELF. I SHOULD LEARN TO LET GO OF IT.
1/6/18
YOU COULD JUST TELL ME YOUR BIRTHDAY.
NOW YOU OWE ME DINNER.
WHAT?!
REMEMBER WHEN I SAID IF YOU ASKED ME WHAT MY BIRTHDAY WAS AGAIN THERE'D BE A PUNISHMENT?
OH DAMN.
1/7/18
COLD BE DAMNED! THERE WAS A RACE!
HACK! WHEEZE!
I WAS SO WEAK AND EVERY BREATH WAS LIKE BEING STABBED.
SNOT
BE IF THERE'S ONE THING I DO WELL AND THAT IS SUFFER
PAIN! BUT I DID IT.

1/8/18
You look tired.
Yeah, I had wierd dreams.
Of what? You planning to go there?
Of India. No
Why?
You can tell a place sucks by all the people you see who have fled it.
Oh doggie kisses!
GLARF!
Oh man, doggy deep throat! Ha ha ha ha ha ha ha.
!
INSPIRATION
The bolt of magical inspiration finally struck me after a lengthy slump.
Tiky Tac Tiky Tac Ticky Tak
I must ride the lightning!
Tick Tac Ticky Tac Ticky Tac Ticky

1/11/18
I HOPE I CAN JUST GET A GOOD NIGHTS SLEEP.
PLEASE, I NEED A GOOD NIGHTS SLEEP
WHO AM I TALKING TO? MYSELF, THAT'S WHO.
1/12/18
I NEVER THOUGHT I'D CARE ABOUT FIXING UP A HOUSE.
SPACKLE.
BUT I MUST ADMIT I'M LEARNING SO MUCH AND I REALLY ENJOY ALL THE IDEAS I HAVE.
I CAN USE A JACK SIDEWAYS TO PUSH THAT BACK.
I CAN'T WAIT TO UNLEASH MY CREATIVITY ON THIS PLACE.
1/13/18
AND.. SEND.
HA. IT WENT THROUGH.
FUCK YOU CITY OF L.A. I WIN.

1/14/18
OH, WHAT A DAY.
RACING WAS SO FUN! EVERYONE HAD A GOOD TIME THE POSITIVE VIBE RULED THE ROOST!
SO FUN!
AFTER WORK I WENT TO IT ON A PROJECT. I WAS SO FURFILLED AND HAPPY IN MY TASKS.
WHAT EVER YOU DO. REMEMBER THIS DAY.
1/15/18
THIS FRAME SHOULD TAKE ME 4 HOURS TO WELD.
CUT CUT MITRE MITRE GRING WELD WELD WELD
OK MAYBE 7 HOURS.
1/16/18
WHAT ARE YOU DOING MEOW MEOW? BEHIND THE TOILET?
THAT MOUSE AIN'T GOING TO COME OUT WITH YOU THAT CLOSE.
YOUR ZEAL BETRAYS YOUR INTEREST.

1/17/18
THAT IS SO RIGHT!
"HAPPINESS IS LOOKING FORWARD TO A ROUTINE"
IT MADE SENSE. AND THE LITTLE THINGS IN LIFE THAT BRING ME JOY, THEY MATTER THE MOST.
1/18/18
I NEED TO WRITE DOWN MY IDEAS
ALL DAY SO MANY IDEAS POP IN MY HEAD. NOT ALL GOOD, BUT SOME ARE.
POP!
I WONDER HOW MANY GOOD IDEAS I'VE LOST BY NOT WRITING THEM DOWN.
LITTLE TO DO LISTS...
AND BIG ONES.
!
ALL THE STUFF IN-BETWEEN - IS CALLED LIFE.
THE CRUEL JOKE.

1/20/18
OK, IT'S 10 BUCKS.
I DON'T HAVE ANY MONEY.
WELL I'M NOT RUNNING A CHARITABLE ORGANIZATION HERE SO I'M KEEPING YOUR BIKE TILL YOU PAY ME. YOU GOT SOME NERVE!
1/21/18
4TH AIN'T BAD.
7 MILES UP & DOWN
! CHARLIE, MOVING SO SLOW?!
ZIPP!
HAHA! 3RD!
1/23/18
I FIXED A FLOOR
I MADE SOUP. I WORKED ON MY BOOK. I WORKED ON WORK, PROMOTED EVENTS & PLANTED SOME ONIONS & POTATOES.
I PLAYED WITH MY KITTIES, WORKED ON MY TRUCK, PAINTED MY FRONT DOOR TO MY HOUSE. AND I ENJOYED EVERY BIT OF IT.
A GOOD DAY.

1/23/18
THE NEW GUY.
WE HAD A NEW GUY ON THE RIDE TONIGHT. HE WAS SLOW. I LIKE TO GO FAST.
HUF HUF HUF HUF
BUT I FIGURED WE ALL WERE THE NEW GUY AT SOME POINT AND WE ALL START FROM ZERO.
IT'S NOT MUCH FURTHER
OK THANKS
1/24/18
CHARLIE?
HA HA
I THINK I DO ROMANTASIZE MY FRIENDSHIPS. THE ONES THAT HAVE MOVED AWAY.
YEAH.
THEY'RE THE ONES I MISS THE MOST.
OK. BYE.
1/25/18
OH LOOK WHO'S BEING FRIENDLY!
ARE YOU HUNGRY KITTY?
FOOD
LATER:
HERE KITTY!
OH IT'S LIKE THAT HUH.

1/26/18
THE TO-DO LIST IS LONG.
WILL I GET IT ALL DONE? I DON'T KNOW IF I'LL LIVE LONG ENOUGH, I HOPE SO.
COFFEE: THE ELIXIR OF LIFE.
BUT I'D RATHER DWELL ON PROJECTS THAN THE LAME WAY PEOPLE HAVE TREATED ME.
1/27/18
THAT WE WILL FLAIL TO NO AVAIL AGAINST THE WORLD. TO FIND LOVE - TO FIND CLOSENESS.
TO FIND TRUTH, TO FIND UNDERSTANDING. TO HAVE FOR A TIME. A SOLID GROUND. ONCE, JUST ONCE TO KNOW WE CAN HAVE ALL THESE THINGS.
IF WE REALIZED THE ONLY THING STOPPING US RESIDED ON THE OTHER SIDE OF A MIRROR
1/28/19
IS THIS THE LAST LAP?
YEAH..
3RD
2ND
GRRR!
AT THE END!
OH MAN YOU DROPPED ME SO FAST! GOOD JOB!
YEP.

1/29/18

HANG ON TIGHT TO MY INNER CHILD.
BZZZZZ

I'VE NEVER STOPPED PLAYING. I COULD PLAY WITH TOYS ALL DAY.
BZZZZZ

JUST NOW MY TOYS CAN MAKE OTHER TOYS.

1/30/18

I SURE DO ENJOY SLEEP.

I WISH I WAS BETTER AT IT. SLEEP IS A TREAT, FOR ME NOT A GIVEN.

PERHAPS THAT IS WHY I ENJOY IT SO.
PERHAPS I SHOULD GET UP.

1/31/18

HANGING OUT WITH OLD FRIENDS MEANS OLD STORIES.
AND THEN!...
OH YEAH

I FORGOT HOW MUCH WE USED TO LAUGH THOUGH.
HE HE HE HE HE HE

THAT'S THE PART I MISS THE MOST.
OH MAN.

2/1/18
DO THIS. DO THAT. DO THIS. DO THAT THEN THIS, THEN THAT.
I DO THE THINGS AND THEN FORGET. TASKS UPON TASKS— IT ALL GETS LOST. I KNOW IT WILL NEVER END
10 DOWN, 500 TO GO.
BECAUSE I'LL JUST AD MORE BEFORE I'M FINISHED.
AND 500 AFTER THAT.
2/2/18
RING RING RING RING RING RING RING
HELLO?
ROBOT
RING RING RING RING RING RI
MAKE IT STOP.
2/3/18
SO MUCH TO DO!
I WAS FEELING A LITTLE OVERWHELMED TODAY SO I WENT HOME AFTER WORK AND WORKED SOME MORE.
EVERY 4 AND THEN 2...
AND THEN I GOT AHEAD.
THE REST IS EASY.

2/4/18
SO POWERLESS AT TIMES. WELL, MOST OF THE TIME.
!
LIFE IS CRUEL LIKE THAT. YOUR MIND CAN GO PLACES YOU'LL NEVER GET TO.
GRRRR
NOT EVEN AN INCH.
HUF. HUF. HUF. HUF.
2/5/18
I TRIED REALLY HARD TO RELAX AND NOT OVER DO IT TODAY.
I LIKE TO GO AND GO AND GO BUT TO HIT THE RESET BUTTON FOR A DAY.
PRRRR
IT WAS MOST LIKLEY A GOOD IDEA.
NOT BAD.
2/6/18
WHERE IS EVERYONE?
YOU SAID BALDOA.
NO, I SAID HAVENHURST!
NO ONE LISTENS ANY MORE!

2/7/18
I JUST WANT TO REMEMBER THAT IS WAS A PEACEFUL DAY TODAY.
DECLINE & FALL OF THE ROMAN EMPIRE VOL 1.
ALL THE RUSHING AROUND WE DO, HOW OFTEN WE FORGET...
ONLY 900 PAGES
...TO TAKA A PAUSE AND ENJOY THE MOMENT.
Hmm.
2/8/18
WORK: 6 AM TIL 6 PM.
RING RING
NOW!
NOW!
SO. HUNGRY. MUST. RESIST. URGE. TO KILL.
GRUMBL
GRUMBL
GRUM
GRUM
GRUMBL
GRUMBL
HOME! FOOD + SILENCE. THANK GOODNESS.
2/9/18
OH I'M WISE BUT YOU'RE WAY UP HERE!
I AM?
I GUESS IF YOU SAY SO.
BUT I DON'T FEEL THAT WAY.

2/10/18
-SO HUNGRY-
WHAT IS GOING ON?
GR
GR
G
LO E
LE
BLE
THE LAST FEW DAYS I'VE BEEN SO HUNGRY.
I JUST ATE FOUR PB+J's AND IT DID NOT FILL THE VOID.
GLARF.
WELL, I CAN SEE MY RIBS BIG TIME SO I GUESS I NEED IT.
I FEEL FAT THOUGH. MID-LIFE OR WHAT?
14 DIRT BAGS + OLD BIKES
+HILLS & BEER (FOR THEM, NOT ME.)
PUBLIC DRINKING
TAP WATER.
EQUAL WHAT LIFE IS ALL ABOUT.
GNAAR GEEEEE REEENN WZZ
LATER:
PURRRRRR

2/13/18
OH THE HUMAN CONDITION—
I SHOULD NOT EAT THIS.
—TO KNOW SOMETHING YOU'RE DOING IS WRONG—
GLARF.
—AND TO DO IT ANYWAY.
OW
GRR
2/14/18
I REALIZE NOW I'M SUCH A NON-CONFORMIST.
THAT WHEN I DEVELOP SOMETHING THAT PEOPLE WANT TO CONFORM TO...
CAN YOU MAKE US SHIRTS?
I REBEL AGAINST THAT TOO.
NO.
2/15/18
YOU DON'T REMEMBER GIVING ME THAT BIKE FOR SO CHEAP?
NO.
I MUST HAVE IF YOU SAY SO.
I GUESS IF I CAN'T REMEMBER DOING NICE THINGS FOR PEOPLE I DO IT ALL THE TIME.

2/16/18
THESE FUCKING PEOPLE
YOU HAVE TO LEAVE IT. REPAIRS TAKE TIME.
YOU HAVE TO WAIT YOUR TURN.
I CANNOT DO IT NOW. TIME. TIME. TIME.
2/17/18
SHE SAID I WAS TOO NICE.
YOU'RE NOT TOO NICE, YOU'RE...
YEAH? DON'T PULL YOUR PUNCHES WITH ME.
...I'M LOOKING FOR THE RIGHT WORD IN YOUR HOUSE HERE...
...YOU'RE A SLAYER.
OH! I LIKE THAT!
2/8/18
A MAGICAL TIME.
MILES UPON MILES OF RIDING, ROLLING HILLS, GRASS + GREAT VIEWS.
AND A CUP OF COFFEE AT THE END TO SEAL THE DEAL.
WHAT? YOU SAY SOMETHING?

2/19/18
I KNOW YOU'RE THERE.
I KEEP BUSY TO KEEP IT AWAY BUT IT CAN CREEP BACK IN AT ANY TIME.
LONELYNESS IS A DULL PAIN THAT RUNS THROUGH YOU LIKE A PIERCING COLD.
AND COLD I WILL BE.
2/20/18
IT'S 45 DEGREES OUT.
DOES NOT FEEL THAT COLD.
NATURAL FUR
IT WAS NOT A BIG DEAL. ANY DEVIATION FROM COMFORT AND PEOPLE GO-A-RUNNING
I WONDER WHEN WE WENT SOUTH. WHAT WAS IT?
WENT ANYWAY.
IT WAS SO COLD BUT I LAYERED UP AND WENT ANYWAY.
NICE SUNRISE.
I THINK I SAW 8 OTHER PEOPLE THAT WORKED FOR THE GIFT WHILE EVERYONE ELSE HID AT HOME.

2/22/18
I DON'T GET EMPTY, AUSTERE SPACES.
?
HOW BORING YOUR LIFE CAN BE IF YOU HAVE NO TRAPPINGS OF ANY INTEREST?
NEAR EMPTY.
A FULL LIFE IS FULL OF STUFF.
MORE LIKE IT.
2/23/18
OH THAT COUGAR MAGNET IS SO FUNNY! THOSE OLD LADIES JUST LOVE YOU!
I KNOW. IT IS RIDICULOUS HOW OFTEN IT HAPPENS.
LATER:
OH, YOU ARE A BEAUTIFUL MAN!
OH MAN!
HA HA HA HA HA HA HA HA HA HA
2/24/18
ON GIVING UP:
I SEE PEOPLE WHO HAVE GIVEN UP ALL THE TIME. GIVEN UP ON THEIR DREAMS, THEMSELVES, ON LIFE.
IT IS SO HARD TO KEEP TRYING. SOMETIMES I ALSO FEEL LIKE OUR PRIVILEGE IN THIS WORLD HAS BLINDED US TO HOW GOOD WE HAVE IT.
THIS IS NOT RIGHT.
AND HOW GIVEN UP ON BEING GRATEFUL IS JUST AS BAD.
HOW'S IT GOING?
THRILLED TO BE HERE!

2/25/18
OH MAN, I HAVE SO MUCH WORK!
IT WOULD GO FASTER IF I DID NOT HAVE TO TALK ABOUT IT ALL DAY.
BUT I'M BLESSED WITH BUSNIESS, THAT'S FOR SURE.
2/26/18
WHERE YOU'D GET THAT SHIRT?
FOUND IT. WHY?
THAT COLOR PATTERN, IT'S VERY TRENDY NOW, THE WAY THE COLORS ARE LAYED OUT.
COFFEE
ARE YOU SAYING I'M TRENDY?
NO, I JUST FIGURED I'D TELL YOU BECAUSE I KNOW YOU'D HAVE NO IDEA.
2/27/18
I'LL MAKE THE SHIRTS THEN!
DO IT!
WHOA I DON'T WANT YOU TO PRANK ME BACK.
WHY?
BECAUSE I KNOW WHAT YOU'RE CAPABLE OF!
HE. HE. HE.

2/28/18
6:30 AM
OH CRAP I LEFT MY GAS CAP AT THE FILLING STATION
I GUESS I'LL NEED TO BUY A NEW ONE OR AT LEAST SEE IF IT'S STILL THERE...
6:15 PM
RIGHT WHERE I LEFT IT!
BUT YOU SHOULD TALK TO THEM, IT'S UNRESOLVED.
IT IS.
CAPSOLITAZION ONLY HAPPENS IN THE MOVIES OR A STORY WHERE THERE'S AN UNDERSTANDING OR CLOSURE.
REAL LIFE IS ALL LOOSE ENDS AND MISSED CONNECTIONS, NO CLOSURE.
3/2/18
I TALKED TO A GIRL ON THE PHONE FOR 3 HOURS.
...
HELL, I DON'T KNOW. WE'RE GOING TO MEET UP IN A COUPLE WEEKS.
SEE YOU THEN.
IT WOULD BE NICE TO BE CLOSE TO SOMEONE AGAIN THOUGH.

3/3/18
RODE IN THE COLD & RAIN.
IT WAS A WET, SLOW, DREARY DAY.
BUT FOR A MOMENT THE SUN POKED THROUGH THE CLOUDS AND RED/ORANGE LIGHT BEAMED THROUGH IN A MAGICAL DISPLAY.
WORTH IT.
HERE, YOU.. GO MAN..
?
I DUNNO TO GOOD DOOR NOT LOCKED SO THEY JUMPED ME
BECAUSE MY MOM IS FROM SAN BER- DO. HOSPITAL
GOTTA GO TO HOSPITAL...
DAMN POOR GUY!
3/5/18
THE LOVE OF A TINY RITUAL.
AFTER GOING OUT IN THE HILLS I LIKE TO GO TO THE SAME COFFEE HOUSE, GET THE SAME THING AND EVEN SITTING IN SAME SPOT.
COFFEE PLEASE.
THERE'S SOMETHING ABOUT MY TINY RITUAL THAT TIES MY LIFE TOGETHER.

3/6/18

LIFE IS A JOURNEY, LIFE IS A CIRCLE, LIFE IS A CHALLENGE, A MYSTERY THEY SAY. IT'S NO MYSTERY PEOPLE ARE LOST.

TO ME AT LEAST, YOU ARE LOOKING FOR THAT MISSING PIECE IN YOUR PUZZLE. SOME CAN LOOK, ON THE OUTSIDE TO HAVE IT ALL BUT BE EMPTY ON THE INSIDE.

MOST OF US SPEND OUR WHOLE LIVES TRYING TO MAKE DO WITH PIECES OF THE PUZZLE MISSING. SAD REALLY, TO NEVER FEEL COMPLETE.

3/7/18

NEXT TOWN OVER IS CALLED VALENCIA. IT IS SO STRANGE, FULL OF WHITE PEOPLE. PLASTIC SURGERY & DYE JOBS.

I FORGOT HOW WHITE FLIGHT PLACES WERE, THEY FEEL LIKE FORIGON LANDSCAPES.

A STRANGE PLACE.

3/8/18

ALL THAT HARD WORK IS PAYING OFF.

3/9/18
I DON'T CARE WHAT PEOPLE SAY, IF YOU ARE NOT A TEACHER, THEN YOU DON'T GET AN OPINION - YOU ARE NOT MY PEER.
IF YOU ARE A BIKE SHOP OWNER OR A WELDER LIKE I AM YOU ARE MY PEER, YOU CAN COMENT.
EVERYONE ELSE CAN FUCK OFF!
3/10/18
AT THE END, I'M GLAD I RELENTED.
RAIN COAT
PLASTIC BAGS
WE HAD A RIDE BUT IT WAS RAINING, SO WE MADE IT SHORTER.
LET'S GO THIS WAY.
BY GIVING IN A LITTLE - I GOT A LOT IN RETURN - I MADE PEOPLE HAPPY.
3/11/18
DRAWING LINES CAN BE HARD - IT IS SO HARD FOR MOST.
OVER TIME THOUGH THAT LINE HAS BEEN THE DIFERENCE POINT BETWEEN ALL THINGS. ONCE DRAWN
THERE IS NO GOING BACK.

3/12/18
NOT TODAY.
IT'S SO HARD TO GET AWAY FROM THE STUPID INTERNET. I JUST WANT TO LIVE SOME. I FIXED MY TOILET & MY TRUCK. I DID SOME CHORES.
KLUNK.
I RODE MY BIKE AND PLAYED WITH KITTIES, AND WELDED SOME BIKE FRAMES BUT I DID NOT GO ON THE INTERNET.
I CHOOSE LIFE INSTEAD.
3/13/18
I JUST THINK THERE'S SOMEONE FOR EVERYONE.
HAHA. WELL I WISH IT WERE TRUE!
I FEEL LIKE I'M DOOMED.
3/14/18
I KNEW THAT GIRL WOULD CANCEL OUR DATE. I WAS ALMOST COUNTING ON IT.
IT'S BLAH BLAH...
LIKE MOST PEOPLE, VERY QUICK TO BUILD WALLS INSTEAD OF BRIDGES.
AND IN DOING SO, YOU NEVER SPAN A SINGLE GAP IN LIFE.

3/15/18
A MAYBE WAS GOOD ENOUGH.
GOT TO HANG OUT WITH THIS COOL GIRL TONIGHT.
HA! HA!
NOT SURE WHAT WAS GOING ON BUT IT WAS GOOD ENOUGH FOR NOW.
NICE HANGING OUT WITH YOU.
YOU TOO.
3/16/18
I FOUND THAT AMP. YOU CAN HAVE IT, IT'S GETTING RUINED OUTSIDE.
I CAN?
YOU'RE SO KIND!
WELL, I'M... TRYING.
HA HA HA HA HA
3/17/18
A DREAM OF RIDING.
I CAN'T WAIT TO GO RIDING TOMORROW BY MYSELF. MY OWN LITTLE ADVENTURE.
WHERE I'M MOST FREE AND ANSWER TO NO-ONE.

3/18/18
I SEE THE TANGLED WEB OF PEOPLE'S LIVES AND AVOID BEFORE I AM SNARED.
SEEING DOWN THE ROAD IS A RARE SKILL, MOST PEOPLE WALK INTO TRAPS THAT WERE OBVIOUS.
I HAVE ALWAYS BEEN GOOD AT SEEING THINGS AT A DISTANCE.
I SEE.
3/19/18
IN A CITY OF MILLIONS... SO STRANGE.
I CAN GO THROUGH IT ALONE SO OFTEN AS IF....
I WAS THE ONLY PERSON ALIVE.
3/20/18
IT SHOULD NOT BUM ME OUT BUT IT DOES. HOW HARD IT IS TO GET CLOSE TO SOMEONE.
IT SEEMS EASY BUT IS NOT. NO ONE EVER WANTS EASY.
Hi.
HELLO.
THEY WANT HELL ON EARTH.
NOW BURN!
OUCH.

*TO ADHERE TO A CODE, YOU LOSE BUT YOU ALSO GAIN THAT YOUR IDEAS AND ACTIONS ARE ONE AND THE SAME.

3/24/18
ARE YOU OK?
WELL MY STOMACH HAS BEEN DOING FLIP FLOPS ALL DAY.
SURE I GUESS. YOU?
WHY?
YOU KNOW AND THAT CALL AT MIDNIGHT.
SURE
JUST SEEING IF YOU'VE MADE IT HOME OK.
DON'T BE SAD.
I'M TRYING. YOU? ALRIGHT THEN? IS THIS WHAT YOU WANT. HAHA THATS HOW IT GOES
NO! NO.
3/25/18
YOU KNOW...
YOU'RE NOT MAKING IT EASY TO RESIST YOU...
PERHAPS I SHOULD STOP TOUCHING YOU..
PERHAPS...IT'S NOT RIGHT.
3/26/18
WHAT A MESS. THESE CRAZY WOMEN—NOTHING MAKES ANY SENSE.
AH.. ENOUGH TIME TO SORT IT OUT, TO THINK...
WELL...THERE'S ALWAYS ANOTHER HILL...

3/28/18
I HATE LAYING DOWN THE HAMMER ON SOMEONE. BUT YOU SOMETIMES YOU HAVE TO.
THINGS HAVE GONE TOO FAR DO YOU JUST TAKE A BEATING?
" I SAID...
OR DO YOU STRIKE BACK?
ENOUGH!
WHAMP
SO IT'S OVER THEN? CAN I KISS YOU?
GREASE
YES!
MOMENTS LATER...
OH! OH WOW! AH!
HA HA YOU WENT CROSSED EYED!
NEVER BEEN KISSED BEFORE LIKE THAT?
NO, NOT LIKE THAT!
HA HA WELL MORE TO COME!
BLAH BLAH BLAH BLAH BLAH BLAH BLAH BLAH BLAH BLAH BLAH BLAH BLAH
BLAH BLAH BLAH BLAH BLAH BLAH BLAH BLAH BLAH BLAH BLAH BLAH BLAH BLAH BLAH
SO, HOW LONG IS IT GOING TO TAKE?
WELL, I NEED BOTH HANDS TO LOOK THROUGH THE CRATES SO I NEED TO PUT THE PHONE DOWN.
YEAH
OOOON...OK

3/30/18
AFTER SO LONG BEING ALONE, TO FALL ASLEEP IN SOMEONES ARMS AGAIN...
THAT IS WORTHY.
ARE YOU OK?
I FORGOT HOW VALUEABLE IT WAS.
YES I AM.
SHE'S SO COOL! WARM, FUNNY, SEXY, SHE MAKES ME LAUGH, SMART, IS FUN TO BE AROUND. A GOOD PERSON, WE THINK ALOT ALIKE.
AWWWW
YOU'RE GOING TO FALL IN LOVE WITH HER!
I HOPE SO...
THESE TROPHIES ARE GREAT ART MAN - IT'S SO GOOD.
ART? WELL, YOU'RE THE ARTIST. WELL I FIGURE IF I'M GOING TO DO AN EVENT I SHOULD MAKE IT DIFFERENT.
A LITTLE EFFORT, WELL IT GOES FAR.

REGAN LIBRARY ENTRY FEE 25⁰⁰
THAT'S A LOT.
OH MAN, FUCK THAT BUTCHER, WELL EVEN IN DEATH HE'S LIKE ALL REBUBLICANS...
STILL ROBBING US LITTLE FOLK AND GIVING IT TO HIS FRIENDS.
WHAT'S THIS?
SEE THAT BUG DIRT BALL, GET IT!
!
GOOD KITTY!
4/4/18
DID YOU DO A SECOND ISSUE OF YOUR ZINE?
NO..
OH, MAX. WHY?
I JUST HAVE NOT BEEN FILLED WITH SELF LOATHING LATELY.
OH A RARE WINDOW OF TIME FOR SURE.
YEAH.

4/5/18
JUST CHIP AWAY.
TAK
TAKY
TAK
NOTHING I'VE EVER DONE IS EASY BUT I KNOW THAT IF I JUST CHIP AWAY AT THINGS A LITTLE AT A TIME.
AT SOME POINT, YOU CAN'T HELP BUT FINISH.
ONE STEP CLOSER...
4/6/18
YOU NEED A BIGGER SHOP.
NO WAY.
BIGGER MESS.
4/7/18
WHILE MOST DON'T LIKE HAVING STRESS, IT HAS BEEN A GREAT TOOL TO DRIVE ME.
THIS THAT THI
THIS THAT
THIS THAT
THIS THAT
THIS THAT
THIS THAT
THIS
THA
THIS
THAT
THI
WITHOUT A MYRIAD OF TASKS AND A SMALL WINDOW OF TIME TO DO THEM IN. THE PRESSURE WOULD NOT BE THERE.
2 DOWN, 8 TO GO.
BZZ
BZ
BZ
BZZ
STRESS CAN BE A SWORD TO CUT THROUGH THINGS, OR TO FALL UPON — YOU CHOOSE

4/8/18

I READ EVERYTHING ON YOUR WEBSITE.
YOU DID?
AND I AGREE WITH EVERYTHING YOU WROTE ON THERE!
!
SCARY
4/9/18
HOW LONG DOES IT TAKE?
BZZZZZZZ
I'VE MADE SO MANY THINGS IN MY LIFE: BIKES, CARS RESTORED, MUSIC, BOOKS & MAGAZINES ETC. AND I KNOW.
SLOW GOING.
IT SIMPLY TAKES TWICE AS LONG AS YOU THINK IT SHOULD.
3 DOWN, 7 TO GO
4/10/18
WE'VE ALREADY GONE 18 MILES!
YEAH THAT'S IT HUH?
!
DOESN'T FEEL LIKE IT THOUGH.

4/11/18
IF IT'S NOT WORKING, THEN WHY HANG ON TO A BROKEN MACHINE?
I DON'T WANT YOU GUYS OVER ANYMORE.
SO MANY PEOPLE, IN LIFE, TRY TO CARRY ON WITH BROKEN MACHINES. NOT ALL THINGS CAN BE FIXED.
YOU GUYS DISRESPECTED MY SPACE AND ABUSED THE RELATIONSHIP.
AAAR
WILL YOU ALLOW YOURSELF TO REMAIN WITH THE BROKEN MACHINES OR CAST THEM OFF AND SEEK FUNCTIONING ONES?
SORRY
OK
4/12/18
TIME AND SPACE ARE THE SAME FOR ALL. ONE'S PERCEPTION + USE OF TIME IS ALL THAT IS DIFFERENT.
NOT ENOUGH TIME.
THERE IS ALWAYS TIME.
THE SAME AMOUNT IS GIVEN EVERY DAY TO EVERYONE. THE ONLY THING IN LIFE THAT IS TRULY EQUAL TO ALL: A UNIVERSAL FAIRNESS.
I DID NOTHING TODAY.
I DID XYZ, 123
AND IT WOULD BE UNFAIR TO YOURSELF NOT TO MAKE THE MOST OF IT.
SO, WHAT'S NEXT?
4/13/18
THIS ASSHOLE... REALLY?
PETITION FOR RESTRICTED PARKING ON MY STREET.
LATER...
WELL, IF I DON'T DO SOMETHING, WHAT GOOD AM I?
WELL WE WENT OUT THERE AND NO ONE SHOWED UP SO WE DID OUR PART.

4/14/18

SOMETIMES YOUR BRAIN JUST ATTACKS YOU FOR NO REASON.

I COULD NOT FIGURE OUT WHY I WAS FEELING WIERD BUT AT LEAST I COULD BE AWARE OF IT AND DO SOMETHING ABOUT IT.

INSTEAD OF LETTING MY MOODS RULE ME, I SHOULD RULE THEM.

SHUT UP BRAIN

4/15/18

IT WENT ON AND ON. A VISION OF ROLLING HILLS + GREEN GRASS.

I'D BEEN HERE COUNTLESS TIMES BEFORE WHEN IT WAS NOT GREEN.

BUT TODAY- WELL IT'S MORE MAGICAL THAN NORMAL.

WOW.

UH - CAN I HELP YOU?

JUST LOOKING

YOU DO THAT PROFESSIONALLY

NO.

YOU SHOULD DRAW ABOUT FAKE NEWS.

ALL NEWS IS FAKE NEWS.

4/17/18
HEY MAN, I'M IN A CRUNCH FOR TIME... MONEY TALKS RIGHT?
MONEY DOESN'T TALK?
NO.
FAIRNESS TALKS.
4/18/18
2 BUCKS.
THANKS.
AFTER 12 YEARS OF HAVING THIS GUY TALK MY EAR OFF I FINALLY GOT SOME MONEY FROM HIM.
4/19/18
SO GOOD TO GET EVERYTHING DONE YOU SET OUT TO DO.
AND THEN TO DO SOME MORE!
LAST ONE!
AND HAVE THE PRESENCE OF MIND TO KNOW IT WAS A GOOD ONE.
ONE LAST THING

4/20/18
OH YOU AIRED UP THE TIRES TOO. HOW MUCH IS IT?
17.
CAR
HERE YOU GO.
THIS IS 30.
YOU WERE ALWAYS NICE TO ME WHEN I WAS A KID.
OH! WELL THANK YOU!

4/21/18
HOW'S IT GOING WITH CHERYL?
OH, IT'S BEEN GOING GOOD— YOU KNOW WHAT IT IS?
IT FEELS HEALTHY.

4/22/18
THAT'S YOUR PERCEPTION.
AND PERCEPTION IS FLAWED...
SAY WHAT YOU WANT.
SO...
I DON'T CARE WHAT YOU THINK ABOUT ME.

4/23/18
THAT SILLY INTERNET AGAIN. MAKING IT SO PEOPLE FROM THE PAST CAN REACH OUT TO YOU — AGAIN.
OH CRAP.
PERHAPS IT MAKES IT TOO EASY, OR WHAT SHOULD NOT BE SAID, BE SAID.
SO SAD.
ANYWAY I FEEL BAD FOR THEM — NOT BE ABLE TO LET GO.
SORRY
4/24/18
HOPE EVERYONE MADE IT.
THAT WAS SUPER FUN!
YEAH.
4/25/18
OH THE PAST AGAIN — ALWAYS THE ROBBER OF THE NOW. HOW IT TRIES TO STEAL YOUR FUTURE.
I TRY NOT TO THINK ABOUT THE PAST. IT IS WASTED ENERGY. WHEN I FIND OLD PICTURES I THROW THEM AWAY.
ONE DAY I HOPE TO ONLY SEE THE NOW, AND FUTURE. BUT NOT WHAT IS BEHIND ME
SORRY, I'M EMPTY HANDED.

4/26/18

LAST ONE!

OH THE JOY OF JOYS, TO TAKE AN IDEA AND TO FINISH IT FROM A-Z. NOTHING LIKE IT

THE SMALLEST CLUB THAT ONE CAN BELONG TO: THE DO-ER'S

DONE

4/0/18

LITTLE NOTES: HOW I REMEMBER IT ALL.

DO.
X Y, 4 Z

PEOPLE ASK FOR SO MANY THINGS FROM ME AND I HAVE SO MUCH I NEED TO REMEMBER SO I PUT NOTES IN MY POCKET.

A SIMPLE SYSTEM I DON'T FORGET TO DO SO I DON'T FORGET.

OH YEAH.

4/28/18

IT'S WORTH A SHOT.

?

I'M LEAVING MY CAT, DIRTBALL THAT HAS A TASTE FOR MOUSE FLESH IN THE HOUSE

WE'LL SEE...

HOPE IT'S WORTH IT.

DON'T PEE ALL OVER THE HOUSE.

MEOW.

4/27/18

I THOUGHT I HEARD MY CAT GETTING MICE. I HEARD NOISES

I DREAMED OF OBSCURE PUNK RECORDS.

THE CAT DID CRAP IN A CHAIR THOUGH.
AH AH

4/30/18

THE SIGN SAYS TO GO NO FURTHER
WE WENT THAT WAY BEFORE.

OK. BUT IT IS PRIVATE PROPERITY. I'D BE MAD IF SOMEONE JUMPED IN MY YARD.

I'M SORRY IT JUST DOES NOT SIT WELL WITH ME, IT'S NOT RESPECTFUL. LETS GO BACK.
OK.

5/1/18

WELL, AT LEAST YOU'RE HONEST.

IT'S FUNNY HOW PEOPLE SAY THAT AT LEAST YOU'RE HONEST...

SHOULDN'T THAT BE THE NORM INSTEAD OF ODD?

5/2/18
OH MY GAWD YOU'VE AGED SO WELL!
?
BABY
LET ME HUG YOU! GIVE ME A HUG! GRRRRRRRR!
OK
NICE TO SEE YOU TOO.
5/3/18
AS WE AGE, IF WE ARE LUCKY, WE MAKE PEACE WITH OURSELVES. OUR WORST ENEMY IS ALWAYS YOU.
SOME WAGE THAT WAR TILL THE DAY THEY DIE. THE GRUMPY OLD PEOPLE HAD LOST THAT WAR.
GRUMBLE GRUMP
BUT TAKE A MOMENT NOW AND GIVE YOUR SELF A HUG. AND START THE PEACE PROCESS: WITH YOURSELF.
OK.
5/4/18
THERE'S SO MUCH TO DO BUT MY BODY SAID NO WAY. I WAS TOO TIRED.
WHEN I FEEL LIKE THIS - I TELL MY-SELF...
JUST ONE DAY.
FOR IT IS TOO EASY TO MAKE JUST ONE DAY TURN INTO A LIFESTYLE.
BACK TO IT!

5/5/18
YOU CAN'T JUST SHOW UP AND EXPECT YOUR BIKE FIXED RIGHT WHEN YOU GET HERE, YOU HAVE TO LEAVE THE BIKE.
BUT I NEED IT NOW...
YOU HAVE TO LEAVE IT. LEAVE THE BIKE. LEAVE THE BIKE LEAVE THE BIKE. IT TAKES TIME. IT TAKES TIME, TIME.
ME, ME ME, ME
NEAR 5 MINUTES LATER...
LEAVE THE BIKE, IT TAKES TIME, YOU HAVE TO LEAVE THE BIKE...
WHAT IS WRONG WITH PEOPLE?
5/6/18
LEVEL UP!
TODAY I LEVELED UP.
YOU GOING UP IN THAT GEAR?
YEAH.
YOU AIN'T GOING TO MAKE IT.
WELL SEE
42 x 18
UP 1100 FEET IN A MILE AND A 1/2 ON A FLATLAND GEAR. DID NOT THINK I COULD...
BUT I DID.
5/7/18
SOMETIMES I WONDER HOW WE CHASE A POIGNANT MOMENT ALL THE TIME AND HOW FOOLISH IT IS.
AH! HA!
AT THE ENDS OF ONE'S LIFE YOU CAN COUNT THOSE MOMENTS ON ONE HAND.
WELL THAT'S ABOUT IT.
PERHAPS WE FORGET TO JUST SIMPLY BE.
IT'S OK.

5/8/10
WHERE'S YOUR BAG MARCUS?
URRR
I'M GOING TO CHANCE IT TONIGHT.
LATER:
HOLD UP! MARCUS GOT A FLAT!
REALLY? NO FUCKING SHIT!
5/9/18
BIG DOG!
!
TOO CLOSE!
HAHA HA CLOSE ONE!
OOF!
5/10/18
I SEE...
A LIFE FURFILLED.. NOT IN THE EYES OF ACCEPTANCE FROM OTHERS BUT IN BEING TRUE TO ONE'S SELF.
THAT GOES AGAINST MY PERSONAL CODE.
IN DOING THAT... THE OTHER THINGS, THEY WILL COME TOO..
HEY!

5/11/18
YOU CAN HAVE ALL THE SKILL TO MAKE SOMETHING BUT NOT HAVE THE MOST IMPORTANT SKILL: THE DRIVE TO DO IT.
WHILE THERE ARE OTHER PEOPLE THAT CAN MAKE THINGS BETTER THAN ME, THEY DON'T DO IT. BUT...
I MADE THIS...
SO IT'S WORSE THAN NOT KNOWING, IT'S SQUANDERING WHAT YOU HAVE.
WHERE'S YOURS?
A COUCH IN MY YARD...
WHAT THE HELL?
OH, YOU'VE GOT TO BE KIDDING ME!
HERE WE GO...
I'VE ONLY HEARD OF ONE PERSON THAT COULD GET UP THIS HILL WITHOUT GETTING OFF THIER BIKE. IT'S THAT HARD.
-HUF. -HUF.
AND NOW I GET TO ADD MY NAME TO THAT LIST.
YEAH.
YOU MADE IT!

5/14/18
OH, YOU GOT THE MOUSE! GOOD BOY!
SQUEE SQUEE
GRRRR
MOMENTS LATER...
YOU LOST HIM! OH, F—!
DON'T PLAY WITH YOUR FOOD SILLY, YOU EAT IT!
HE HAD A RELAPSE.
OH NO.
WHAT CAN YOU DO? NOTHING. WHEN SOMEONE IS SICK YOU ARE POWERLESS TO HELP THEM.
WISH I COULD DO SOMETHING...
ALL I CAN DO IS BE SAD.
5/16/18
CLACK.
CLACK!
!
I'VE NOT BATTLED IN SO LONG I FORGOT HOW MUCH I LOVE IT.

5/17/18
SO MUCH TO DO!
EVERY MORNING, I PACK A WEEKS WORTH OF TASKS IN THE AM
IT IS STRESSFULL BUT AT THE SAME TIME...
JUST WHO I AM.
TIME TO GO TO WORK.
5/18/18
OH POOR DAVE.
I HAVE TWO MONTHS TO LIVE...
WASTED AWAY TO NOTHING AND HIS LIFE CUT SHORT SO.
AND HOW POWERLESS YOU ARE TO DO ANY- THING ABOUT IT
5/19/18
DO YOU LIKE ME ENOUGH TO FIX MY BRAKES TOO?
UMMMM...
I DON'T LIKE ANY ONE WELL ENOUGH TO WORK FOR FREE.

5/20/18
IS THAT MY CAT? IT LOOKS SORT OF LIKE HIM.
ALL DAY...
CAN'T WAIT TO GO HOME AND CHECK.
WORRY WORRY WORRY WORRY WORRY WORRY WOR
ALL FOR NOTHING...
THERE YOU ARE!
PRRRRR
DAVE PASSED AWAY..
OH OH OH OH NO.
VIA E-MAIL NO LESS.
IS OUR HUMANITY CHEAPENED BY TECHNOLGY?
5/22/18
YEAH. DAVE DIED.
ALL DAY.
DAVE DIED.
AND A LITTLE PART OF ME DIED TOO.

5/23/18
YEAH, I KNOW IT'S A DRAG BUT IT IS LIKE I KEEP SAYING..
MAKE THE MOST OF YOUR TIME HERE, DON'T SQUANDER IT...
AS YOU NEVER KNOW WHEN YOUR TIME IS OVER.
5/24/18
JUST LISTEN...
NO THE HISTORY IS THERE I SAW ON YOU TUBE A SPACE SHIP NEAR THE SUN IS MAKING THESE WIERD P IN THE SK THE WAS
TO SOME ONE FOR A WHILE
A GIANT SPHERE AND A HELICOPTER FLEW AROUND IT- TWICE.
AND THE CRAZY WILL SHOW.
AND THE FLYING TRIANGLE-IT'S REAL! THE PENTAGON RELEASED THE DRAWINGS
5/25/18
A LITTLE THOUGHT...
HOW CAN I SOLVE THAT?
AND THE SOLUTION COMES TO YOU...
I GOT IT!
THE BUILDING OF THOSE BRIDGES IN ONE'S MIND - IT IS IT'S OWN REWARD.
SO GOOD.

5/26/18
COME OUT TO THE CAR...
OK?
MY BIKE! *
* STOLEN IN 2016
I'D NEVER THOUGHT THAT I'D SEE YOU AGAIN!
5/27/18
I USED TO LAY AWAKE AT NIGHT AND THINK OF MY STOLEN BIKE.
NOW THAT I HAVE IT BACK IT IS LIKE A BAD PART OF MY LIFE'S EQUATION IS ONCE AGAIN IN BALANCE.
IF LIFE, BEING LIKE A PUZZLE, ONE GETS A LONG MISSING PIECE THAT FITS. WELL, IT'S NICE.
5/28/18
UP AND UP FOR 60 MILES.
I WAS UNABLE TO RIDE IT ALL — I HAD TO WALK SOME.
SO TIRED.
BUT I DID NOT QUIT EVEN THOUGH I WANTED TO.
HAVE A HOT DOG
OK

5/29/18
I SHOULD WRITE THAT DOWN...
I FIGURE I GET 10 GOOD IDEAS A DAY AND ONLY REMEMBER 1 OR 2 OF THEM.
PERHAPS I SHOULD WRITE THAT DOWN.
5/30/18
I'M GOING TO FORGO THE BREAST PLATE.
OK
WAK
ARRG!
REGRET DITCHING THE ARMOR HUH?
OOOOON
I LOOKED AT YOUR WEBSITE, I FOUND A TYPO.
OH REALLY? A TYPO HUH?
I'M OVER IT. ARE YOU?

6/1/18
NOT IN HERE...
SOME WHERE ELSE. SO MUCH STUFF.
I THINK MY STUFF OWNS ME, NOT THE OTHER WAY AROUND.
OH BARF!
WHAT A WAY TO START THE DAY, CLEANING UP VOMIT.
OK. LET THE GAMES BEGIN!
OK 350 + 45 is 395
HERE'S 500. IT'S ONLY 395"
I KNOW
YOU'VE ALWAYS BEEN COOL TO ME SO I WANT YOU TO HAVE IT.

6/4/18
AHH! YOU PUT A CHIP CLIP ON MY NIPPLE!
HA HA HA HA
HERE YOU GO!
AHH! MY ARM!
THAT WAS FUNNY!
YES!
6/5/18
NEVER LAY DOWN YOUR SWORD.
NEVER GIVE UP ON WHO YOU ARE AND BE TRUE TO YOURSELF.
I'M NOT DOING THAT.
IN DOING SO, YOU MAY LOSE A BATTLE HERE OR THERE BUT YOU'RE SURE TO WIN THE WAR.
I'LL JUST BE ME.
6/6/18
OH BICYCLE, HOW I LOVE THEE.
YOU TAKE ME TO ALL THE QUIET PLACES I CAN GO AND ALL THE MENTAL ISLAND RETREATS ONE NEEDS IN THIS LOUD WORLD.
MANKINDS LAST INVENTION THAT STILL HAS SOME HUMANITY BUILT INTO IT.

6/7/18
THAT'S NOT GOOD.
BLARP.
THIS IS NO GOOD.
¡%¥?!3@#!
HOW DO YOU LIKE IT?
THIS IS GOOD.
6/8/18
LOOK AT THIS IDIOT. BACKED INTO THAT OTHER CAR... AND LEAVING!
WHICH IS PARKED NOT IN A PARKING SPACE.
SO I GUESS THEY ARE BOTH ASSHOLES AND DESERVE EACH OTHER,
6/9/18
WHAT? OH NO! THAT'S AWFUL!
WHY IS IT THAT SO MANY PEOPLE I KNOW ARE SICK AND DYING?
WHEN WILL IT END? IT SEEMS TOO MUCH.

6/10/18
A DAY WHERE ALL THINGS WORK AGAINST YOU - IT HAPPENS.
WHY IS THIS NOT WORKING?
GETTING MAD OR BREAKING THINGS NEVER DOES ANY GOOD. INSTEAD
JUST FIGURE IT OUT.
AND WHILE YOU MAY NOT FIX A THING TODAY BY KEEPING A COOL HEAD - YOU FIX YOURSELF
AH... THEY ARE LABLED BACKWARDS
GO AHEAD AND TURN ON THE WATER!
OK
SQUE SQUE
ACK
WOOSH!
OH! OH. HA HA HA HA HA HA!
6/12/18
WITH MY LIFE INSURANCE, IF I DIE I GET 180,000...
NO, YOU WON'T GET ANYTHING BECAUSE YOU'LL BE DEAD.
NOTHING.
HA HA HA!

6/13/18
ALL AROUND YOU...
MAN WHAT AN A-HOLE!
YOU CAN'T BEAT THEM OR JOIN THEM, BUT YOU CAN CHOOSE...
COFFEE PLEASE
...NOT TO BE ONE OF THEM.
THANK YOU.
NO, THANK YOU!
6/14/18
WOOSH!
I GOT A NEW AIR-ASSIST TOILET.
WOW!
I NORMALLY DON'T LIKE NEW THINGS BUT THIS, WELL IT'S PRETTY
AMAZING.
6/15/18
I CAN GRAB A RADIATOR HOSE AND NOT GET BURNED.
OH, YOU'D DO GOOD ON SURVIVOR!
I'D JUST KILL EVERY ONE AND EAT THEM.
I'M JOKING.

6/19/18
THE SILLIEST THINGS THAT I THINK ARE JUST SO-SO JUST TAKE OFF... FOR SOME REASON...
SO-NO 40 BOOKS SOLD IN A DAY!
AND THE THINGS I PUT A LOT OF WORK INTO OFTEN SEEM TO GO NOWHERE.
HOW LONG HAVE YOU DONE THAT ZINE?
18 YEARS.
REGARDLESS THOUGH, TO GIVE UP, WELL, THAT'S NOT AN OPTION.
!
AND 18 + TO GO...
6/20/18
I HAVE A FLAT - HOW LONG IS IT GOING TO TAKE? I HAVE TO MEET SOMEONE YOU KNOW? CAN YOU GET TO IT AND...
I COULD HAVE BEEN 1/2 WAY DONE WITH IT BY NOW.
OH.
WELL, WHAT ARE YOU WAITING FOR? GO GET YOUR BIKE.
OH!
6/21/18
ALWAYS LOOK PAST THE ACTION - THAT'S WHAT I LIKE TO DO.
I DON'T GET MAD OFTEN OR TAKE THINGS PERSONAL WHEN PEOPLE ARE ANGRY OVER SOME SMALL THING
YOU DID IT TO YOURSELF.
BECAUSE MOST OF THE TIME...
IT'S NOT ME, IT'S YOU...

6/19/18
HERE'S YOUR FINISHER BUTTON.
COOL!
WHERE'S MINE?
YOU DIDN'T FINISH.
I FINISHED IN THE PAST.
BUT YOU DID NOT FINISH TODAY RIGHT? OK THEN.
6/20/18
THE BOOK OF LIFE - EVERYONE THINKS THEY HAVE ONE, IS IT THAT EASY? WELL, NO OF COURSE NOT.
THE BOOF OF LIFE
IT MADE ME NEARLY CRY WHEN I FIGURED OUT WHAT THE REAL BOOK OF LIFE IS. THE TRUTH BEING A HARD ONE.
WHAT DOES IT SAY?
OH DAMN
IT WON'T BE EASY.
6/21/18
I DON'T KNOW WHEN - I DON'T KNOW
BUT...
I'LL SAY IT AGAIN! NO MAGIC WAND. NO CRYSTAL BALL I CAN'T SEE INTO THE FUTURE.
WORDS DO NOT ALTER THE UNIVERSE OK?! THE HELL MAN.

6/22/18
TELL ME YOUR PHONE NUMBER SO I CAN PICK UP, I DON'T NORMALLY ANSWER MY PHONE.
WELL, YOU NEED TO DO ME A SOLD THEN—
YEAH?
ANSWER YOUR PHONE.
6/23/18
TODAY I WENT AND SAW MIDGET WRESTLING
AND ALL I CAN SAY IS IT WAS COOL.
WOW
6/24/18
INTERNET IS DOWN.
I HAVE A LOVE/HATE RELATIONSHIP WITH THE INTERNET.
I NEED YOU BUT HATE YOU.
AND NEED WILL OFTEN WIN OUT.
RATS ATE THE CORD.

6/25/18
THINGS GET DERAILED, THEY DO.
SO IT IS GOING TO HAPPEN - COUNT ON IT.
SCREEEEEE
BUT DO YOU GET BACK ON TRACK OR MAKE A HOME IN THE WRECKAGE?
6/26/18
TACOS
THE COMPUTERS ARE DOWN, WE HAVE TO GO ELSEWHERE.
ELSEWHERE,
THAT'S STUPID, WHY COULD THEY NOT JUST WRITE IT DOWN
I GUESS THAT WAS TOO HARD FOR THEM TO WRAP THEIR HEADS AROUND.
6/27/18
I HEAR YOU RAT..
AHN!
GUESS I'M NOT SO TOUGH AFTER ALL

6/28/18
TRAPS LAYED OUT WHERE I SAW HIM GO COVERED IN WET PEANUT BUTTER.
MOMENTS LATER...
WAK! WAK!
HERE'S WHAT VICTORY LOOKS LIKE YOU LOSER.
?
6/29
OK, ANOTHER PASS
OK.
CHUG CHUG CHUG
HOURS IN...
.080 THAT'S GOOD.
IT'S TOO WEAK, BARELY TAPPED IT AND IT BROKE!
OH, BACK TO THE DRAWING BOARD.
6/30/18
THE MENTAL CHECKLIST
DID I DO WHAT I NEEDED TO? DID I DO MORE? DID I MAKE PEOPLE HAPPY?
DID I DO WHAT I SAID I WOULD? DID I WORK HARD TO GET THINGS DONE?
AND DID I REMEMBER TO ENJOY IT?
WELL I HOPE SO.

7/1/18
I DID NOT EXPECT TO WIN...
HUF HUF HUF HUF
BUT BY NOT GIVING UP AND TRYING AS HARD AS I COULD...
HUF HUF HUF
I DID.
1ST PLACE!
HEY, LOOK AT THAT OWL CANDY JAR
YOU WANT IT? I'LL BUY IT FOR YOU. IT'S YOURS.
THAT WAS THEN, WHAT ARE YOU DOING NOW?
NO MATTER WHAT WE TRY, WE CAN'T LIVE IN THE PAST. WE MUST LIVE IN THE NOW.
YOU'RE NOT THERE...
SO BEST TO MAKE THE MOST OF IT...
YOU'RE ONLY HERE, NOW.

7/4/18
?
CRACK!
GUESS I'M RIDING SINGLE SPEED
THE BICYCLE GODS HAVE SPOKEN!
I'VE BEEN PUSHING THIS BIKE IN AND OUT FOR MONTHS. WHEN'S THIS GUY GOING TO COME GET IT?
LATER THAT DAY...
MY FRIEND DROPPED OFF A BIKE A COUPLE OF MONTHS BACK...
YEAH?
HE DIED.
MYSTERY SOLVED.
TODAY I THREW OUT SOMEONE'S LIFE.
ALL MY FRIENDS THINGS I WENT THROUGH AND TOSSED A LOT OUT, THEN MADE A BIG PILE FOR GOODWILL.
UF!
IN THE END THERE WAS NOT MUCH LEFT. SAD & STRANGE ALL AT ONCE.
POOR GUY.

7/7/18
NOT TO WORRY, PAUL IS HONEST TO A FAULT.
?
I DON'T SEE HOW BEING HONEST IS FAULTWORTHY.
AND IF SOMEONE DOES NOT LIKE THAT THEN, WELL, I DON'T NEED THEM.
7/8/18
IT WAS 117 DEGREES YESTERDAY.
SO?
YOU DON'T CARE?
I HAVE NOT HAD AIR CONDITIONING SINCE I MOVED OUT OF MY PARENTS HOUSE 27 YEARS AGO.
JUST DEAL WITH IT - COMFORT IS OVERRATED.
5:45 AM
NOON.
100°F
SO MUCH MORE TO DO
BUT WORTH THE SWEAT FOR A CLEAN SPACE.

7/10/18
WAK
WAK
WAK
MADE iT!
DID YOU GET CUT UP?
YEAH BUT IT WAS WORTH IT.
WAK!
SORRY ABOUT YOUR LEG!
WHAT?
OH. I AM HUH, OH WELL
I CAN SEE IF I HAVE ONE iN STORAGE BY TOMORROW
THAT'S OK.
WHAT DOES THAT MEAN? THAT'S OK. YES LOOK OR THAT'S OK DON'T LOOK.
NO DON'
COMPLETE SENTENCES ARE AWESOME.
SOMETiMES

7/13/18
I'D NEVER WANT A CHANCE TO DO IT ALL OVER AGAIN.
OUR MISTAKES AND HOW WE DEAL WITH THEM ARE MORE IMPORTANT THAN OUR SUCESSSES...
THE FIRE OF FAILURE TEMPERS ONE INTO A HARDEND VERSION THAT CAN NEVER BE OTHERWISE.
ARE YOU OK?
YEAH.
7/14/18
IS LIFE A RACE? WE DO COMPARE ONE TO ANOTHER, SO IT WOULD SEEM - PERHAPS. BUT SHOULD WE RUN?
AT THE END ONE WILL LOOK BACK WITH REGRET OF FOOTSTEPS NOT TAKEN. BUT SELDOM DO WE COMPARE TO OTHERS AT THAT POINT.
SO SURE, IT'S A RACE BUT ONLY IN THAT YOU RUN YOUR RACE WELL, ITS THE ONLY ONE YOU GET.
7/15/18
AFTER I DO A RACE I KNOW I DID MY BEST BECAUSE I CANT STOP EATING.
IN A LIFE WHERE I DENY MYSELF THINGS ALL THE TIME...
COOKIES?
NAH
I LIVE IN A REALM WHERE A TREAT IS TRULY A TREAT.
A SPECIAL MOMENT.

7/16/18
THE TO DO LIST IS SO LONG.
IN BEING MIRED IN ENDLESS TASKS I MISS OUT ON THINGS, PEOPLE MOSTLY
MISSED YOUR CALL
LEAVING 2ND MESSAGE.
BUT THEY DON'T KNOW I'M SILENTLY WORKING FOR THEM ALL THE TIME.
THEY'LL LIKE THIS.
7/17/18
YOU LOOK SO HEALTHY, YOU EAT RIGHT?
MOST OF THE TIME.
AND EXERCISE? YOU LOOK GREAT!
SURE. ALL THE TIME.
HA HA HA
THE DEAL IS I MAY LIVE THE SAME NUMBER OF YEARS ANYONE DOES BUT I WANT TO BE ABLE TO WIPE MY OWN ASS TILL THE END.
7/18/18
I MISSED YOUR CALL...
I CALLED YOU 5 TIMES! PICK UP YOUR PHONE OR SET IT UP TO GET MESSAGES. YOU JUST WASTE TIME BY DOING THIS.
USE IT RIGHT OR DON'T USE IT AT ALL

7/19/18
AH - A LITTLE REJECTION IT'S FUNNY.
OK THEN.
OVER TIME, I'VE JUST GOTTEN USED TO BEING REJECTED - IT'S OK THOUGH. I THINK CHASING ACCEPTANCE CAN BE WORSE...
...SO BUSY LOOKING FOR APPROVAL BY OTHERS YOU FORGET WHO YOU ARE.
"2 LIKES"
7/20/18
IT IS EASY TO FORGET HOW SOME OF THE BEST THINGS YOU HAVE ARE THINGS YOU DO ALL THE TIME.
WHERE BIG, SWEEPING ARCS MAY GET YOU TO A MILE STONE.
IT'S THE STEPPING STONES THAT COMPRISE MOST OF THE JOURNEY.
7/21/18
WHAT A WASTE OF TIME!
HOW MUCH TIME YOU GONNA SPEND TALKING ABOUT WHAT OTHER PEOPLE ARE DOING? DON'T WORRY ABOUT THEM.
PERHAPS ONE SHOULD BE WORKING ABOUT ONE'S SELF A LITTLE MORE EH?

7/22/18
HUF HUF HUF HUF
YOU GOT 2ND!
I DID? WHAT HAPPEND TO STEVEN? HE WAS AHEAD OF ME!
LATER.
WHAT HAPPENED TO YOU?
I DID 4 LAPS.
OH.
DUDE, IT WAS 3 LAPS
YEAH
7/23/18
DO YOU WANT TO WATCH A MOVIE?
SURE.
WHAT DO YOU WANT TO SEE?
SOMETHING THAT DOES NOT SUCK.
!
7/24/18
YOU GOT TIME TO FIX A FLAT?
SURE.
I HAVE MONEY!
...
YEAH, THAT'S HOW IT WORKS.
!

7/25/18
THERE WILL NEVER BE ENOUGH TIME.
SO MUCH TO DO.
I'LL NEVER RUN OUT OF IDEAS OR THINGS TO DO. LUCK? OR A CURSE? WELL AT LEAST I DON'T HAVE TO WONDER ABOUT WHAT TO DO WITH MY TIME.
AT LEAST I FINISH THINGS, NOTHING BE WORSE THAN TO JUST TALK ABOUT THINGS AND NOT DO THEM.
BZZZ
BZZZ
7/26/18
HM HM HM
SO STRANGE... I AM JUST SMILING FOR NO REASON.
OH! I GUESS I'M HAPPY. SOMETIMES WE FORGET
HE HE HE HE
7/27/18
A CRUTCH, A CAGE OR A SET OF WINGS. YOU GET TO PICK ONE WHEN THINGS DON'T GO YOUR WAY.
I'M LEAVING YOU.
YOU CAN USE IT AS A CRUTCH AND SLOW EVERYTHING YOU DO OR A CAGE AND BE HELD TO THE PAST
I'LL NEVER LOVE ANOTHER.
OR A SET OF WINGS AND JUST MOVE ON.
ONWARD AND UPWARD

7/28/18
OH, YEAH...
TED NUGENT...
?
I'M NOT HAVING THAT! NO MORE TALKING ABOUT CLASSIC ROCK THERE ARE MORE THAN 12 CRUSTY OLD BANDS OUT THERE!
WHEN WILL IT END! FUCK THE BEATLES! TAKE THAT NOISE OUTSIDE BUT NOT HERE!
7/29/18
AROUND EVERY CORNER...
SOMETHING NEW!
I DON'T REALLY GET BOREDOM THAT MUCH. THERE ARE SO MANY PLACES IN MY LOCAL AREA I HAVE NOT SEEN YET...
AND SO MANY THINGS I HAVE NOT YET THOUGHT OF THAT I WILL, IN THE FUTURE, WANT TO DO.
7/30/18
PAINTING MY KITCHEN TOOK OVER 10 HOURS, IT WAS HARD WORK - AT THE END I WAS POOPED.
ALL I KNEW IS I HAVE SO MUCH MORE TO DO IN THIS LIFE, MUCH FURTHER TO GO...
½ DONE...
..AND TO EXPECT MY JOURNEY TO NEVER END.
... AND A WHOLE LIFETIME TO GO.

7/31/18
OH THE MONTH LONG HEAT WAVE JUST KILLED IT - JULY IS A BANNER MONTH FOR ME BUT IT WAS DOWN.
THEN I DIVIDED MY IN STORE HOURS BY MY GROSS INCOME AND WOW! I MAKE A GREAT WAGE.
THAT'S A LOT OF MONEY!
AND MOST OF ALL I'M DOING WHAT I WANT TO DO.
NOT BAD.
IT'S NICE HANGING OUT WITH YOU KITTIES IN MY ROOM.
PRRRR
BUT ONE OF YOU PEED ON MY BED.
SO OUT YOU GO!
8/2
5 MINUTES OF:
AND ANOTHER IN 2 DAYS SAX THREE DAYS WHY CAN'T YOU TELL ME BLAH BLAH BLAH BLAH BLAN BL BLAH BL BLAH
OK! I CAN'T HELP YOU! I'M HANGING UP NOW!
HOW MUCH SHIT CAN YOU TAKE?

8/3/18
HA!
IT WAS SO GOOD TO BATTLE AGAIN WITH YOU, IT'S BEEN DECADES.
NO HAND SHAKE.
GIVE ME A HUG MAN— WE'RE BROTHERS.
HA HA HA
8/4/18
OK. GIVE IT A TRY.
CHUGGA CHUGGA
ALL RIGHT, IT'S RUNNING!
CHUGGA CHUGGA
OK SO COOL! POTENTIAL POTENTIAL! POTENTIAL!
8/5/18
80 HOURS A WEEK WAS TOO MUCH, I NEED A LIFE TOO
IT'S TOO MUCH.
THESE BIG COMPANIES DON'T CARE ABOUT US. YOU'RE JUST A RESOURSE
ARE YOU LIVING FOR YOU OR FOR THEM?

8/6/18
IT'S SO HOT!
So?
ROLLED AROUND OVER 10 MILES IN THE NOON DAY SUN, 100 DEGREES...
SO WHAT?
PEOPLE ARE SUCH PUSSIES!
8/7/18
UP THE HILL AND THROUGH THE TUNNEL...
DOWN THE DIRT ROAD TO THE HIDDEN PATH.
TO OUR DESTINATION: ADVENTURE.
CLOSED! BUMMER!
PIZZA
CLOSED
8/8/18
HOW CAN I PACK IT ALL IN?
THERE IS SO MUCH I AM WORKING TOWARDS, TO MAKE ENOUGH TIME IN THE DAY.
3 MINUTES LEFT TO DO THAT...
AND SOMEWHERE IN THE MIDDLE....
HEY, I FEEL PRETTY HAPPY RIGHT NOW.

8/9/18
HE WAS REALLY HAPPY WITH THE TRUCK. HE DID NOT KNOW IF YOU'D STICK TO THE DEAL BUT I TOLD HIM YOUR WORD WAS YOUR BOND.
YOU'RE NOT LIKE ANY ONE ELSE, LIKE THAT, YOU KNOW; A RARE BREED.
I GUESS SO.
I WAS TOLD ONCE THAT YOU SHOULD NOT BE REWARDED FOR WHAT YOU SHOULD BE DOING ANYWAY.
FLAT!
THEN!
OOF!
COFFEE FIXES EVERYTHING!
8/11/18
ONE OF THE BEST PARTS OF SUMMER IS THE NIGHT TIME BIKE RIDE. FOR ME THAT IS.
THE SENSATION OF AIR AND MOTION INSTEAD OF JUST SITTING NEXT TO A FAN.
BE YOUR OWN FAN.

8/12/18
OH TIME, HOW I WORK AGAINST THEE. I'LL NEVER HAVE ENOUGH TO DO WHAT MUST BE DONE.
HAVING A SENSE OF PURPOSE; SO FEW HAVE IT, ONCE YOU FIND ONE IT WILL POSSES YOU.
SO MUCH TO DO.
IT WILL OWN YOU. YOUR TIME WILL NEVER BE YOUR OWN.
SO LITTLE TIME.
8/13/18
ALL RIGHT, YOU MADE IT!
HUF HUF HUF HUF
LOOK AT THE VIEW! ALL THE TREES DOWN THERE, LOOKS LIKE A FOREST.
GLUG
YEAH IT IS PRETTY COOL...
WHAT DO I HAVE TO COMPLAIN ABOUT?
I MUST ADMIT MOST THINGS ARE GOING WELL. I'VE GOT A GOOD LIFE, LIVE BY MY OWN RULES.
I GUESS I'M HAPPY THEN? I THINK I'LL JUST ROLL WITH THAT IDEA.

I WISH I KNEW.
ALL I KNOW IS I DON'T KNOW WHAT WILL HAPPEN NEXT. WE ALL THINK WE DO, BUT CHANCE IT IS ALWAYS AROUND THE CORNER.
WHAT EVER HAPPENS IN LIFE AT THAT MOMENT YOU ARE ALWAYS IN THE NOW NO MATTER WHAT YOU'D LIKE IT TO BE
SO LIVE IT.
PACKAGE FOR YOU.
THANKS?
LOOK AT ALL THESE COMICS! WOW!
SOMEONE WAS THINKING OF ME!
C'MON BOB!
I'M GOING TO BE LATE TO WORK!
NO YOU WON'T
IT'S 10:23
OK OK.
YOU'LL HAVE TO DROP ME OFF AT WORK AND COFFEE

8/18/18
ALL THAT HARD WORK WILL PAY OFF THEY SAY. I WONDER.
I'VE GOTTEN A GOOD PAY OFF FOR SURE. BUT IT SEEMS..
...LIKE THE HARDER I WORK THE MORE OF IT I HAVE TO DO. I WONDER WHERE THE BALANCE POINT IS.
8/19/18
I THINK I KNOW WHY I LIKE DOING BIKE RACES; AN ANALOGY FOR LIFE.
YOU SUFFER.
HUF HUF HUF HUF GASP WEEZE HUF
AND YOUR GOAL IS AN UNOBTAINABLE SPECK IN THE DISTANCE.
SO FAR AWAY.
8/20/18
SEEKING THE MAGICAL EQUATION: WHAT EVERY ONE IS LOOKING FOR.
WILL YOU FIND THAT LAST PIECE OF YOUR LIFE'S PUZZLE?
OR WILL YOU REALIZE THAT IT WILL NEVER BE ENOUGH.
NEXT PUZZLE.

8/21/18
WHERE'S MAX?
I'LL GO LOOK.
ALL THE WAY BACK UP THE MOUNTAIN...
LATER
HE'S OK. HE WENT ANOTHER WAY.
OK. EXTRA CREDIT.
8/23/18
OH SLEEP, TAKE ME AWAY FOR A SPELL AS I HAVE TOILED SO HARD TODAY - I NEED THE REST.
EVERY NIGHT I THINK OF ALL THE THINGS I GET TO DO AND LOOK FORWARD TO THEM.
SO I GUESS THAT MAKES THINGS OK RIGHT?
8/23
YOU KNOW I BRAG ABOUT YOU A LOT.
REALLY?
I'M PROUD THAT YOU'RE MY FRIEND.
YOU ARE?
OH, WOW, WELL... THANK YOU!

8/25/18
YOU STILL DRAW?
YEP.
THAT'S GOOD.
IT'S EASY LIKE BRUSHING MY TEETH, I JUST SIT DOWN AND DO IT.
LATER:
I HAVE NO IDEA WHAT TO DRAW.
8/26/18
THROW IT OUT.
MORE TRASH.
ONLY TO MAKE ROOM FOR MORE GARBAGE.
8/27/18
RISE EARLY
RIDE: MILES - ALONE
SOMETIMES YOU JUST NEED A BREAK - FROM EVERYONE ELSE.

8/27/18
IT'S ALL IN THE DETAILS, YOU MADE THE EFFORT I SEE.
YOU NOTICED!
OF COURSE! THAT IS THE LIFE EQUATION. IN ORDER TO GET SOMETHING OUT OF LIFE...
...YOU MUST PUT SOMETHING IN...
CHOMP CHOMP CHOMP
8/28/18
I DON'T HAVE TIME FOR PEOPLE'S BULLSHIT
ONCE SOMEONE BECOMES A NEGATIVE INTERGER IN MY LIFE'S EQUATION I GET THEM OUT OF MY WORLD.
THERE ARE PLENTY OF WORTHY, GOOD ONES SO WHY WASTE YOUR TIME ON THE BAD ONES?
TRUE.
8/29/18
SHAKING THE RUST OFF IS A GOOD THING
I THINK WE TEND TO DABLE IN THINGS AND NOT STICK WITH THEM ENOUGH.
THE ONLY WAY TO KEEP SOMETHING ALIVE IS FOR IT TO NOT GATHER ANY RUST.
WHO'S NEXT?

OH MY LITTLE BIKE SHOP, HOW YOU'VE MADE ME EVERYTHING I AM - I FORGOT HOW I'D BE LOST WITHOUT YOU.

HOW I'VE LAYED ON THE FLOOR IN THE BACK IN TIMES OF DISPAIR AND BEEN THERE FOR PEOPLE WHEN THEY HAVE NEEDED ME, OFTEN NOT FOR BIKE REPAIR
IT'S OK.

I SAT IN A PILE OF USED TIRES AND LOOKED AROUND REALIZING HOW TRULY RICH I AM - BEYOND ANYTHING I COULD HAVE EVER HOPED FOR.

I'VE NEVER SEEN YOU ON A GEARED BIKE BEFORE. I HAVE TO TAKE A PICTURE.
REALLY?
I SAW YOUR BIKE IN YOUR TRUCK, GEARS HUH? ARE YOU GETTING OLD?
REALLY?
WHAT THE HELL, I RIDE A GEARED BIKE ONE TIME AND GET A RATION OF SHIT FROM EVERYONE!

TO PUT OFF AN IDEA OR ACTION IS FOR IT NOT TO BE DONE.
I'LL DO IT LATER.
IN A WORLD FULL OF DISTRACTIONS ONE WILL FORGET...
WHAT WAS THAT THING?
..AND ADD ANOTHER THING TO THE PILE OF THINGS THAT WILL NEVER BE DONE.
CAN'T REMEMBER...

9/2/18
GOOD RIDE COFFEE?
I LOST MY KEYS ON THE TRAIL.
I WAS TRYING TO DO A SHORT ONE BUT OH WELL, EXTRA CREDIT.
NO KEYS. PLAN B. I'LL TAKE YOU HOME.
OK
WUB WUB WUB
WUB WUB WUB
9/3/18
WE RODE 45 MILES TODAY. 25 TO START AND ABOUT 18 FINISHED.
I THINK THAT IT DOES NOT MATTER HOW LONG OR HARD YOU GO.
BUT THAT YOU SHARE IT WITH OTHERS
THERE YOU ARE.
9/4/18
HELLO MORRIS! KITTY KITTY!
OH WHAT'S THAT? YOU WANT SOME LOVINS?
PRRR PRRR
EVERYONE, EVEN CATS NEED A LITTLE TOUCH NOW & THEN.

9/5/18
I CAN GO ON AND ON.
I COULD. THERE IS SO MUCH TO DO, SO MUCH TO LEARN, TO TRY. I SIMPLY CAN'T GET WHY ANYONE WOULD BE BORED.
ALL YOU HAVE TO DO IS LOOK OUTSIDE YOUR FRONT DOOR. TAKE A STEP.
9/6/18
THAT'S IT!
THE DECLINE + FALL OF THE ROMAN EMPIRE VOLUME III
I HAD STARTED THESE IN DECEMBER AND TOOK A BRAKE AFTER TWO. IT IS 2700 + PAGES LONG.
THE CAUSE OF THE GOTHS HAD BEEN IRREVOCABLY JUDGED IN THE FIELD OF XERES: AND IN THE NATIONAL DISMAY, EACH PART OF THE . . .
BUT TODAY .. I FINISHED.
PEOPLE HAVE NOT CHANGED ONE BIT.
IS THIS A COVER BAND? LETS GO!
WHY DO THAT? WHY SPEND ALL THOSE YEARS LEARNING HOW TO PLAY AN INSTRUMENT JUST TO COPY SOMEONE ELSE' MUSIC?
I'D RATHER PUSH ALL MY GEAR IN MY FRONT YARD AND BURN IT THAN DO THAT!

9/8/18
ARE YOU OK? YOU LOOK WORN OUT.
I'M JUST TIRED.
ARE YOU OK?
REALLY TIRED REALLY TIRED.
BUT...
CAN I JUST BE TIRED? OK?
9/9/18
I SEEK AN EVERY-DAY ADVENTURE.
I DON'T THINK YOU NEED TO TRAVEL THE GLOBE TO HAVE AN ADVENTURE. IN FACT, I THINK IT COMES EASIER IF YOU BUILD THAT IDEA AT HOME.
AND MAKE IT IN YOUR HEART & HEAD SO YOU CAN TAKE IT WITH YOU WHEREVER YOU ARE, EVEN AROUND THE CORNER.
HA HA HA
9/10/18
TO FORGET TO ENJOY THE MOMENT: A CURSE UPON US ALL.
EVERYTHING ELSE
THE MOMENT
WITH SO MUCH IN OUR HEADS, WE MAY MISS A CHANCE TO ENJOY A MOMENT.
IF WE COULD JUST GO FROM MOMENT TO MOMENT AND ENJOY IT, WELL WOULDN'T LIFE BE WONDERFUL?

9/11/18
. ALL DAY I WAS OFF: SAYING THINGS WRONG, FORGETTING STUFF, DROPPING THINGS
LATER I NOTICED THERE WAS A QUIET, SULLEN WAY ABOUT MY FRIENDS. WE RODE BUT DID NOT SAY MUCH.
AND I GOT A FLAT A FEW BLOCKS FROM MY HOUSE. JUST ONE OF THOSE DAYS WHERE THINGS ARE OFF.
THE HELL?
9/12/18
I HAD CRAZY DREAMS LAST NIGHT, I WAS BEING ATTACKED BY MEN WITH LONG GREY HAIR
ONE ASAILANT I KILLED WITH A QUICK-RELEASE SKEWER.
THE OTHER, I RAN OVER WITH AN SUV. I DON'T EVEN OWN ONE.
HEH HEH.
BLAP!
9/13/18
I DOUBT MY SELF TOO MUCH I GATHER BUT SOMETIMES...
WELL THAT IS GOOD ENOUGH.
I GUESS I SHOULD NOT WORRY TOO MUCH ABOUT IT, WHO ELSE IS EVEN PUTTING IN 1% OF THE EFFORT I AM?
I DO WONDER WHY NO ONE ELSE IS EVEN TRYING - LAZY.

9/14/18
GOOD BYE
NO!
THATS WHAT PEOPLE NEVER SEEM TO GET.
ANANA
I LIKE BEING AROUND GOOD PEOPLE BUT IF YOU'RE NOT...
I DON'T NEED YOU.
9/15/18
I JUST WANT TO THANK YOU FOR FIXING MY BIKE SO GOOD. IT'S BETTER THAN NEW.
REALLY?
I TOOK IT TO SO MANY HIGH END BIKE SHOPS AND IT NEVER WORKED RIGHT.
THAT'S SAD REALLY THAT NO ONE ELSE WANTED TO DO A GOOD JOB.
9/16/18
NOTHING IS OWED TO YOU - ONE CAN DO EVERYTHING RIGHT AND STILL GO DOWN HILL IN FLAMES.
IF SOMEONE IS NICE TO ME OR KIND. I NEVER EXPECT IT BUT ALSO NEVER TAKE IT FOR GRANTED.
FOR ME? THANK YOU!
AND IF YOU HAVE TO DEAL WITH MEANESS, I JUST LOOK AT IT LIKE A CHALLENGE.
SOMETHING TO GET THROUGH.

9/17/18
IT'S NOT FAIR!
PEOPLE LIKE TO SAY THAT: OF COURSE THINGS AREN'T FAIR, THEY NEVER WILL BE. WHAT THEY REALLY MEAN IS THEY DON'T GET WHAT THEY WANT.
TO BE FAIR IS A PATH THAT CAN ONLY BE WALKED ALONE. DO YOU REALLY WANT THAT?
9/18/18
UP TWO PEAKS
AND TWO GREAT VIEWS...
SO PRETTY.
AND A BAG OF 50¢ BREAD TO FINISH OFF THE ADVENTURE.
PB+ BREAD, ANYONE?
50¢
9/19/18
SO TIRED, I SHOULD DO A SHORTER RIDE.
BUT I'M TIRED BECAUSE I'VE BEEN SLACKING OFF.
SO I SHOULD DO MORE TO GET BETTER THEN.

9/20/18

FATE, DESTINY, ETC. I THINK PEOPLE THINK THAT THERE IS SOME SORT OF COSMIC REASON OUT THERE. SOME CALL IT GOD RIGHT?
THINGS HAPPEN FOR A REASON

SUCH AN EGO TRIP TO THINK THAT THERE IS A PLAN OR AN IDEA AND YOU OR WE ARE PART OF THAT PLAN.
DO THEY?

TO THINK THAT THERE IS SOMETHING INSTEAD OF NOTHING IS FOLLY.
OR ARE YOU PLACING VALUE TO EVENTS WHERE THERE IS NO VALUE?

9/21/18

TODAY I MADE A BICYCLE FORK. IT WAS MY SECOND ONE—

NOW THERE ARE MOST LIKELY BILLIONS OF BICYCLE FORKS THAT HAVE BEEN MADE.

BUT ONLY A COUPLE THAT I MADE MY SELF.

I JUST CLEANED THE TOILET, SO YOU COULD TRY AND AIM BETTER.

HEY, SOMETIMES IT GOES IN STRAIGHT AND THEN A FAN, THEN 90 DEGREES. I CANT DO MUCH ABOUT THAT.

YOU COULD LOWER YOURSELF...
REALLY?
WELL MY DICK'S NOT THAT BIG YOU KNOW.

9/23/18
YOU WANT TO GO A LITTLE FURTHER?
SURE!
I'LL ALWAYS WANT TO RIDE A LITTLE MORE, GO A LITTLE FURTHER FOR ME, RIDING BIKES IS LOVE.
AND ONE CAN NEVER GET ENOUGH OF THAT.
LET'S GO UP ONE MORE HILL.
9/24/18
TO ACT UPON YOUR DREAMS THAT IS WHERE THE MAGIC IS.
I COULD DO THAT NEXT.
YOU CAN TAKE YOUR DREAMS AND ACT UPON THEM...
I CAN DO THIS AFTER I DO THAT.
AND IN DOING SO, YOU'LL ALWAYS HAVE SOMETHING TO LOOK FORWARD TO.
CAN'T WAIT TO DO IT ALL.
9/25/18
A FEW MINUTES - IT SEEMS LIKE A TIME TO SQUANDER BUT NO! A FEW MINUTES IT TAKES...
...TO DO A QUICK CHORE OR LIFT SOME WEIGHTS OR CHIP AWAY AT A PROJECT
AND A FEW MINUNTES HERE AND THERE, WELL, THAT WILL ALWAYS ADD UP.
BOOK PROJECT

9/26/18
DARK MOODS ARE JUST PART OF ME - I SPEND WAY TOO MUCH TIME, TRYING IN A STATE TO REAP JOY OUT OF LIFE...
AND NOT GETTING A RETURN.
THE BREAD I MAKE IS... LACKING.
BUT REST ASURED, I WILL GET UP TOMORROW AND.
TRY AGAIN.
9/27/18
THE CRUCICLE OF EVERY DAY CRAP YOU HAVE TO ENDURE, SOMETHING WE ALL HAVE TO DEAL WITH.
YOU CAN LET THESE THINGS MELT YOU DOWN INTO USELESS SLAG.
SSSSSSSS
OR BE CAST ANEW, BETTER THAN BEFORE.
9/28/18
IT IS ON THE THIRD SUNDAY OF THE MONTH.
WHEN IS THE NEXT ONE?
NEXT MONTH.
DO YOU KNOW THE DATE?
NO, YOU HAVE TO LOOK AT A CALENDAR.
I CAN'T DO EVERY THING FOR YOU MAN

9/29/19
HOW WE FORGET THINGS FROM THE PAST THAT BROUGHT US JOY.
DUM DUM BUD
HOW MUCH TIME WE SPEND MAKING LOVE TO IDEAS.
I NEED TO DO MORE OF THIS...
ONLY TO FORGET THEM?
9/30/19
ON MY WAY
KLICKY CLACK
ALL THE WAY INTO LA AND HE FLAKED. OUT- NO SHOW.
BUT I HELD UP MY END OF THE BARGAIN.
10/1/19
NOW IS NOW. THERE IS NOTHING ELSE.
FORK IS LOOKING GOOD.
BZZZ
WHILE WE MAY WORK TOWARDS THE FUTURE, ALL WE DO IS BE IN THE MOMENT THAT WE ARE IN. MOMENT TO MOMENT.
LOOK BACK 10, 20 YEARS AND DO YOU THINK YOU'D BE WHERE YOU ARE NOW? THAT IS WHY NOW IS ALL WE HAVE.
I NEVER THOUGHT I'D DO THIS.

10/2☰/18
ONE'S OWN LITTLE UNIVERSE SPANS OUT, HOW WELL DO YOU FIT IN YOUR OWN WORLD?
THAT'S THE CRUEL JOKE! PEOPLE JUST MINE THEMSELVES IN SELF-MADE RUTS.
IF YOU DON'T LIKE YOUR WORLD, CHANGE IT.
10/3/18
I'M NOT SO SURE THE WHOLE "LIFE IS SHORT" THING REALLY FLIES UNDER SCRUNITY-
IS IT?
IF IT WERE SHORT, WE WOULD NOT WASTE SO MUCH OF OUR TIME WATCHING TV OR MAKING WAR, OR DO OTHER THINGS TO KEEP US OCCUPIED.
PERHAPS 10% OF YOUR LIFE IS SPENT REALLY LIVING, THE REST IS SQUANDERED. SO IS IT SHORT OR LONG?
10/4/18
OH THOSE CREATIVE JUICES, HOW THEY GIVE ME PURPOSE.
I THINK THE KEY IS TO MOVE FROM THING TO THING. SO EVERYTHING YOU DO FEELS FRESH
MAP LOOKING GOOD.
AND THUS YOU KEEP LIFE INTERESTING
AND FUN!

10/5/18
OK, ADD THAT UP.
IT'S BEEN A COUPLE OF YEARS BUT IT LOOKS LIKE I'M GOING TO PLAY D&D AGAIN.
30 YR OLD BOOK
CAN'T HELP BUT BE A LITTLE EXCITED BY THE PROSPECT.
10/6/18
ALL THE LOW-HANGING FRUIT HAS BEEN PLUCKED.
IF EVER IT WAS HARD TO GET AHEAD IT IS NOW. NOTHING IS GOING TO BE EASY.
BUT THAT FRUIT, ONCE GOTTEN IS ALL THE SWEETER.
CHOP CHOMP
10/7/18
SHALL WE PLAY A GAME?
FOR THOSE THAT HAVE FORGOTTEN TO MAKE YOUR OWN FUN.
LAST LAP!
YOU HAVE LOST YOUR WAY...
WHAT ARE YOU DOING?
HAVING FUN.

10/8/18
WELL THAT WAS A GOOD EVENT! EVERYONE HAD FUN, NO ONE GOT HURT. I'D CALL THAT A VICTORY.
A BUNCH OF LITTLE VICTORIES, DO THEY ADD UP TO A BIG WIN? NOT SURE....
BUT THEY DO ADD UP
10/9/18
WOOH! YEAH E.T. WENT THAT WAY!
HAHA A BMX JOKE!
HA HA
AT LEAST SOMEONE HAS A SENSE OF HUMOR.
10/10/18
HEY NO TOUCHING. LET ME TEST RIDE A BIKE.
UMM
WELL IT'S BEEN HOURS - A CHEAP PRICE TO GET RID OF HER.
WOW SHE BROUGHT IT BACK.

10/12/18

LITTLE LIVES LIKE GRAINS OF SAND WITH THEIR LITTLE DRAMAS...

THE WALES OF HISTORY WASH OVER AGAIN AND AGAIN AND SUCH THINGS ARE LOST IN THE SANDS OF TIME..

BE NOT A GRAIN OF SAND - BUT A ROCK AND YOUR LIFE WILL RISE ABOVE THE REST.

ROUND AND ROUND.

24 LAPS IS A MILE. RODE MORE THAN THAT, 60 OR SO? MORE PERHAPS...

EACH TURN - AND SOME FUN WAS HAD - THUS IS THE GOAL.
THAT WAS AWESOME!

GREAT RIDE BUT I'M STARVING!

AT HOME...
THERE'S NOTHING TO EAT BUT CAT FOOD.

SO BE IT.
?

10/14/18
IT WAS WORTH IT TO LOOSE SLEEP..
PFFT!
AND CARRLY ALL THE EXTRA WEIGHT 4 MILES UP.
JUST TO HAVE A CUP OF COFFEE AT THE TOP OF THE MOUNTAIN
THE BIG LITTLE JOY.
10/15/18
I HATE BURBANK! THESE PEOPLE...
I TOO HATE BURBANK...
SOMETIMES IT'S THE HATE THAT BRINGS US TOGETHER!
10/16/18
OK GET THAT RAT!
POKE.
F - MINUS CATS. GREAT JOB.

10/17/18
WELL, I BELIEVE IN KARMA
NOT ME
YOU SHOULD DO GOOD THINGS BECAUSE THEY ARE GOOD THINGS, NOT BECAUSE YOU CAN GET A REWARD.
ALL YOU CAN DO IS FOCUS ON YOU. TO BE YOUR BEST. PEOPLE ARE NOT BETTER NOW THAN THEY WERE IN THE PAST.
10/18/18
OPEN ONE DOOR AND...
AND SEE ANOTHER
FOR EVERY DOOR YOU OPEN WILL ALLOW YOU TO OPEN OTHERS, TO SEE MORE, DO MORE...
AS LONG AS YOU KEEP OPENING - KEEP GOING. OTHERWISE ITS EASY TO ENTER A ROOM...
WITH NO DOORS..
10/19/18
3 STEPS BACK...
ALWAYS STRIVE TO GO FORWARD - ROLL THE DICE AND YOU MAY GET TO MOVE AHEAD...
AND IF YOU HAVE TO GO BACK A FEW SPACES, WELL, A CHANCE TO MAKE REPEATED STEPS A LITTLE BETTER..

10/20/18
ROLL TO HIT
GOT TO PLAY D+D AGAIN - WHAT A TREAT, HOW I MISSED IT SO.
NEVER ABANDON, THE THINGS THAT GIVE YOU JOY - YOU OWE IT TO YOURSELF.
OK, NOW YOU SEE...
10/21/18
THE TRUTH IS OUT THERE - PEOPLE LIKE TO SAY THAT. THEY DO
BUT IS IT? THEN WHY IS THE TRUTH SO ILLUSIVE? ARE WE CLOSER OR FURTHER AWAY?
PERHAPS WE COME UP WITH A COMFORTABLE NARRATIVE AND CHOOSE TO ACCEPT IT
10/22/18
KA-CHUK KA-CHUK
FINALLY HAD SOME TIME TO USE MY NEW TOOLS TO MAKE A BIKE FRAME.
DREAMS CAN COME TRUE.
OH YEAH

10/23/18
GATHER UP GODS OF MONEY.
GO TO THE BANK.
DEPOSIT THIS PLEASE...
..TO WRITE A CHECK AND GIVE IT TO THE GOVERNMENT.
MAIL
10/24/18
UP AND UP - NO REASON, I WAS IN A MOOD. WE NEVER REALLY KNOW WHY.
*#?,
BUT I WENT TO THE BIKE AGAIN AND AFTER A COUPLE GOOD CLIMBS..
WELL, THINGS BEGAN TO LOOK BETTER.
LIKE A CHARM.
10/25/18
MORRIS IS LOOKING A LITTLE SLOW.
HIS WATER WAS OUT, THAT MAY BE IT.
GRROOWLL
BACK TO NORMAL

10/26/18
ON A SUNNY DAY IN "FALL" ON A MOUNTAIN
AROUND 6 MILLION OTHER PEOPLE.
NO OTHER CYCLISTS.
ALL MISSING OUT.
OK. TWO JOGGERS
10/22/18
I'M WARNING YOU, YOU'RE PLAYING WITH FIRE.
OH YEAH?
POKE POKE POKE POKE
I TOLD YOU.
10/28/18
I HAVE TO PAT MYSELF ON THE BACK TODAY. I DON'T LIKE TO BUT TODAY I DID SOMETHING WORTHY OF CELEBRATION.
WHEN ONE WORKS HARD AT A GOAL - WE OFTEN FAIL, WE DO. OR WE QUIT, THINKING WE CANNOT DO WHAT WE SET OUT TO DO - WE DO.
I CAN'T
BUT WHEN WE GET THERE IN THAT RARE INSTANCE IT IS WORTH TAKING TIME OUT TO FEEL ACCOMPLISHED.

10/29/18
PRRRRRRRR
THE LITTLE JOY OF HAVING SOMETHING IN YOUR LIFE..
HA HA!
..THAT ASK FOR SO LITTLE IN RETURN.
MEOW.
10/30/18
MAN THAT WAS SO COOL, WHAT A FUN RIDE!
IT WAS.
AND THAT IS WHY WE DO IT.
10/31/18
THE WORLD IS FULL OF ½ ASS ATTEMPTS AT ACTION.
IN THE END, ONLY THE THINGS THAT ARE DONE MATTER
WUB WUB WUB WUB
IF WHAT I SAY IS TRUE THEN WHAT YOU FINISH IS PROOF OF LIFE, NOT JUST LIVING
PROJECT

11/1/18
THINKING IS OUT THE WINDOW. NOW MANY PEOPLE REACT INSTEAD.
FOOD
REVIEW
OF COURSE I BLAME TECHNOLOGY, THE EASE WE CAN GET INFORMATION AND GIVE IT MAKES US IMPULSIVE.
MY IMPULSE IS THIS WILL NOT GET BETTER, I CAN ONLY HOPE FOR SOME BALANCE.
PERHAPS.
11/2/18
AS THE WORLD BURNS..
I SEE PEOPLE ALL CAUGHT UP IN EACH OTHERS FIRES, THEY BURN EACH OTHER.
I COULD CARE LESS ABOUT SUCH STUFF AND THAT MAKES MY WORLD..
WAY COOLER.
10 DOLLARS! THAT'S STEEP!*
* ½ OF WHAT OTHERS CHARGE
WELL, YOU CAN SHOP AROUND YOU KNOW.
REALLY?
NEVER GOING TO WIN AM I?
...

11/4/18
UP AT 5AM - ALL DAY A PUSH: TO DO A LITTLE MORE.
IN EACH DAY, PUSH A LITTLE MORE, TAKE YOUR GOOD ENERGY AND HELP PUSH THINGS ALONG
HERE YOU GO.
AND AT THE END OF 12 OR 14 HOURS YOU CAN BE SURE YOU DID MORE THAN MOST.
OK. THAT WAS A GOOD ONE.
FLIP
HMM
OK, I WENT THROUGH ALL THE VOTING MATERIAL AND CAN NOW MAKE A QUASI-INFORMED CHOICE.
DAMN MICES! I KILL ONE AND ANOTHER SHOWS UP.
ALL SORTS OF TRAPS ARE USED. YOU HAVE TO USE THEM ALL TOGETHER.
POISON!
THE MESSAGE IS CLEAR!
WE'RE NOT SHARING.

11/7/18
OK, DON'T SAY DYE.
PEOPLE ARE NOT LIKE THEY WERE...
YES, I'D AGREE.
YEAH.
PEOPLE TODAY WOULD NOT START TWO WORLD WARS AND KILL UNTOLD MILLIONS.
11/8/18
DOES IT MATTER? I'M NOT SO SURE.
I THINK LIFE IS JUST LIFE. ONLY IN THE END DO WE TRY AND LOOK AT OUR LIFE AND GIVE IT SOME SORT OF MEANING.
IS PURPOSE JUST A SELF MADE TITLE? I DOUBT THERE IS ANYTHING ELSE.
11/9/18
YOU REMEMBER ME? YOU SAVED ME OUT THERE.*
YEAH. KYLE RIGHT?
*2 YEARS AGO
THAT'S AMAZING! HOW YOU REMEMBER!
I DUNNO.
I'M CURSED NOT TO FORGET ANYTHING.

11/10/18
DUM
DUM
DUM
I FORGOT HOW MUCH I ENJOY PLAYING MY BASS. HOW CAN I HAVE BALANCE TO JUST ENJOY THINGS?
WELL, THIS IS A GOOD A PLACE TO START AS ANY.
OH FUN HOW YOU ARE THE ONLY TRUE THING ON THIS EARTH.
HA HA HA HA HA HA
TO ME AT LEAST, THE MOST NOBLE CAUSE IS TO CREATE A LITTLE FUN IN THIS LIFE, TO BE A BECON AGAINST ALL THE BADNESS IN THE WORLD.
IF YOU DO THAT WORK, ALL THE OTHER GOOD THINGS WILL FALL IN PLACE BEHIND IT. A LIGHT OF TRUTH IN A SEA OF DARKNESS.
YOU ARE CRAZY MAN, COMING UP WITH THIS...
YEAH.
WELL, SOME ONE HAS TO BE.
THATS WHY I LOVE YOU.

11/13/18
SMOKE FROM BRUSH FIRES IN THE AIR...
HOWLING WINDS...
BUT WE'RE DUMB LIKE THAT, WE RODE ANYWAY.
FUUCCCKK!
WELL I GUESS I'M ALL GROWN UP NOW.
INVESTING MY MONEY IN SOME FUND LIKE AN OLD MAN, SITTING IN A NO
BANK IS GOOD
EITHER
THEY ARE BOTH EVIL SO WHAT DOES THAT MAKE ME?
SORRY MORRIS
MRRRrrH!
sock
THAT PAW HAS GOT A NASTY ABCESS!
MRRRRRR!
CHEAPER THAN A VET BILL - ALL BETTER.
PRRRRRR

11/16/18
ONE MORNING:
GLAD TO BE OUT RIDING.
GLAD TO BE DRAWING AND DRINKING COFFEE.
GLAD TO BE WELDING BIKE FRAMES.
11/17/18
A PLAN WITHIN PLANS
I DON'T THINK I WAS VERY CREATIVE WHEN I WAS YOUNG I THINK I LEARNED HOW TO UNLOCK MY CREATIVITY...
NOW I CAN PLAN AND PLAN - THE IDEAS THAT WERE ONCE FEW ARE SO MANY, A GIFT I LEARNED TO GIVE TO MYSELF.
LAST ONE.
B2
TTT!
SO GOOD TO GET SOMETHING THAT WAS LONG OFF YOUR LIST - OFF...
BUT THE FEELING, IT IS SHORT.
SO MANY THINGS TO GO.

11/19/18
I DON'T KNOW WHAT TO DO WITH YOU!
YEAH.
THATS BEEN GOING ON MY WHOLE LIFE WITH EVERYONE I KNOW. WHAT TO DO WITH ME.
AND NO ONE FIGURED IT OUT YET.
11/20/18
IT'S 10.50
YOU SHOULD HAVE SAID THAT ON THE PHONE.
I DID.
WHAT MADE YOU THINK I WOULD FIX YOUR BIKE FOR 50¢ THE COST OF A SPOKE?
I HAVE NO MONEY.
WELL I DON'T WORK FOR FREE - THIS IS NOT A CHARITY, IT IS A BUSINESS.
THE HELL?
11/21/18
WAK
WAK WAK WAK WAK WAK WAK WAK
DID IT MOVE?
NOT ONE MM. OH WELL.

11/22/19
UP AND UP WE CLIMB
9 MILES OF STEEP, ROCKY TRAIL.
HUF. HUF HUF
AT THE TOP, MAGIC HAPPENED. SOME GUY WAS THERE AND GAVE ME A WARM TAMALE.
F-THAT! BLURCH!
OH YOU HAVE NOT CHANGED A BIT SINCE I'VE KNOWN YOU.
WELL I GOTTA BE ME RIGHT?
YOU FIXED IT! AND SO FAST!
IT'S MY JOB.
I THINK THE BEST CURRENCY YOU CAN HAVE IS MAKING PEOPLE HAPPY.
THANKS!
THE RETURN ON YOUR INVESTMENT IS HIGH Y YEILD
I'LL BE BACK!

11/25/18
I CAN GO OUT FRONT AND GET A REFIL RIGHT?
NO
SO YOU'RE SAYING EVEN THOUGH YOU CAN SEE ME, IF I GO OUT THE DOOR I HAVE TO PAY?
1.39
I GUESS I'M STAYING IN THEN.
11/26/18
IT'S NOT A GOOD TIME.
AGAIN?
TWO TIMES NOW I TRIED TO VISIT ONE OF MY FRIENDS THAT IS DYING AND GOT TURNED AWAY.
THERE WILL NEVER BE A "GOOD TIME."
11/27/18
I'M WRITING THAT DOWN!
OH TO REMEMBER IT ALL AND THEN DO IT ALL.
THAT WOULD BE HUGE.
PROJECT #512.

11/28/18
SAVE SAVE AS..
AND ... SAVE!
I AM SO POSSESED BY AN IDEA. IT IS A BLESSING AND A CURSE.
THAT UNTIL I FINISH IT, THE IDEA OWNS ME.
MUST FINISH..
11/29/18
LISTEN!
HARUGGG!
OHOH!
LET'S MAKA A MOVIE OF HIM GOING PSYCO ON ME.
OK
LATER
OK IT'S DONE.
SO COOL WE TALKED ABOUT IT AND THEN DID IT.
11/30/18
HAVE SOME SOUP.
SO GOOD.
AHH. SO GOOD. IF I COULD STRING THESE LITTLE GOOD THINGS END TO END.
IT WOULD END SO WELL...

12/1/18
ARE WE HAVING FUN YET?
FUN IS NOT SOMETHING THAT LANDS ON YOUR LAP, YOU HAVE TO GO OUT, AND SEEK IT OUT.
NO FUN YOU GET HANDED TO YOU WILL BE WORTHY OR LEAVE A LASTING IMPRESSION- BUT THE KIND WORKED FOR. IS GOLDEN
12/2/18
IT SHOULD NOT BE A BIG DEAL, I'M JUST DOING MY JOB AFTER ALL.
WELL IT IS HARD TO COME BY.
WELL, IT SHOULD BE EXPECTED, NOT SPECIAL.
12/3/18
DONK DONK
OK OK I GET IT.
I'LL PLAY WITH YOU.

12/4/18
GOOD
DAD
HOWDY, THERE IS WATER LEAKING OUT OF YOUR HOUSE.
GOOD
DAD
OH REALLY? HOW ABOUT I SEND YOU 10,000 EMAIL SPAM YOU DICKHEAD!
I GUESS I CAN GO BOTH WAYS IN THE SAME DAY.
12/5/18
NO.
I AM A CYCLIST, I SHOULD RIDE MY BIKE, NOT DRIVE.
REAL CYCLISTS ARE KNOWN TO GET WET!
12/8/18
TWO DAYS OF SITTING INSIDE - RAIN SUCKS
CAN'T LOOK AT THIS COMPUTER ANYMORE, AM I WEAK?
OR DO I JUST KNOW WHAT I WANT.

12/7/18
1 NIGHT
2 SETS OF WEAPONS: FOAM SWORDS & SURIKENS
3 NINJA BIKE RIDERS
12/8/18
A MERRY "BEARY" HOLIDAY, THAT IS WHAT SHE WANTS?
YEP.
THIS IS THE DUMEST PROJECT EVER.
UH HUH
SO THIS IS WHAT YOU HAVE TO LOOK FORWARD TO WITH MENOPAUSE.
UH HUH
12/9/18
I SAW YOU RIDING THAT BIKE- YOU'RE STRONG STRONG!
I GUESS
JUST BEEN DOING IT FOR A LONG TIME.
I HOPE IT WILL NEVER GET OLD.

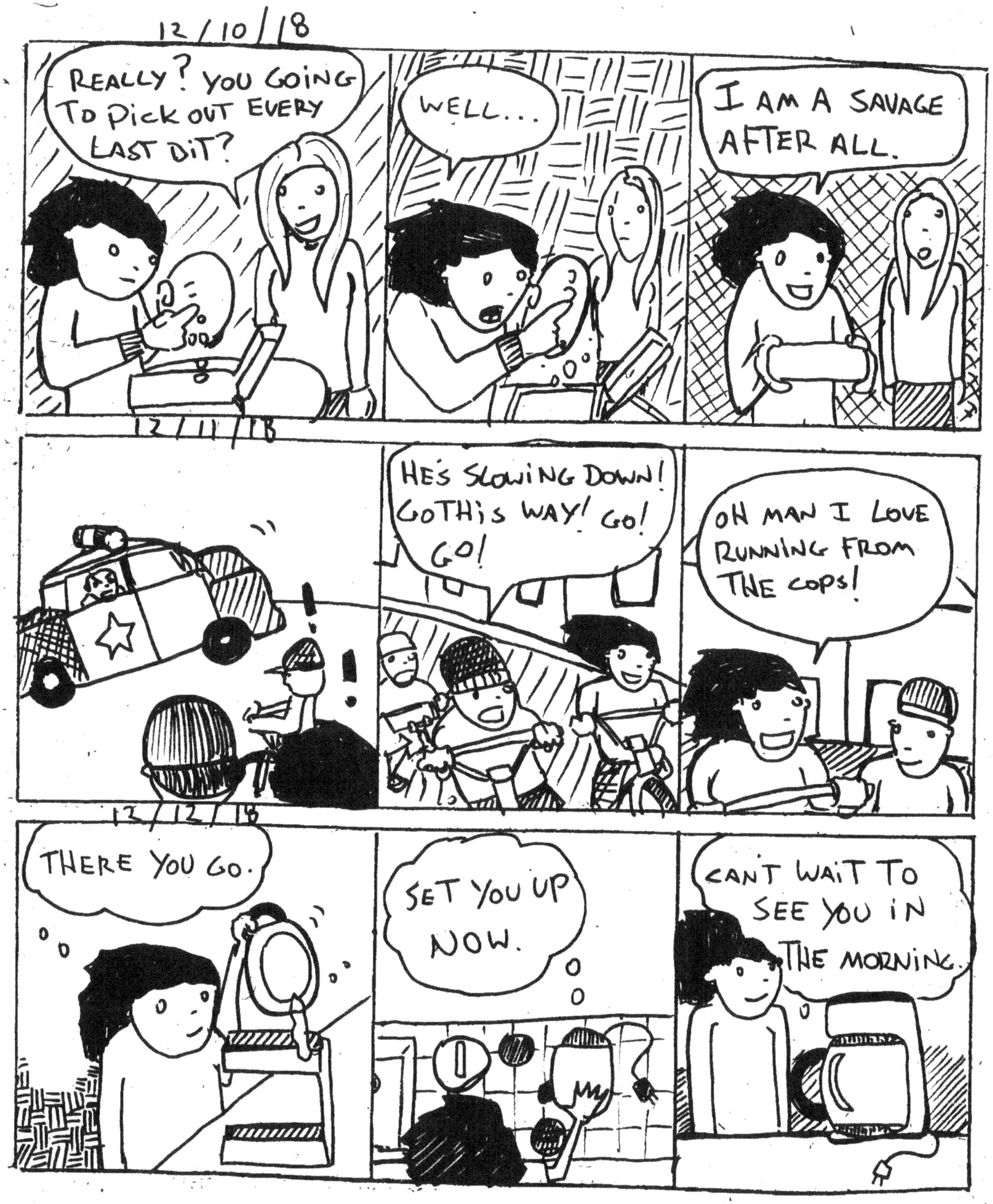

12/10/18
REALLY? YOU GOING TO PICK OUT EVERY LAST DIT?
WELL...
I AM A SAVAGE AFTER ALL.
HE'S SLOWING DOWN! GO THIS WAY! GO! GO!
OH MAN I LOVE RUNNING FROM THE COPS!
THERE YOU GO.
SET YOU UP NOW.
CAN'T WAIT TO SEE YOU IN THE MORNING.

12/13/18
OK, AND SEND.
SEE THAT MEOW MEOW? I JUST MADE 120 BUCKS.
JUST CAUSE I SAID YES.
Prrn
WE CAN RIDE BIKES THERE
WE CAN AND WE SHOULD RIDE BIKES THERE - ANYWHERE THAT IS.
NOTHING ELSE CAN GET YOU TO WHERE YOU NEED TO GO UNDER YOUR OWN POWER WITH SUCH EASE AND GRACE.
THOSE CHEEZ-ITS ARE SO GOOD.
I KNOW, SO ADDICTIVE...
SO FULL
GLARMPH.

12/16/18

12/17/18

12/18/18

12/19/18

I WANT A BIKE. BUT MY BOY FRIEND GOT KILLED FOR HIS BIKE, HE WAS IN A GANG.
OH.
HE HIT ME THOUGH SO I LEFT BUT THE HEART WANTS WHAT THE HEART WANTS YOU KNOW? SO I WENT BACK.
SURE.
LOVE IS THE ANTITHESIS OF REASON.
12/20/18
SURREY TO BOTHER YOU CAN YOU SPARE 5 DOLLARS
5 BUCKS?
WHAT HAPPENED TO "CAN YOU SPARE SOME CHANGE"?
12/21/18
I THREW SOME OF THE BURNT COOKIES IN THE TRASH.
GASP!
YOU DID NOT DIG THOSE OUT OF THE TRASH...
MUNCH MUNCH
!

12/22/18
OH WELL, HE'S A FUCK UP, WORLD'S FULL OF THEM.
THE THING THAT GRATES ME IS SO MANY PEOPLE SPEND SO MUCH TIME ON WHAT OTHER PEOPLE ARE DOING WRONG.
AND THEY SHOULD BE FOCUSING ON THOSE AREAS FOR THEMSELVES, INSTEAD.
12/23/18
A LIFE ANALOGY: RIDE UP A HILL
HUF HUF HUF.
EVERY HILL REQUIRES YOU PUT IN AN EFFORT. NO CLIMB IS FREE. ONCE TO THE TOP, THE REWARD IS BRIEF HOWEVER...
HUF HUF
FOR THERE ARE MANY HILLS TO GET UP.
12/24/18
6AM? NOT 6:30?
6.
I NEED SLEEP BUT TIME TO GET THINGS DONE...
WELL, I NEED THAT MORE
TIME TO DO SHIT.

12/25/18
CHUG CHUG
INSTEAD OF OPENING PRESENTS I MADE A PRESENT FOR MYSELF.
Looks Good
I HAD AN IDEA AND IT LEFT MY HEAD & IS NOW IN THE FLESH.
12/26/18
BZZZZZZ
WELD WELD WELD
NOW THAT'S A SHELF!
12/27/18
MY OLD COMPANION 1986 HONDA - 400K MILES RAN LIKE A CHAMP. I'VE HAD IT 24 YEARS..
GREW UP IN THIS CAR. IT WAS BOUGHT NEW BY MY DAD AND GIVEN TO ME. AS HIS HEALTH GAVE OUT HE'D ASK ME AS A POINT OF PRIDE. I GUESS.
YOU STILL HAVE THE HONDA?
TODAY I GAVE IT TO A FRIEND IN NEED. IT WAS TIME. HE'S GONE SO IS THE CAR. STILL IN THE FAMILY THOUGH.
SEE YOU OLD PAL.

12/28/18
GLORIOUS SHELVES..
SPENT 3 DAYS MAKING SHELVES FOR ALL MY BOOKS. IT IS GOING TO BE GREAT TO..
...FIND A BOOK WHEN I NEED IT.
ALL PART OF MY SELF IMPROVEMNT PLAN - A LIFE-LONG PROJECT.
IN THE RIGHT DIRECTION.
12/29/18
Books.
AND Books.
AND Books!
12/30/18
LOOK AT ALL THOSE LEAVES.
I SHOULD RAKE THOSE LEAVES.
BUT IT IS MY TIME OFF. CHORES CAN WAIT, THE LEAVES WILL BE THERE BUT THE FREE TIME WON'T

12/31/18
LOOK BEYOND, INTO THE FUTURE.
FOR THE PAST IS GONE FOREVER AND CAN NEVER BE LOOKED UPON THE SAME AGAIN
ALL YOU WILL EVER HAVE IS THIS MOMENT. SO REMEMBER...
ENJOY IT.
1/1/19
WE RODE BIKES ALL DAY, 40 MILES AND WE STOPPED FOR FOOD.
FRIES
I WAS JUST SITTING THERE LISTENING TO MY FRIENDS AND A WAVE OF HAPPINESS WASHED OVER ME.
HMM.
I JUST LIKE TO REMEMBER THOSE MOMENTS AS THEY ARE FEW.....
GLARF.
1/2/19
YOU TAKE THESE BIKES OUT AND IN EVERY DAY?
YEP.
OH MAN, THAT LOOKS LIKE SUCH A HASSLE!
NOT REALLY.
IT'S CALLED WORK FOR A REASON.

1/3/.19
GOOD NEWS, JAG'S OUT OF THE SURGERY.
WENT OK?
THEY CUT HIS HEAD AND ZAPPED OUT TWO TUMORS..
OH.
LIFE - THERE'S NO GUARANTEE, WE ARE OBLIGATED TO LIVE IT.
1/4/19
HOW ABOUT 200 FOR BOTH.
NAH
IT'S ONLY 8 DOLLARS MORE, WHY PEOPLE DO THAT?
BECAUSE, THEY DON'T KNOW...
...THAT IF I GIVE IN 15 DOLLARS A DAY, 5 DAYS A WEEK AFTER 20 YEARS IS 72,000. MY 72,000.
1/5/19
YOU NEVER WANT TO WAIT YOUR TURN!
I'VE DONE THIS WITH YOU A DOZEN TIMES - NO MORE. YOU CAN LEAVE YOUR BIKE AND WAIT YOUR TURN.
OR YOU CAN GO AWAY.

1/6/19
CAN I HAVE ONE OF YOUR PAN COOKIES?
SURE.
THAT'S TWO NOT ONE.
THEY WERE STUCK TOGETHER.
I THINK I'VE BEAT YOU FAIR AND SQUARE ONCE.
NAH. I GOT A FLAT.
DURING THE RACE...
GASP WHEEZE!
SO, LOOKS LIKE I BEAT YOU FAIR AND SQUARE HUH?
I GUESS SO
GTN
3RD
OH WELL.
THERE IS SO MUCH YOU CAN'T CONTROL IN THIS LIFE, YOU WILL LOSE OFTEN.
X#?@!
JUST FOCUS ON THE THINGS THAT BRING YOU JOY AND THE STUFF THAT GETS BY WON'T BE SUCH A BIG DEAL.

1/9/19
THE WORLD IS SO STRANGE, THERE IS SO MUCH WE DON'T KNOW.
WHAT WAS THAT?
SOMETIMES I HAVE A VISION IN A DREAM TAKE PLACE IN REAL LIFE.
I'VE DONE THIS BEFORE.
AND THEN I..
WONDER WHICH IS REAL
I SEE WHY PEOPLE HAVE PETS.
PRRRR
THEY DON'T JUDGE YOU TOO HARSHLY, THEY JUST WANT YOU TO BE THERE
PRRRR
STUDENT DISCOUNT?
NO DISCOUNTS.
WHAT IF I TRADE YOU SOME PANTS?
SORRY, NO TRADES
IF YOU DO IT FOR 90 I'LL COME RIGHT OVER..
OH GEE - I DON'T THINK SO...

1/12 1:19
SURE THING.
CAN I GET A RIDE?
CAN I CATCH A RIDE TO THE RACE?
SURE!
CAN I GET A RIDE TO THE RACE?
YEP.
AN TO BE THE PIED PIPER OF FUN
!
HUF HUF HUF
I'LL TAKE 3RD ANY DAY.
RAIN AGAIN, SO STUCK INSIDE.
WELL, I CAN WORK ON SOME INDOOR PROJECTS..
HOW PEOPLE SIT AROUND EACH DAY ON PURPOSE BEATS ME.
HOPE I'LL NEVER KNOW.

1/15/.19
I'M NOT A MINIMALIST, I'M A MAXIUMIST!
I WANT MORE THINGS TO DO MORE STUFF MORE HORIZONS TO GET TO, MORE IDEAS AND MORE FINISHING OF THINGS!
I WANT THE MOST OF THE RIGHT THINGS, MORE IS BETTER!
WHAT IS THE STRIKE OVER NOW?
CLASS SIZE.
WELL I WOULD LIKE TO GO ON STRIKE BUT I'M THE BOSS OF ME.
SO I JUST HAVE TO SUCK IT UP AND TAKE MY LUMPS.
IT RAINED ALL DAY FOR DAYS NOW AND THINGS JUST GROUND TO A HALT.
I SAT AROUND READING ALL DAY AT WORK.
DOUBT I'LL MAKE A BUCK.
WELL 10 BUCKS WAS O.K.
BETTER THAN ZERO.

1/18/19
10 DOLLARS! I CAN'T DO THAT!
NO LESS.
WHAT CAN YOU DO FOR ME?
HAND YOU BACK YOUR RIM AND HAVE A NICE DAY!
ARE WE COOL THEN?
NO.
I TOLD YOU NOT TO TREAT ME THE WAY YOU HAVE. I GAVE YOU AMPLE WARNINGS - OVER AND OVER AGAIN.
. . .
YOU DID THIS TO YOURSELF. I'M HANGING UP NOW.
SOMETHING YOU HAVE TO TAKE OUT THE TRASH.
WHERE IS EVERYONE?
DID I WIND UP IN FRONT?
LOOKS LIKE I WON!

1/21/19

IT'S WORKING.

;CUGCHUG;;;

MADE SOME GOOD PROGRESS ON SO MANY DIFFERENT THINGS.

YOU WORE SO MANY HATS TODAY.

JUST ONE HAT: THE HAT OF SOMEONE WHO TRIES.

1/22/19

HOBO LAYERS

T-SHIRT
2 FLANNELS
1 JACKET
GLOVES

WE RODE THROUGH THE NIGHT. NO ONE ELSE WAS DUMB ENOUGH TO BE OUT IN COLD AND HOWLING WINDS.

BUT IT WAS OURS.

1/23/19

NEED MORE BLANKET?

UH HUH.

YOU'RE A BLANKET HOG YOU KNOW THAT? A BLANKET HOG.

I KNOW. I CAN ADMIT THAT.

1/24/19

WE FORGET.

IT IS SO EASY TO HANG ON TO THE BAD MOMENTS IN LIFE.

AND SO EASY TO FORGET ALL THE GOOD ONES.

CHINEESE ACROBATS

SO MUCH STRENGTH AND SELF-DICIPLINE. YOU CAN'T HELP BUT ADMIRE THIER PROWESS.

ALSO KNOWING THAT YOU HAVE LESS THAN 1% OF THEIR SKILL. WELL, IT'S HUMBLING

WOW.

AN ALLEN!

ALL THE OLD ROAD BIKES I'VE WANTED AND HERE IS THE ONE.

OH WHAT A GREAT DAY!

IT'S YOURS!

IT is!

1/27/19.
EVERY DAY...
I TRY TO HANG ON TIGHT TO THE CHILD-LIKE WONDER OF THE WORLD.
AND NOT BECOME ONE OF THE JOYLESS MASSES.
HOW AM I DOING?
HA HA HA HA HA HA HA HA HA HA
1/28/19
OH LOOK!
TWO ART POSITION DOLLS ON THE CURB. THESE THINGS COST BUCKS!
ONE MORE ADVANTAGE TO RIDING A BICYCLE! GROUND SCORES!
1/29/19
AN ADVENTURE RIDE.
TO COUNT, THERE HAS TO BE SOME SORT OF TRAVERSE INTO A WOODED AREA AT NIGHT.
AND THERE HAS TO BE SMILES.
AWESOME!

1/30/19
WE SHOULD CELEBRATE THAT YOU REPLLED A HOME INVADER.
WE SHOULD.
YEAH PIZZA!
WHAT'S MORE LIFE-AFFIRMING THAN PIZZA?
2/1/19
MAGIC NETE BOOK
I DON'T KNOW WHY I NEVER DID IT BEFORE BUT I TOOK A NOTE BOOK TO WORK.
AN IDEA!
AND NOW ALL THE THINGS IN MY HEAD HAVE A PLACE TO GO.
2/3/19
YOU GIVE ME A GOOD PRICE.
PRICES ARE FAIR, NO HAGGLING.
DON'T WORRY, I'M NOT JEWISH.
!
HEY! I DON'T WANNA HEAR THAT KIND OF TALK YOU GOT ME?

2/3/19
YOU RODE YOUR BIKE IN THE RAIN?
YEAH
THERE ARE FLOODS RIGHT NOW! YOU CRAZY!
YEAH...
SO...
...
2/4/19
OF COURSE I'D RIDE MY BIKE IN THE RAIN, IT SEEMS SILLY NOT TO.
I LIVE A MILE + 1/2 FROM WORK. I HAVE FENDERS AND A RAIN COAT. WHEN YOU GET WET, WHAT DO PEOPLE DO? TAKE A SHOWER.
SO I TAKE A FREE ONE INSTEAD.
NOT SO BAD.
2/5/19
WE CARRY A BURDEN OF OUR OWN CHOOSING.
I THINK WE CAN MAKE OUR LIVES EASY OR HARD, SIMPLE OR DIFFICULT - WE CHOOSE THAT PATH THOUGH, NONE ARE POWERLESS.
I WILL CARRY A HEAVY LOAD.
TO KNOW THAT IF WE DO BURDEN OURSELVES, IT IS BECAUSE...
...I WANT TO

2/6/19
SO COLD!
RIGHT!
THAT'S THE WRONG WAY!
OH NO IT'S NOT.
WARM NOW
2/7/19
OF COURSE BY DOING NOTHING YOU'RE JUST AS BAD.
IF YOU DON'T TAKE ACTION THEN YOU'RE PAYING LIP SERVICE TO BEING MORAL.
BUT YOU ARE NOT ACTING MORAL.
2/8/19
SO MUCH TO DO
A PILE OF TASKS HIGH ABOVE ME
CURSED TO NEVER BE DONE.
OR BLESSED WITH THINGS TO DO ALL THE TIME.

2/8/19

WRRRRRR
INSIDE THE SHELF
WRRRRRR
OH SHIT.
FSSS
2/9/19
6 AM OFF TO WORK
BEING SELF EMPLOYED MEANS YOU WORK ALL THE TIME.
BUT YOU WORK FOR THE BEST BOSS; YOURSELF.
10/19
MY FACE HAS NEVER BEEN THIS COLD!
LATER: YOU GOT CAUGHT IN THE RAIN? WAS THE RIDE WORTH IT?
OH. OH YEAH.

2/11/19
I DON'T WANT TO TALK ABOUT THINGS...
...I WANT TO DO THINGS
EVEN RAKING LEAVES UP IS BETTER THAN HAVING ANOTHER CONVERSATION WITH SOMEONE ABOUT THINGS...
...THAT THEY WILL NEVER DO.
SURE YOU WILL
2/12/19
THEY ARE PARTYING IT UP OVER THERE!
YEAH
AREN'T WE HERE TO ENJOY IT?
2/13/19
NICE CLEAN BED!
HEH.
HA HA
SOON TO BE INHABITED BY ONE DIRTY HUMAN.

2/14/19
OH MORRIS YOU SICK BUDDY?
MRRRR
WELL YOU'RE MY LITTLE FUZZY CHILD.
I HAVE TO TAKE CARE OF YOU.
2/15/19
HE'S OK. HE'S FIGHTING A VIRUS BUT HE SHOULD BE GOOD.
THANK GOODNESS
I FELT BAD BUT BECAUSE IT MADE ME SO SAD AND I FELT MORE SAD ABOUT A CAT THAN SOME FRIENDS THAT PASSED AWAY THIS YEAR.
SORT OF MADE ME WONDER IF SOMETHING IS WRONG WITH ME.
2/16/19
TO LAUGH OUT LOUD IS SUCH A GIFT.
HE HE HE
LIFE CAN BE SO SERIOUS, SO LAUGH WHEN YOU CAN...
HE HE HE
...AND MAKE YOUR SPACE A LITTLE BRIGHTER..

2/17/19

2/18/19

2/19/19

2/20/19

33° OUT - RODE ANYWAY.
ONE THING I'VE LEARNED IS JUST TO GO OUT AND MAKE YOURSELF DO THINGS
HUH NUH HUH
I'VE NEVER REGRETED IN LIFE, PUTTING FORTH THE EFFORT.
SO GOOD.
2/21/19
IT'S SNOWING!
THERE'S SNOW!
OK?
I'LL BELIEVE IT WHEN I SEE IT.
2/22/19
HERE YOU GO
333 OUT OF 1000
COOL!
I GUESS I'LL JUST DO FOLDING NOW AND GET IT DONE.
ALL DONE. THAT'S HOW WE DO IT.
WHEW!

2/23/19
THE EXPONENTIAL EFFORT IS THE ONLY WAY YOU CAN GET A GOOD RESULT.
RESULT
TIME
THE ONLY WAY TO THE TOP OF THE MOUNTAIN IS TO CLIMB TO THE TOP.
ANYTHING LESS AND YOU'RE STILL NOT THERE.
2/24/19
SO WORN OUT, I HAVE SO MUCH TO DO THOUGH...
I'LL JUST SIT HERE FOR A MINUTE...
OH. HELLO?
PRRRR
I NEED TO DO MORE OF THIS.
2/25/19
CLIKATY CLAKITY CLICKAITY CLACKITY
I HATE HAVING AN IDEA THAT IS UNFURFILLED. IT EATS AT ME...
YEARS LATER FINALLY GETTING AROUND TO IT.
BUT ONE CAN ONLY GO HUNGRY FOR SO LONG.
AND 12 HOURS LATER WE'RE ALMOST THERE.

2/26/19
COOL SHIRT!
HA! WELL MY BROTHER GAVE IT TO ME TO SHOW YOU AND HE SAID IF YOU MENTIONED IT, I AM SUPPOSED TO GIVE IT TO YOU.
ROSS
SO HERE YOU GO.
COOL!
ROSS
2/27/19
DIRTBALL!
I COULD NOT WAIT HOWEVER.
OH WORRY
LATER...
MEEEEW!
OH THANK GOODNESS
2/28/19
BE KIND.
HERE YOU GO.
PEOPLE SAY IT BUT TO BE IT, WELL THAT TAKES WAY MORE STRENGTH THAN BEING A JERK.
THANKS!
ARE YOU STRONG ENOUGH?

3/1/19

CAN I COME BACK AND TALK TO YOU AGAIN?
SURE.
SO STRANGE THAT PEOPLE HAVE TO GO OUT OF THEIR WAY TO HAVE A GOOD CONVERSATION.
SEE YA.
I'VE HEARD THIS SO MANY TIMES NOW IT MUST BE TRUE.
MORE RAIN.
I NEED TO RIDE MY BIKE.
IT GOES BEYOND NEED; IT IS LIKE MISSING A LIMB.
YES, RAIN OR SHINE.
IS THE EVENT STILL GOING?
THE NEXT DAY
LOOK! THE SUN IS PEEKING OUT!
THE BICYCLE GODS ARE SMILING ON US!

3/4/19
LET'S GO UP THERE OK?
NUF NUF NUF
WENT UP THIS TRAIL A 100 TIMES.
BUT NEVER STOPPED TO TAKE IN THE VIEW.
3/5/19
NO RAIN YET WE RIDE!
HA HA HA!
WE WET.
3/6/19
THE CHAOS OF THE MIND.
NOTHING LIKE HAVING YOUR ROUTINE GOING SOUTH TO RUN YOU OFF THE TRACKS..
NEED. OUTSIDE.
JUST KEEP IN MIND IT IS IN YOUR HEAD.
FIND THOSE TRACKS.

3/7/19
AND DONE!
WUMP
OH ANOTHER BOOK DONE. AND ANOTHER AND ANOTHER!
THE BEST THING ABOUT FINISHING A BOOK
IS BEING ABLE TO START ANOTHER.
3/8/19
SUN IS OUT!
OUT WHERE I NEED TO BE!
I'M LUCKY BECAUSE I KNOW THE LOCATION OF MY MAGICAL PLACE
3/9/19
PIZZA!
SHOULD WE BE EATING HEALTHY?
NOT, WHEN WE'RE GAMING.

3/10/14
DID YOU RIDE YOUR BIKE HERE?
YEAH
BUT IT'S RAINING, DO YOU WANT A RIDE?
OH NO, A LITTLE RAIN WONT BOTHER ME MUCH.
SUM UP ONE'S LIFE IN PARTS: ALL TEMPORARY.
THE GOOD, THE BAD, AND ALL IN BETWEEN. A STRING OF IDEAS, FEELINGS, STATES OF MIND: ALL FOR A SMALL TIME.
A SMALL TIME, YOURS AND ALL PARTS OF WHO YOU ARE - DONT FORGET THAT.
FOR NOW.
3/12/14
SO ADDICTED TO: ACHIEVEMENT!
ONCE YOU GET THE TASTE, YOU'LL NEVER HAVE ENOUGH. BUT NOW, MORE.
WELL, IT'S BETTER THAN OTHER VICES, AT LEAST YOU HAVE THINGS TO SHOW FOR IT.

3/13/19
WELL, I HAVE TO TELL PEOPLE THAT ALL THE TIME.
AMAZING.
SO YOU'RE A TEACHER JUST SO YOU KNOW IT DOES NOT GET BETTER.
THANKS FOR RUINING MY DAY.
ANY TIME.
3/14/19
DEALING WITH PEOPLE CAN BE A CHALLENGE.
REALLY?
BUT I HAVE TO REMIND MYSELF THAT THE BAD ONES, THEY ARE FEW.
AND TO MAKE SURE TO SPEND TIME WITH THE GOOD ONES.
SLAM!
3/15/19
I'LL DO A PODCAST OF YOU.
UM OK.
SO, THAT'S HOW I SEE IT.
I'LL SEND IT TO YOU
NO NEED.
ONE MORE VOICE INTO THE VOID.

3/16/19
ARE PRICES NEGOTABLE?
NEVER
WHY?
WHY SHOULD THEY BE?
3/ /19
NO, THANK YOU.
I DON'T LIKE TO INDULGE IN THINGS TOO MUCH. I THINK GIVING IN MAKES YOU SOFT.
TOO MUCH.
NOT HAVING EVERY WHIM CATERED TO. WELL THEN YOU DON'T FORGET THE GOOD THINGS YOU DO HAVE.
STAY HUNGRY
3/18/19
A GOOD DAY = DIRTY HANDS.
WASH THEM OFF AND THEN YOU KNOW YOU DID A LOT.
FZZZZZ
YOU MADE SOMETHING OF YOURSELF THAT DAY— YOU DID REAL THINGS IN THE REAL WORLD. IT MATTERS.

3/19/19
A LITTLE DE-COMPRE-SSION AFTER A GOOD DAY.
AND WHY NOT? I WANT TO STOP AND THINK ABOUT WHY IT WAS A GOOD DAY - PROCESS IT.
Ooo
AND REMEMBER WHY.
OH YEAH
3/20/19
SO TIRED, AND WET OUT BUT RODE ANYWAY.
NATURE'S CANVAS WAS PAINTED IN HUES OF GREEN, BLUE, YELLOW AND PURPLE. WILD FLOWERS ABOUND.
IT IS A THEME I KEEP GOING BACK TO BECAUSE GOOD THINGS ARE WORTH REPEATING.
3/21/19
TO GO THROUGH LIFE WITHOUT A RUDDER, HOW AWFUL
I KNOW WHERE I WANT TO GO AND SOME IDEA OF HOW TO GET THERE.
CAN YOU SAY THE SAME?

3/22/19
ROLL ATTACKS!
WE GAMED ALL NIGHT.
YES
MOUNTIAN DEW?
LIKE BACK IN THE DAY.
YOU SLAY THE EVIL WIZARD!
3/23/19
THE BASE LINE - SO IMPORTANT.
SO TIRED...
WHAT EVER IT IS - FOOD, SLEEP, SHELTER, COMFORT, A SHOWER, A TIDY PLACE ETC. MAKE SURE IT IS GOOD.
OR NOTHING ELSE IS.
WHOLE DAY MISS FIRING.
3/24/19
LET'S KEEP GOING.
SO WE DID 20-22 MILES? NOT SURE. WILD FLOWERS WERE EVERY WHERE.
IT IS ALWAYS BETTER TO TRY THAN TO DOUBT - WHO KNOWS WHAT YOU'LL GET.

3/25/19
MAN I USED TO HATE YARD WORK.
BUT IT IS MY YARD NOW.
SO I GUESS THAT IS OK.
3/26/19
WHAT A MESS
office of FINANCE
THIS IS GOING TO BE AN EPIC BATTLE.
HERE YOU GO.
JUST SIGN HERE. IT WAS OUR FAULT, YOU OWE NOTHING
WOW. THAT WAS EASY.
3/27/19
SO HUNGRY
NO FOOD.
NOM NOM
FUCK IT.
CHOMP CHOMP
?

3/28/19
NO DRAKES!
THAT BUSH WILL DO.
WUMP!
OOOF!
3/29/19
MMM SO GOOD
AH... A CUP OF COFFEE...
MY LITTLE REWARD TO MYSELF.
3/30/19
HOLD STILL
OH, DON'T BOTHER.
THAT'S A FULL-TIME JOB.

3 31/19

I DON'T THINK I AM TALENTED OR REALLY GOOD AT MUCH. THE ONE THING THAT I DO THOUGH IS LOOK AT THE HORIZON.

WHEN I LOOK AT THINGS I SEE WHERE IT COULD GO AND HOW GETTING THERE CAN LEAD TO MORE AND MORE.

IN THE DISTANCE IS WHERE I LOOK, KNOWING THAT REACHING THAT HORIZON ONLY EXPOSES ME TO A DOZEN NEW ONES.

4/1/19

HAVE NOT MADE A TO-DO LIST IN A WHILE.

OH, AND THAT & THAT, AND THAT, AND THAT..

30 THINGS ALREADY, DAMN.

4/2/19

THROUGH SECRET PASSAGES

SEEKING ADVENTURE.

AND PIZZA.

4/3/19
SOMETIMES, TRYING TO MAKE PEOPLE HAPPY IS A FOOLS ERRAND.
NO TRADES MEANS NO TRADES.
BECAUSE WHAT THEY WANT FROM YOU IS A PART OF YOURSELF.
THAT IS MY DAY TO GO RIDE.
A PART OF YOU, THAT YOU'D BE A FOOL TO GIVE.
IT'S TOO MUCH.
I WORK ON 10,000 DOLLAR BIKES, GOT MY START MAKING WHEELS FOR HARLEYS.
UH HUH.
I NEED A PAIR OF PLYERS
FOR WHAT?
WHATS THIS? YOU TRYING TO SHIM A SEAT POST WITH A SHOE STRING? YOU NEED TO MOVE ON.
CAFE
MEOOOOOW
YOU HAVE FOOD, WHAT IS IT?
MEOOOO
OH YOU JUST WANT SOME LOVING!

4/6/19

'LITTLE GREEN TRUCK HELPING ME ALONG
HAD IT 16 YEARS OR SO NOW, IT'S SLOW AND SMELLS LIKE GAS.
BUT IT GETS THE JOB DONE.
MY LITTLE HELPER.
4/7/19
ON BIKE.
YOU SERVED ME SO WELL. NOW YOUR TIRE + HUB IS RUINED AND YOUR CRANKS NOW GROAN LIKE AN OLD SHIP.
BUT I WILL MEND YOU BECAUSE YOU ARE MY BEST FRIEND AND ALLY IN THIS WORLD.
4/8/19
OK, I FEEL LIKE I GOT ENOUGH DONE.
A CURSE TO NEVER FEEL LIKE YOU DID ENOUGH. SO RARE.
NOT ENOUGH.
WILL I GO THROUGH LIFE ALWAYS UNSATIFIED WITH MY EFFORTS?

4/9/19
WOOOOOOSH
THIS WIND SUCKS.
BUT THERES NO PLACE I'D RATHER BE.
4/10/19
I HATE WHEN I'M OFF.
WUMP
I HAD TO KEEP TELLING MYSELF THAT I HAD NO REASON TO BE IN A BAD MOOD.
BUT HOW CAN YOU ESCAPE YOURSELF?
I REALIZED I DON'T BELIEVE IN THE PAST. MY PAST.
HISTORICAL EVENTS, SURE. BUT HOW THEY REALLY WERE WHO KNOWS FOR SURE.
MY ABILITY TO SEE THINGS TRUE IS FLAWED AND SO IS MEMORY SO I KNOW WHAT I THINK I KNOW IS WRONG.
WAS IT GREEN? OR RED?

4/12/19
YOUR TURN
EAT! EAT!
THIS IS THE BEST BOARD GAME EVER!
4/13/19
?
!
RULE 1. DON'T MAKE EYE CONTACT WITH THE CRACK HEADS.
COULD NOT HEAR HER ANYWAY. OH WELL.
CAN'T SEE THE TRAIL
HA HA HA HA!
TO LAUGH LIKE A CHILD - IS GOLD.

4/15/19

WRRRRR
THAT MAY WORK.
AHH! PROOF OF CONCEPT!
WING WING WING
DO YOU HAVE A BACK PACK?
NO
THAT'S A LOT OF BEER MAN.
WELL IT WILL TASTE BETTER AFTER HAVING TO CARRY IT ALL THE WAY ACROSS TOWN.
YEAH, I WAS ATTACKED BY A GANGSTER BUT I KILLED HIM - I GOT 13 YEARS.
. . .
WHAT DO YOU SAY? HE HAD A LOT OF TIME TO PROCESS. HOW AWFUL.
. . .
ONLY A FOOL WOULD THINK SAYING ANYTHING WOULD DO ANY GOOD.
DAMN

4/18/19
I WASHED EVERY DISH & UNTENSIL I OWNED.
TOOK A WHILE....
BUT IT WAS GLORIOUS.
NEATO
4/19/19
THE NEW TRAIL
DISCOVERING A NEW TRAIL IS LIKE FINDING A SECRET.
?
WHAT WILL IT REVEAL?
OOOH
4/20/19
IT'S 4:20
YEAH.
HITLER'S BIRTHDAY.

4/21/19
OOF!
YOU OK?
YEAH, I AM.
4/22/19
SCOOP)
DOING SOMETHING PRODUCTIVE IS SO REWARDING, EVEN DOING CHORES...
.IS BETTER THAN NOT KNOWING WHAT TO DO.
4/23/19
WE RODE THROUGH THE WASH.
WE WERE NOT SUPPOSED TO.
BUT WE DID ANYWAY.
INNER CHILD INTACT.

4/24/19
"THERE ARE SO MANY THINGS IN LIFE THAT WILL REMAIN UN-RESOLVED.
AND THEY BEAT YOUR WELL BEING LIKE A HUGE HAMMER.
BUT TAKING YOUR LUMPS MAY BE YOUR ONLY OPTION AT TIMES.
4/25/19
THAT HAS TO BE IT.
AT LEAST I'M WILLING TO TRY.
LET'S SEE.
AND IN TRYING YOU'D BE AMAZED AT WHAT YOU GET.
I FIXED IT.
YOU DID?
4/26/19
THIS IS JESUS PAUL, WHAT'S YOUR LAST NAME I THINK YOU'RE ONE OF MY SONS.
HUH?
DO YOU NEED HELP WITH SOMETHING?
NO. I JUST MISS YOU.
OH.
OK THEN.
?????

4/27/19
PRRRRRR
THE LITTLE JOYFUL MOMENTS....
PRRR PRRRR
HOW WE FORGET.
PRRRRR
4/28/19
FEELS GOOD TO BE STRONG.
4/29/19
SO MUCH TO DO.
WILL I EVER GET IT DONE?
TO NOT TRY THOUGH, NOT AN OPTION.

4/30/19
SOMETIMES I'M DOING SOMETHING I LOVE AND MY HAPPINESS EVAPORATES.
I GOT HOME AND LOOKED AT PICTURES OF VINTAGE MTN BIKES AND I FELT BETTER.
COOL.
THERE'S NO POINT. JUST YOU, AT TIMES, WON'T MAKE SENSE, EVEN TO YOURSELF.
5/1/19
WOO
AAH!
OH YEAH, GOT SKILLS TONIGHT!
5/2/19
AN EPIC BATTLE
A MONTH-LONG JOURNEY THROUGH MANY PERILS
BUT VICTORY AT LAST.
LAUNDRY IS DONE.

5/3/19
ARE YOU HAPPY I SAID WE SHOULD RIDE BIKES THERE?
WELL YEAH...
RIDING BIKES ALWAYS MAKES ME HAPPY.
5/4/19
I DON'T KNOW HOW LONG IT WILL TAKE.
WELL SURE, SOME TIME BUT THE TALKING ABOUT HOW LONG...
.. JUST MAKES IT TAKE THAT MUCH LONGER.
5/5/19
ONE OF THE THINGS ABOUT WORKING WITH THE PUBLIC IS YOU SEE HOW PEOPLE ARE.
SURE.
I'LL BE BACK.
NOT.
A PATTERN WILL COME TO LIGHT- SLOWLY YOU BECOME AWARE OF IT.
LAST TIME I SEE HIM.
I GUESS AT THIS POINT IT COMES AS NO SURPRISE.
NO GREAT LOSS

5/6/19
THERE ARE NO SUCH THING AS THE "GOOD OLD DAYS" WHAT A LIE WE TELL OURSELVES.
THE GOOD OLD DAYS...
IN THE PAST, YOU LOOKED TOWARD THE FUTURE AND AS THAT IDEA OF WHAT SHOULD COME TO BE DID NOT. LE TURN TOWARDS THE PAST.
I REMEMBER.
WITH FLAWED EYES AND EARS AND A FLAWED MEMORY BANK WE HAVE ONLY FUZZY SNAP SHOTS OF THE PAST AND WE ONLY HAVE THE NOW.
WAS THAT RIGHT? HMM?
5/7/19
GO THIS WAY!
NOW THAT WAY!
WHY?
WHY NOT?
5/8/19
SOMETIMES I FORGET HOW GOOD I GOT IT.
11 DOLLARS AN HOUR.
IT'S GOOD TO LISTEN TO OTHER PEOPLE IF ONLY JUST TO GET PERSPECTIVE.
DAMN.
AND THAT WILL MAKE A BETTER PERSON OUT OF YOU.
THINGS AREN'T SO BAD.

5/9/19
STRESS
I HATE STRESS — I HAVE MORE THAN MY FAIR SHARE, HOW IT WEARS ME DOWN.
YES I DO THIS
I WISH I'D GET BETTER AT DEALING WITH IT THOUGH.
SOME DAY.
5/10/19
HOW MUCH WAS IT?
25.
YOU SNUCK IN?
YEAH..
VENUES DIE IF THEY DON'T MAKE MONEY YOU KNOW.
5/11/19
PUURRRR
...
PRRRRR
OH DID YOU GET YOUR WET PAWS ON MY DRAWINGS? OH WELL.

5/12/19
DO YOU THINK WE CAN STOP 1/2 WAY DOWN TO LOOK AT NATURE?
YOU MEAN DRINK YOUR BEER.
WELL, I HAVE TWO LEFT.
AH WOOOA!
YOU HAVE TO GO IN FRONT!
YOU HAVE TO SEE THE BUTTERFLIES!
WHAT TO DO WITH THESE BOOKS..
I'LL TAKE THEM IF YOU DON'T WANT THEM.
SURE.
REALLY! OH YOU MADE MY DAY!

5/15/19
I DON'T FEEL SPECIAL NOR DO I WANT TO. I AM AGAINST THE IDEA.
I AM ONE OF BILLIONS. BILLIONS OF PEOPLE. IT IS SO ARROGANT TO THINK YOU'RE ABOVE IT ALL.
ONLY THE EGO CAN MAKE YOU NOT SEE YOURSELF IN THE PROPER CONTEXT.
ONE OF MANY.
5/16/19
RAIN?
SO MUCH FOR WELDING.
WELL, THERE'S OTHER THINGS TO DO.
PRRR
5/17/19
JACOB'S TUMOR WENT INTO HIS SPINE.
HE HAS A FEW MONTHS LEFT.

5/18/19
LIFE MUST BE LIVED. IT MUST. REAL LIFE DEMANDS YOU LIVE A FULL LIFE.
THAT YOU DIG AND SCRAPE AND LEAVE NO STONE UNTURNED. THAT YOU DO IT ALL.
TO DO OTHERWISE IS TO CHEAPEN YOUR OWN LIFE EXPERIENCE
5/19/19
IT'S RAINING, YOU STILL WANT TO GO?
HELL YEAH.
ALL THIS MUD!
HAHA HAHA HA
SO GLAD I'M HERE RIGHT NOW.
5/20/19
I GOT IT.
YOU'RE CRADELING THAT OLD CAR PART LIKE A BABY.
MY FUEL PUMP BABY

5/21/19
ALL THE ADVENTURE ONE CAN HAVE...
AT THE PRICE
WOOOOU
...OF AN EFFORT
THAT WAS AWESOME!
5/22/19
JAGG PASSED AWAY LAST NIGHT.
WHAT DO YOU DO?
UN HUH HUH HUH HUH
YOU BE SAD, IT MEANS YOU CARED.
HUH HUH HUH HUH
5/23/19
WAM!
CLUNK!
TOOK 3 WEEKS BUT I GOT YOU OUT.

5/24/19
CAN YOU MAKE A VESSEL FOR JAGE'S ASHES? WITH BIKE PARTS?
SURE.
WELD
HOPE IT IS GOOD ENOUGH.
5/26/19
IN MY NEVER ENDING QUEST TO GET E-BIKES OFF TRAILS, I FIGHT ON ALL FRONTS.
PARK SERVICE GOT BACK TO ME.
IT IS A WAR FOUGHT ON MANY FRONTS
ONE BATTLE LOST.
BUT WE MUST KEEP FIGHTING..
ANOTHER SALVO FIRED.
MAIL
TO QBP
5/27/19
I TRIED TO, I DID BUT I THINK BY NOW I SHOULD KNOW BETTER, I SHOULD.
OK, THAT'S IT.
I FINISHED MY RIDE PREP AND I TRIED TO SIT AND DO NOTHING, TAKE IT EASY.
HMM
IT WAS TERRIBLE.
FUCK.

5/27/19
UP AND UP WE WENT.
HUF HUF
60 MILES, 3 MOUNTAIN PEAKS. 25 STARTED, NOT ALL FINISHED.
WE'RE TURNING OFF.
OK.
BUT WHAT A REWARDING EXPERIENCE TO GET TO THE END.
HARD ONE.
5/28/19
SOMETIMES IT IS EASIER TO BE SAD AROUND YOUR PETS THAN PEOPLE.
PRRRR
TO NOT HAVE TO TALK, THAT IS THE MAIN THING. TALKING IS SO WORTHLESS. I DON'T KNOW WHY PEOPLE CAN'T SEE THAT.
...
WHAT IS THE VALUE OF WORDS ANYWAY? I FIGURE THEY SHOULD BE MUCH LOWER THAN PEOPLE THINK.
PRNN.
5/29/19
IT KEPT RINGING AND RINGING.
RING
BUT I JUST STONE WALLED HIM. ANOTHER SOLICITOR, I HUNG UP ON HIM AND HE MUST HAVE LOST HIS MIND.
PERSISTENT!
RING
HE CALLED OVER 20 TIMES BUT HE WAS NOT ABLE TO CONQUER MY IRON WILL.
YOU'LL HAVE TO DO BETTER THAN THAT!

I'M READING A BOOK ON SURFING. I DON'T REALLY CARE FOR THE BEACH THAT MUCH ANYMORE.
THE HISTORY OF SURFING
BUT IT IS INTERESTING THOUGH. HOW IT ALL DEVELOPED AND ALL THE CHARACTERS ALONG THE WAY.
HMM
THE HISTORY OF SURF
BEING AT THE POINT WHERE ONE WAS AWARE THAT YOU WERE THERE WHEN IT WAS BECOMING SOMETHING MUST HAVE BEEN VERY EXCITING
I'LL CALL YOU WHEN IT'S DONE.
TEXT ME.
I CAN'T GET MESSAGES.
OH REALLY!
HOW ABOUT SETTING YOUR PHONE UP TO GET THEM? -WHAT THE HELL?
IS THAT SLICE OF PIZZA IN THE FRIDGE?
YEAH
HAVE YOU BEEN THINKING ABOUT IT?
ALL DAY.

6/2/19
UM-PA-PA-UM PA-PA
WHO IS PLAYING MEXICAN MUSIC OUTSIDE?
HEH.
MEXICANS CHERYL. MEXICANS PLAY MEXICAN MUSIC THEY ARE A FESTIVE PEOPLE YOU KNOW.
HAHA
6/3/19
VAROOM!
ON
SO GOOD JUST TO FIX SOMETHING YOURSELF.
GAS GAUGE IS OFF BUT IT RUNS.
EVEN IF YOU CAN PAY SOMEONE IT IS WORTH MORE TO PAY YOURSELF WITH A SENSE OF ACHIEVEMENT.
OK THEN.
6/4/19
YOU THINK THAT THINKING ABOUT AN IDEA OR TALKING ABOUT WILL MAKE IT COME ABOUT.
NO. I DON'T BELIEVE IN ESP OR ESPN, OR ANYTHING.
TALK DOES NOT MAKE THINGS HAPPEN, IT IS PRETTY LOW ON MY VALUE SCALE.

6/5/19
I FORGOT MILK!
SKEERR.
THAT WAS CLOSE! CAN'T GO WITHOUT COFFEE IN THE MORNING!
6/6/19
JAGG'S DEAD? WHA? NO WAY. REALLY? NO.
I FIND MYSELF IN THIS PLACE TOO OFTEN NOW— THE BRINGER OF HEAVY NEWS.
YEAH
BUT A BURDEN THAT ONLY MEANS YOU ARE HUMAN BY BEING WILLING TO CARRY IT.
SORRY.
6/7/19
HOLY SHIT HAHA!
AN OLD FRIENDS, SO GOOD TO HAVE THEM.
SO WHAT'S NEW?
HUM HUH
SOMETIMES BEING REMINDED OF THE PAST MAKES ME BE GLAD IT IS THE NOW.
HE'S NEW!

6/8/19
"OK THEN - DOES IT MATTER? ? ? ? ? ? ? ? ? ? ? ? ? ? ? ? ? ? ? ?
EVERYTHING AROUND ME JUST DISOLVES INTO AN INERT STATE. PEOPLE SEEK IT - TO BECOME NOTHING.
AND THEY GET WHAT THEY SEEK MORE OFTEN THAN NOT.
WHAT'S NEW?
NOTHING.
6/9/19
I CAN'T EXPECT OTHERS TO UNDERSTAND HOW AWFUL IT FEELS NOT TO BE MOVING FORWARD.
NEW IDEAS, THE DOING OF THINGS IS SO IMPORTANT - ALL I CAN SEE IS THE HORIZON AND WANT TO GET THERE TO SEE MORE.
ON THE OTHER SIDE OF THE COIN - MOST PEOPLE WANT A SIMPLE LIFE WHERE NOTHING HAPPENS BUT COMFORT AND PREDICTABILITY - DIFFERENT WORLD.
6/10/19
I HATE NEGATIVE EMOTIONS, GETTING INTO A FIGHT WITH SOMEONE CLOSE TO YOU IS THE WORST.
I'VE NEVER RECOVERED FROM A SINGLE ONE, EACH BATTLE LEAVES A WOUND THAT WILL NOT HEAL.
HUF HUF HUF
AND I'VE BEEN WOUNDED TOO MUCH

6/11/19
WELL, IT'S BALANCE.
I LIKE THAT.
THAT IS WHAT IS EVERYONE SEEKS IS SOME SEMBELANCE OF BALANCE IN THIER LIVES...
...THAT ALL THINGS ARE WHERE THEY NEED TO BE.
6/12/19
TODAY I BUILT A WHEEL AT HOME INSTEAD OF BUILDING IT AT WORK
IT WAS RELAXING AS I SOLVED ONE PROBLEM WITH MY HANDS..
I SOLVED ANOTHER WITH MY HEART.
I NEED TO MAKE IT RIGHT.
WE'LL GO UP THE CANYON
OK
SO WE DID
CRANK CRANK CRANK
I FORGOT HOW HARD THIS WAS!

6/14/19
I'M GIVING YOU THIS BIKE.
YOU CAN'T GIVE ME THAT!
YES I CAN.
YOU TURNED ME ON TO THIS GREAT THING AND I WANT TO RETURN THE FAVOR.
SO TAKE THE BIKE, IT IS MY WAY OF SAYING THANK-YOU.
LOOK, DON'T CALL TO SEE IF I'M BUSY IN 10 MINUTES
IF I COULD SEE INTO THE FUTURE 10 MINUTES I'D LINE UP WINNING LOTTERY TICKETS ONE AFTER ANOTHER.
AND NEVER HAVE TO ANSWER THE PHONE AGAIN.
OOOOO!
YOU OK?
YEAH SAGE.
I SMELL LIKE SAGE, I GUESS I DON'T HAVE TO TAKE A SHOWER NOW.

6/17/19
IT WAS FUN
YEAH
THAT'S THE KEY TO HAPPINESS...
HAVING SOMETHING TO LOOK FORWARD TO.
6/18/19
IT IS A RE-OCCURING THEME IN LIFE..
TO RIDE AND HAVE ADVENTURES. TO GO PLACES OTHERS DO NOT GO, I'VE MENTIONED IT 100'S OF TIMES.
RAD!
BUT GOOD THEMES ARE WORTH REPEATING.
ANOTHER REWARDING EXPERIENCE.
6/19/19
THE BIGGEST LIAR TO YOURSELF IS YOU.
YOU WILL TELL YOURSELF TO NOT DO THINGS. TO BE LAZY, TO EAT BAD, NOT EXERCISE ETC.
YOU LIE AND SAY THE PATH OF LEAST RESISTANCE GOES TO A GOOD PLACE, BUT IT ALWAYS LEADS TO NOWHERE.
DEAD END.

6/20/19
A LIFE. WHILE IT SEEMS SO IMPORTANT, I GATHER IT IS NOT.
SO MANY LIVES AND SO MUCH TIME. HUMANITY IS NOT EVEN A COMMA IN THE SENTENCE THAT IS THE UNIVERSE.
WE ARE HERE NOW AND IN A BLINK OF TIME ALL WE EVER DID IS GONE FOREVER. WE ARE AT THE END OF TIME AND SOON WILL BE LEFT BEHIND BY IT.
6/21/19
HEY NICE BIKE YOU GOT ANY THING TO SMOKE?
NAH
I'M THE NICEST GUY YOU KNOW I CAN SHAPESHIFT INTO ANOTHER FORM..
SORRY I'LL BE HOME SOON.
NO ONE THERE
OK HAVE A GOOD DAY.
BIKE, YOU'RE COMING WITH ME.
OH FAIRNESS. I WILL ALWAYS BE IN YOUR VANGUARD. IN THE THICK OF BATTLE AGAINST THEM.
THE SELFISH, THE SELF CENTERED, THE UNFAIR OF THE WORLD.
UNTIL MY SWORD IS CHIPPED AND CRACKED AND I AM CARRIED OUT ON MY SHIELD, I WILL FIGHT FOR YOU.

6/23/19
SIR, I CAN HELP YOU? SIR I CAN TAKE YOU? SIR?
COFFEE PLEASE.
I WAS AHEAD OF YOU
YOU WERE PLAYING WITH YOUR PHONE, THEY CALLED YOU 3 TIMES— SO THATS ON YOU MAN.
6/24/19
I KNOW IT IS IN MY HEAD, BUT I HATE FEELING LIKE I DID NOT GET ENOUGH DONE.
IT GNAWS AT ME AND I FEEL LIKE I HAVE FAILED MYSELF.
NOT LIKE LOOKING FROM THE OUTSIDE, YOU'D KNOW.
YOU DID ALL THAT?
EH
6/25/19
THIS WAY!
WE WENT THROUGH CHUTES AND TRAILS, IN DITCHES AND OVER HILLS.
AND WE CAN SAY THAT WE WERE TRULY ALIVE.
GOOD RIDE?
FUCK YEAH!

6/27/19
SO, YOU HAVE ANY VICES?
NOPE. DON'T DRINK, SMOKE OR DO ANY DRUGS.
I LIKE COFFEE. I QUIT FOR A YEAR SO I WAS SURE IT DIDN'T OWN ME. I LIKE TO READ A LOT.
I GUESS I JUST WANT TO GET THE MOST OUT OF LIFE, THAT I'M ADDICTED TO.
6/28/19
I'M GOING TO WIN THE LOTTERY AND MAKE THIS PLACE HUGE!
WE'LL PUT A STORAGE BIN IN THE BACK AND CLEAN IT UP.
CLEAN?
WELL, I'M NOT GOING TO HOLD MY BREATH.
6/29/19
NEED IT NOW.
YOU HAVE TO WAIT YOUR TURN.
NEED IT. NOW.
THIS WILL NEVER END, WILL IT?
BUT SO IS ME NEVER GIVING IN.
BYE.

6/30/19
I DON'T NEED THIS BOOK TO FIX BIKES.
How To Fix
BUT YOU'RE JUST STARTING OUT.
How To Fix
SO I'D LIKE YOU TO HAVE IT.
THE BURDEN
I'D SAY THE THING THAT HELPS ONE ALONG THE BEST IS HOW TO CARRY A BURDEN.
BECAUSE EVERYONE YOU SEE IS CARRYING ONE TOO.
GO SLOW
WELD WELD
WELD
AFTER A YEAR OF GETTING ALL THE PARTS TOGETHER IT IS NOW COMING TOGETHER.
ALL I HAVE TO EAT IS HOT DOG BUNS
BUT IT WAS WORTH THE WAIT.
AT LONG LAST.

7/2/19
THIS RIDE IS SO HARD! YOU'RE TRYING TO KILL ME?!
I'M NEW
HARD? THIS WAS AN EASY ONE.
EASY?! WHA??
HA HA HA
7/3/19
I'M LOANER AND TIRE WILL TO DO.
OH BOY.
I'VE FOUND FEW PEOPLE A SANE AND EVEN LESS ARE RATIONAL.
COO-COO
HANG ON TO THE GOOD ONES.
TOTALLY NUTS.
7/4/19
IT IS FUNNY.
HELLO!
EVERYWHERE I GO I SEE PEOPLE THAT KNOW ME.
LONG TIME NO SEE.
I GUESS I MUST BE DOING SOMETHING RIGHT.
PERHAPS.

7/5/19
RARELY DOES AN IDEA JUST POP IN MY HEAD, I GET THEM BY WORKING IT OUT.
I THINK YOU CAN GET GOOD AT COMING UP WITH IDEAS BY PRACTICING THE THOUGHT PROCESS
LIKE ANYTHING OVER TIME YOU GET GOOD AT IT.
!
7/6/19
THE EFFORT.
I DON'T KNOW WHEN I LEARED THAT THE EFFORT IS WHAT MATTERS. IT MUST BE EXPENETIAL AND/OR
ANYTHING LESS IS SIMPLY NOT ENOUGH.
7/7/19
SO MUCH HARDER THAN NORMAL.
EVEN DOWNHILL IS HARD
6TH PLACE. NOT BAD BUT I KNOW I CAN DO BETTER.
GASP
WEEZE

7/8/19

WHERE DID THAT WOUND COME FROM?
BECAUSE I GOUGE, CUT, BURN & SCRAPE MYSELF SO OFTEN I COULD NOT REMEMBER WHERE IT CAME FROM.
? ? ? ? ? ? ? ?
ALL I KNOW IS SMALL WOUNDS ARE JUST PART OF LIFE.
OH WELL
7/9/19
WORLDS APART.
SO MANY OF MY FRIENDS HAVE MADE THE TRANSITION TO ADULTHOOD.
HERE'S THE BABY PICTURES
AND I STILL RESIDE IN THE FAIRY REALM.
THAT'S COOL.
ANOTHER ONE GONE.
7/10/19
THE KEY TO SUCCESS IS HAVING DIGNITY
IT IS?
YEAH—HAVE THE DIGNITY TO WANT TO DO A GOOD JOB.
HMM.. THAT DOES MAKE SENSE.

7/11/19
OK- I RE-TAPPED THE THREAD ON YOUR CRANK, ADJUST THE BRAKES AND PUT THE PEDALS ON.
DO I OWE YOU ANYTHING?
YEAH, THAT'S HOW IT WORKS
7/12/19
THE TRAIL WAS MOSTLY ALL MINE, ONLY ONE OTHER GUY ON A BIKE
I LIKE TO MAKE THE MENTAL NOTE TO MYSELF THAT THE JOYFUL THINGS WE DO IN LIFE ARE FLEETING AT BEST.
AND THUS NOT TAKE THEM, WHEN THEY APPEAR, FOR GRANTED.
NICE DAY.
7/13/19
HOW MUCH?
85.
70.
NO
85?
YEP.
ALL-DAY-!

2/14/19
KEEP GOING!
HUF HUF
ONE MORE LAP!
P.5.1
NOT QUITTING...
AS LONG AS IT TAKES!
GLUG GLUG
2/15/19
A LITTLE SENSE OF ACHIEVEMENT- HOW SO MANY MISS OUT ON IT.
PEOPLE WHO WORK IN OFFICE SPACES MAY NEVER SEE HOW THEY MADE SOMETHING HAPPEN. JUST COGS.
BUT TO TAKE AN IDEA AND MAKE IT REAL- THAT IS ONE OF THE MOST REWARDING EXPERIENCES ONE CAN HAVE.
2/16/19
THAT WAS AWESOME!
THAT'S WHAT IT IS ABOUT.
HAVING LIFE- AFIRMING EXPERIENCES

7/17/19
DON'T FORGET.
FORGETTING IS AN ODD THING - MOST PEOPLE SPEND A LOT OF TIME AND MONEY FORGETTING THINGS.
GLUG GLUG
SOME OF US ARE DOOMED TO NOT FORGET A THING.
YOU REMEMBERED!
YES, CURSED WITH A GOOD MEMORY.
7/18/19
DO YOU HAVE A FAMILY?
NO.
I THOUGHT YOU DO, WHY DON'T YOU HAVE A FAMILY?
I DON'T WANT ONE.
MAKE IT WITH 3 ADJUSTABLE POINTS MUST TAKE 29" WHEELS & 27" WHEELS LOOK LIKE A CRUISER MUST MAKE A LIST OF PARTS & TOOLS.
FRAME & FORK FIXTURE, MILL, 4130 TUBING FORK DROPOUTS, REAR DROPOUTS · TUBING BENDERS, HOLE SAWS AQUIRE ALL... FIGURE OUT CUTS ETC.
A YEAR LATER
STEP 1 DONE.

7/20/19
"WITH MACHINES I HAVE ALMOST UNLIMITED PATENCE
Hmmm
THEY CAN, FOR THE MOST PART, WITH A GOOD EYE AND SKILLED HANDS BE GUIDED BACK TO USEFULNESS...
THAT DID IT.
HUMAN BEINGS CANNOT
WILL YOU BE BUSY WHEN I GET THERE?
7/21
7 MILES UP AND UP.
HUF HUF HUF
AND THEN DOWN & DOWN
SLOW IS FAST.
ANOTHER LIFE-AFIRMING-POSITIVE EXPERIENCE
7/22/19
OH MEOW MEOW WERE YOU LOCKED INSIDE?
WELL NOT YOUR FAULT YOU CRAPPED IN THE HOUSE. NOT ON MY BED PLEASE.
OH! BY THE TOILET! GOOD KITTY!
AHH THE LITTLE THINGS.

7/23/19
"I DON'T WANT TO FORGET THE GOOD TIMES.
WOAH!
I WANT TO SAVOR EACH MOMENT, GET THE MOST OUT OF WHAT IS GOOD IN THIS LIFE.
AND NOT LET THE BAD THINGS CLOUD THE MANY GOOD THINGS THAT DO HAPPEN, THAT WE TEND TO FORGET.
THAT WAS GOOD.
7/24/19
WHAT TO DO?
WHAT TO DO NEXT? MOST PEOPLE DON'T HAVE MUCH TO DO SO THEY BECOME PASSIVE TV/INTERNET WATCHERS. SO SAD.
FOR ME AT LEAST, HAVING THAT NEXT THING IS THE BEST THING IN LIFE - TO LOOK FORWARD TO SOMETHING.
NEXT & NEXT.
7/25/19
HEY PJ, WHAT'S IN THE BAG?
FRENCH FRIES.
FOR YOU!
ATH SOUM!

7/26/19
"SO MANY KINGDOMS HAVE RISEN AND FALLEN IN THE EONS OF TIME I FIND MY PLACE IN TIME TO MEAN LESS & LESS.
WILL OUR LAND BE HERE IN 100 YEARS? OR A 1000? DOUBTFUL. SOME OTHER PLACE WILL RISE TO THE FRONT OF THE WORLD.
IN CONTEXT, I TRY NOT TO FORGET THAT I AM FORTUNATE TO BE HERE, NOW.
COULD BE WAAAAY WORSE.
7/27/19
OUT OF MY NORMAL CONDITIONER TRY THIS ONE.
BIG POOF
OK THEN.
7/28/19
ONE MORE THING TO GIVE AWAY...
?
FOR ALL THE HARD WORK YOU DO, FOR PUTTING THIS ON...
FOR ME?
THANK YOU!

7/29/19
Prnn.
OK
Prnn
PRrnn
I GUESS TYPING IS OUT FOR NOW.
Prnn
7/30/19
LIFE IS GOOD.
IS IT SO? IF I THINK IT, WILL IT COME TRUE? IS IT HERE AND I DON'T SEE IT.
LIFE IS GOOD?
I GATHER IT IS BECAUSE WHAT YOU MAKE OF IT IS UP TO YOU.
LIFE IS GOOD.
BECAUSE THAT IS WHAT I WORK FOR SO IT IS AN IDEA MADE REAL.
7/31/19
I NEVER FEEL MORE ALIVE OR AT PEACE WHEN I'M HAVING AN ADVENTURE.
THE ADVENTURE DOES NOT HAVE TO BE EPIC. A LITTLE ONE IS GOOD.
LET'S GO THAT WAY!
AND A LITTLE GOOD, WELL, I KNOW HOW TO SPREAD THAT AROUND.

8/1/19
I NEED TWO TIRES AND TUBES
OK
YOU DON'T EVEN WANT TO KNOW WHY. SLASHED. MY WIFE DID IT.
I DON'T
OH
HA HA. THAT'S LOVE I GUESS
8/2
YOU HAVE BRAKE CABLE?
YEAH
HOW MANY STRANDS ARE IN THE CABLE?
HA HA HA HA HA HA HA!
...
8/3/19
DON'T FORGET HOW LITTLE THINGS BRIGHTEN YOUR DAY.
BEEP BEEP.
COFFEE'S READY.
AND MANY LITTLE THINGS STRUNG TOGETHER MAKE THINGS GREAT.
A LITTLE CUP OF JOY.
AND IF YOU DO IT LONG ENOUGH, WELL THAT'S A GREAT LIFE.
GOOD PLACE TO START.

8/4/19

DIRTBALL NO!

I HAVE NOT EVEN FLUSHED YET.

YOU ARE DISGUSTING JUST LIKE YOUR OWNER

MEOW

THAT IS THE FARTTHEST I'VE GONE ON A BIKE.

YEAH?

THE MORE YOU DO IT, THE EASIER IT GETS.

SIP.

I SEE THAT GLEAM IN YOUR EYE!

HA HA HA

WELL HE HAS THE COMMON CURSE OF MIDDLE AGE MEN.

THEY GET THIS IDEA THAT THIER OPINIONS HAVE VALUE TO OTHERS.

SIMPLY IS NOT TRUE.

8/7/19
IT WILL REQUIRE DEEP THINKING.
I DON'T FEEL LIKE I'M THAT SMART BUT I DO TAKE THE TIME TO REALLY THINK THINGS THROUGH.
MORE EFFORT.
I AT LEAST UNDERSTAND THAT THE ANSWER MAY NOT BE AN EASY ONE TO DISCOVER.
PERHAPS
FOR
MY TOIL WILL NOT BE REMEMBERED. MANY HAVE TOILED BEFORE ME.
BUT THOSE OF US THAT DO, TOIL WE ARE CLOSER TO THE GROUND THAN OTHERS
FINISHED.
I WENT TO A RETRO ARCADE.
I REMEMBER PLAYING A LOT OF THESE GAMES AND BEING GOOD AT THEM
BUT I WAS NOT NOSTALGIC.

8/10/19
STAYING AHEAD.
HUF HUF HUF
STAYING AHEAD SEEMS LIKE A RACE YOU CAN'T WIN BUT IN DOING SO YOU MAY NOT HAVE THINGS POUNCE ON YOU.
AH!
AND IT IS MUCH HARDER TO CATCH UP THAN TO JUST STAY AHEAD
WE SHOULD GET THEM TO COME OUT OUR WAY.
YEAH.
THEY'D LIKE IT.
THOSE OTHER PLACES ARE JUST A BUNCH OF HOMOGENOUS CORPORATE BARF.
AWFUL.
HA HA
8/12/19
SO MUCH LIES AHEAD
SEEING THE HORIZON IS A BLESSING AND A CURSE. YOU CAN SEE ALL THAT YOU WANT TO DO
AND SEE HOW YOU'LL NEVER GET TO DO IT ALL.
SIMPLY NOT ENOUGH TIME.

8/13/19
40 MILES WE WENT OUT AND BACK OVER DARK ROADS & BUSY NEON TOURIST TRAPS.
LITTLE TWINKLING LIGHTS AMONG THE LIGHTS OF CARS.
LITTLE LIGHTS OF FREEDOM.
I SHOULD JUST DO IT NOW.
WHEN SOMETHING NEEDS TO BE DONE JUST DO IT NOW. WHY WAIT TILL THE NEED BECOMES DIRE?
WON'T TAKE LONG.
WHY MAKE MORE STRESS FOR YOURSELF? DON'T WE HAVE ENOUGH OF THAT ALREADY?
DONE & DONE.
8/15/19
WHAT MAKE SENSE.
THE EASY ROAD
THE HARD ROAD.
THE PATH THAT IS EASY BEARS POOR FRUIT IT MAY SEEM LIKE THE BEST PATH TO TAKE.
SO SO.
BUT ONCE YOU SUMMIT THE HARD PATH, ALL OTHER PATHS BECOME APPEARENT.
EASIER NOW.

8/16/19
DIRT BALL NO!
OH SHIT!
I'LL GO AROUND!
MOMENTS LATER
YOU GOT HIM!
THAT WAS A CLOSE ONE!
HEHE
LOOK AT THESE PEOPLE WHEN THEY GO TO AN ART GALLERY THEY BREAK OUT THIER "ART" CLOTHES OR WHAT?
LIKE THEY RAIDED THIER GRANDMOTHERS WARDROBE SO THEY CAN LOOK ARTY - SO PRENTENTIOUS!
LET'S CHECK THAT LEG.
OK LOOKS GOOD
WELL ONE LESS THING TO WORRY ABOUT TO BE REPLACED BY ANOTHER

8/19/19
SOMETIMES I WONDER WHY I PUT SO MUCH EFFORT INTO THINGS.
I COULD BE PASSING BUT WOULD I FEEL LIKE LIFE WAS WORTH
ONE MORE.
SOMEHOW I DOUBT I'D SEE A GLIMMER OF HAPPINESS BY BEING A SQUARE.
8/20/19
LIFE IS GOOD. I GET TO RIDE BIKES WITH FRIENDS, JUMP CURBS, DO WHEELIES ETC.
WE GET TO EAT PIZZA, JOKE AROUND. PLAN AN ADVENTURE - ENJOY OURSELVES.
AND ALL AROUND US IS HOMELESSNES. GRINDING POVERTY, DRUG ADDICTION AND LONELYNESS. NOT TO FORGET IS KEY.
8/21/19
GRRR
?
OH NO MEOW MEOW! YOU GOT A RAT, GET OUTSIDE WITH THAT!
GOOD BOY.

3/22/19
THE SENSATION THAT I'M MOVING TOO SLOW IN LIFE.
MY MIND RACES AHEAD BUT I MUST SIT BACK AND WATCH THINGS DEVELOP SLOWLY.
IT WILL TAKE WEEKS TO FINISH
WHILE OTHERS SEE PRODUCTIVITY I SEE UNFINISHED BUSINESS.
WEEKS!
8/23/19
IT'S 17
HOW ABOUT 15?
NO CAN DO. HAVE A GOOD DAY NOW*
15.
* MEANS GO AWAY.
I WONDER IF WE ACTUALLY THOUGHT THAT WOULD WORK.
8/24/19
IS THAT TRUMP WITH A BICYCLE?
WHY DON'T YOU READ IT?
INSTEAD OF WASTING MY TIME ASKING ME WHAT IT IS, YOU COULD JUST READ IT.
I'M NOT WASTING YOUR TIME.
YOU'RE DOING IT RIGHT NOW!

8/25/19
IT WAS A METH INDUCED PYCHOSIS..
SO I LISTENED TO THE WHOLE TALE. IT WAS OUT THERE... AND LONG.
IF I CUT HER UP THEN THE TV SHOW WOULD STOP.
ALL I CAN SAY IS..
I'M GLAD I NEVER DID DRUGS.
8/26/19
WILL THE FALL OF BERLIN BOOK BE REMOVED FROM MY HOUSE NOW THAT YOU FINISHED IT?
UH HUH
YEAH THAT'S THE THING ABOUT BOOKS..
THERE'S ALWAYS ANOTHER ONE.
9/22/19
I REALIZED I DON'T REALLY MISS PEOPLE THAT ARE OUT OF MY LIFE FOR WHATEVER REASON, I AM MISSING AN IDEA.
THE IDEA THAT YOU CAN HANG ON TO THOSE HAPPY MOMENTS AND THOSE MOMENTS REPRESENT THE WHOLE SPAN OF THAT LOST RELATIONSHIP.
1=8? YES.
AND THE IDEA THAT ANY MOMENT OR MEMORY OF A MOMENT CONSISTS FOR WHAT IT REALLY WAS FOR THE WHOLE SPAN — I KNOW THIS NOT TO BE TRUE.
1=0

8/28/19
I TOLD A GUY WITH AN E-BIKE TODAY I WOULD NOT HELP HIM.
YOU? DID.?
YES I DID.
I PUT MY PRINCIPLES BEFORE PROFIT.
8/29/19
I'D SEE HIM IN HIS GARAGE AS I RODE BY.
TV
I FIGURE HE WAS RETIRED. HE'D BE OUT THERE ALL THE TIME - DOING NOTHING. SITTING.
THE OUTCOME WAS AS PREDICTED...
IF YOU DON'T KEEP MOVING, YOU DIE.
8/30/19
I LOVE THIS PLACE!
IF THERE WERE MORE PLACES LIKE THIS THE WORLD WOULD BE A BETTER PLACE!
HMMM.

8/31/14

YOU'RE LIKE NO ONE ELSE.

YEAH?

I'M SURE THEY SAID THE SAME THING ABOUT HITLER.

9/1/14

OK THANK YOU
THANK YOU
YES. THANK YOU.
YOU'RE WELCOME.
OK BYE
OK
OK
YES.
OK THANKS.
OK
THANKS.

SO MUCH TALKING IT WILL NEVER END, WILL IT?

I JUST WISH PEOPLE WOULD LISTEN TO THEMSELVES TALK. PERHAPS THEY'D SAY LESS BUT SAY IT WELL.

9/2/14

4 MILES UP NEAR 100°...

HOW COME ONLY THE SKINNY GUYS ARE AT THE FRONT?

WELL, ONE LEADS TO ANOTHER

BIKE
BIKE

9/3/19
I" NEED SOME TUDES BUT I'M ON A SCOOTER, DO YOU THINK I'LL MAKE IT BEFORE YOU CLOSE?
I'M ON A SCOOTER. I HEARD YOU. ARE YOU SCOOTING HERE OR TALKING ABOUT SCOOTING HERE?
YOU KNOW TALKING ABOUT IT WON'T GET YOU HERE FASTER.
9/4/19
THE TIME YOU LOSE HAVING TO DEAL WITH PEOPLE'S B.S. HOW MUCH HAVE I LOST?
TO ME AT LEAST, IT SEEMS LIKE IT TAKES LESS ENERGY TO DO SOMETHING RIGHT THAN TO DO IT WRONG.
WHY DID YOU NOT JUST SAY THAT IN THE FIRST PLACE?
BUT WHAT DO I KNOW? I'M THE CRAZY ONE RIGHT?
IT DOES NOT NEED TO BE THAT HARD!
9/5/19
YOU'LL LIVE A LONG TIME DOING THAT.
THAT'S THE THING HUH? PEOPLE ARE OBSESSED WITH LIVING A LONG TIME...
..BUT NOT WITH LIVING WELL.
THAT'S DEEP!
HA!

9/6/19
A VOW TO STAY IN THE FIGHT,
ANYONE CAN LEAVE THE BATTLE AT ANY TIME. MANY DO. BUT THE NARROWER PATH...
...ONLY ALLOWS ONE TO MOVE FORWARD OR DIE TRYING.
CLARK
I HAVE TO GIVE THIS BACK TO YOU.
OK?
I HAVE TO MOVE OUT OF MY HOUSE MY DAD WENT TO JAIL.
WHAT?
OH NO MAX, WHAT HAPPENED?
I'LL TELL YOU LATER.
9/8/19
DON'T FORGET...
SO GLAD I REMEMBERED TO WASH THIS DISH. IT'D BE UNFAIR FOR CHERYL TO DO IT.
REMEMBERING IS CARING.

ALL I HAVE LEFT IS THE VAN.
IT WILL HAVE TO WORK.
YOU GOT ALL THAT SHIT IN THERE?!
YEP!
CONQURED THAT CHALLENGE!
YEP.
9/10/19
LOOKS LIKE A DIRT ROAD, LET'S TRY IT.
LOOK! A SHOOTING STAR!
COOL!
WHAT? WHERE ARE YOU GOING?
DOWN!
9/11/19
WORKING WITH THE PUBLIC CAN TEST ANYONE'S RESOLVE.
REALLY?
I HAVE MY WEAK MOMENTS.
HOW ABOUT SO?
HOW ABOUT YOU GO AWAY?
THEN I GO HOME AND MY LITTLE PALS ARE HAPPY TO SEE ME - IT'S GOOD.

9/12/19
YOU SHOULD BE A SPERM DONOR.
WHAT?
YOU'RE JUST SO SMART, DON'T YOU THINK SOMEONE WOULD WANT TO HAVE A KID LIKE YOU?
HMM
THAT'S NOT GOING TO HAPPEN.
13 NINJAS
IN A MOON LIT SKY ON BIKES.
SHURIKENS FLEW, PEDALS TURNED, SWORDS SWUNG. THERE WAS THRILL, ADVENTURE, SWEAT, AND OF COURSE, SMILES
CAN I RETURN A BIKE. SHE DOES NOT LIKE IT.
I DON'T TRY AND SELL THINGS TO PEOPLE BUT YOU MADE A CHOICE -
A CHOICE YOU'RE HELD ACCOUNTABLE FOR..

9/15/19
I GOT TO DO WHAT I WANTED TO DO TODAY.
I AM JUST REMINDING MYSELF THAT MANY PEOPLE DO NOT GET TO DO WHAT THEY WANT TO DO.
YOU CAN'T GO RIDE YOUR BIKE TODAY!
AND NOT TAKE THAT FREEDOM FOR GRANTED.
9/16/19
WHAT DO YOU KNOW?
SO LITTLE.
I'VE READ 1000 OR MAYBE 1000 BOOKS AND...
STILL ONLY KNOW I KNOW NOTHING.
ONLY SLIGHTLY UP FROM HERE.
THE BEST DEFENSE VS. A BUMMER LIFE IS TO GO OUT AND DO THINGS.
OH SHIT!
HAVE ADVENTURES. EXPLORE. TRY HARD. SEEK THE NEW. HAVE A CURIOUS MIND.
WHERE DOES IT GO?
I DON'T KNOW, LET'S FIND OUT.
SHARE WITH OTHERS. MAKE LAUGHTER, EVOKE POSITIVITY. WELL, A PIPE DREAM BUT A GOOD PLACE TO START.
HA HA HA HA HA!

9/18/19
WHAT HAPPENED TO THAT GUY?
HE ASKED TO BE TAKEN OFF THE GROUP TEXTS SO HE HAD A PROBLEM AND SAID NOTHING OR THERE WAS MOST LIKELY NOTHING WRONG BUT HE MADE UP A PROBLEM THAT WAS NOT THERE.
EH GROW-UP
EITHER WAY...
FUCK EM'
9/19/19
THANKS FOR THE REFERENCE, CAN I BUY YOU LUNCH?
NAH.
YOU CAN BUY ME LUNCH IF YOU GET THE JOB.
LATER...
I'M BUYING YOU LUNCH.
OH YEAH! CONGRATS!
9/20/19
3 BUCKS
HOW ABOUT 2?
REALLY? YOU'RE GOING TO GRIND ME FOR A DOLLAR?!
I'M POOR.
YEAH, WELL I DON'T WANT TO JOIN YOU. 3 BUCKS.

9/21/19

ALL RELIGION IS A CONTRADICTION OF NATURE.

ALL LIFE IS TIED TO THE CHANGE OF THE SEASONS, THE MOVEMENT OF THE PLANET AROUND THE SUN. CYCLE AFTER CYCLE, BIRTH DEATH & RENEWAL. RELIGION TRIES TO GO AGAINST THAT.
RUMB+LE!

HOW MANY GODS HAVE CAME AND WENT THROUGH THE EONS AND NATURE JUST BRUSHED THEM ASIDE. SO, WHICH ONE IS TRUTH?

9/22/19
I KNEW IT WOULD BE HARD.
HUF HUF
HUF
HUF

BUT I WENT ANYWAY.
¡HUF HUF HUF

BECAUSE I KNEW I COULD.
HUF HUF

9/25/19

ANYTIME? THE TIME CAN ONLY BE NOW...
NOW.

THE PAST AND THE FUTURE CAN ONLY BE SEEN THROUGH A LENZ. WHAT YOU THINK YOU SEE IS OUT OF FOCUS.

BUT NOW, WELL IT HAS THE BEST CHANCE OF BEING SEEN CLEARLY.

9/24/19
WAS A 'CYOTE
?
PEOPLE TELL ME THE MOST AMAZING THINGS
WE WERE GOING TO KILL HER BUT I GOT HER TO COME AROUND.
LIFE NEVER CEASES TO BE INTERESTING.
WOW
9/25/19
WELL, I'M INTO TESLA + SPACE X AND WHAT THE FUTURE WILL BRING.
TECHNOLOGY WILL MAKE THE WORLD A BETTER PLACE.
YEAH? I DON'T THINK GIZMOS MAKE PEOPLE HAPPY. SUICIDE'S UP THAT'S FOR SURE.
9/26/19
MEOW.
IT'S 5 AM...
MEOW.
I GUESS THAT'S NOT TOO EARLY TO BE FED.
MEOW

9/22/19

WE EXPLORE AN IDEA.
FACTOR IN 2 DOLLARS FOR HARDWARE.
THINKING OF EVERY ANGLE IS IMPORTANT.
WE CAN USE SCAVENGED CARDBOARD FOR PACKAGING.
DEEP THINKING, A THING OF THE PAST IS REQUIRED.
WE FORGOT X, Y, + Z
OH YEAH.
9/28/19
BE A POSITIVE FORCE IN THE UNIVERSE.
NOT FOR PRAISE OR A REWARD. THEY ARE NICE THOUGH.
YOU'RE THE BEST ONE.
DO IT BECAUSE IT IS THE THING TO EXIST FOR
WELL THANK YOU!
9/29/19
20 + MILES TOTAL.
BUT THE VIEW...
HOW'S IT GOING?
WELL IT'S WORTH IT.
COULDN'T BE BETTER

9/30/19

10/1/19

10/2/19

10/3/19
IT DOES NOT MATTER WHERE YOU LIVE - IT IS JUST A PLACE.
WHAT YOU DO WITH IT IS UP TO YOU.
I KNOW I'D MAKE THE FUN WHEREEVER I WENT.
10/4/19
FLAT.
WENT THROUGH 6 PATCH KITS AND ALL HAD NO GLUE.
SOME CYCLIST I AM.
FINALLY FOUND ONE.
IF I CAN'T DO THIS WHAT GOOD AM I?
10/5/19
10 MINUTES LEFT, WHAT CAN I DO?
WHAT CAN'T I DO? STARTING SOMETHING, ANYTHING IS BETTER THAN DOING NOTHING.
SWEEP
SWEOP
WEEP
SW
SO THAT IS WHAT I'LL DO.

LAST LAP, WE GOT THIS...
HUF HUF
WOOOH!!
I KNOW I GAVE IT MY ALL - THAT'S WHAT COUNTS.
HOW DO YOU FEEL?
TIRED BUT GOOD.
OK YOU AND ME MR. BROOM.
I MAKE WAR WITH THE BROOM, THERE IS SO MUCH TO BATTLE...
AND TO AN END, TO MAKE PEACE THAT IS THE HARDEST PART.
HAPPENED SO FAST.
WUMP!
I PICKED MYSELF UP AND CHECKED FOR INJURIES. ~ THEN I REFLECTED ON HOW DANGEROUS MY LIFE CHOICES ARE.
I'M OK.
FUCK IT.

10/9/19
THE MAZE OF LIFE: WILL WE EVER SOLVE IT?
MOST STICK TO A RIGID WAY TO NAVIGATE.
ONLY LEFT TURNS.
FEW REALIZE THERE IS NO GETTING OUT.
WHEREVER I AM IS WHAT MATTERS MOST.
10/10/19
IT WILL NOT LAST.
I DOUBT THE USA WILL LAST ANOTHER 500 YEARS, PERHAPS LESS. CAN WE EVEN IDENTIFY WHAT MAKES US - US?
ROME FALLS...
WE SURVIVE ON A FUZZY IDEA AT BEST, OUR WORLD IS FRAGILE.
WE WILL TOO.
10/11/19
FUN WAS HAD.
IF YOU DO ANYTHING IN THIS WORLD, BE THE FUN STARTER.
HA HA HA HA
AND THE WEIGHT OF THE WORLD IS JUST A LITTLE BIT LIGHTER DO TO YOUR EFFORTS. IT IS WORTH IT.
THANK YOU!

10/12/19
OUT IN THE HILLS — A POINT OF LIGHT.
AWAY FROM EVERYONE ELSE. JUST US.
AND THE ECHO OF LAUGHTER.
HE
HA
HA
HE
HA
HE
HA
HE
10/13/19
OH I'M 55, I CAN'T GET UP HERE WITHOUT AN EBIKE.
SEE THAT GUY THERE? HE'S 72 YEARS OLD — HE PEDALED UP HERE.
10/19/19
I HOPE THIS WORKS.
THEY ARE NOT THE SAME. I HOPE I CAN MAKE IT WORK.
IT WORKED!
VAROOM!
DODGE

10/15/19

YOUR BODY OR MIND MAY BE COMPROMISED AT ANYTIME. IT WILL NOT LAST, THAT YOU CAN COUNT ON.

BUT THAT IS NO REASON TO GIVE UP, TO RETREAT FROM THE FREY. NO; KEEP ONE'S SWORD SHARP.

GO TO WHERE THE FIGHTING IS THE THICKEST. THERE AND ONLY THERE WILL ANY VICTORY YOU GAIN BE WORTHY.

10/16/19

WHAT IS AN ARTIST? A ARTIST IS SOMEONE THAT MAKES GETTING IN THEIR OWN WAY A LIFESTYLE CHOICE.

S.

I DON'T REALLY BELIEVE IN ART THOUGH. THE IDEA THAT ONE'S CREATIVE OUTPUT HAS EXTRINSIC VALUE IS ABSURD.

NEW CANVAS $35°°

ONE PAINTED ON. $3.°°

ARTISTS ARE VENERATED SELDOM WHEN THEY ARE ALIVE TO REAP THE REWARDS. IF YOU CAN'T TAKE ANY JOY OUT OF IT IN SOME OTHER WAY THEN WHY BOTHER.

10/17/19

I GUESS I NEED TO DO A LITTLE MORE THEN.

WHILE I SEE MANY PEOPLE TRYING TO DO LESS, I WILL TRY AND FIGURE OUT HOW TO DO MORE.

SEE THIS ALL THE TIME.

IF YOU'RE NOT WILLING TO DO MORE THEN YOU'RE STAGNANT, AND IF YOU'RE STAGNANT THEN YOU'RE DEAD.

MORE MEANS MORE.

10/18/19
I'LL BE SHORT AND SWEET
5 & 1/2 MINUTES LATER...
BLAH BLAH BLAH BLAH.
KILL ME NOW
BLAH BLAH BLAH
10/19/19
WE HAVE THIS GAME WITH PIZZA.
YOU HAVE TO GO DOWN IN LEVELS. EMPTY EACH BOX - CLEAR EACH LEVEL BEFORE YOU CAN MOVE DOWN TO THE NEXT.
ONE CAN NOT GO DOWN TO THE LOWER LEVELS TO GET THE SLICE THEY WANT, THEY HAVE TO EAT THEIR WAY TO IT.
GLMPH.
10/26/19
LIFE: A GAME WITHIN A GAME.
ALL ROLES TAKEN IN LIFE CAN BE VIEWED AS A GAME. YOU ARE A SON, AN EMPLOYEE A LOVER, A FRIEND, A EATER OF TACOS; EACH ONE A GAME.
ALL ONE AND ALL WITHIN EACH OTHER SOME WILL EVEN KEEP GOING BEYOND YOUR YEARS IF YOU PLAY WELL.
BURP!

10/21/19
I HAVE NOT HAD TIME TO PLAY IT.
OK
I DON'T EXPECT ANYONE TO HAVE ANY SORT OF FOLLOW-THROUGH IF NOT FOR SOME SELFISH SELF-INTEREST. JUST A TRUE-ISM.
D O O
BUT I KNOW I CAN RELY UPON MYSELF.
TRUE TOO.
10/22/19
WE SHOULD GO LEFT AT THE BOTTOM OF THE HILL.
BUT IF WE GO RIGHT THERE'S THAT WHOLE WINDY DOWN HILL SECTION.
THAT MEANS MORE RADNESS. WE HAVE TO GO WITH THAT ON GROUNDS OF RADNESS ALONE.
YES. YOU'RE RIGHT.
10/23/19
I THINK I WILL DO BETTER TODAY.
WAK
AH
HMM..THINKING ABOUT IT ACTUALLY WORKED.

6/27/19
I EXPECT THAT SOME WEIRD THING WILL POP UP WHEN TRYING TO COMPLETE A LONG TERM GOAL.
HMM
BUT I ALSO EXPECT TO SURMOUNT THAT PROBLEM.
HERE YOU GO.
WHAT'S THIS?
OWL SOCKS? IT'S NOT MY BIRTHDAY YOU KNOW.
IF I SEE SOMETHING THAT REMINDS ME OF YOU, IT DOES NOT NEED TO HAPPEN ON A GIVEN DAY, I JUST DO IT.
10/28/19
WITHOUT THINKING PEOPLE JUST PASS ALONG AN IDEA.
IF YOU VOTE FOR A 3RD PARTY YOU'RE THROWING YOUR VOTE AWAY!
BUT THEY DON'T HAVE AN IDEA THEM SELVES, THEY ARE SAYING SOMETHING — MINDLESSLY.
REALLY?
IT IS THE LACK OF THINKING THAT IS DISTURBING.
WHO HAS THE MOST TO GAIN BY THAT IDEA?

WHAT
U MADE A KITTY LAST YEAR.
WELL I'LL MAKE ONE THIS YEAR TOO.
S TO SHIP?
THAT ONLY MEANS ONE THING! THEY ARE MAKING IT OVERSEAS
WELL, I CAN DO THAT TOO.
TAKY TAK
OH HELLO?
PRRRRRH
FOOD BOWL IS FULL.
I GUESS HE JUST WANTS SOME ATTENTION.
PRRR
NOOM
10/22/19
10/29/19

10/30/19
You look one step away from being accused for homeless.
NA NA NA
OH, I HAVE.
BUT TO REALLY WIN THAT GAME I NEED SOMEONE TO HAND ME SOME MONEY.
10/31/19
TRICK OR TREAT.
GRR..
WAAAH!
JOD (WELL DONE.
I'VE SEEN PEOPLE MAKE COMENTS.
OH THEY DO. THOSE COMENT PEOPLE.
WHAT THE REAL QUESTION IS THAT IS THIS THE PART WHERE I'M SUPPOSED TO CARE?

11/2/19
I HAD THIS CLOCK FOR 20 YEARS AND IT FINALLY...
SO I FOUND ONE ON E-BAY TO REPLACE IT.
OH!
WHEN I FIND A THING I LIKE, I DON'T LOOK ANY FURTHER.
NOTHING LIKE WHAT YOU'RE USED TO.
I DIG SOME OF THE HOMELESS WAYS, YOU KNOW ONE THING I'VE SEEN?
?
THEY ALL HAVE AN AWESOME HEAD OF HAIR!
I THINK YOU'RE ON TO SOMETHING!
THERE IS NO EASY WAY OUT.
I FIGURE I'M LUCKY BECAUSE I KNOW THIS LIKE I KNOW NOTHING ELSE.
I WONDER HOW MANY PEOPLE GO THROUGH LIFE LOOKING FOR A MAGIC BUTTON THAT DOES NOT EXIST.

11/5/19
THE EARLY DARK— HOW IT EVOKES AN PRIMAL FEAR IN PEOPLE AND THEY SHUT THEMSELVES INTO THEIR HOMES
NOW THAT THE CLOCKS HAVE MOVED BACK IT IS DARK SO FAST, I CAN SEE THE MOOD SHIFT ALREADY.
BUT FOR THOSE OF US WHO VENTURE OUT IN IT, WE HAVE TO SHARE THE SPACE WITH A SCANT FEW!
I CALLED YOU.
YEAH?
BUT I THOUGHT IT WAS SOME AUTOMATED THING SO I DIDN'T LEAVE A MESSAGE.
WELL, THAT'S WHAT I CALL HARD WORK PAYING OFF.
DO YOU THINK HE'S READY TO RIDE WITHOUT TRAINING WHEELS?
FSSSSS.
I MEAN I WANT HIM TO DO THINGS WHEN HE'S READY TO DO THEM?
PERHAPS A LITTLE GUIDANCE.
HOWEVER, I DON'T KNOW ANYTHING ABOUT RAISING KIDS NOR DO I WANT TO KNOW.

11/02/19
I'm NOT WAITING 2 HOURS TO MAKE MY BIKE WORK
WELL, SOUNDS LIKE I'M NOT WORKING ON YOUR BIKE EVER AGAIN.
x!?#!!
GOOD RIDDANCE.
I WISH I HAD YOU TO DRIVE TO DO THINGS.
IT'S EASY, JUST TAKE A TASK THAT HAS 1000 STEPS DO ONE EVERY TWO DAYS..
..IN 500 DAYS YOU'RE DONE - I LOOK AT EVERYTHING LIKE THAT.
SOMETIMES YOU WONDER WHY YOU DID NOT DO IT SOONER.
50 BUCKS.
CLICK.
WE'RE JUST A MINOR THREAT!
I'LL NEVER HAVE TO HEAR ANOTHER EAGLES SONG AGAIN.

11/11/19

"WE KNOW ENOUGH TODAY TO KNOW THAT THERE IS INFINITE ROOM FOR BETTERMENT IN EVERY HUMAN CONCERN. NOTHING IS NEEDED BUT COLLECTIVE EFFORT AND MUTUAL TOLERATION..."
THE OUTLINE OF HISTORY
"OUR POVERTY, OUR RESTRICTED SURROUNDINGS OUR INDECISIONS & INDECISIONS, OUR QUARRELS & MISUNDERSTANDINGS ARE ALL THINGS CONTROLLABLE AND REMOVABLE BY CONCERTED HUMAN ACTION: BUT WE KNOW AS LITTLE HOW LIFE WOULD FEEL WITHOUT THEM AS SOME POOR, DIRTY, ILL-TREATED, FIERCE SOURED CREATURE BORN AND BRED AMIDST THE CRUEL AND DINGY SURROUNDINGS.

... EACH ONE WHO BELIEVES THAT BRINGS THE GOOD TIME NEARER, EACH HEART THAT FAILS DELAYS IT...

11/12/19

HAVE WE BEEN OVER THIS BEFORE?
NOPE.
HOW ABOUT THIS TRAIL?
HA HA WOAH! NOOO!
SEE? AFTER ALL THESE YEARS, STILL NEW ADVENTURES.

11/13/19

DID YOU WATCH THE DETH MOTO VIDEO?
YEAH, I PUT IT ON FACEBOOK.
MMM FACEBOOK, CONSIGNED TO THE VOID.

11/14/19

AS AN EXERCISE, IT WOULD BE GOOD TO LOOK AT SOMETHING THAT MADE YOU LAUGH EVERYDAY.

HA HA!

LIFE HAS BECOME TOO SERIOUS TO SO MANY TOO OFTEN.

STRESS!

BUT TO LAUGH JUST A LITTLE, WELL IT CAN'T HURT.

HE HE HE HE HE

11/15/19

PRRR...

THOSE LITTLE JOYFUL MOMENTS.

PRRR...

TO EXTEND THEM END TO END FOR ONE'S WHOLE LIFE, THAT WOULD BE THE GOAL.

11/16/19

DID SHOTGUN MIKE PASS AWAY?

TIKY TAK.? TICKY? TAK.

DAMN.

11/17/19
THE FEW.
HE SHOULD BE HERE SOON.
THERE ARE FEW PEOPLE THAT YOU CAN COUNT ON.
WHEN YOU FIND ONE, HANG ON.
THERE HE IS.
HA HA HA
HA HA HA
A LITTLE SILLYNESS GOES A LONG WAY.
AHH TO BE A KID AGAIN JUST FOR A TIME.
TIME SPANS SO LONG IT STILL AMAZES ME I'VE BEEN ON THIS PLANET NEAR 50 YEARS.
IT DOES NOT FEEL LIKE IT. BEING A CHILD SEEMS LIKE YESTERDAY.
I'VE DONE SO MUCH? I'VE DONE SO MUCH. AND FEEL LIKE I'VE DONE SO LITTLE.
AND GETTING OLD SEEMS SO DISTANT, BUT I'M HERE A SPIT IN TIME.
WE CAN ONLY GO FORWARD.

11/20/19
I JUST WANTED TO CALL AND SAY HOW MUCH I LIKE THE BIKE AND WHAT A GOOD JOB YOU DID. THANK YOU.
THANKS FOR ALL THE HELP YOU'VE GIVEN ME - I'VE GOT MY LIFE BACK TOGETHER!
OH!
A LITTLE PRAISE...
A FORM OF CURRENCY, MOST ARE IN A STATE OF POVERTY
11/21/19
ARE YOU THERE?
I'M HERE.
WHY WOULD I NOT BE AT WORK? IT MAKES NO SENSE TO SEE IF I'M HERE. WHERE ELSE WOULD I BE?
11/22/19
I'D LOVE TO TALK MORE BUT I HAVE TO JAM.
I UNDERSTAND
I KNEW YOU WOULD.
SO FEW DO.

11/23/19
HAPPY HOLIDAYS!
ALREADY WITH THAT CRAP?
WHEN IS IT TOO SOON?
11/24/19
FUN IS A MENTALITY. YOU WILL HAVE FUN.
THIS WILL BE COOL
YOU WILL NOT HAVE FUN.
THIS IS GOING TO SUCK.
CHOOSE WISELY.
FUN IT IS.
11/25/19
TO FINISH.
A FEW MORE.
NO MATTER WHAT ANYONE SAYS ABOUT WHAT YOU DO - IF YOU FINISH SOMETHING.
I DON'T KNOW ABOUT THAT PROJECT.
THEN YOU'RE A STEP ABOVE THE REST.
YEAH? WHERE IS YOURS?

11/23/19
HAPPY HOLIDAYS!
ALREADY WITH THAT CRAP?
WHEN IS IT TOO SOON?
11/24/19
FUN IS A MENTALITY: YOU WILL HAVE FUN.
THIS WILL BE COOL
YOU WILL NOT HAVE FUN:
THIS IS GOING TO SUCK.
CHOOSE WISELY.
FUN IT IS.
11/25/19
TO FINISH.
A FEW MORE.
NO MATTER WHAT ANYONE SAYS ABOUT WHAT YOU DO - IF YOU FINISH SOMETHING.
I DON'T KNOW ABOUT THAT PROJECT.
THEN YOU'RE A STEP ABOVE THE REST.
YEAH? WHERE IS YOURS?

11/26/19
AAA!
LOW BRIDGE!
WHERE'S THE TRAIL?
LIFE: GIVEN TO SO MANY AND GRASPPED BY SO FEW.
THAT WAS AWESOME!
SURE WAS.
ARE YOU PAUL FROM SIMI VALLEY?
YEAH?
WE TALK, WE GREW UP IN THE SAME NEIGHBOR-HOOD. HE GETS ME UP TO SPEED ON ALL THE KIDS I GREW UP WITH AND TOTALLY FORGOT ABOUT.
HE GOT SHOT!?
I FEEL BAD BECAUSE I DON'T RECONIZE HIM.
IT'S BEEN 30 YEARS. YOU ARE SUCH AN ASS.
I'M RIDING IN SNOW!
WE'RE TURNING AROUND
WELL, SOMETHING NEW IS ALWAYS AROUND THE CORNER!

11/29/19
IT IS JUST FINE TO SAY NOTHING. I DON'T GET THIS NEED PEOPLE HAVE TO FILL THE SILENCE WITH WORDS.
IT'S COLD NOW.
ONE CAN SAY ANYTHING PERHAPS. NOT SAYING SOMETHING SAYS MORE THAT WORDS ARE USED BEST..
...WHEN USED WISELY.
I NOTICED.
11/30/19
EXCUSE ME, ARE YOU IN A BAND?
NOT FOR MANY YEARS.
I THOUGHT YOU WERE SOMEONE..
YEAH?
JOHN OATS.
!
MAN YOU ARE STRONG!
ANYONE CAN DO IT
E BIKE
IT'S IN THE MIND.
HMM
A BATTLE YOU LOST RIDING THAT E-BIKE YOU CHOAD.

12/2/19
YOU NEED TO WATCH OUT! TWO HUSKIES ARE OUT THERE AND BIT MY DOG!
OH SHIT THERE THEY ARE!
BACK HOUNDS!
IT'S JUST EGO
IT IS. I HAD TO TAKE A HARD LOOK AT MYSELF AND SEE WHY PEOPLE NEED SO MUCH VALIDATION NOW.
POST
AND DO I NEED VALIDATION TOO? OR IS JUST DOING WHAT I'M DOING GOOD ENOUGH WITHOUT ANYONE ELSE KNOWING ABOUT IT?
12/4/19
I HAD TO CONTINUE MY JOURNEY. IF WHAT I AM DOING IS ONLY VALUEABLE BECAUSE IT IS APPROVED BY OTHERS IS IT TRULY VALUEABLE TO ME?
I DON'T WANT TO BE ANOTHER VICTIM OF ALL THIS NARCISSITIC SELF-ANGGRANDIZING NAVEL-GAZING THAT HAS CONSUMED SO MANY OTHERS.
I WANT MY CHOICES TO BE VALID UPON THIER OWN MERITS

12/5/19
AHH..THE REAL WORLD.
THE INTERNET WORLD IS THE BLACK VOID. ANYTHING PUT THERE IS LOST FOREVER.
RAKING LEAVES IS GOOD.
I CAN MOVE THINGS HERE TO MUCH BETTER EFFECT AND IT WILL HAVE REAL VALUE.
12/6/19
I'VE BEEN ON THAT GEARED BIKE FOR TOO LONG.
NOW YOU'RE WEAK.
YEAH . . . .
12/7/19
I CAN'T GET HOW IRRATIONAL PEOPLE ARE!
NEH
YOU'RE ASKING TOO MUCH.
IF SOMEONE IS RATIONAL, I LOOK AT THAT AS A BOON.

12/8/19
LET'S TURN AROUND HERE.
OK
LOOK AT THE CLOUDS! HEAR ALL THE BIRDS
OH IT IS SO GOOD TO BE ALIVE.
12/9/19
YOU'D MAKE A GREAT DAD!
YEAH RIGHT.
BUT YOU'RE SO SMART THE WORLD NEEDS MORE PEOPLE LIKE YOU.
THAT'S NOT TRUE.
THAT IS THE MOST ARROGANT THING I'VE HEARD ALL WEEK. THAT ONE PERSONS' CHILD WILL TIP THE SCALES OF HUMANITY SO GREATLY, AND IT WOULD BE MINE. GET REAL
12/10/19
GOOD IDEAS & THEMES ARE WORTH REPEATING.
WAAAAA
SO MANY REPEAT BAD THEMES. I TRY AND REPEAT THE GOOD.
THAT WAS RAD!
WHICH ONE YOU CHOOSE? WELL, LIKE ALL THINGS IN LIFE, UP TO YOU.

12/11/19
DEALING WITH OTHERS CAN BE HARD WHEN YOU DON'T BELIEVE IN PREFERENTIAL TREATMENT.
NO CUTS IN LINE, SORRY.
EVERYONE ELSE WANTS TO BE SPECIAL, TO HAVE AN ADVANTAGE. THEY WANT YOU TO AGREE WITH HOW THEY FEEL.
CAN'T YOU...
IT IS A NARROW PATH. ONE YOU MUST WALK ALONE.
I COULD, BUT IT IS UNFAIR.
OH WOW J.D!
WE CATCH UP.
I'M RIDING MY MOTORCYCLE TO THE ARTIC CIRCLE.
AH! I'M SO GLAD YOU'RE STILL YOU.
HMM
TODAY I FOUND A PAIR OF GLASSES ON A TRAIL
SOMEONE IS MISSING THESE.
I PUT A "FOUND" AD ON CRAIGSCLIST, BUT I DOUBT THEY WILL LOOK.
WORTH A TRY.

THESE CHIPS ARE STALE.
MUNCH MUNCH
HMM.... THEY ARE.
CHUM CHUM CHUM
MMM.. CHEWY.
CHOM CHOM CHOM CHOM CHOM
ALL HAIL THE NEW GOD!
?
THE ONLY GOD THESE PEOPLE BELIEVE IN...
. . .
THE GOD OF COMMERCE.
DIRT BALL!
WHERE IS HE?
WORRY WORRY WORRY
LATER
THERE YOU ARE!
MEOW!

12/17/19
OH SHIT!
HELP
A FEW MINUTES LATER:
DID I CRASH?
I'M OK TO RIDE.
YEAH
NO!
MUROOOUW.
OK I'LL LET YOU OUT— YOU GOTTA BE FREE.
I TOTALY UNDERSTAND.
YOU DID THAT TO A FAT CHANCE?
IS IT BAD?
IT'S A COLLECTOR ITEM!
OH.
NO YOU WON'T
I'LL FIX IT
OH, YE OF LITTLE FAITH!

12/ 20/ 19
THAT DOG WAS WEARING A BODY SUIT.
LIFE NEVER STOPS TO BE INTERESTING!
12/ 21/ 19
ARE YOU READY FOR THE HOLIDAYS?
SURE. I DO NOTHING LIKE I ALWAYS DO. I AVOID ALL GATHERINGS, GIVE NOR ACCEPT NO GIFTS
SO, I'M READY ALL YEAR ROUND.
12/ 22/ 19
FAIRLY OFTEN I GET A REMINDER THAT MANY PEOPLE ARE NOT RATIONAL.
I NEED SOME TIME.
I HAVE TO LOOK AT IT AS A TEST TO NOT MAKE ME ONE OF THEM.
I CAN'T KNOW HOW LONG.
I DO, AT TIMES, FEEL OUT NUMBERED.
TALKING ABOUT IT ONLY ADDS TIME TO THE EQUATION.

12/23/19
CAREFUL
IT WAS NOT WISE TO TRY AND WELD ON A WET DAY BUT I DID IT ANYWAY
FEEL A JOLT.
BZZZ
AT TIMES THE RISK YOU TAKE IS THE TRUE DEFINER OF WHAT YOU ARE.
GOT THAT DONE.
12/24/19
A RARE MOMENT WHEN I LET SOMEONE GO THERE ARE NO TEARS. I THOUGHT I SHOULD CRY BUT IT DID NOT HAPPEN.
RARE HONS
SOMETIMES THINGS JUST RUN THIER COURSE AND YOU KNOW IT'S DONE.
RETURNING THINGS
IT'S NOT HOLLYWOOD AFTER ALL. I THINK LOOSE ENDS ARE MORE COMMON THAN A MOMENT OF CLARITY.
SAD.
12/25/19
PERHAPS I WAS ACTING OUT OF ANGER.
HELLO?
I WAS - ANGRY ALL DAY.
I'M SORRY.
THEN THE FOG OF ANGER LIFTED AND REASON RETURNED.
ME TOO.

12/22/19
WELL THAT'S IT.
JUST ME AND YOU AGAIN.
12/28/19
I JUST HAD TO ADMIT TO MYSELF MY ROLE IN THE RUINATION OF MY RELATIONSHIP WITH CHERYL.
MY FOLLY IS TO KNOW WHAT I'VE LOST TOO LATE AND TO BE BLIND TO THE VALUE OF WHAT I HAD.
I WILL CARRY THE SHAME AND REGRET OF IT TO MY FINAL DAYS...
12/29/19
I CAN SEEK SALVATION IN WHAT I KNOW: THE RIDE.
THERE WILL BE ROUGH PATCHES, ROCKS, DITCHES, CRASHES & SMOOTH PARTS, GRUELING PARTS, EASY ONES, JUST LIKE IN LIFE.
BUT IF YOU DON'T GIVE UP, YOU'LL HAVE ONE HELL OF A RIDE.
IN THE RIGHT DIRECTION.

12/29/19
WHAT DAY IS IT?
FOR ONE WHO IS A SLAVE TO PLANS AND THE MARKING OF TIME. TO LOSE TRACK OF THE DAYS WAS A BREAK. ? ? ? ? ? ? ? ? ? ?
I AM ON BREAK - A REVELATION:
TIME ONLY HAS VALUE IF YOU GIVE IT VALUE.
12/30/19
I DO IT ALL THE TIME, I PUSH MYSELF TOO HARD AND GET SICK.
...
SO I SAT AROUND WATCHING YOU TUBE VIDEOS.
NOTHING CAN BE PROVEN.
AND CAME TO THE LOGICAL CONCLUSION:
NOTHING ON HERE CAN BE SUBSTANTIATED AS FACT.
12/31
LAST ONE.
TO DEFINE A GOAL. SET A TIME OF COMPLETION AND THEN CARRY IT OUT.
YEAR+ LONG PROJECT.
IN DOING SO YOU GAIN A VISTA THAT MAKES MANY OTHER ROADS APPEARENT.

1/1/20
IT'S TYPE 2 FUN.
THAT SOUNDS LIKE SOME INTERNET SHIT.
WHEN YOU TRY AND QUANTIFY FUN YOU PUT LIMITATIONS ON IT. BY GIVING IT STRUCTURE YOU PUT THE IDEA IN A CAGE.
NOW WITH A LABEL YOU LOSE THE CHANCE TO SHARE DISCUSSION BECAUSE YOU CAN NOW RATE YOUR FUN AND RELATE IT TO SOMEONE IN A PHRASE THAT CAN BE PUT ON A BUMPER STICKER.
1/2/20
1st WORK CALL OF THE YEAR.
HELLO.
WHEN I GET THERE WILL YOU BE BUSY?
I HAVE NO WAY TO KNOW THAT.
IT NEVER ENDS.
1/3/20
MY FRIEND IASO CAME FROM JAPAN AND ONE OF HIS GOALS WAS TO COME TO YOUR SHOP.
REALLY?
FOR REAL!?

1/4/20
AH! A CAPER!
I HAVE NOT DONE A CAPER IN SO LONG...
IT FELT GOOD TO GO HOME.
NO BICYCLES
1/5/20
PERHAPS I'M JUST BETTER OFF ALONE.
IT IS SAD BECAUSE I FEEL LIKE MY CAPACITY TO LOVE IS MY STRONGEST CHARACTERISTIC.
AND UNDER SCRUTINY, I DON'T THINK I'M VERY GOOD AT IT.
PERHAPS TOO STRONG.
1/6/20
I BUILT A BIKE, DID A BUNCH OF ORGANIZING MADE MY SELF TIRED JUST DOING THINGS.
I ROTATED THE TIRES ON MY VAN, DID PAPER WORK. DID DISHES, FINISHED MY BOARD GAME DESIGN. ALL DAY.
THEN I MADE A GIANT TO DO LIST AND WORKED MY WAY BACK INTO A LONELY EXISTANCE.
HRMM

1/7/20
YOU TIRED?
YAWN.
YEAH I DON'T SLEEP WELL LAST 2 NIGHTS WERE NO SLEEP.
WELL YOU EXERCISE A LOT AND EAT WELL, WHAT IS IT?
MY DUMB HEAD.
1/8/20
I GET THESE NOTIONS TO SELL EVERYTHING AND JUST LIVE IN A VAN. SEE THE WORLD.
BUT THEN I REALIZED YOU CAN'T RUN FROM YOURSELF.
AND THE GOOD THINGS IN LIFE. THEY ARE MOST LIKLEY RIGHT IN FRONT OF YOU, YOU'RE JUST NOT LOOKING.
1/9/20
A GREAT TOOL: THE TO-DO LIST.
TO DO
1 2 3 4 5 6 7 8
WHEN I HAVE A MOMENT, I TAKE A LOOK.
I CAN DO THAT NOW.
TO DO
AND DO A LITTLE MORE THAN I THOUGHT I COULD.
NEXT?

1/10/20

I WAS GOOD.

I WANTED A SECOND CUP OF COFFEE BUT I KNEW THE SHORT TERM JOY WOULD BE FOLLOWED BY A NIGHT OF LOW SLEEP AND GETTING UP TO PEE OVER AND OVER AGAIN.

SO I SUMMONED MY WILL POWER AND SAID NO. IN DOING SO, I GAINED SO MUCH.

1/11/20

YOUR HEART JUST WALKS OUT ON YOU.

FOR NOW, BEING ALONE IS NOT SO BAD. I CAN SEE THE ROAD AHEAD.

A WELL TRAVELED, LONELY ROAD THAT I'VE BEEN DOWN OFTEN.

1/12/20

WHAT LAP ARE YOU ON!?

5

NO, YOU WENT ONE EXTRA LAP!

?

GUESS I WAS HAVING TOO MUCH FUN THEN.

1/13/20
YOU HAVE COFFEE GRINDERS?
BACK ON THE LEFT.
SO MANY
OOH NEXT LEVEL!
1/14/20
PERHAPS I COULD DO A BOOK OF THE FIRST 10 YEARS.
ALL OF THEM? OR JUST THE GOOD ONES?
YOU CAN'T EDIT LIFE, MAX.
1/15/20
DO YOU WANT TO COME OVER AND WATCH A MOVIE?
NO.
WHAT GOOD WILL COME OF IT? I NEED TO MAKE PEACE WITH THE IDEA THAT I WILL BE BETTER OFF ALONE.
A MONASTIC LIFE WILL BE A LIFE OF LOVE AS WELL, PERHAPS IT WILL BE BETTER.
PRRR.

1/16/20
Crak!
OH MAN, I BROKE MY KICKSTAND OFF MY CRUISER.
I GUESS I'VE NEGECTED YOU TOO LONG.
1/17/20
I DID NOT WANT TO GO. I HAVE BRUISED RIBS AND IT HAD RAINED THE NIGHT BEFORE. IT HURT TO BREATHE DEEP.
HUF HUF
BUT I WAS GREETED BY THE PURPLED VIOLET HUES OF A NEW DAY. THE COLD CRISP AIR AND SOLITUDE WAS SO BEAUTIFUL....
I KNEW THEN I HAD MADE THE RIGHT CHOICE.
GLAD TO BE HERE.
1/18/20
I THROW A LOT OF IDEAS OUT THERE INTO THE VOID.
MOST NEVER RETURN.
BUT WHEN ONE DOES IT IS SUCH AN REWARDING EXPERIENCE.

1/19/20

AH, TO BE THE FUN MERRY MAKER. HOW VALUEABLE IT IS TO OTHERS.

I THINK IF YOU CAN MAKE OTHERS HAPPY YOU'RE DOING ONE OF THE MOST IMPORTANT THINGS FOR HUMANITY.

BY BRINGING A LITTLE JOY INTO PEOPLE'S LIVES THE WORLD IS JUST THAT MUCH BRIGHTER.
THANK YOU!

1/20/20

I SAW SHE CALLED BUT DID NOT CALL BACK.

I'M SAYING IT NOW BECAUSE I'M SURE I'LL CHANGE MY MIND LATER BUT COMPANIONSHIP. IT JUST WEIGHS ME DOWN.

IT WEIGHS SO HEAVY ON MY HEART THAT I CANNOT CARRY ANOTHER OUNCE OF SORROW.
OOF!

1/21/20

HERE'S A GIFT FOR YOU.
?

OH! HAHA. I THINK YOU SHOULD PASS THIS ON TO SOMEONE ELSE.
WEED

I'VE NEVER DONE ANY DRUGS IN MY LIFE. THANK YOU THOUGH.

1/22/20
WHAT AN ORDEAL OTHER PEOPLE CAN BE. THE CLOSER YOU ARE, THE WORSE IT GETS.
SEEMS LIKE SO MUCH WASTED TIME + ENERGY. LOW YIELD, HIGH ENERGY OUTPUT. NOT A GOOD RETURN.
THUS I PUT MY ENERGY INTO CAN HAVE A GOOD RESULT AS LONG AS NO ONE ELSE IS INVOLVED.
1/23/20
PERHAPS A MONASTIC LIFE THEN?
A LIFE DEVOTED TO STUDY, CONTEMPLATION, WORK, CHARITY.
PERHAPS A FORK IN THE ROAD LEADS TO THE SAME PLACE.
1/24/20
YOU MARRIED? HAVE ANY KIDS?
HEH. HE'S KNOWN ME A LONG TIME, NO.
HA!
THAT IS FOR GROWN-UPS.
IF THAT WORKS FOR YOU.
IT DOES
PETER PAN FOREVER

1/25/20
OUT IN THE WOODS AT NIGHT - ALONE,
SO LITTLE NOISE AND A LITTLE FEAR OF WHAT YOU CAN'T SEE.
BUT IT WAS VERY PEACEFUL.
I SHOULD DO THIS MORE OFTEN.
1/26/20
AN IDEA
I LOVE HOW MY MIND CAN TRAVEL WITH AN IDEA AND IN TIME PEOPLE WILL CROSS CONTENENTS AND EVEN OCEANS TO TAKE PART IN YOUR IDEA. JAPAN KANAS
I DON'T THINK I CAN FEEL MORE FLATTERED AND HONORED THAN I DO RIGHT NOW.
1/27/20
EXCUSE YOU!
GO ON OPPOSSUM - OUTSIDE.
NOW I SEE WHERE ALL THE CAT FOOD HAS GONE.

1/28/20
IS THIS THE GUY WHO DOES CHICKEN HEAD ZINE.
YES?
THIS IS AARON COMETBUS
!
I'VE BEEN READING YOUR ZINE FOR OVER 20 YEARS NOW!
HAHA!
1/29/20
SO WHAT'S YOUR FEEL THEN ON HOW IS IT GOING?
80% SAY NO CASH FLOW.
THEY CAN'T GET OR WON'T GET A LOAN THEY HAVE TROUBLE MAKING MONEY.
THAT MANY BUSINESSES AREN'T MAKING MONEY, THAT'S BAD!
REAL BAD.
1/30/20
I TRIED SO HARD
I DID.
BUT YOU CAN'T GIVE UP ON WHO YOU ARE.
I LOVE YOU.

1/31/20
YOU MARRIED? HAVE A GIRL FRIEND?
NOT ANY MORE.
THATS GOOD. BEST TO STAY THAT WAY.
MY WIFE MADE ME WAIT FOR TWO HOURS AT A REPAIR SHOP BEFORE SHE PICKED ME UP.
WHY DOES EVERYONE SAY THAT?
2/1/20
MAY AS WELL FINISH THIS.
ANYTHING TO KEEP MY MIND OFF HOW I'M ALONE AGAIN.
AND HOW I'M GOING TO STAY THAT WAY.
2/2/20
MORE LOVE NOTES, IT IS NOT HELPING.
I'M LOOKING IN THE BOX OF MY HEART AND TRIED TO PUT IT BACK TOGETHER
AND I SEE THERE ARE NOT ENOUGH PIECES LEFT TO COMPLETE THE PICTURE.

2/3/20
I RODE AND RODE.
IT WAS COLD AND WINDY BUT I WENT UP TWO MOUNTIAN PASSES ANYWAY BECAUSE I TOLD MYSELF I COULD.
JUST ME AND MY TRUSTY FRIEND: MY BICYCLE.
2/4/20
WANT SOME CAKE?
I GUESS.
I CAN'T REMEMBER THE LAST TIME I HAD CAKE.
LATER THAT NIGHT:
HAVE SOME CAKE GUYS
WHAT ARE THE ODDS?
2/5/20
ARE YOU OK?
PLEASE BE OK.
ALL I HAVE LEFT IS A 4 LEGED CREATURE THAT WILL TAKE ME AS I AM. I HAVE NOTHING ELSE.

2/6/20
PEOPLE RUN FROM THE BEAR OF BADNESS, THEY FEAR IT.
OVERTIME, BAD IS JUST THE OTHER SIDE OF GOOD. I GRAB THE BEAR AND IT RENDS ME...
AS I LAY THERE BROKEN, NEAR DEATH, AS LONG AS I LIVE, IT IS PART OF LIFE THAT I EMBRACE.
TAKE THE BAD TOO, YOU MUST.
2/7/20
OK. IT'S ON!
AHNN! OH SHIT!
WHAT DO YOU THINK?
I THINK IN 5 YEARS NO ONE WILL BE OUT SIDE.
2/8/20
ZZZ
ZZZ
A QUIET NIGHT, NODDING OFF IN A CHAIR...
TO BE ABLE TO DO THAT. IT CAN BE LOOKED UPON AS A PRIVELAGE.
ZZZ

2/9/20
I'M ALMOST DONE WITH THE NEW ZINE.
COOL!
I'M WORKING ON IT!
BUT MAINLY I'M WORKING ON MYSELF.
2/10/20
A DOCTOR VISIT.
I GUESS I'M OK MY VARIOUS NUMBERS WERE BETTER THAN FOUR YEARS AGO.
WHAT THE HELL
HDL? ADL?
AND THE SORENESS IN MY BACK WAS JUST MUSCLES SO I'M NOT DYING YET.
WELL, THAT'S A RELIEF!
2/11/20
WHEN WE CATCH A SHOPLIFTER, WE CALL IT STATS.
?
NOT A SHOPLIFTER? STATS?
I JUST LEARNED SOME SECRET THEFT PROTECTION JARGON!

2/12/20
I DON'T NEED IT.
NEGATIVITY IS A NARCOTIC JUST LIKE ANY DRUG.
IN THE END IT DESTROYS YOU.
2/13/20
I TOLD YOU OVER AND OVER THIS IS YOUR PROJECT. DID YOU LOOK FOR WHAT YOU NEEDED BEFORE ASKING ME? NO? OK THEN.
IF I LOOK THEN I'M WORKING ON YOUR BIKE AND I COULD HAVE DONE A 100 BIKES IN THE TIME YOU HAVE TAKEN. YOU NEED TO LEARN, NOT ME.
EVERYTHING YOU NEED IS OUT THERE IF YOU LOOK. BUT YOU ARE BY BEING LAZY, TAKING MY TIME. MY VERY FINITE + PRECIOUS TIME AND I WON'T ALLOW THAT.
2/14/20
M
SOMEONE TOSSED OUT THIER WHOLE LATINA/FEMMIST ARTIST PERSONA... HUM
FRIDA
SCORE!

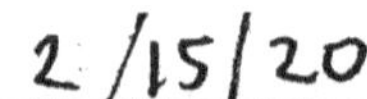

2/15/20
AS I THRASH ABOUT AT NIGHT TRYING TO SLEEP
I REALIZED THAT OF THE TIMES I'VE FOUND MYSELF CRYING IN A FETAL POSITION, 9 OUT OF 10 THERE WAS A WOMAN INVOLVED.
THE REVELATION DID NOT MAKE ME ANGRY OR BITTER TOWARDS WOMEN, JUST SAD. SAD THAT IT HAS TO BE SO NEEDLESLY HARD.
2/16/20
TODAY I IDULGED.
PEDAL HARDER.
WHY NOT? MORE COFFEE?
IT'S BEEN A YEAR SINCE I ATE HERE, IT WAS TIME I DID.
2/17/20
GREAT VIEWS.
CLEAR SKYS + SUN.
HOW WE FORGET TO GO OUT AND ENJOY LIFE, WILL IT PASS YOU BY?
NOT IF I CAN DO ANYTHING ABOUT IT.

2/18/20
AAAAHHH!
LOOKOUT! WOAH!
SOMETIMES IT DOES NOT MATTER WHAT YOU ARE DOING, BEING ALIVE IS ENOUGH.
2/19/20
I HAVE TO CUT MY RIDE SHORT SO I CAN GET SOME DRAWING DONE.
I HAVE TO CUT MY DRAWING SHORT TO FIX MY VAN.
A WORTHY SACRIFICE
VAR oom!
2/20/20
I WAS SO READY TO BE ALONE TONIGHT AND JUMP INTO A PROJECT BUT FRIENDS COME BY
I THINK YOU CAN HAVE VERY LITTLE IN THIS LIFE BUT BE RICH IN FRIENDS.
AND YOU'D BE WEALTHIER THAN MOST.

2/21/20
EVERY DAY".
OK DONE!
A LITTLE XTTRA, A LITTLE OF FINISHING THINGS. A LITTLE OF GETTING CLOSER TO GETTING SOMETHING DONE. A LITTLE ADVENTURE EVERY DAY.
WITHOUT, YOU REPEAT THE MANTRA OF THE LIVING DEAD.
JUST ANOTHER DAY.
2/22/20
HAVE NOT HAD A PB+H IN FOREVER
DIRTBALL! YOU DON'T WANT THAT!
OK, I GUESS YOU DO.
CHOMP
2/23/20
AMAZING!
NOTHING BRINGS ME SO MUCH JOY AND INNER PEACE THAN BEING OUT IN NATURE ON MY BIKE.
A MOMENT TO STOP AND RECONIZE HOW LUCKY I AM THAT I CAN HAVE SUCH A THING IN MY LIFE.

2/ 24 /20
THE INVITE WAS THERE BUT I WOULD NOT DO IT.
NO
I HAVE TO ANSWER THE PHONE ALL DAY, 6 DAYS A WEEK. I HATE THE PHONE MORE AND MORE.
GRRR
RING!
SO THERE WAS NO WAY I'D PICK ONE UP ON MY DAY OFF.
FUCK THAT.
RING!
2/25/20
WONA! AAH!
HA HA HA HA
THANK-YOU BICYCLE FOR BEING YOU.
2/26/20
SOMETIMES YOU SLIP—WE ALL DO, BUT GETTING BACK ON TOP OF THINGS IS THE HARDER PART.
NEED TO DO THAT SECOND CLIMB.
AS LONG AS WE CAN SUMMON THE WILL TO RE-ALIGN OURSELVES WE CAN DO WELL.
NOT SO BAD.
THE CHOICE IS UP TO US.
I WONDER WHY I DID NOT PUSH MYSELF A LITTLE MORE?

2/20/20

WHEN YOU HAVE SOME TIME AND WONDER WHAT TO DO.
MAY AS WELL GET THAT DONE.

WHATEVER IT IS, WHY WAIT? JUST GO AHEAD AND DO IT, GIVING INTO HOW YOU FEEL AT THE MOMENT WILL MEAN YOU GET NOTHING DONE.
EVER.

BUT THE FEELING ONE GETS BY FINISHING SOMETHING FEELS WAY BETTER OVER TIME THAN A TEMPORARY MOOD YOU'RE IN.
DONE + DONE.

2/28/20

CRUISE NIGHT!

I'M GLAD I GOT OUT...

...AND BROKE FROM MY ROUTINE.

DODGE

KLUNK!

SO MANY WHEELS. I HAVE 2, 3, 4 LIFE TIMES WORTH OF OLD BIKE PARTS. I'LL NEVER LIVE LONG ENOUGH TO USE THEM ALL.

I HATE TO WASTE ANYTHING BUT I MUST LET GO OF THINGS
OH WELL.

3/1/20
YOU NEED TO WATCH YOUR LANGUAGE.
THAT SHIT...
OH YEAH? IT'S MY HOUSE SO I CAN SAY WHAT I WANT. FUCK FUCK FUCK FUCK FUCK FUCK FUCK FUCK FUCK
I LOVE YOU MAN!
3/2/20
I DON'T KNOW HOW MANY FEET I CLIMBED OR HOW MANY MILES I RODE. BUT I RODE.
I WENT WAY PAST MY COMFORT & ENDURANCE ZONE.
ALL I CAN THINK OF IS PEANUT M&MS
BUT I KNEW IT WAS A GOOD RIDE BECAUSE WHEN IT IS GOOD, I WANT TO CRY.
HOLD IT IN.
3/3/20
OOOOOOOH!
THAT WAS RAD!
IT WAS!
OH ADVENTURE, WHERE WOULD I BE WITHOUT YOU?

3/4/20
HERE YOU GO!
WOOOO!
IT'S LIKE BEING A KID AGAIN!
MY WORK IS DONE HERE.
3/5/20
I THINK I'M DONE WITH WOMEN.
TYPE TYPE
TYPE TYPE
I THOUGHT ABOUT IT. I HAD HUNG OUT W/ CHERYL AND FELT LIKE HAVING A GIRLFRIEND WAS THE LAST THING I WANTED.
BIKES
I DON'T BELIEVE IN ANY FAIRY TALE NONSENSE WHERE THERE IS A PERSON FOR EVERYONE. I'M LIVING PROOF OF THAT.
I'M CHOOSING TO BE OK WITH IT.
3/6/20
THIS IS PAUL FROM ATOMIC CYCLES
I WAS JUST GOING TO CALL YOU
YOU. LISTEN. NOW.
BEGINING TOMORROW, I'M CHARGING YOU 1 DOLLAR A DAY FOR STORAGE. YOU'VE HAD YOUR BIKE HERE FOR 6 MONTHS, 8 MONTHS? TOO LONG AGO. I WILL ONLY TAKE CASH FOR YOU.
AS YOU'VE PROVEN TO BE UNTRUSTWORTHY, I DON'T WANT TO HEAR ANY EXCUSES YOU HAVE WASTED ENOUGH OF MY TIME, ENERGY AND RESOURCES. SO A DOLLAR A DAY.
YOU'RE RIGHT.

3/9/20

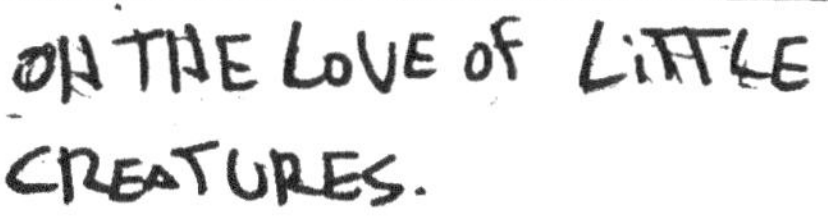

OH THE LOVE OF LITTLE CREATURES.

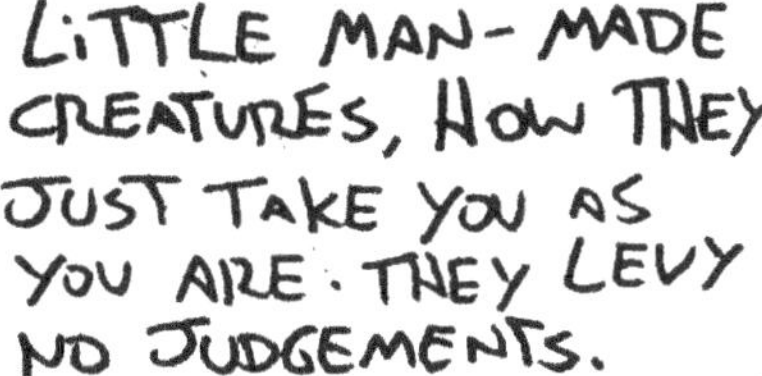

LITTLE MAN-MADE CREATURES, HOW THEY JUST TAKE YOU AS YOU ARE. THEY LEVY NO JUDGEMENTS.

AND THEY HOLD YOU IN HIGH ESTEEM FOR JUST BEING THERE I SEE THE APPEAL.

3/8/20

THE LIBERATED MIND.

THE LIBERATED MIND CAN LOOK AT THINGS AND MAKE THE MOST OF THEM. THEY SEE WAYS TO ENJOY LIFE IN EVERYTHING THEY ENCOUNTER.

THE CLOSED MIND ONLY WAITS TO BE TOLD WHAT TO THINK. WHICH ONE ARE YOU?

3/9/20

I DID IT ALL. I RODE. I DREW. I WELDED AND I FIXED A BENT FRAME (MOSTLY).

I VISITED A PAL, I MADE A DEAL AND KEPT MY WORD. I GOT A BUNCH OF BIKE PARTS FOR WORK FOR CHEAP. I UNLOADED EVERYTHING.

I FINISHED A ZINE. I READ A BOOK, I DID SOME DISHES. BY 9 PM I GOT EVERYTHING DONE I SET OUT TO DO SO I GOT ONE MORE THING; I SATIFACTION OF A DAY WELL SPENT.

3/10/20
RACING HOME BEFORE THE RAIN I KNEW THE RIDE WAS OUT FOR TODAY SO I OWED IT TO MYSELF TO MAKE THE NIGHT COUNT.
WHEN YOU SQUANDER TIME, YOU ROB YOUR SELF OF A REAL CHANCE TO LIVE. TO BE CREATING, TO BE A FOOL IF NEED BE SURE, TO TRY? YES!
TO FAIL WOULD TO BE NOT TO TRY. ONLY IN NOT TRYING DOES ONE REALLY FAIL. TO LIVE IS TO TRY - FAILURE ONLY COMES IN GIVING UP.
3/11/20
GET UP - NO RAIN! THAT MEANS..
RIDE!
BAD WEATHER MAKES YOU WANT TO STAY IN BUT I HAD TO OVER-RIDE MY FEELINGS - THEY OFTEN BETRAY WHAT IS GOOD FOR YOU.
IN THEN TO DO A THING YOU LOVE IS THE MOST IMPORTANT THING FOR BEING HAPPY.
THAT'S THE GOAL.
3/12/20
MY OVER-REACHING THEME IN LIFE IS I WANT TO BE A HAPPY PERSON.
SO YOU KNOW WHEREEVER THAT JOURNEY IS TAKING ME...
THAT'S WHERE I'M GOING.

3/13/20
IT WAS GOOD.
FOOSH
IT WAS GOOD TO GET DOWN ON MY HANDS AND KNEES AND REALLY CLEAN UP MY WORK SPACE.
THERE ARE POTATOES HERE SPROUTING ON THE CARPET.
TAKING SOME PRIDE IN WHAT YOU DO IS A GOOD THING.
HAVE NOT SEEN THE FLOOR IN AGES.
3/14/20
OK. ROLL TO HIT.
WE PLAYED D&D AGAIN, WE ALL MISSED IT.
SHE DEFLECTS YOUR ARROW.
AWW!
THE MAIN DIFFERENCE IS NOW I GO TO BED ALONE AT THE END.
STILL A GOOD TIME.
3/15/20
HARDER THAN NORMAL.
YEAH, ALL WET.
I'LL TELL YOU THOUGH.
I'M SO GLAD TO BE OUT HERE RIGHT NOW.

3/16/20
I JUST WANT TO FINISH IT.
WHY DO SOMETHING IN STAGES WHEN YOU CAN KNOCK IT OUT IN ONE SHOT?
WHY INDEED.
DONE & DONE.
3/17/20
LET'S MAKE A RIGHT UP HERE
ARE YOU FEELING THE DESPERATE ENERGY OUT THERE TOO?
YEAH.
3/18/20
OH THOSE AMAZING MACHINES.. !!!!
HUMANITY CAN BE SO CREATIVE
HOW DID THEY EVER THINK OF THAT!
I JUST WISH WE'D PUT AS MUCH ENERGY INTO GETTING ALONG.

3/19/20
CITY WILL SHUT DOWN
WHAT?
BIKE SHOPS ARE ESSENTIAL...
?
WELL LOOK AT THAT! I'M FINALLY ESSENTIAL.
3/20/20
THE PLAGUE HAS BEEN GOOD TO ME, I MUST ADMIT. I SHOULD NOT BE HAPPY ABOUT IT THOUGH
I KNEW IT WOULD. IN 2008 WHEN THINGS CRASHED I WAS KILLING IT.
I'M A BOTTOM FEEDER AND THE BOTTOM IS BIGGER THAN EVER.
3/21/20
JUST SHUT UP ABOUT IT! ALL YOU DO IS COMPLAIN!
YOU'RE LIKE EVERYONE ELSE JUST RUN YOUR MOUTH OVER AND OVER BUT DO NOTHING ABOUT IT.
IF YOU'RE NOT GOING TO DO ANYTHING ABOUT IT, HAVE THE COURTSEY TO SUFFER IN SILENCE.

3/22/20
HERE YOU GO, THANKS.
I'LL HELP SOMEONE. GIVE A LOT TO A POINT THAT IS. I WANT TO SEE A RETURN ON MY INVESTMENT YOU KNOW.
HOPEFULLY THAT WILL HELP.
AT SOME POINT THEY HAVE TO TRY.
THE REST IS UP TO YOU.
3/23/20
THAT'S TWO.
WAS SO GLAD TO GET OUT AND RIDE TOO LONG OFF THE BIKE IN THIS SCARE. THERE WAS NO ONE OUT.
CAN'T DENY THE SOLITUDE WAS VERY NICE.
ALL MINE.
3/24/20
HEY?!
WHAT ARE YOU DOING HERE NOW? YOU LOOK SO HAPPY?!
I GOT LAYED OFF!
OH! HAHA!

3/25/20
WHEN YOU SPEND SO MUCH TIME GETTING AROUND PROBLEMS ON A DAILY BASIS, YOU DO YOUR HOMEWORK.
SO NOW THAT THINGS ARE A LITTLE OUT OF THE NORM IT IS EASY TO FIGURE OUT BECAUSE MENTALLY, YOU'RE READY.
AND BEING READY IS WHERE IT IS AT.
3/26/20
YOU DID ANOTHER 16 HOUR DAY, STAY HOME AND SLEEP IN SOME.
YOU'RE GOING TO MAKE YOUR SELF SICK IF YOU DON'T TAKE IT EASY.
OK BODY. I HATE WHEN YOU'RE RIGHT.
3/26/20
WELL THAT WAS NO BIG DEAL
BZZZ
IT WAS NOT. I GET IN MY OWN WAY THINKING THAT SOMETHING I'VE DONE SO MANY TIMES WILL BE A BIG CHORE
SELF DOUBT IS THE BIGGEST ANCHOR IN ONE'S MIND.
LOOKS GOOD.

3/28/20
YOUR INTERNET IS SO SLOW!
IT IS?
YOU'VE GOT WIRELESS AND AN EITERNET CABLE HOLD ON!
WOW! IT HAS NEVER BEEN THIS FAST BEFORE!
3/29/20
5 PM. TIME TO GO HOME!
WORK HAS BEEN INSANE. SO BUSY. THIS CONTAGEN HAS FORCED SO MANY PEOPLE OFF THEIR COUCHES AND ONTO A BIKE.
NECOL STOPS
RENT
IT'S BEEN GREAT BUT I'M BEAT. SUCCESS CAN RUIN YOU TOO.
NOW NOTHING.
3/30/20
60 MILES AND SOME PALS.
WE TOOK OUR TIME.
FARMERS MAR
BECAUSE ONE SHOULD NOT FORGET TO ENJOY IT.

3/31/20
HAVE YOU SEEN HIM? MISSING
CALL HIS FRIENDS
OH MAN!
YOU PUT CHRIS ON A MILK CARTON!
TO LAUGH, WELL NOT MUCH IS GOLDEN IN THIS WORLD BUT A FEW MOMENTS CAN BE HAD WITH AN EFFORT.
4/1/20
DO YOU HAVE YOUR ARM GUARD ON?
NO.
I'LL MOST LIKLEY GET WACKED THERE AND REGRET IT.
AAG!
4/2/20
LOOK AT THIS PLACE! I JUST CLEANED IN HERE, WHAT HAPPENS?
WORK HAPPEND. I'M TOO BUSY TO KEEP THINGS TIDY.
I WORK WITH MY HANDS. NOT MY MOUTH YA KNOW.

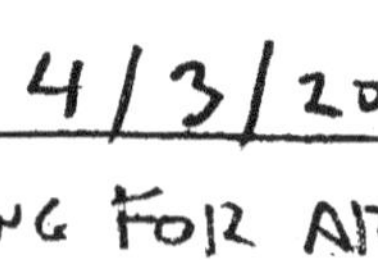

4/3/20
Looking for artwork for a flyer.
But I knew that was the path of least resistance— the easy way
None of these are right.
And that is not the way to go.
I'll have to do it myself.
4/4/20
It was easy.
Coaster made from USPS box
I don't know why I doubt myself but I do. Is it better to not be sure you're sure?
Perhaps one can be unsure that being sure can also be the same as being blind to mistakes. It's called wisdom.
4/5/20
That's one peak, let's go all the way to the other side.
OK
You want to go all the way up there?
Why not?

4/6/20
CAN YOU HEAR US?
YEAH.
YES
?
YES
OK LAST WE LEFT OFF YOU HAD CLEARED OUT THE CITADEL AND DEFEATED THE GHOST IN RED ARMOR.
WE USED SKYPE TO PLAY D&D. WE ARE IMPROVISING. I MUST ADMIT IT IS NOT SO BAD.
4/7/20
OK. KEEP TALKING THEN.
WORDS DON'T FIX THINGS. THINK OF ALL THE TREATIES AND TRADE AGREMENTS THAT GOT SO CASUALLY DISCARDED. JUST WORDS.
I'VE SPENT SO MUCH TIME MASTERING WORDS ONLY TO REALIZE IT IS A SWORD WITH A BROKEN TIP.
4/8/20
TO HAVE GOOD FRIENDS SUCH A GIFT.
SOME PLYWOOD PERHAPS.
CAN DO
AFTER INTERACTING WITH 1000'S OF PEOPLE, HAVING PEOPLE IN YOUR LIFE THAT TRULY ADD TO THE QUALITY OF YOUR LIFE EXPERIENCE IS SO RARE.
I HAVE! HUMANS.
A GOAL! TO BE COUNTED AS ONE OF THEM.
HAHA ALREADY! SO GOOD!

4/9/20

THERE IS A PLAGUE UPON THE LAND. IT IS CALLED FEAR.
WASH YOUR HANDS!

FEAR OF WHAT MAY HAPPEN WILL CAUSE PEOPLE TO DO STUPID THINGS. THE MASS HYSTERIA IS THE REAL CONTAGIAN.
6 FEET.

HOPEFULY, WE WILL NOT DO THINGS THAT WE LIVE TO REGRET.
ARE YOU AFRAID?
NO.

4/10/20

ANY LESS?
NOPE.

IT NEVER CEASES TO AMAZE ME THAT PEOPLE WILL HAGGLE WITH ME. OVER AND OVER AGAIN. EVERY DAY.
NO LESS.

AND 1000'S & AND 1000'S OF PEOPLE WILL FAIL OVER AND OVER AGAIN.
ADD YOUR NAME TO THE LIST.

4/11/20

YOU'RE RIDING TOMORROW? WHERE ARE YOU GOING?

59 MILES UP OVER SANTA SUSANA PASS AND THEN.. AND THEN.. AND THEN..

NEVER MIND.

4/12/20
OH SHIT!
YOU OK?
YEAH. WHAT A FALL!
MAN, I WISH I HAD SEEN THE WHOLE THING!
HA HA HA HA HA
4/13/20
BANK
OF ETERNAL SLAVERY
LINE.
I HAVE AN APPOINTMENT, DO I HAVE TO WAIT?
NO GO ON IN
NK
NAL SLAVER
WELL IT IS THE ONLY TIME IT IS OK TO WALK INTO A BANK WITH A MASK ON!
4/14/20
YOU CAN'T STAY HERE.
LATER...
COPS!
OK, WE TAKE THE HINT.

4/15/20
Hmm
FOOOOO...
I TAUGHT MYSELF HOW TO WELD WITH A TORCH TODAY.
THAT'S NOT RIGHT, I NEED TO LOOK IT UP.
WITH SOME HELP FROM YOUTUBE.
OH! A NEUTRAL FLAME!
4/16/20
NEVER EXPERIENCED SUCH A DEMAND FOR MY WORK. I'VE NEVER BEEN THIS BUSY THIS MANY DAYS IN A ROW.
I FEEL GOOD BECAUSE I DID NOT STRESS - I DID AS MUCH AS I COULD AND KEPT THE SHOP AFLOAT.
YOUR BIKES ARE DONE.
ALREADY!
BEING GOOD AT SOMETHING FEELS GOOD. I HIGHLY RECOMMEND YOU TRY IT.
KICK-ASS
4/17/20
WHAT AN ADVENTURE.
TAKING A WRONG TURN TOOK ME DOWN A WET CANYON. UP AND DOWN I WENT. SOAKED, I FOLLOWED THE WATER TO CIVILIZATION.
GLAD TO BE BACK ON DRY LAND. I'D NOT FORGET THE LITTLE ADVENTURES I DISCOVER, THEY MAKE LIFE WORTH LIVING.

4/18/20
SOMETIMES YOU JUST DRAW A BLANK ON WHAT TO DO NEXT.
EVERY DAY WE WANT TO BE INSPIRED TO HAVE A MAGIC MOMENT. TO HAVE SOME DRIVE.
SOMETIMES THOUGH TO BE ABLE TO JUST GET TO THE NEXT DAY IS ALL YOU GET.
TOMORROW
4/19/20
OK, I CAN SIT DOWN FOR A WHILE.
I'VE BEEN ON MY FEET FOR 12 1/2 HOURS FIXING BIKES. I DON'T MIND THOUGH.
I'M NEVER GOING TO BE IN THIS MUCH DEMAND AGAIN SO I'D BE A FOOL NOT TO MAKE THE MOST OF IT.
4/20/20
WE'D NEVER BE ABLE TO RIDE THAT ROAD NORMALLY NOW THAT THERE ARE NO CARS, WE CAN.
A ONCE IN A LIFE-TIME OPPROTUNITY!

4/21/20
!
EVERYONE STOP!
WAIT?
HUN?
THERE'S A SKUNK IN FRONT OF US!
WE CAN WAIT.
YEAH
4/22/20
CAN I COME IN WITHOUT MY MASK ON?
SURE COME ON IN. IT'S OK.
I'M OVER IT.
4/23/20
ARE YOU OK?
YEAH, I JUST NEED TO RELAX FOR A MINUTE.
WINNING AT CAPATIALISM IS KICKING MY BUTT.

4/24/20
THAT WAS A GOOD SCORE.
6K WORTH OF PARTS FOR A HUNDRED BUCKS!
IT'S NICE TO WIN ONCE IN A WHILE.
4/25/20
NOT NOW. HA HA!
YOU'LL NEVER GET IT TODAY. YOU HAVE TO LEAVE IT LIKE I ALWAYS SAY. LOOK AT ALL THESE BIKES.
WHEN WILL YOU LEARN YOU HAVE TO WAIT YOUR TURN?
4/26/20
WASA MATTER? YOU TIRED?
GEARS
NO GEARS
HUF HUF HUF.
IT IS GOOD TO FEEL STRONG.
DID IT.

4/27/20
THERE'S JUST TOO MUCH PRESSURE TO PERFORM AT THIS VERY HIGH LEVEL. OTHER COUNTRIES, PEOPLE RELAX, THEY TAKE BRAKES HERE WE GO GO GO.
AND HERE WE HAVE MENTAL ILLNESS, SUICIDE. PEOPLE ARE NOT HAPPY THAT IS FOR SURE.
WE SPEND OUR LIVES WORKING TO PAY BILLS FOR THINGS WE DON'T NEED. IT IS HOLLOW.
4/28/20
IS MY BIKE DONE?
DID I CALL YOU?
NO
OK THEN. NOT DONE.
...
4/29/20
I WONDER ABOUT HOW I SEE THE WORLD. SOMETIMES I WILL KNOW SOMEONES NAME BUT HAVE NEVER MET THEM BEFORE.
MY NAME IS CHARLES
OR I THINK ABOUT SOME ONE AND THEY SHOW UP.
HEY!
ODD.
I WONDER IF I THINK I SEE THINGS OR IF THEY ARE REALLY HAPPENING. IS MY PERCEPTION FALSE? OR AM I FOOLING MYSELF.
HMM

4/30/20
GETTING USED TO IT. THE CONSTANT 12-14 HOUR DAYS ON MY FEET. THE PHONE (THAT I HATE) RINGING CONSTANTLY
RING
I'VE GOTTEN USED TO PEOPLE PILED UP WAITING FOR ME TO OPEN. AND USED TO NOT FINISHING EVERYTHING.
YOU NEED TO GIVE ME 10 MINUTES.
I'VE NEVER HAD TO WORK THIS HARD THIS LONG BUT I'M GETTING USED TO IT.
5/1/20
LOOK, I CAN'T TAKE A BIKE BACK A SECOND TIME, I CAN'T RUN MY SHOP ON THE CAPRICIOUS WHIMS OF A CHILD.
NOT A CHILD, A WOMAN.
OH.
EVEN WORSE.
5/2/20
WHERE LIFE TAKES US, MOST OF US KNOW AS WE GO DOWN ON THE BOAT OF LIFE ON A SLOW MOVING STREAM.
EVEN THOSE THAT ENTER TO A LIFE OF CRIME OR DRUGS TAKE A KNOWN PATH. IT MAY SEEM LIKE THERE ARE TWISTS AND TURNS. THE COURSE IS PREDICTABLE - THEY WILL CAPSISE THEIR CRAFT.
ONLY A TRUE ADVENTURER GETS TO GO THROUGH LIFE WITH THEIR OAR IN THE WATER AND GO PLACES. PLACES THAT CAN ONLY BE SEEN UNDER YOUR OWN POWER.

5/3/20
I THINK MEN ARE MORE HONORABLE THAN WOMEN.
REALLY?
I THINK UNDER SCRUTINY, ALL PEOPLE ARE DISPICABLE.
I'D HAVE TO AGREE WITH THAT.
5/4/20
Look out!
oof!
You ok?
YEAH.
THAT WAS AWESOME!
5/5/20
THE PAY OFF.
OH WOW.
SLAVING AWAY, WORKING SO HARD; THE INCREASED DEMAND IS HUGE.
I'VE NEVER MADE THAT MUCH MONEY IN MY LIFE.
AND I MET THE CHALLENGE INSTEAD OF MAKING EXCUSES. SO THERE'S THE YIELD.
DON'T THINK I CAN KEEP IT UP FOREVER BUT FOR NOW.

5/6/20
WITH NO STREET LIGHTS ONLY LIT BY THE MOON AND OUR BIKE LIGHTS WE WORKED UP THE CANYON.
NOT SEEING ANYTHING WAS PART OF THE ADVENTURE. WHAT YOU DON'T KNOW MAKES IT WORTH IT.
I THINK WE GO THAT WAY.
A LIFE THAT IS INTERESTING - THAT IS THE LIFE WORTH LIVING.
5/7/20
CAN YOU FIX THIS?
I CAN'T NOW BECAUSE ITS NOT FAIR.
I DON'T CARE FAIR OR NOT, CAN YOU DO IT NOW.
NO.
5/8/20
BARELY MADE IT PAST 9 PM. SO TIRED.
SO MUCH TO DO AND THINGS KEEPING ME UP LATE.
SURE I'LL HELP YOU.
A RARE TIME: A NIGHT FOR ME AND ME ALONE.

5/9/20
33 BIKES LEFT TO FIX...
I HAVE NEVER BEEN THIS BUSY - NOT BY A LONG SHOT. THERE WAS NO WAY I'D EVER KNOW IT WOULD BE LIKE THIS.
BUT I KNOW ONE THING. STAY CALM.
YOU'RE BIKES ARE DONE.
WOW!
5/10/20
OH WOW.
THE WILD FLOWERS WERE AT THEIR BEST. NEVER SEEN SO MUCH COLOR - SO GLAD WE GOT TO SEE IT ALL; NATURE'S SPLENDOR.
THE WORLD IS A WONDEROUS, BEAUTIFUL PLACE - ALL YOU HAVE TO DO IS GO OUT AND LOOK.
AMAZING.
5/11/20
A PUNISHING CLIMB/PUSH UP HILL.
ANOTHER AWESOME VIEW
ALWAYS WORTH IT.
ON THE WAY HOME, 45 MILES & 6500 FEET OF CLIMBING I KNEW..
I'M FEELING HAPPY.

5/12/20
MAN DOWN!
MOMENTS LATER.....
ARE YOU OK?
OH YEAH! I FEEL GREAT!
5/15/20
MY COOKIE JAR. MINE.
ALL THOSE YEARS I SPENT TOILING AWAY - NOW MY SKILLS ARE IN DEMAND.
YOU SHOULD HIRE SOMEONE.
IT ONLY MAKES SENSE THAT I REAP MY REWARD
NO WAY, I'M NOT LETTING ANYONE GET INTO MY COOKIE JAR
FOOOOM...
ALMOST OUT.
WAK!
WAK!
HOURS LATER, AFTER SOAKING.
GOTCHA!

5/15/20
IT IS A CHALLENGE, THE WORK IS LONG, THERE ARE NO BRAKES.
I DOWN, 38 TO GO.
BUT THAT IS ALL IT IS; A CHALLENGE. I'M NOT GOING TO BE A MARTYR TO THIS WHOLE THING AND ACT LIKE I'M DOING SOMETHING EXTRA OR I'M SPECIAL.
YOUR BIKE IS DONE.
LEAVING THE 100TH VOICE MAIL NO ONE WILL LISTEN TO
BECAUSE I CAN ASSURE YOU, I'M NOT.
NOR WILL I EVER BE.
5/16/20
SPACE AND TIME DON'T HAVE ANY MEANING UNLESS YOU DO SOMETHING WITH THEM.
I'M NOT TALKING ABOUT PHONY FORCES THAT PEOPLE GIVE WEIGHT TO, BUT WHAT YOU PUSH FORWARD WITH YOUR TIME HERE.
TO-DO LIST
ONCE YOU HAVE MEANING, SPACE AND TIME BECOME MUCH MORE VALUEABLE TO YOU THAN SOMEONE THAT WATCHES TV ALL DAY.
5/17/20
HOW'S GOING BACK TO WORK?
ENH.
IT JUST SEEMS WRONG NOW, LIKE I'M NOT LIVING.
YEAH.
IT IS A SHAME WE SQUANDER OUR LIFE FORCE DOING THINGS WE THINK WE NEED TO DO BUT BRING US NO JOY.

5/18/20
MY GAME IS HERE!
A 1000 GAMES. I THOUGHT IT WOULD TAKE MORE ROOM.
ME TOO.
WE CELEBRATE?
AFTER I SELL ONE.
5/19/20
YOUR GAME? HOW MUCH?
25
GAME of TRUTH
I'LL TAKE IT
COOL!
ONE DOWN, 999 TO GO.
5/20/20
WHERE DO YOU WANT TO RIDE?
DUNNO
WELL... I LIKE GOING IN THE DIRT.
ME TOO!

5/21/20
JUST BEFORE DARK I MADE IT HOME. I HAVE NEVER STAYED LATE TO GET THINGS DONE BUT THERE IS 5 TIMES MORE WORK THAN USUAL.
I WAS GLAD I DID. I GOT A DELIVERY I NEEDED AND TOOK IN MORE WORK.
YES!
UPS
WHY NOT DO WHAT EVER IT TAKES TO MAKE THINGS WORK BETTER.
A LITTLE EXTRA EFFORT GOES A LONG WAY.
5/22/20
THAT'S A GREAT IDEA.
THE LOVE OF IDEAS AND THE ACTING UPON THEM - THAT IS MY TRUE CALLING
THEN WE CAN DO 1, 2, 3, ETC!
THE THING IS, ANYONE CAN UNLOCK THINGS IN THEIR MIND AND SET THEM FREE. BUT FEW DO.
I DON'T KNOW.
5/23/20
WHY CAN'T YOU JUST DO IT? IT IS EASY?
SURE IT IS. FOR ME. YOU CAN JUST LEAVE IT, JUST LIKE EVERYONE ELSE WITH ALL THE OTHER REPAIRS THAT ARE JUST SO EASY THAT NO ONE CAN DO THEM.
SO, YOU CAN JUST WAIT YOUR TURN, JUST LIKE EVERYONE ELSE OR JUST KEEP MOVING.

5/24/20
WE ARE DOOMED.
NOT BECAUSE WE WILL DESTROY OUR SELVES OR THE WORLD. THE WORLD DOES NOT NEED US.
WE ARE DOOMED BECAUSE WE ONLY CARE ABOUT OURSELVES
5/25/20
WE DID THE HELL RIDE. I MADE UP THE ROUTE AND IT LIVED UP TO ITS NAME SAKE.
I DON'T THINK I HAVE EVER DONE A RIDE THAT HARD. MY LEGS CRAMPED UP SO BAD AT THE END.
BUT I'LL TELL YOU, IT WAS SOMETHING ELSE.
5/26/20
7-11
E E E E E E E E E E E E E E E E
AHH
7-11
WHAT IS THAT NOISE? IS IT SUPPOSED TO BE A HOMELESS DETERENT?
E EE EE EE EE EE EE EE EE
E E E E E E E E
YEAH IT'S WORKING SO WELL

5/22/20
I BROUGHT YOU A GIFT.
YEAH?
IT'S CHOCOLATE COVERED HONEYCOMB TRY IT!
OK
OMGUH SOO SWEEEE
5/28/20
JUST KEEP GOING.
MAY AS WELL FINISH IT.
WE CAN ONLY MOVE FORWARD IN LIFE SO WHY NOT DO IT?...
OK DONE!
...WITH SOME FORCE BEHIND IT.
ANOTHER DAY NOT SQUANDERED.
5/29/20
DON'T WORRY, I'LL DO IT IN ORDER.
I KNOW YOU HAVE INTEGRITY
IT ANNOYS PEOPLE TO NO END THAT I HAVE INTEGRITY.

5/30/20
THE DIRTY BIKE.
THE DIRTY BIKE IS LOVED BECAUSE IT IS USED. ANYTHING THAT IS NOT USED IS NEGELECTED AND NEGLECT IS NOT LOVE.
SO GET YOUR BIKE DIRTY AND LOVE IT AND IT WILL LOVE YOU BACK.
5/31/20
CLOSED
CLOSED
CLOSED
?
RIOTS SHUT THINGS DOWN - IT'S NOT A PROBLEM. I DON'T HAVE EXPECTATIONS ABOUT A LOT OF THINGS
SO I DON'T EXPECT HUMANITY TO STOP BEING AWFUL.
6/1/20
I'M LONELY, I MISS YOU
?
SEEMS TO BE GOING AROUND. I HAVE 3 EX-GIRLFRIENDS THAT I'VE BEEN CHATTING WITH ON-LINE. IT FEELS OK THERE, ALSO LAME PERHAPS.
BUT I KNOW THEY REMEMBER A FALSE IDEA OF ME. NOTHING MORE.
EVER FORWARD.

6/2/20
A KNOCK AT MY DOOR.
KNOCK KNOCK
IT WAS MY FRIENDS WHO VIOLATED CURFEW TO COME SEE ME.
HEY!
WOULD YOUR FRIENDS RISK GETTING ARRESTED TO COME SEE YOU? I MUST BE THE WEALTHIEST MAN ALIVE.
6/3/20
WHAT I SHOULD DO...
THAT WORD "SHOULD" IT IS A WALL, A MAZE, A CROSS. IT MAKES PEOPLE INERT OR WALLOW IN REGRET. MAKES ONE FEEL LESS THAN WHEN SHOULD TURNS INTO DID NOT.
WHEN IT SHOULD TURN INTO..
I DID.
6/4/20
WHAT DAY OF THE WEEK IS IT?
HA!
YOU DON'T KNOW? YOU'RE LIVING THE LIFE.
I AM A SLAVE TO TIME HOWEVER.

6 / 5 / 20
THE LAST THING I WANTED TO DO WAS GO RIDE.
I WAS SO TIRED.
BUT I TOLD MYSELF I WOULD.
AND IF YOU CAN'T EVEN TRUST YOURSELF HOW CAN ANYONE TRUST YOU?
6 / 6 / 20
THAT IS A COOL RAIN COAT YOU HAVE.
I HAVE TWO, YOU CAN HAVE ONE.
REALLY?
I ONLY NEED ONE.
6 / 7 / 20
I NEED TO PUT IT SOME PLACE SAFE.
LATER.
WAK!
OH SHIT!
OF COURSE THAT HAD TO HAPPEN LIKE THAT.

6/8/20
DO YOU KNOW WHERE WE ARE?
NO IDEA
WE WERE LOST AND PAST THE POINT OF NO RETURN.
?
BUT WE KEPT OUR HEADS AND AFTER MANY HOURS, WE GOT OUT
THIS IS THE WAY.
6/9/20
I WAS TIRED. I SHOULD BE. I RODE 70 MILES YESTERDAY, WORKED FROM 5:30 AM TILL 6 PM TODAY, THEN RODE ANOTHER 20 MILES.
BUT I WANTED TO STAY UP A LITTLE LONGER WHEN I GOT HOME.
NOT 10 YET
IF I WENT TO BED BEFORE 10 PM I'D JUST FEEL OLD.
SO TIRED.
6/10/20
I SHALL NOT BE TAMED.
I THINK THAT IS THE BEST WAY I CAN SUM MYSELF UP. I WILL NOT BE TAMED, I WILL BE FREE.
I WILL REMAIN TRUE TO MYSELF AND A SLAVE TO NO ONE.
WOOOO!

6/11/20
JUST LIKE ANYTHING, YOU GET OUT OF PRACTICE THEN YOU GET RUSTY. THAT INCLUDES THINKING AND THINKING ABOUT IDEAS.
YOUR BRAIN IS PLASTIC SO YOU CAN TRAIN IT TO THINK ABOUT THINKING JUST LIKE YOU CAN PRACTICE GUITAR.
SO BEFORE YOU SIT DOWN AT HOME TAKE A 1/2 HOUR AND JUST SKETCH OUT IDEAS. IT IS PUSH-UPS FOR THE MIND.
6/12/20
THE WAY YOU TALK TO PEOPLE IS SO FUNNY!
YOU'RE SO DIRECT! NO ONE ELSE IS LIKE THAT!
NO?
HOW THE HELL ELSE ARE YOU GOING TO SAY WHAT YOU NEED TO SAY?
6/13/20
YOU WANT LUNCH? YOU DON'T HAVE TO DO THAT!
HERE'S THE COFFEE YOU WANTED.
REALLY?
PEOPLE WERE KIND TO ME TODAY, I'M NOT GOING TO FORGET THAT.

6 14/20
THEY ARE RIPE!
I GOT SOME TOMATOES TO SEED AND I PUT THEM IN A SALAD AND ATE THEM.
I MUST SAY IT WAS A REWARDING EXPERIENCE.
CHOMP
6 15 20
OH, A SINGLE SPEED, YOU'RE THE MAN!
I'M NOT SO SURE. JURY'S OUT ON THAT ONE.
SURE.
ALWAYS QUESTION.
6 16 20
BUT I'M SPECIAL.
NO ONE IS SPECIAL NO ONE. YOU CAN ONLY MAKE YOURSELF SPECIAL BY MAKING YOURSELF THAT WAY BY HOW YOU TREAT OTHERS.
AND EVEN THEN, IT IS ONLY FOR THAT PERSON FOR THAT MOMENT IN TIME. THEN YOU REVERT TO NON-SPECIAL STATUS WITH THE REST OF US.

6/17/20
THIS IS THE BEST BIKE SHOP I'VE EVER BEEN TO

I CAN'T DENY THAT I LOVE HEARING THAT. I WANT TO BE GOOD AT WHAT I DO. I DON'T EXPECT TO BE RECOGNIZED THOUGH.
THANKS!

BUT PRAISE IN SMALL DOSES IS A FORM OF CURRENCY I WILL ACCEPT.

6/18/20
FUCKING PEOPLE FUCKING PEOPLE FUCKING PEOPLE.

FUCKING PEOPLE FUKI- FUCKING PEOPLE FUCKIN PEOPL FOKINO PEOP LE FUCK FU FUCKI

WELL, MY BIKE NEVER DROVE ME NUTS.

6/19/20
JUST GET IT DONE.

JUST GET IT DONE. WHY WAIT? THERE IS SO MUCH TO DO. ONE LESS THING TO DO.

ONLY TO ADD A FEW...
NEVER ENDS...

6/20/20
A WEEEEK!?
SO MUCH ENDLESS BLEATING. I WONDER HOW MUCH TIME PEOPLE WASTE COMPLAINING ABOUT THINGS.
1 WEEK.
IF YOU KNEW IT NEVER DID ANYTHING WOULD YOU DO IT AGAIN?
UNDERSTAND?
6/21/20
THE GOOD NOISES...
OOOHOW!
DEEP DOWN INSIDE WE ARE STILL CAVE MEN - WHEN SOMETHING HAPPENS THAT HITS US ON A PRIMAL LEVEL WE JUST MAKE NOISE.
OOOR!
IT IS A GOOD NOISE. LANGUAGE FAILS UP AT THAT MOMENT AND OUR TRUE SELF IS SEEN.
GRUNH!
6/22/20
WE'LL NEVER GET THERE FROM HERE.
GETTING LOST IS PART OF THE FUN.
HOW BORING WOULD LIFE BE IF YOU KNEW WHAT LAY AROUND EVERY CORNER.
LES'I GO THIS WAY.

6/23/20
THAT WOULD BE SINCIRE FROM SOMEONE THAT HAD A HAIRCUT.
BIKE JERSEY
A HAIRCUT?
WHAT THE HELL IS THAT SUPPOSED TO MEAN?
6/24/20
WHAT ARE YOU HERE FOR?
DOES ANYONE KNOW? I'D HOPE YOU'RE NOT HERE JUST TO CONSUME THINGS, THAT MEANS YOU'RE NOT ADDING ANYTHING.
SOME ARE LUCKY ENOUGH TO HAVE AN IDEA THOUGH.
I'M HERE TO HELP.
6/25/20
CAN YOU JUST LOOK AT IT, IT IS A QUICK FIX.
NO.
IT IS NOT A QUICK FIX, YOU HAVE TO WAIT YOUR TURN.
BUT IT'S EASY.
SURE. EASY. FOR. ME.

6/26/20
I HAD NO IDEA WHAT I MADE LAST MONTH.
I'VE BEEN TOILING AWAY AT SUCH A PACE WHERE I DID NOT HAVE TIME TO LOOK.
SO I FIGURED I NEEDED A MENTAL COOKIE TO KEEP GOING.
MOST $ I'VE EVER MADE.
6/27/20
I LOVE TALKING TO YOU, I GET SO CENTERED.
MANY PEOPLE HAVE SAID THAT TO ME. I FIND IT ODD TO BE LOOKED UPON AS AN ANCHOR...
YOU DO?
BECAUSE INSIDE IT IS TOTAL CHAOS.
6/28/20
HOW YOU FEEL ABOUT SOMETHING IS A CHOICE.
BUT I NEED IT NOW.
NO WAY.
I OFTEN CHOOSE NOT TO EXPEND ENERGY ON HOW VILE PEOPLE ARE. I KNOW WE'RE DOOMED.
NO CAN DO.
SO I'M CHOOSING TO NOT TAKE IT PERSONAL. - I FEEL IT IS ON THEM, NOT ME.
C-YA!

6/29/20
TODAY WAS FULL OF:
NEW PLACES.
YOU EVER RIDE HERE BEFORE?
NOPE
NEW FACES.
I KNOW YOU I BOUGHT SOME BIKE PARTS FROM YOU!
COOL!
NEW ADVENTURES.
TO A GREAT RIDE!
6/30/20
YOU THINK BECAUSE YOU PUT YOUR NAME ON SOMETHING YOU MADE THAT YOU'LL BE IMMORTAL-IZED? DOUBTFUL
MY STORY
HOW MANY THINGS SPAN A GENERATION, A MOMENT? DO YOU THINK BRITNEY SPEARS WILL BE THOUGHT OF IN 100 YEARS?
WHO?
YOU SHOULD DO SOMETHING BECAUSE YOU REAP JOY OUT OF IT, NO OTHER REASON MATTERS.
7/1/20
I DON'T CARE WHAT YOU THINK ABOUT HOW I RUN MY SHOP.
YOU CAN WAIT YOUR TURN - LIKE EVERY ONE ELSE OR DO THE REPAIR YOUR SELF!
CONFORM TO MY WAY TO DO THINGS, NOT YOURS, DIG?

6/31/20
IT HURTS A LITTLE.
YEAH..
JUST WAIT TILL YOU'RE AN ADULT.
WHERE EVERY DAY IS PAIN.
?
I FLIP-FLOPPED THE DATES HERE SO THESE TWO PANELS ARE BLANK (WELL, THEY WERE.)
IT IS 4/1/24 TODAY SO THIS LAST BIT OF STUFF IS IN THE NOT TOO DISTANT PAST. I DON'T REALLY ENJOY THE REVIEW LIKE I MENTIONED BEFORE.
OOOH.
BAD.
HOW I DO COMICS IS AS FOLLOWS:
I THINK OF AN IDEA OR SOMETHING FUNNY HAPPENS DURING THE DAY
NO.
BUT
I TRY AND REMEMBER WHATEVER IT WAS THROUGHOUT THE DAY. I DO FORGET SOMETIMES OR NOTHING OF NOTE OCCURS.
?
BEFORE I GO TO BED. I PENCIL IN MY COMIC FOR THE DAY. SOMETIMES I NOD OFF WITH THE CLIPBOARD ON MY CHEST
AND SOMETIMES IT IS TOTAL GIBBERISH. BUT ONE A DAY? YES.
THIS MAKES NO SENSE.

7/2/20
YEAH KITTIES!
IT IS SO GRATE TO HAVE SOME FUZZY PALS AROUND THE HOUSE.
BECAUSE NO MATTER WHAT PEOPLE SAY, THEY DON'T WANT TO BE ALONE.
7/3/20
FINALLY SOME REST!
A HOLIDAY MEANS A FUN DAY BUT I NEEDED TO REST SO BAD. MY BODY SAYS SO.
SO I'M GOING TO LISTEN FOR ONCE.
7/4/20
HERE I AM BEING A COUCH POTATO.
DANK CAT MEMES 9
I DON'T KNOW HOW PEOPLE DO THIS ALL DAY...
DANK CAT MEMES 10
CAN'T WAIT TO FEEL BETTER.
DANK CAT MEMES 11

7/5/20
THE TIME AND ENERGY YOU GIVE TO OTHERS IS WHAT MAKES YOU SPECIAL TO THEM.
HERE YOU GO
ALL THAT?
YEP
I DON'T KNOW WHY PEOPLE CAN'T SEE THIS PART OF LIFES EQUATION.
GREAT TIME.
THANKS.
IT'S NOT WHAT YOU GET. IT'S WHAT YOU GIVE
...
7/6/20
ARE YOU SLEEPY?
CAN'T KEEP YOUR EYES OPEN HUN?
GOOD NIGHT.
A WEEK?! THAT IS SO LONG...!!
SURE, YOU THINK YOU HAVE A MONOPOLY ON BEING A SELFISH PRICK?
WORLD IS FULL OF YOU DICKHEADS

7/8/20
YOU DID THAT?
IF YOU HAVE A HEART WARMING STORY, I SAY SNARE THEM.
SHE SAID SHE'D GIVE ME THE HOUSE IF SHE COULD.
IF YOU CAN INSPIRE SOMEONE, THAT IS SURE THERE IS NOT ENOUGH TO GO AROUND.
YOU CAN DO IT.
7/9/20
I HAVE NEVER FELT SO TIRED IN MY LIFE.
IT IS A CHALLENGE TO GET THROUGH IT ALL. I HOPE TO LOOK BACK AND LAUGH.
THAT WAS SOMETHING!
BUT FOR NOW, I JUST ACHE.
7/10/20
I'M TRYING TO HELP YOU.
YOU ALWAYS GIVE ME ATTITUDE!
THERE ARE OTHER BIKE SHOPS YOU KNOW I CAN GO THERE!
WELL...
I GOT NO PROBLEM WITH THAT.
?

7/11/20

YESTERDAY.
HERE YOU GO!
?

IT WAS AMAZING - OVER A DECADE + ½ WORTH OF MY EVENT FLYERS, T-SHIRTS, BUTTONS ETC... 100's OF PAGES.
COASTER

THANK YOU.. "SNIFF"
IT'S OK. I COULD HAVE BEEN WATCHING T.V. INSTEAD.

2/12/20

I THOUGHT YOU KNEW - SHE DIED.

IT IS A BUMMER TO LAY SOME HEAVY NEWS ON SOMEONE...
WHEN? WHY?

BUT IN FAIRNESS.. THEY DESERVE TO KNOW.
A COUPLE YEARS BACK - CANCER.

2/13/20

THAT HAS TO BE IT!

MY MORNING COFFEE IS MAKING ME FEEL SO BAD. I THINK THE MACHINE IS FULL OF GUNK OR MOLD THAT IS POISONING ME.

SO TODAY I CLEANED IT OUT REALLY GOOD. I HOPE IT DOES THE TRICK.
BECAUSE I'M ADDICTED.

7/14/20
I KNOW IT HAS NOT BEEN A WEEK
I CALLED YOU
NO NO. NONE OF THAT. I DON'T HAVE TIME FOR YOU TO SEE YOUR WAY GOD BETRAYED YOU.
? ? ?
I CALLED YOU. YOU'RE HERE NOW, LETS GET YOUR BIKE.
HAVE YOU HEARD OF OBOKOTE BEAVER?
NO?
BLISTERING HARDCORE FROM JAPAN
CHILLS RAN DOWN MY SPINE.
I HAVE TO HAVE THAT.
YOU CANNOT SAY YOU WILL DO SOMETHING AND BE SURE YOU CAN BECAUSE YOU CANNOT CONTROL THE FUTURE.
IF YOU SAY YOU'RE GOING TO BE SOMEWHERE BUT YOUR CAR WON'T START WHAT THEN? YOUR CAR DOES NOT CARE ABOUT YOUR LOVE.
WRRR RRR
CERTAINTY IS UNCERTAIN, THAT IS CERTAIN.
I'M NOT GOING TO MAKE IT

7/17/20
?
NEVER SEEN THAT BEFORE.
DOWN I WENT AND I WAS SO GLAD I DID. THE PATH UNFOLDING BEFORE ME IN A NEW ADVENTURE.
OH BICYCLE, HOW I OWE THEE THE WORLD.
7/18/20
THAT'S A GOOD IDEA.
THE THING IS TIME. I'LL NEVER HAVE THE TIME TO IMPLEMENT ALL THE IDEAS I HAVE.
BUT I'LL ALWAYS HAVE TIME TO DO SOME OF THEM.
7/19/20
IF YOU MUST BELIEVE IN ANYTHING - BELIEVE IN FUN.
WHEN PEOPLE ARE HAVING FUN THERE IS NO HATE, ONLY JOY. THERE IS PEACE & LOVE.
HaHaHa.
FUN HAS NO MALACE, FUN ONLY HAS FRIENDS

7/20/20
?
THAT GUY JUST GAVE ME 2 DOLLARS BECAUSE HE THOUGHT I WAS HOMELESS.
THAT'S A WIN.
7/21/20
POOF!
. . .
!
HE ATE SHIT.
I'M GOOD!
7/22/20
THAT WAS THE MOST FUN I'VE HAD IN MY LIFE!
IT SEEMED LIKE IT COULD NOT BE TRUE. SURLY HES HAD MORE FUN SOMEWHERE
BUT IF IT WERE TRUE. WELL THEN AT LONG LAST I'D BE ONTO SOMETHING.
REALLY WOW!

7/23/20
THE TEMPLE OF THE SELF.
HOW MUCH TIME DO WE SPEND ALONE WITH OURSELF? WITH OUR OWN THOUGHTS, IN OUR OWN HEAD IN OUR OWN SPACE.
NOT ENOUGH. AND IF YOU CAN'T GO TO CHURCH THEN HOW CAN YOU CENTER YOURSELF.
BALANCE.
7/24/20
YOU'RE THE BEST ONE!
I AM?
YOU'RE REALLY GOOD AT WHAT YOU DO
IF YOU SAY SO...
7/25/20
HE'S CUTE.
HE IS.
BUT HE HAS TO GO.

7/26/20
!
SKID!
!
MISSED ME BITCH!

7/27/20
THERES SHADE HERE.
I KNOW BUT I'D LIKE THE VIEW, MORE UP.
I WANT IT TO BE MEMORABLE.

7/28/20
HUF HUF.
PUSH PUSH
HOW'S THE VIEW?
SO WORTH IT.

7/29/20
THE ONLY THING STOPPING YOU IS YOU.
I NEED TO DO SOMETHING BESIDES GO TO WORK, WE ALL DO THAT.
I WONDER WHAT THE WORLD WOULD BE LIKE IF WE GOT OUT OF OUR OWN WAY.
I CAN DO THAT.
IT WOULD BE A WONDERFUL PLACE, THAT'S FOR SURE.
WELL, IT'S NICE TO DREAM...
7/30/20
IF YOU DON'T CARE ABOUT A THING OR IDEA, IT HOLDS NO POWER OVER YOU.
I SAW THIS ON FACEBOOK
I DON'T HAVE FACEBOOK.
I FAIL TO SEE HOW PEOPLE DON'T GET THAT. YOU GIVE THINGS POWER OVER YOU BY GIVING THEM VALUE THEY DON'T REALLY HAVE.
I DON'T CARE WHAT GOES ON THERE.
IN THE END IT IS YOUR CHOICE.
IT MEANS NOTHING TO ME...
8/1/20
THE UNINHIBITED MIND IS THE FREE MIND. THERE IS THE LAW OF THE LAND BUT BEYOND THAT, WE LAYER MANY MORE RULES UPON OURSELF.
VEGAN
IF YOU CHOOSE TO NOT FEEL LIKE YOU HAVE TO JOIN IN A COMMONLY HELD IDEA THEN IT HOLDS NO POWER OVER YOU.
MY NEWEST CAR IS FROM 1989
THEN YOU CAN DEVOTE MENTAL ENERGY TO THINGS THAT ACTUALLY MATTER
WANT TO RIDE BIKES?
YES!

8/2/20
I FEAR WE WILL NEVER GET THERE, TO THE PLACE WE NEED TO BE.
MACHINES, TECHNOLOGY AND GADGETS WILL NOT AVAIL US TO ENLIGHTENMENT, WE ARE STILL SAVAGES
HUMANITY CANNOT SIMPLY PUT THE HUMANITY ASIDE TO BE MORE HUMAN.
8/3/20
THE BEAST
1940's BRIDGEPORT MILL. SUCH A DEAL BUT SO HEAVY, WE HAD TO PUSH IT WITH MY VAN.
CAR TIRE
VAROOOOM
USING EVERY OUNCE OF STRENGTH AND BRAINS I HAD, I GOT IT TO IT'S NEW HOME.
I WON.
8/4/20
OKI DOG!
WE'RE ALMOST THERE.
NOOOOOO!
OKI DOG
CLOSED

8/5/20
WELL, YOU HAVE TO TRY...
IF YOU DON'T EVEN TRY YOU'LL NEVER KNOW IF IT WILL WORK OUT OR NOT. WHY WOULD YOU NOT WANT TO GIVE IT A SHOT?
DAY DREAMING ABOUT AN IDEA ONLY HAS SO MUCH VALUE - THE REAL TREASURE IS IN DOING SOMETHING.
8/6/20
CAN I JUST BORROW YOUR TOOL?
GRRRR
NO, BECAUSE YOU WON'T KNOW HOW TO DO IT THEN I HAVE TO HELP YOU. THEN I HAVE TO HELP YOU AND STOP WHAT I'M DOING MAKING YOU FIRST IN LINE...
...WHICH YOU ARE NOT, YOU ARE BOTH IN LINE SO YOU STILL HAVE TO WAIT YOUR TURN LIKE EVERY ONE ELSE, IT'S NOT FAIR.
8/7/20
I'M SORRY
FUCKING DOG ON FUCKING LEASH YOU FUCKING PRICK

8/8/20
YOU'RE VERY NICE.
IT'S EASIER TO BE THAT WAY RIGHT?
I'D SAY IT TAKES WAY MORE STRENGTH TO BE KIND THAN TO BE A JERK.
8/9/20
DO YOU KNOW WHERE THE CAVE IS?
CAVE?
THERE'S A CAVE UP HERE WITH A SWING.
WHITE MAN'S WORDS. THEY MEAN NOTHING TO ME.
8/10/20
?
WHATS UP WITH THESE BOOKS?
THEY ARE FREE.
FREE BOOKS OH YEAH!

8/11/20
WE RODE THROUGH AN ABANDONED BATTING CAGE.
EYES PEERED OUT FROM THE HUT THROUGH BROKEN GLASS
SURREAL
8/12/20
OVER AND OVER AND OVER
IT WILL BE A WEEK..
AND OVER AND OVER AND
WE'RE GOING OUT OF TOWN, I CAN GIVE YOU MORE MONEY..
OVER AND OVER AND OVER
NO, YOU CAN'T IT'S NOT FAIR TO THE PEOPLE THAT CAN BARELY AFFORD ME.
8/13/20
CA- CHUNK!
I GOT A BUTTON MACHINE - THE BEST ONE MONEY CAN BUY. I KNOW THE VALUE OF GOOD TOOLS
THEY CAN TAKE YOU PLACES.

8/14/20
I'm LOOKING ALL OVER FOR A CASE OF TUBES.
I THOUGHT I WAS LOSING MY MIND - SO MUCH WORK, I AM MAKING MISTAKES.
DID THE GET THROWN OUT?
IN THE END THE TRUTH WAS NOT SO BAD.
I PUT THEM IN A DRAWER.
8/15/20
DID I FORGET SOMETHING?
I WONDER ABOUT ALL THE THINGS I WANTED TO DO AND FORGOT OR ALL THE GOOD IDEAS I HAD THAT WERE LOST TO THE VOID.
I WONDER IF IT MATTERS OR NOT, WOULD MY LIFE BE ANY DIFFERENT?
8/16/20
CLICK.
DONATE
THERE IS SO MUCH BAD OUT THERE ON THE INTERNET. SO MUCH EVIL, WE HEAR ABOUT IT ALL NOW.
FEELINGS OF SADNESS AND POWERLESSNESS ARE ABOUND. AND WHAT DO WE DO? WELL SOMETHING - DO SOMETHING

8/17/20
WHEN YOU DID A LOT AND FINISHED THINGS, YOU KNOW IT WAS A GOOD DAY
WHEN YOU HELPED OUT SOME PALS AND GAVE YOUR TIME TO OTHERS, IT WAS A GOOD DAY.
THANKS!
WHEN YOU CAN LAY DOWN AT NIGHT KNOWING YOU PUT A LITTLE GOOD OUT THERE, IT WAS A GOOD DAY.
8/18/20
I MADE "RADNESS KITS" FOR EVERY ONE ON OUR BMX RIDE. WE HAVE BEEN DOING IT FOR OVER 11 YEARS.
RADNESS KITS!
RAD!
YOU GET A LONG SLEEVE T-SHIRT, A PATCH, POSTER, STICKERS, BUTTONS AND A ZINE.
LITTLE TOKENS OF JOY TO GO WITH YOUR MEMORIES, WHAT MORE COULD YOU WANT?
8/19/20
INTERNET DOWN?
THERE WAS MY CAT, HANGING OUT.
?
HELLO.
INTERACTING WITH HIM WAS A MORE REWARDING EXPERIENCE.
PRRR

8/20/20
WHEN I DON'T EAT ENOUGH I PAY THE PRICE. I GET SO HUNGRY I HAVE TO KEEP EATING.
AND EATING
GARF
AND EATING TO NO AVAIL. I REALLY NEED TO PACE MY SELF BETTER.
8/21/20
AFTER NEARLY 5 MONTHS OF CONSTANT WORK I GOT TO SIT DOWN FOR 5 MINUTES.
MY FEET WERE SMOLDERING
NEVER HAVE THEY HURT SO
I LOOK FORWARD TO THE LITTLE THINGS LIKE BEING ABLE TO SIT AND READ FOR A SPELL
8/22/20
THANK YOU FOR HAVING FAIR PRICES
THEY HAVE TO BE.
NOT EVERONE DOES, THAT, IT IS RARE.
I GUESS
THE WORLD IS AN UNFAIR PLACE SO IF YOU WANT IT TO IMPROVE, YOU MUST START WITH YOURSELF.

8/23/20

BEING LAZY ONLY MAKES YOU HAVE DOUBLE THE WORK LATER.

PEOPLE THAT ARE INDUSTRIOUS ARE ALWAYS FORGING AHEAD AND THAT TAKES LESS EFFORT.

THAN SOMEONE WHO IS ALWAYS TRYING TO CATCH UP.

I WAITED TOO LONG.

8/24/20

UP AND UP

I WANTED TO QUIT SO BAD BUT IT WAS A CHALLENGE THAT I SET FOR MYSELF.

42:18

AND BY NOT QUITTING, I PROVED MY WORTH.

HARDEST CLIMB EVER.

8/26/20

OUR SPOT.

IN SOME NEW RICH AREA THEY HAVE A PATIO AND SOME BENCHES. THESE PEOPLE WILL NEVER USE THEM.

TURN YOUR LIGHTS OFF.

SO WE SNEAK IN AND MAKE IT OURS.

8/26/20
SCREECH!
?
OF COURSE I DID NOT SEE MY CAT AROUND AND BEGAN TO FEAR THE WORST. NORMAL TACTICS TO MAKE HIM COME OUT DID NOT WORK.
TAP TAP
CATS
OF COURSE, NOTHING WAS WRONG.
HELLO!
PRRR
8/27/20
I FEEL BAD FOR PEOPLE THAT ARE SLAVES TO BAD IDEAS.
HMM
LA DWP BILL
LIKE HAVING GRASS IN AN ARID PLACE LIKE L.A. THROWING MONEY DOWN A HOLE.
ELETRIC USAGE $163.28
WATER USAGE $ 6.93
THE ONLY HOLE MY MONEY SHOULD GO IN IS THE HOLE WHERE MY POCKET IS.
8/28/20
YOU MIND IF I BLOW UP YOUR BATHROOM?
GO AHEAD.
I DON'T WANT TO STINK UP YOUR PLACE..
NO WORRIES
I'VE BEEN FARTING ON YOU GUYS ALL NIGHT.

8/29/20
IS THERE... SOMETHING OUT THERE?
PEOPLE ARE SO DESPERATE TO HAVE SOMETHING OUT THERE. A GOD. A GREAT LOVE. A HOPE. OVER AND OVER THEY LOOK OUT AND NOT GET WHAT THEY WANT.
PERHAPS THEY ARE IN THE WRONG PLACE-THOSE THINGS, THEY ARE LOCATED WITHIN.
8/30/20
WE HEAR YOU'RE GOOD AT FIXING BIKES.
I HOPE SO BY NOW.
MANY PEOPLE, MOST I'D SAY, PINE TO GET SOME RECOGNITION FOR ANYTHING-MOST GET LITTLE OR NONE.
NICE HAT.
SO AT LEAST THERE, I'D SAY, I'M A WEALTHY GUY..
OK-THANK YOU.
8/31/20
I JUST NEED TO DO IT THE RIGHT WAY.
DOING THINGS THE RIGHT WAY IS A MASTER STROKE IN BECOMING AN ELIGHTENED INDIVIDUAL
YOU SAVE TIME AND HAVE THE ASURANCE THAT WHAT YOU DID WILL WORK RIGHT. TO MESS WITH THE FORMULA JUST PAINS YOU IN A CORNER.

9/1/20
ADVENTURE IS AT YOUR FINGER TIPS, ALL YOU HAVE TO DO IS REACH OUT A LITTLE FURTHER THAN OTHERS.
WHILE OTHERS ARE AT HOME, YOU CAN BE OUT DOING SOMETHING IN YOUR BACK YARD YOU'VE NEVER DONE BEFORE.
BUT FIRST - ONE MUST TAKE THAT FIRST STEP.
9/2/20
FOR DECADES, THE WISE MAN LISTENED.
AFTER MUCH CONTEMPLATION, HE SPOKE.
HE'S GOING TO SAY SOMETHING!
SHUT THE FUCK UP.
9/3/20
I'VE NEVER DONE ANY DRUGS IN MY LIFE
NO ONE HAS EVER NOT BEEN SURPRISED BY THAT - NO ONE.
REALLY? FOR REAL? THAT IS ADMIRABLE!
BUT IN THE END;
EH. IT IS JUST A CHOICE.

9/4/20
I'M TOO NICE...
NO ONE IS TOO NICE, THINK WHAT YOU GOT BECAUSE I HELD MY HAND OUT.
WOULD ANY OF US BE HERE NOW ON THIS MOUNTAIN HAVING THIS MOMENT IF I DID NOT HAVE MY HAND OUT?
9/5/20
WHEN YOU DO TOO MUCH, I AM PAST MY BEDTIME.
I WILL NOT BE ABLE TO SLEEP IN, NEVER COULD.
5:30
BUT IT IS JUST ONE DAY - ONE DAY OUT OF MANY....
9/6/20
THE CARDS YOU'RE DEALT. THEY COULD BE HIGH OR LOW CARDS.
YOU CAN TRADE BAD ONES FOR GOOD IN LIFE OR MESS UP BY TRADING THE GOOD ONES FOR BAD - UP TO YOU.
ALSO IN THE HAND YOU'RE DEALT YOU GET TWO MORE CARDS: THE EXCUSE CARD AND THE SOLUTION CARD. WHICH ONE WILL YOU PLAY?
SOLUTION

9/7/20
IT WAS THE BEST RIDE. WE HAD A LITTLE BIT OF EVERYTHING. THE PACING WAS GOOD — EVERYONE AGREED.
THE BEST RIDE.
WE HAD CHALLENGE, ADVENTURE, FUN, EXPLORATION, THE UNKNOWN, SWEAT, SMILES AND A SENSE OF ACCOMPLISHMENT.
THE BEST PART IS A SHARED EXPERIENCE THAT CAN NEVER BE TAKEN FROM US.
THAT WAS AWESOME!
9/8/20
I FINALLY STARTED ANSWERING THE PHONE AGAIN AT WORK AFTER 5 MONTHS.
ARE YOU THERE?
I HOPED THE TIME AWAY WOULD HELP BUT IT DID NOT. PHONES ARE DUMB.
HOW LONG WILL IT TAKE?
AND THE PEOPLE THAT USE THEM, DUMBER.
I DON'T KNOW.
WHY NOT?
9/9/20
WHATS THE PROBLEM? I FIXED THE CRANK LIKE YOU SAID. YOU SAID NOTHING ABOUT BRAKES.
IF YOU WANT THEM FIXED, SURE BUT IT'S MORE MONEY.
WHAT? FOR FREE?
IT'S NOT BUY ONE GET ONE FREE. WHAT'S WRONG WITH YOU?

9/10/20

HOW THE INTERNET IS A SWORD TURNED UPON THE USER.

SNIK!

ONE LOOKS AT WHAT EVERYONE ELSE IS DOING (IF THEY REALLY ARE THAT IS) AND CAN ONLY FEEL MORE OUT OF TOUCH AND MORE ALONE.

IT IS USED TO CONNECT PEOPLE BUT IN REALITY IT DRIVES US FURTHER APART.

9/11/20

OH MEMORY LANE, HOW IT LEADS YOU DOWN UNFAMILIAR ROADS.

THE SNAPSHOTS OF YOUR MIND LEAVES OUT SO MUCH DETAIL. WE CAN LAUGH AT THE IDEA OF ONE'S MEMORY BUT NOT THE TRUE FACKS OF EVENTS

WHAT WE REMEMBER IS WHAT WE WANT TO REMEMBER. A PICTURE IN A YELLOWD GLASS FRAME AT BEST.

9/12/20

THERE SEEMS TO BE A DRIVE TO MAKE PEACE WITH BEING UNPRODUCTIVE. THAT IT IS OK TO DO NOTHING.

BEING LAZY IS A CURSE. YOU STRUGGLE ALL YOUR LIFE NOT TO BE ENSLAVED BY SLOTH.

I SHOULD DO SOMETHING.

AND IF YOU DON'T YOU CAN BE SURE WHEN YOU LOOK BACK AT YOUR LIFE YOU'LL SEE..

NOTHING.

9/13/20
FUN WILL NOT COME TO YOU, YOU MUST GO OUT AND SEEK IT.
AND FUN TAKES A LOT OF EFFORT. ONE MUST PUT IN THE WORK OR FUN YOU WILL NOT HAVE.
I KNOW THIS, SO I GET TO HAVE FUN, EVERY WEEK, ONE FUN THING AFTER ANOTHER. SO MANY MISS OUT.
9/14/20
ONLY 3 WEEKS AWAY, I NEED TO GET THIS DONE!
I WON'T HAVE TIME TO COLOR THE FLYER...
NO... I WILL MAKE IT HAPPEN!
9/15/20
OOOF!
OH MAN, YOU OK?
NEARLY EVERYONE ELSE FELL DOWN THE SLOPE. I CAN'T SAY IT WAS NOT FUNNY.
HE HE HE.

9/16/20
THE CURSE OF THE "SMART" GUY!
ALWAYS SO CLEVER - A KEEN MIND, SURE.
I'VE SEEN A LOT OF "SMART" PEOPLE FEEL THAT THEY SHOULD BE FURTHER ALONG THEN THEY ARE.
WHAT'S HE GOT THAT I DON'T?
BUT THE MASTER STROKE OF INTELLIGENCE IS FIGURING OUT WHAT PATH TO WALK. IF YOU'RE SO SMART, WHY CAN'T YOU FIGURE OUT A WAY TO GET THERE?
SO TIRED...
I DID A LITTLE BIT MORE TODAY. I TRY TO DO A LITTLE BIT MORE EVERY DAY.
OK. DONE.
AND THERE LIES ALL THE DIFFERENCE IN THE WORLD.
I STEP CLOSER.
NOT A NORMAL NIGHT.
YAAH!
NOT MANY PEOPLE CAN SAY THEY DRESSED UP LIKE NINJAS AND BATTLED EACH OTHER ON BICYCLES.
BUT WE CAN.
HA HA HA HA!

9/19/20
HELLO
IS MY BIKE GOING TO BE DONE TODAY?
I DON'T KNOW. WHAT I DO KNOW IS, I CANNOT WORK ON YOUR BIKE WITH A PHONE IN MY HANDS INSTEAD OF MY TOOLS..
...
HERE!
IS THAT A PILLOW?
AND A WHITE CASE?
YEAH!
WELL, THAT WON'T LAST LONG IN MY WORLD.
?
I THINK I MADE A WRONG TURN THERE. WE'RE AT THE OCEAN.
WE'LL HAVE TO CLIMB OVER AGAIN I GUESS.

9/22/20
ALL DAY LONG PEOPLE WERE JERKS, SOME THING WAS OFF FOR SURE.
ON THE ROAD THERE WAS CAR CHASINGS, BURN OUTS AND HONKING OVER AND OVER AGAIN
BEEEP
BUT WHEN I GOT HOME I WAS GREETED BY MY LITTLE FRIENDS AND ALL WAS WELL.
PRRRR
9/23/20
I LOVE THAT ALBUM! IT GIVES ME GOOSE PIMPLES JUST TALKING ABOUT IT!
I HAVE THEM ON MY LEGS!
ME TOO!
9/24/20
ARE YOU A SAGATARIOUS?
NO.
THE THING IS, ONLY ONE PERSON HAS EVER GUESSED RIGHT AND IT WAS SOME DRUGGIE IN PASSING
SO I'D SAY YOU CAN'T PUT PEOPLE IN A CATAGORY AND EXPECT IT TO FIT.

9/25/20
HOW'S IT GOING?
YOU KNOW THE USUAL. WAGING AN UNWINABLE WAR AGAINST THE LOWER I.Q.'S THAT ROAMS THE EARTH.
I FEEL YOU.
9/26/20
THAT GUY IS OUTSIDE AND LOCKED OUT OF HIS PARENTS HOUSE?
YEAH, THEY BOARDED UP THE WINDOWS ON THEIR OWN HOUSE
THEY GOT THE CHILD THAT THEY DESERVE.
9/27/20
OH SHIT MY FRAME IS CRACKED!
IF YOU HAD A RATCHET STRAP YOU CAN HOLD IT TO- GETHER
I DO
BEER
HOPEFULLY I'LL SURVIVE

9/28/20
THE DAY STARTED OUT WRONG.
WHERE IS THAT CHARGER? I HAVE SO MUCH TO DO!
BUT AS THE DAY WENT ON.
FOUND THAT, WELDED THAT, FINISHED THAT, MADE SOME PROGRESS ON THAT.
BY ACTION AND WILLFUL CHOICE I MADE IT A GOOD DAY.
I CAN BE MY OWN BEST ALLY OR ENEMY, MY CHOICE.
9/29/20
WHAT A GOOD DAY TO ENJOY THE LITTLE THINGS. WE RODE BIKES.
THEN WE HAD PIZZA AND THREW FIREWORKS AROUND.
POP
POW
I LAYED BACK AS WE LAUGHED - HAPPY TO BE ALIVE AMONG FRIENDS.
BUGS
9/30/20
CAN YOU HELP ME?
I'M TRYING TO LET THE AIR OUT OF THIS KIDDIE POOL AND CAN'T DO IT.
I'LL TRY.
HERE YOU GO. THERE IS A SECOND VALVE HERE. ALL SET.
OH THANK YOU!

10/1/20

THE WALKING STICK OR THE CANE? WHICH ONE DO YOU CARRY?

THE THINGS YOU TAKE IN LIFE TO HELP YOU ALONG CAN EASILY TURN FROM THE AID OF A WALKING STICK TO THE DEPENDENCE OF A CANE.

BE WISE ENOUGH TO KNOW WHEN TO LET GO.

10/ 2/ 20

HMMM

AH ANOTHER BOOK FINISHED. THE BEST PART IS BEING ABLE TO PICK UP ANOTHER ONE.
WHICH ONE.?

EACH ONE TAKES YOU TO A NEW WORLD. HOW ONE CAN TRAVEL TO DISTANT TIMES AND LANDS AND NOT LEAVE ONES HOME IS MAGIC.

10/ 3/ 20

FINALLY GOT MY SAMPLES.

SO MUCH BACK AND FORTH OVER A YEAR OF GETTING IT RIGHT. THEN THE SAMPLE GETS LOST IN THE MAIL - TWICE!
THE NOTE OF DOOM

I MADE MYSELF SICK WITH WORRY AS I WENT TO THE POST OFFICE. I FELT LIKE I'D CRY IF IT WAS LOST. SAD TO BE LET DOWN.

10/4/20
HOW TO WIN..
THINK OF WHAT YOU'D LIKE TO DO.
?
MAKE A PLAN ON HOW TO DO IT.
AND THEN INACT YOUR PLAN.
10/5/20
YOUR PAD IS IN THE GUTTER!
?
I HAD THOUGHT IT WAS LOST FOR GOOD. BUT THERE IT WAS ON MY STREET..
AMERICAN EAGLE
TRY NOT TO LOSE IT AGAIN.
10/6/20
WELL WE'RE HAVING A WACKY DETN-MOTO BIKE PARTY AT MY HOUSE BRING YOUR FRIENDS.
THAT'S SO COOL YOU'RE SO INCLUSIVE I DON'T GET THAT MUCH IN LA.
OH... WELL MOST OF US ARE NATIVES

10/7/20
THINKING ABOUT HOW GOOD COFFEE IS GOING TO BE TOMORROW.
I CAN ONLY TRY AND BE WISE BY SEEING HOW LUCKY I AM TO HAVE A SIMPLE THING TO LOOK FORWARD TO THAT GIVES ME JOY...
...KNOWING THAT SO MANY GO THROUGH LIFE WITH NOTHING GOOD ON THE HORIZON.
10/8/20
I'VE BEEN WATCHING A LITTLE PLANT ON MY KITCHEN WINDOW AND TODAY IT FELL OUT.
I THOUGHT IT WAS DEAD, BUT ON A WHIM I PUT IT BACK IN THE SOIL.
AND TO MY SURPRISE, IT SPRANG BACK TO LIFE! THE WORLD IS AN AMAZING PLACE.
10/9/20
THE GREATEST GIFT YOU CAN GIVE SOME ONE IS TO BE A GOOD FRIEND.
IF YOU CAN GIVE TO YOUR FRIENDS, IT IS WORTH A 1000 TIMES WHATEVER YOU MAY GET BACK.
THANK YOU.
WHILE DOING SO WON'T PUT YOU IN THE HISTORY BOOKS, YOU'RE MAKING THE WORLD JUST A LITTLE MORE FILLED WITH LOVE AND JOY IF YOU DID NOT.

10 | 10 | 20

I WON'T DO MYSELF A DISERVICE AND ACT LIKE I KNOW SOMETHING WHEN I DON'T

I DON'T KNOW.

I THINK IT IS TOO EASY TO THINK YOU KNOW SOMETHING AND HAVE CONFINDANCE THAT CAN TURN INTO ARROGANCE.

CAN'T YOU GUESS?

I'D RATHER NOT.

ALL I KNOW IS WHAT LIES AHEAD AND WHAT I DON'T KNOW IS A VAST OCEAN IN FRONT OF ME.

10 / 11 / 20

THE CHALLENGE

WAS TO RIDE 4 MILES UP ON A 1978 MONGOOSE 40 POUND 20" BMX BIKE AND NOT PUT A FOOT DOWN. DRESSED LIKE A CHICKEN.

CHALLENGE ACCEPTED.

MADE IT.

10 / 12 / 20

SPLIT THE PAPER IN 1/2 AND WRITE DOWN ALL THE THINGS YOU HAVE THAT ARE GOOD AND ALL THE BAD THINGS YOU CAN'T SEEM TO GET AROUND.

YOU WILL QUICKLY SEE THAT THE GOOD THINGS WILL BE IN GREATER NUMBER THAN THE BAD THINGS

BUT THE BAD THINGS CARRY MUCH MORE WEIGHT.

10/13/20
IN A SEWER SOMEWHERE..
OH LORD JESUS NO!
COME ON!
HA HA HA HA HA HA
10/14/20
YOUR BEST REVENGE AGAINST THE ONES THAT HAVE WRONGED YOU IS TO LIVE WELL.
GLAD YOU'RE HERE.
ME TOO
BE HONEST AND FAIR. MAKE THE MOST OF YOUR TIME HERE. LIVE WELL. THE ONES THAT HAVE WRONGED YOU, THEY WILL WRONG OTHERS.
YOU LYING SACK OF SHIT!
THEY WILL MAKE THEM SELVES ALONE IN THIS WORLD AND THE ONES THAT LIVE WELL, THEY WILL BE THE TRULY RICH ONES. YOU CHOOSE.
10/15/20
WHAT HAVE YOU BEEN UP TO?
I DIDN'T TELL YOU? I GOT MARRIED.
WHAT A TERRIBLE DREAM.
BLINK BLINK

10/16/20
THE FREEST YOU CAN BE IS WHEN YOU DENY ALL MECHINISIMS OF CONTROL. PEOPLE TRY AND TELL YOU WHAT TO DO — YOU DENY THEM.
NO WAY.
WE NEED IT NOW.
EVERYONE ELSE PLAYS THIS STUPID GAME WHEN THEY TRY AND CONTROL PEOPLE BY TELLING THEM WHAT TO DO.
YOU KNOW WHAT YOU SHOULD DO..
BUT ONCE YOU SEE THE RTNROUGH THE RUSE, WELL, IT IS EASY TO AVOID.
DON'T WORRY ABOUT WHAT I'M DOING.
Dick.

10/17/20
STILL GOT A GIRLFRIEND?
NOPE.
OH, THERE'S SOME ONE FOR EVERYBODY.
I DON'T BELIEVE IN YOUR FAIRYTALE OPTIMISIM, SORRY.

10/18/20
YOU ALWAYS HAVE SOMETHING TO LOOK FORWARD TO HUH?
YEAH.
WELL YOU HAVE TO MAKE THAT HAPPEN. NO ONE WILL HAND IT TO YOU. IF YOU HAVE THAT ALWAYS THEN IS THAT NOT A GOOD LIFE?
YOU'RE THE ONLY ONE THAT THINKS THAT WAY, YOU KNOW?
TOO BAD I GUESS.

10/19/20
WAY DEEP IN A MOUNTIAN ROAD WE RAN INTO SOME COWS.
THE BULLS WOULD STARE BUT WE WOULD STAND THERE AND HOLD OUR GROUND.
THE PSYIC DUEL WON, THE COWS WOULD FLEE.
10/20/20
I GOT THE MILEAGE DOWN SEE?
WE TOOK THE UPPER ROUTE, THAT WAS THE MIDDLE ROUTE.
Bike
SO IT WAS LONGER?
SO OVER 70
70?
I THOUGHT IT WAS 48!
70+
NO WONDER MY KNEES HURT.
10/21/20
MAKE A PROMISE TO MYSELF - I HAVE TO -
TO BE HAPPY AND LOVE LIFE. TO NOT DWELL IN SADNESS, PAIN OF LOSS OR LONELYNESS. TO MAKE THE GOOD GO TO THE GOOD.
I OWE MYSELF THAT MUCH - JUST TO BE KIND TO MYSELF, TO WASH AWAY THE TEARS THAT HOLD ME BACK AND MOVE ON.

10/22/20
A GOOD CONVERSATION IS HARD TO FIND.
NICE TO TALK TO YOU.
YOU TOO
MOST PEOPLE WANT TO MONOLOG, NOT LISTEN.
SO WHEN YOU FIND A GOOD ONE, HOLD ON TIGHT.
CAN I COME BACK HERE, JUST TO TALK?
SURE!
10/23/20
THAT'S NOT GOOD!
SO MUCH BULLSHIT JUST COMES AND COMES...
THAT IS FUCKED UP
SO MUCH FOR SLEEPING TONIGHT.
10/24/20
MMMM
I THINK YOU'RE GETTING THE HANG OF IT.
WRRRRRRR
LEARNING A NEW THING IS AWESOME WHEN THE MINDS EYE IS OPEN THAT IS WHEN
HMMM

10/25/20
THROUGH THAT GATE!
YOU EVER GONE THIS WAY BEFORE?
NOPE
SEE? NEW ADVENTURE RIGHT IN OUR OWN BACK YARD!
10/26/20
LATER:
YOU'RE ALL SET. NO LEAKS, YOU DID A GOOD JOB.
GAS CO
WELL COMING FROM A PROFESSIONAL I'LL TAKE THAT AS A COMPLIMENT.
10/27/20
NEW DISCOVERIES ARE THE BEST.
A TRAIL WHEN FOUND IS NOT NEW.
OOOOOH!
BUT IS NEW TO YOU.
THAT WAS RAD!

10/28/20
THE LONELY ROAD.
UNLIKE THE ROAD TO NOWHERE, THIS ROAD SADDLES YOU WITH A DULL PAIN
ONE YOU MUST GET USED TO BECAUSE THERE IS NO OTHER ROAD TO TAKE.
10/29/20
PRRRRR
WHO'S THIS HANDSOME BOY?
PRRRRR
I REALIZE NOW, THAT THESE CATS ARE ALL I GOT NOW.
10/30/20
THE THEME IS "I DID IT ANYWAY"
I WAS TIRED BUT I RODE MY BIKE ANYWAY.
AFTER WORK I FINISHED A STEP IN A PROJECT AND CLEANED UP EVEN THOUGH I WAS TIRED. I DID IT ANYWAY.
HOW YOU FEEL IS TEMPORARY, WHAT YOU PUT OUT IN THE WORLD IS NOT.

10/31/20
HALLOWEEN -
WE WAITED ALL NIGHT FOR ANYONE TO COME OVER.
D+D!
NO ONE DID
THE PAST IS A FUZZY SNAP-SHOT AT BEST.
THE FUTURE IS ON THE HORIZON AND ALSO CANNOT BE SEEN CLEARLY.
BUT NOW, NOW CAN BE SEEN WITH SOME AMOUNT OF CLARITY - WHAT DO YOU INVEST IN?
I WANT TO TAKE A PICTURE OF YOUR SPACE
THE LAYOUT IS ART, IT IS INTERESTING.
IT IS? OK I'LL GO WITH THAT.

11/3/20
WHERE IS EVERYONE?
HIDING OUT.
THERE IS SUPPOSED TO BE CIVIL UNREST BUT THERE IS NOTHING.
PERHAPS PEOPLE ARE WORN OUT.
11/4/20
HERE, MY BROTHER WANTS TO TALK TO YOU ABOUT THE BIKE.
GROAN
HOW IS THE CONDITION OF THE BIKE?
I DON'T KNOW. I JUST GOT IT AND HAVE NOT LOOKED AT IT YET. IF I HAVE MY HANDS ON A PHONE THOUGH, I'LL NEVER KNOW.
OOOOON
5/20
AHH.. LIFE IS GOOD!
IT IS WHAT YOU MAKE OF IT.
NOW IS THE TIME TO HEED MY OWN ADVICE.

11/6/20
AS TIME HAS GONE ON, I TRY AND LIVE WITH LESS COMFORT. I DON'T WANT TO BE TOO COMFORTABLE
SO YEAR OLD CHAIR
NO HEAT OR AC
TOO MUCH COMFORT MAKES ONE SOFT. ALSO WHEN COMFORT BECOMES THE NORM YOU DON'T REAP ANY JOY OUT OF IT AS IT HAS BECOME SOMETHING IN THE BACKGROUND.
TEMP 68°
I WANT TO REMEMBER THE TIMES I FELT GOOD OR WARM OR WHEN I WAS NOT, SO I CAN VALUE THE TIMES WHEN I AM.
11/7/20
OK THAT IS DONE.
TAKI TAK
FEW THINGS IN LIFE BRING MORE SATIS- FACTION THAN GETTING SOMETHING DONE. I LIVE FOR COMPLETION
NEXT STEP.
ONCE FELT, THE FEELING NEEDED TO BE EXPERIENCED OVER AND OVER, IT'S A GOOD ADDICTION TO HAVE.
11/8/20
BREAKFAST IS ON ME FOR FIXING MY WHEEL ON THE TRAIL, IT IS THE LEAST I CAN DO..
OK.
YOU'VE FED US SO MANY TIMES AT YOUR EVENTS.
WELL, I DO THAT BECAUSE IT IS WHAT I WANT TO DO, I'M NOT LOOKING FOR RECIPROCATION.

11/9/20
TURN TURN
1000TH OF AN INCH
THE MILL IS AMAZING
W12R
12 12 12
OH HOW I LOVE THIS MACHINE!
11/10/20
!
BRAND NEW! SCORE!
CA
OVER AND OVER IT IS THE LITTLE THINGS LIKE A GROUND SCORE THAT MAKE YOUR DAY.
11/11/20
YOUR BIKE IS IN SOME JAPANESE MAGAZINE. YOU DID NOT KNOW THAT?
NO?
WHAT THE?
SEE?
HOW IS THIS HAPPENING?

11/12/20
THERE IS NO ONE OUT THERE.
I CAN INTERACT WITH PEOPLE FOR A TIME.
BUT A MOMENT LATER, IT IS JUST ME AND THE CATS.
11/13/20
I THINK ABOUT ALL THE EMOTIONAL PAIN AND SUFFERING OTHER PEOPLE HAVE CAUSED ME.
I'M LEAVING.
HOW HUMANITY CAN BE SO CASUALLY CRUEL..
BUT.. WHY?
I ASK MY SELF THAT EVERY DAY. WHY? THERE IS NO ANSWER.
11/14/20
LOST ANOTHER ONE TODAY. CANCER - ALWAYS CANCER. I FEEL LIKE IT IS MUCH WORSE THAN THEY LET ON.
I HAD TO STOP AND THINK ABOUT ALL THE GOOD TIMES I HAD WITH HIM.
LET ME ASK YOU A QUESTION...
AND THOSE MOMENTS IN THE END, IT IS WHAT WE LIVE FOR.
SO LONG PAL.

11/15/20
LET'S DO THE EXTRA CREDIT.
WOOOOO
WOOOOO
THAT WAS AWESOME!
AND ONLY ADDED 40 MINUTES TO OUR RIDE. WE SHOULD DO IT MORE OFTEN.
11/16/20
SPENT THE DAY TOSSING SOMEONE'S LIFE INTO A DUMPSTER—
WENT THROUGH EVERY THING AND FILLED MY VAN WITH SOME GOODIES
IT IS OK THOUGH— ONE DAY MY LIFE WILL BE THROWN OUT TOO.
WEB
WOB
WUB
WUB
DUMP ALL
11/17/20
I AWOKE TO SEE MY BELOVED TRUCK IN A BALL OF FIRE.
IT WAS SURREAL FOR SURE. I WAS SUPER CALM ABOUT THE WHOLE THING
GO BACK
DRUNK DRIVER
BECAUSE I KNEW THE TRUTH
SORRY ABOUT YOUR TRUCK
LIFE HAS DOLED OUT MORE SAVAGE BEATINGS TO ME THAN THIS.

11/18/20
I GOT TWO PRACTICE KATANA'S
ON!
ALL THOSE YEARS OF PRACTICE WITH THIS SWORD CAME BACK TO ME
oof
GAVE EVERYONE A SURPRISE THAT NIGHT FOR SURE.
11/19/20
I OWE THE IRS A MILLION IN BACK TAXES.
!
IF THEY SHUT US DOWN AGAIN I DON'T KNOW WHAT I'LL DO!
!
ONLY TIME WILL TELL. FOR NOW, UNCERTAINTY AND FEAR ARE ON THE PLATE.
11/20/20
THAT FUNNY THING I SAID - I CAN'T REMEMBER.
HOW MUCH GOOD GETS FORGOTTEN IN THE WORLD BY BEING DISTRACTED BEFORE ONE CAN COMMIT TO MEMORY.
FOR LEASE
WELL, I DON'T KNOW THAT EITHER.

11/18/20
READING A BOOK ON HOW TO BE HAPPY SEEMS SILLY BUT I HAVE TO ADMIT, I'M MISSING SOMETHING...
I WANT TO BE HAPPY MORE THAN ANYTHING. A QUEST I'M ON- ENDLESS SEARCHES...
ONE DAY, I HOPE I FIND IT.
11/22/20
WHO WANTS A BELLY RUB?
DA BELLY RUB!
PLURRLR
NEVER FORGET TO TAKE IN THESE LITTLE MOMENTS OF JOY.
11/24/20
I TOLD A GIRL ABOUT YOU!
NOT INTERESTED.
I THINK I'VE SUFFERED ENOUGH FOR ONE LIFE-TIME.

11/24/20
TAKE ME TO MY SLEEP SCAPE WHERE I CAN REST.
AND DREAM.
AND ESCAPE FOR A LITTLE WHILE.
11/25/20
SORRY ABOUT YOUR CAT.
JUST THE TIP OF THE ICEBERG.
WELL, LOOK UP, THINGS GET BETTER, DON'T THEY?
YEAH
I GUESS THEY DO.
11/26/20
ONE MORE BEER AND I'LL GO.
5 BEERS LATER...
ONE MORE BEER AND I'LL GO.
?
YOU SAID THAT 5 BEERS AGO - TIME TO CUT YOU OFF.

11/27/20

YOU ARE THE MOST AUTHENTIC PERSON I KNOW.
REALLY?
THE ONLY ONE.
REALLY?
THAT MAKES ME SAD.
11/28/20
ONE DAY WE'LL PIN YOU DOWN AND MAKE YOU WATCH ALL THE TV YOU HAVE NOT SEEN.
WHY WOULD YOU DO THAT? I HAVE NOT NEEDED IT FOR 30 YEARS, SO WHAT?
I HAVEN'T MISSED FUCKING SHIT.
11/29/20
HUF HUF
AWWW
ANA, IT'S GOOD TO BE ALIVE.

11/30/20
AM I THAT BAD?
AGAIN, I PUT ON MY WELL WORN COAT OF LONELYNESS. I'VE WORN IT MOST OF MY LIFE.
NO ACCEPTANCE.
ITS WEIGHT AND ILL-FIT HAVE BECOME SOMETHING TO CARRY.
JUST ME.
STICKING WITH THINGS IS SO IMPORTANT.
YOU CAN TRY AND FAIL, SURE AND THEN TRY AGAIN AND AGAIN.
ONE MORE TIME.
YOU ONLY LOOSE WHEN YOU QUIT.
12/2/20
I HATE GOING THROUGH THE MOTIONS.
THE SAYING "JUST ANOTHER DAY" IS A DEATH RATTLE TO ME.
JUST ANOTHER DAY.
EXCITEMENT AND INSPIRATION ARE IN SOME DARK CORNER SOMEWHERE, BUT NOW THEY ILLUDE ME.
?

12/3/20
L E F G D F C T
F D P L T C E O
P E I O L C F T R
SOMEONE TOLD ME TO EXERCISE MY EYES BY READING SOMETHING UP CLOSE AND THEN AT A DISTANCE.
IT WORKS! HOPEFULLY GLASSES WILL BE A WAYS OFF....
12/4/20
IT WAS ONLY 5 BUCKS, HE STARTS WALLOWING AROUND ON THE FLOOR...
WHAT RACE WAS HE?
?
THE HUMAN RACE.
12/5/20
SO COLD TONIGHT!
RIGHT ON CUE.

12/6/20
THAT WITCHER SHOW SUCKED.
?
ONLY ON DAYS WHEN I'M SUPER TIRED WILL I WATCH SOMETHING
I KNOW HE SAID IT WAS DAD, WHAT THE HELL...
YOU JUST NEED TO MAKE UP YOUR OWN MIND ON THINGS.
NOT BAD.
12/7/20
CRACK!
?
OH MAN I CRACKED MY FRAME.
I CAN'T HELP FEELING A LITTLE PROUD ABOUT IT BEING 6 IN A ROW NOW.
12/8/20
OH BOY A SOLICITOR
I HAVE THIS OFFER...
MOMENTS LATER.
NA NA NA NA NA NA
I WASTED 2:47 OF HIS LIFE.

. . .
I JUST DON'T WANT TO BE FORGOTTEN.

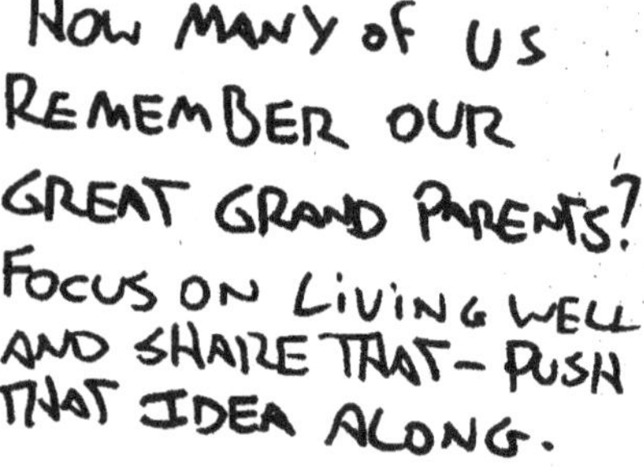
IN 100 YEARS TIME YOU AND EVERYONE YOU KNOW AND WHAT THEY DID WILL MOST LIKELY BE FORGOTTEN. HAVING CHILDREN WON'T SOLVE THAT.
HOW MANY OF US REMEMBER OUR GREAT GRANDPARENTS? FOCUS ON LIVING WELL AND SHARE THAT - PUSH THAT IDEA ALONG.

SO YOU DON'T THINK THERE IS SOMETHING AFTER THIS LIFE?
NO

THAT IS WHAT I DON'T GET. EVERYONE IS SO FOCUSED ON WHAT HAPPENS AFTER YOU DIE, WHAT ABOUT WHEN YOU ARE ALIVE?

YOU CAN'T GO BACK TO THE PAST NOR CAN YOU SEE INTO THE FUTURE - BUT NOW - RIGHT NOW, IS ALL YOU HAVE. PERHAPS PEOPLE SHOULD DO THAT WELL?

WHEN SOMEONE IS POSSESED BY AN IDEA, THEY ARE CALLED MADMEN

AN IDEA, ONCE MADE FIRTILE IN THE BRAIN, MUST GET OUT OR IT WILL ROT THE MIND OF THE POSSESOR.
MUST DO

FOR THOSE THAT HAVE NO IDEAS, THEY WOULD HAVE NO IDEA
WHAT IS WRONG WITH YOU?

12/12/20
NEVER SEEN THAT BEFORE.
?
AFTER FIXING SO MUCH A NEW MECHANICAL CHALLENGE... OOO
SPINNING THE WHEEL ACTIVATES THE BRAKE.
..IS NOT THAT MUCH OF A CHALLENGE.
IT'S DONE.
REALLY?!
12/13/20
WOOOOOOOOOO!
FUMP!
OH THAT WAS GOOD.
SO GLAD I CAN BE HERE RIGHT NOW...
12/14/20
SQUEEEE!
60 MPH
WE'RE GOING OVER 60 IN THE CORNERS.
THIS IS FUN BUT I THINK I'M CAR SICK.

12/15/20

I WISH PEOPLE WOULD STOP TRYING TO BE CLEVER. MORE THAN AN AVERAGE NUMBER OF PEOPLE THINK THEY HAVE MORE THAN AVERAGE INTELIGENCE.

ALL DAY LONG PEOPLE TRY AND OUTWIT ME AND ALL DAY LONG THEY FAIL.

I'M NOT THAT SMART. JUST SMARTER THAN THE PEOPLE THAT THINK THEY ARE SMARTER THAN ME.

12/16/20

WHAT IS RIGHT? WHILE WE MAY HAVE SOME SORT OF CODE WE FOLLOW, WE OFTEN IMPOSE MORE RULES UPON OURSELVES THAN SOCIGITY DOSE...

WHAT YOU CHOOSE TO STAND FOR (IF ANYTHING) IS UP TO YOU FOR THE MOST PART. IDEAS OF WHAT IS RIGHT IS SOLO TO YOU, BUT YOU ARE NOT OBLIGATED TO BUY.

WHAT IS RIGHT? HOPE SOMETHING IS. UP TO YOU.

12/12/20

DARKNESS AND COLD COMPOUND THE WAR IN MY HEAD. I AWOKE NOT WANTING TO - BE ANYTHING

BUT I KNEW A FEELING IS JUST A TEMPORALY THING. AS I BUSIED MYSELF WITH POSITIVE THINGS THE LIGHT BEGAN TO LEND AID TO MY PLIGNT.

AND BY THE TIME DARKNESS ROLLED AROUND AGAIN, I FELT OK. TAKE SOLACE IN THE LITTLE BATTLES YOU WIN EACH DAY AS THEY CAN TURN INTO A VICTORY.

12/18/20
THATS MY SON
I CAME ALL THE
WAY FROM CHICAGO
NOT TO HAVE ME
FIX YOUR BIKE THOUGH?
YES, I'VE
HEARD ABOUT
YOU.
WHAA?
12/19/20
wrnhn
I GOT A EXPENSIVE
VACCUM FOR FREE-
I HAVE A 6×6 PIECE
OF CARPET AND A 3
FOOT ONE IN THE HALL.
IT'S OVERKILL.
WOW
THIS THING
KICKS ASS!
12/20/20
HOME MADE
COOKIES?
YES!
TAKE A FEW, I
DON'T WANT TO TAKE
THEM
HOME
WITH
ME.
NOT A PROBLEM.

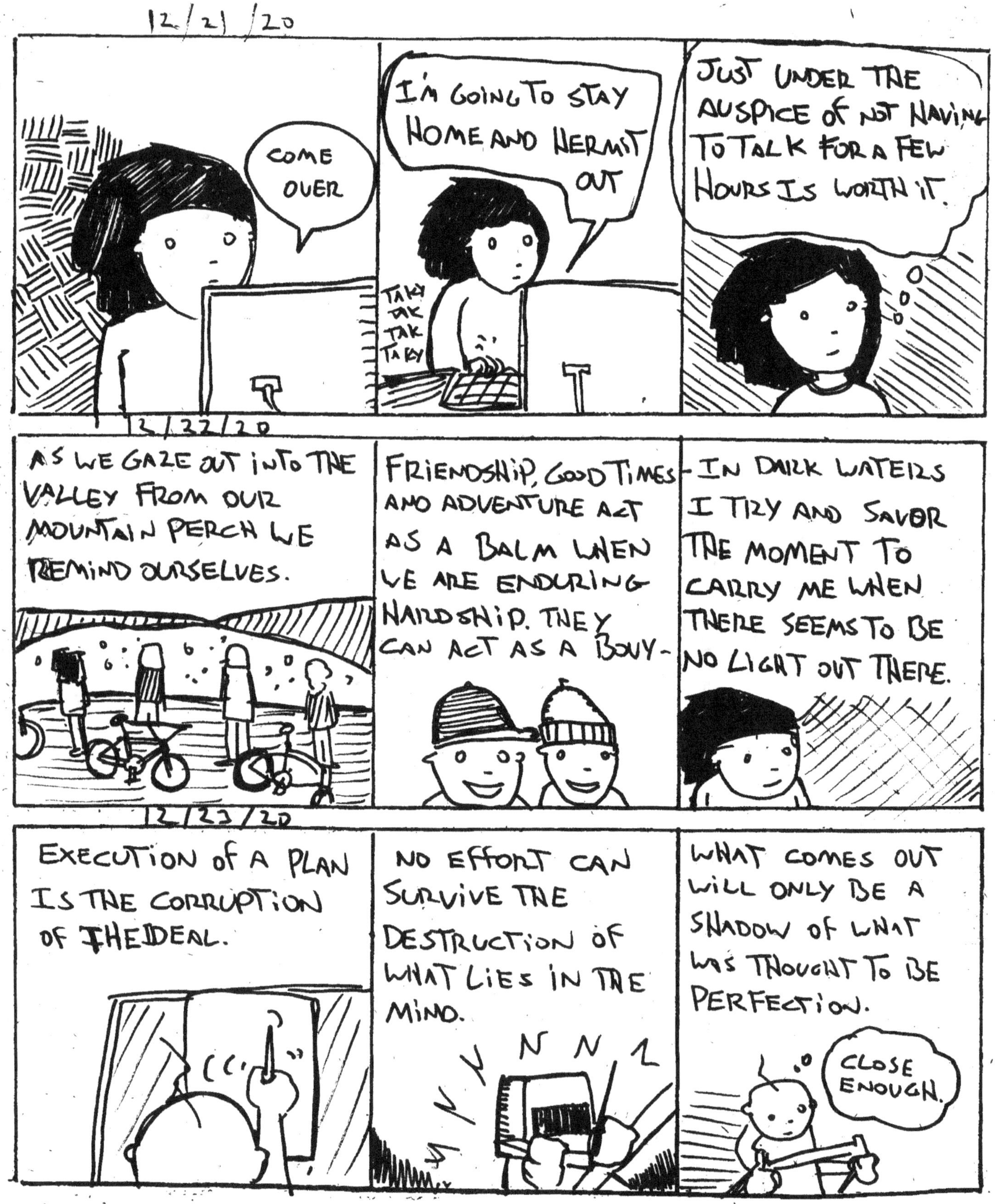

12/21/20

12/22/20

12/23/20

12/27/20
UP AND UP IT NEVER SEEMED TO END.
THEN DOWN AND DOWN ON TREACHOUS TERRAIN.
IT TOOK ALL DAY BUT IT WAS WORTH IT.
RAD!
12/28/20
ARE YOU WEARING A RAIN SUIT?
YEAH
HOW IS IT?
WELL, ITS DOING ITS JOB!
12/29/20
KNOWING WHERE THE ROAD ALWAYS GOES IS NO FUN.
?
I THINK IF WE WERE CERTAIN OF EVERYTHING WE'D LOSE THE WILL TO LIVE.
EVERYTHING IS KNOWN, WHY BOTHER?
ADVENTURE, EVEN IN A SMALL WAY IS ESSENTIAL TO OUR BEING
WHAT'S NEXT IS WHAT MATTERS MOST.

12/30/20
AHH. THE MODERN WORLD.
WHEN SOMEONE DIES NOW THEY DON'T GET A WAKE OR ANY SPECIAL EULOGY - NO.
THEY GET AN INSTAGRAM EUGOLY INSTEAD.
SOMETHING A-MISS
MISS YOU
12/31/20
WORTH A TRY.
I TRIED COOKING IN A POT INSTEAD OF THE SLOW CROC-POT. I WANTED SOUP SOONER.
THE HIGHER HEAT REALLY BROUGHT OUT THE FLAVOR. I WAS PLEASNTLY SURPRISED.
GOOD!
END OF A WEEK OFF
I'D LIKE A 'NOTHER WEEK.
SO I ADDED UP MY MOST HARDEST YEAR.
I MUST LOOK AT IT AS A REWARD FOR STAYING STRONG EVEN WHEN I DID NOT WANT TO.
NOT DAD.

This is the mystery page. It had two 2016 dates and one 2012 date. I think it belongs in 2012 but by the the time I found it, I had already

completed book two that has 2012 in it. I felt like I was short a page in 2012 however all can do is include it here at the back of this book.

Not like I'm unlocking the great mystery of humanity in these pages, I'm not. Just a few days documented out of a life. Nothing more.